THE ESSENTIAL COLLEGE PROFESSOR

THE ESSENTIAL COLLEGE PROFESSOR

PROFESSOR

A Practical Guide to an Academic Career

Jeffrey L. Buller

JOSSEY-BASS
A Wiley Imprint
www.josseybass.com

Published by Jossey-Bass
A Wiley Imprint
989 Market Street, San Francisco, CA 94103-1741—www.josseybass.com

Jossey-Bass books and products are available through most bookstores. To contact Jossey-Bass directly call our Customer Care Department within the U.S. at 800-956-7739, outside the U.S. at 317-572-3986, or fax 317-572-4002.
Jossey-Bass also publishes its books in a variety of electronic formats. Some content that appears in print may not be available in electronic books.

Library of Congress Cataloging-in-Publication Data

Buller, Jeffrey L.
    The essential college professor : a practical guide to an academic career / Jeffrey L. Buller.
        p. cm.
    Includes bibliographical references.
    ISBN 978-0-470-37373-6 (pbk.)
        1. College teachers—United States.   2. Universities and colleges—United States—Faculty.   3. College teaching—Vocational guidance—United States.   I. Title.
    LB1778.2.B85 2010
    378.1'202373—dc22
                                                                              2009031946

FIRST EDITION
PB Printing   10 9 8 7 6 5 4 3 2

CONTENTS

Part IV: The College Professor as Citizen

THE AUTHOR

JEFFREY L. BULLER is dean of the Harriet L. Wilkes Honors College at Florida Atlantic University. He began his administrative career as honors director and chair of the Department of Classical Studies at Loras College in Dubuque, Iowa, before going on to assume a number of administrative appointments at Georgia Southern University and Mary Baldwin College. Dr. Buller is the author of *The Essential Academic Dean: A Practical Guide to College Leadership* (Jossey-Bass, 2007), *The Essential Department Chair: A Practical Guide to College Administration* (Anker, 2006), and *Classically Romantic: Classical Form and Meaning in Wagner's* Ring (Xlibris, 2001). He has also written numerous articles on Greek and Latin literature, nineteenth- and twentieth-century opera, and college administration. Serving from 2003 to 2005 as the principal English-language lecturer at the International Wagner Festival in Bayreuth, Germany, he is widely known as an entertaining and popular speaker on such topics as international culture, music, literature, and higher education.

INTRODUCTION

At times the work of a college professor can seem a bit like manual labor: no one gives you very much job training; you're just expected to figure it out somewhere along the way. It's not that college professors don't devote many years to advanced training in their academic disciplines. Through coursework, examinations, and the creation and defense of a dissertation, faculty members at colleges and universities know the content, methods, and theories of their fields extremely well. Nevertheless, many of the things they're expected to do throughout their careers—interview for a job, design a syllabus, teach an auditorium full of freshmen, chair a committee, use technology to promote student learning, write a book proposal, resolve a conflict with a colleague, develop a new course—aren't included in the standard graduate school curriculum. Most college professors develop these skills largely by observing others who demonstrate them, imitating successful examples, discovering how not to follow bad examples, adopting some by trial and error, and eventually improving.

Certainly, this approach has produced some excellent college professors over the years. But as a method of professional development, it does take a great deal of time, and time—particularly when the tenure clock is running—is a commodity that most faculty members really don't have. Fortunately, this situation is improving in graduate programs. A number of institutions have revised their doctoral programs to focus not merely on research but also on effective ways of teaching their disciplines to others. Practical experience as a teaching assistant is increasingly preceded by explorations of which pedagogical approaches work most effectively in introductory courses, service courses, and other types of instruction needed by nonmajors. Future faculty members are exposed to strategies in course design, ongoing assessment to promote maximum student learning, techniques of securing external sources to support research, and many of the other skills that will continue to serve them throughout their careers. Moreover, even after the new faculty member is hired, many colleges and universities have expanded what were once woefully inadequate faculty orientation programs into full first-year faculty experience programs. Centers for teaching excellence have been transformed into comprehensive centers of professional development, providing advanced training on how to write grant proposals, manage an academic department, promote maximum student engagement, and lead strategic change.

In addition, nearly every institution has discovered the benefits of mentorship programs in which new faculty members learn from the experience of a more senior colleague. Sometimes faculty mentors are assigned formally; at other times these relationships are simply encouraged and allowed to develop more informally. Even in the best mentorship systems, however, one oversight can still be found: far too often no one asks, "But who will train the trainers?" As a result, new college professors often report that what they learned from their mentors was only of marginal value or that they stopped meeting with their senior colleagues after only a few sessions. By not providing professional development to mentors in what new college professors really need to know, the senior faculty members were left to act on their instincts. And certain people's instincts are, quite frankly, better than others. The hope of most new college professors—finding the perfect mentor who will "tell it like it is," who will explain clearly what a faculty member's priorities should be and then point out when those priorities should change; who will make it his or her most important goal, not to be proved right, but to help the new faculty member succeed; and who truly understands (not just *says*, but truly understands) that the needs of no two college professors are alike—is still often unfulfilled.

Think of this book as being the paperback equivalent of that perfect mentor.

Like its companion volumes, *The Essential Department Chair: A Practical Guide to College Administration* (2006) and *The Essential Academic Dean: A Practical Guide to College Leadership* (2007), the current work focuses not on abstruse theories about how colleges and universities *should* work, but on real-life choices that every faculty member has to make. I've tried to condense to its most essential form advice that I've given to hundreds of faculty members over the years, as well as the information that I've provided in dozens of workshops on such topics as effectiveness in teaching, taking your scholarship to the next level, being an excellent academic citizen, working collaboratively with colleagues, setting priorities and making plans, unleashing your inner creativity, and negotiating the sometimes arcane systems that institutions have in place for tenure, promotion, and post-tenure review. My goal was to create a single volume that can be useful to college professors of all kinds, regardless of their disciplines, the type of institutions they serve, or the number of years they've been working in their careers. Having a single resource to which all college professors can turn provides many benefits. It allows faculty members to explore what they have in common rather than the differences that divide them into isolated departments, disparate colleges, and separate institutions. It serves as a counterargument to the idea that simply because people work in different fields and different types of schools, they don't have a great deal to learn from one another. And it makes it possible for professional development centers to adopt a single resource for their faculty training programs rather than a shelf of books for each discipline, academic rank, and institutional mission. Inevitably, however, any book that tries to embrace the academic profession as a whole will occasionally indulge in generalizations that are inappropriate for specific individuals or programs. Even in these cases, however, it can be extremely useful to see what often occurs at other institutions and in other disciplines as a basis for a conversation with a mentor, supervisor, or department chair about what the precise expectations are for a college professor with your background and in your position.

The Essential College Professor has been designed so that you can use it in many different ways:

- You can read it straight through from cover to cover, as later topics build incrementally on the principles introduced in earlier chapters.

- You can consult it as a reference book, picking it up from time to time when you want to find advice on how to deal with a particular challenge or to make best use of a special opportunity. If you decide to use the book in this manner, you'll find numerous cross-references throughout the text, guiding you to the chapter in which each topic was first introduced or where a certain concept is dis-cussed in greater detail.

- Faculty development programs could use this book as part of their orientation activities for new faculty members, throughout the year as part of a first-year faculty experience program, or as a common text in a faculty training program conducted by a center for teaching excellence or institute for professional development.

- Graduate programs can adopt the book to help prepare students for what they are likely to encounter if they pursue academic careers.

- Departments or colleges may wish to use this text as the basis for workshops, discussion groups, or faculty reading and discussion circles.

- Teaching circles, scholarship networks, and service alliances, all of which are discussed in the pages that follow, might find this book useful in their efforts at colleague-based support and encouragement.

In other words, *The Essential College Professor* has been written for both the individual reader and for people who are discussing this material as members of a larger group. Each chapter is as brief and self-contained as possible. As in the rest of the "Essential" series, my goal is to provide you with as much clear, concise information as you can absorb in ten minutes or less.

Scattered throughout the book you will find several essential principles that are formatted as follows:

Essential principles are the key ideas that can help you succeed in a variety of academic situations. These are the principles to which you'll want to give particular attention when you face your own opportunities and challenges.

Essential principles are designed to be short and easily remembered, but they are not mere platitudes. All of them have been tested in actual situations and have proven their value. Even if you disagree with one or two of them, they deserve your serious and thoughtful attention.

I've had the opportunity to work with an amazing group of creative and dedicated faculty members at Loras College in Dubuque, Iowa; Georgia Southern University in Statesboro, Georgia; Mary Baldwin College in Staunton, Virginia; and Florida Atlantic University in Boca Raton, Florida. This book is dedicated to all of them, but particularly to the incredible faculty of the Harriet L. Wilkes Honors College in Jupiter, Florida, from whom I have learned so much and who frequently serve as the positive role models described in the pages below. Individuals who contributed specific ideas and insights to this book include the following faculty members from Georgia Southern University: Rebecca Davis, political science; Peggy Hargis, sociology; Barbara Hendry, anthropology; Sandra Peacock, history; Anastatia Sims, history; and Georgina Hickey, formerly of Georgia Southern's Department of History and now an associate professor at the University of Michigan–Dearborn; and Ruth Thompson, formerly of Georgia Southern's Department of History and now a senior counsel to the attorney general for the state of Tennessee. Faculty members at the Wilkes Honors College at Florida Atlantic University whose insights and talent have particularly shaped the following chapters include: Jacqueline Fewkes, anthropology; Paul Kirchman, biology; Kevin Lanning, psychology; Terje Hoim, mathematics; Michelle Ivey, chemistry; and Eugene Smith, chemistry. Staff members on the MacArthur campus of Florida Atlantic in Jupiter, Florida, who also contributed to this book in many ways include: Phil Cromer, assistant director of counseling; April Mistrik, assistant director of academic support services for biology; Dianne Reeves, associate vice president for development for the northern campuses; and Sandy Ogden, executive secretary in the Wilkes Honors College. Christian T. Weisser, associate professor of English at Penn State Berks, provided valuable insights about techniques for teaching writing. In addition, thanks are due to John N. McDaniel, dean of the College of Liberal Arts at Middle Tennessee State University, and his twin brother, Thomas R. McDaniel, senior vice president, professor of education, and acting dean of graduate studies at Converse College in Spartanburg, South Carolina, who offered to write and contribute the summary comments that appear near the end of Chapters 6 and 22. I'm indebted, too, to the three anonymous referees who provided Jossey-Bass with many constructive suggestions that helped make this book even more useful. Finally, I'm endlessly grateful to my extremely patient editor and the world's most engaging cheerleader, Carolyn Dumore, who first suggested this series of books and then provided the expertise and support that made these volumes a reality.

Regardless of whether you're hoping to become a college professor, are relatively new to the faculty, or are already well established in your career, I hope that you will find a great deal of constructive and useful advice in the following chapters. Each year offers us a new beginning in academic life, and this can be the year that you start attaining the goals you've always had for yourself as a teacher, scholar, and academic citizen. Even better, now can be the time to set goals even higher than you ever imagined possible and then to exceed those goals. This book will explain many of the hows and whys of academic life, but *what* you will achieve is ultimately up to you. No matter what you decide your goal will be, I hope you find the path you follow in attaining it to be rewarding, satisfying, surprising, and unquestionably worth the effort.

THE ESSENTIAL COLLEGE PROFESSOR

APPLYING FOR A FACULTY POSITION

Searches for full-time faculty positions at North American colleges or universities frequently elicit fifty to two hundred applications. From that pool, institutions will usually invite three or four candidates to on-campus interviews. Of those finalists, one candidate will end up being hired, unless the search is canceled, postponed, reopened, or extended. In other words, even for positions where you are extremely well qualified, there is a very small chance that you will receive an interview, and an even slimmer chance that you'll be offered a contract. That is the reality of applying for an academic job today. But the picture is not as bleak as it seems. There are actually several ways of improving the odds that a search committee will give your application high priority and that you will be granted a telephone interview or even a chance to visit the campus as one of the finalists.

Decide Where to Apply

The first factor you should consider when applying for faculty positions is which specific positions to apply for. Many applicants are not selective. They blanket institutions with generic-looking applications for any jobs they can find in their field. Because they do not address the issues that are most important to that institution, their applications are overlooked by search committees. So, the first thing you should do when applying for a job is to focus your energies on those positions for which you are most suitable, carefully crafting applications tailored to those announcements. The precise method you use to select these positions will be different depending on whether you are a graduate student looking for an initial full-time position, an established faculty member hoping to find a better opportunity, or a senior faculty member looking for the greater challenge of an extremely prestigious appointment. If you are relatively inexperienced, you should not narrow your job search too restrictively, taking a chance on a number of institutions that *could* be a good fit and keeping an open mind about the regions of the country in which you are willing to work. The important question for you to consider is "Is this position a proper match for my qualifications?" not "Is this position located in my ideal part of the world?" If you are more established as a faculty member, however, you can afford to focus your search a great deal; you may end up being surprised by the number of telephone interviews and campus visits you are asked to make, and it can be difficult to balance your job search with your current responsibilities. Moreover, experienced faculty members are less likely to be searching for just any job than to be interested in a particular type of job, and this kind of search requires great selectivity.

Regardless of whether you are just starting out or far more experienced, there is one essential principle that you should always keep in mind:

Never apply for any faculty position that you have no intention of taking if it is offered.

Faculty searches are expensive and time consuming, both for candidates and for the institution. Even if you have your travel expenses paid, you will need to spend time away from your current duties, incur at least some expense because of dry-cleaning costs or additions to your wardrobe, and be called on to prepare new copies of your curriculum vitae, course materials, and evidence of scholarship. The institution will be investing significant expense and personnel time on you, and you will leave a very poor impression if it appears that you were never serious about the position in the first place. Academia is a surprisingly small world, and people at one institution often know their colleagues elsewhere. A poor reputation that you establish in one search can "follow" you when you interview for another position that you really want.

As you consider which jobs to apply for, ask yourself the following questions:

- Is this position at an appropriate level for someone with my experience and in a discipline that is closely related to my background and training?

- Can I make a persuasive case to someone who does not know me that this position is suitable for someone with my credentials?

- Can I realistically see myself accepting this position, giving it my best effort, and taking all the steps necessary to succeed in this position?

Sometimes people who are about to conduct a job search wonder whether it is ever appropriate to apply to an institution that has not already posted a vacancy. The truthful answer is that although there is probably no great harm in applying to an institution that has not advertised a position in your field, there is also probably no great benefit to be gained from doing so. Academic institutions cannot afford to create new positions whenever interesting applications come their way. The announcement of a vacant position occurs only after an extended and sometimes highly politicized process. By sending an application to a college or university and asking to be kept in mind for future positions, you are unlikely to have any real effect on your chances of being hired. At best, you may encounter an institution that has a need in your area for a part-time instructor or a semester-long sabbatical replacement. More commonly, however, you will simply receive a response stating that no vacancies are currently available and your application materials will be discarded.

Prepare Your Application Materials Carefully

Because nearly every successful application for a full-time faculty position has been submitted in response to an advertised search, where do you learn about current vacancies in your field? The answer to that question depends on your specific academic discipline. In many fields there are professional associations that publish listings of current positions and usually even offer job placement services. The associations may also post announcements for positions on their websites or in publications specific to each discipline. In other fields, scholars tend to rely on advertisements that appear in the *Chronicle of Higher Education*. Published weekly, each issue of the *Chronicle* covers a broad range of academic and administrative issues while also including a large section of advertisements for academic positions. The *Chronicle*'s website (www.chronicle.com) provides access to many of these job listings, as well as the opportunity to sign up for weekly updates of newly advertised positions in your field. These updates may be customized so that you only receive announcements containing certain key words (such as "Asian history" or "assistant professor") or concerning positions in certain parts of the country.

Once you learn of a position that has been announced, read the job description carefully. It is tempting, particularly in an initial job search, to use the mail merge function of your word processor and create a hundred or more application letters that are identical except for the name and address of the institution. These are precisely the letters that are least likely to attract the attention of a search committee. Remember that your letter will probably be one of fifty to two hundred. For this reason, a generic letter will simply be less effective than a letter that takes into consideration the specific focus of the position as stated in the advertisement and that has been directed toward that particular program's individual needs and situation. Read the advertisement for language that distinguishes it from other positions. For instance, if an institution states in its advertisement that it is "part of a multicampus environment," try to address that distinctive feature in your letter. If your undergraduate or graduate institution maintained several campuses, mention that you are familiar with and appreciate such a learning environment. If you don't have any direct experience that you can cite, mention that you would enjoy the rich complexity of being part of a multicampus environment. The key factor is to relate in some fashion to whatever is unique about the advertisement. Institutions are charged per word for these position announcements, and they rarely waste verbiage on factors that are not important to them.

Here is an example of how to read an advertisement for an academic position. Although the language has been drawn from actual postings, the sample below is a composite with phrasing drawn from many different advertisements. The institution is fictitious, and the discipline is highly unlikely, to say the least.

> *Necrology:* Tenure-track position at the rank of assistant or associate professor. A Ph.D. in necrology, obituary studies, or a closely related field is required by the starting date of the position, August 10, [YEAR]. Applicants should have demonstrated a commitment to research and graduate-level teaching. Duties will include supervision of internships and theses, instruction in an area closely related to the applicant's specialty, and service to the department's graduate program. The successful applicant will be expected to seek external funding for professional activities. Applicants should send a cover letter, curriculum vitae, three letters of reference, and a representative sample of refereed research (such as an article, book chapter, or book) to: C. U. Layter, Chair, Department of Necrology, Research One University, Mapleton, Verhampshire, 05555. Application materials may also be submitted electronically (PDF, Microsoft Word document, RTF, or plain text) by sending them as email attachments to culayter@researchone .edu. Review of applications will begin on October 15, [YEAR], and will continue until the position is filled. Research One University is an Affirmative Action, Equal Opportunity Employer.

As you read ads like this one, use a highlighter to identify phrases that speak about the level of teaching that is involved, the balance of responsibilities between instruction and research, the institution's commitment to diversity, the importance of technology for teaching or doing research, and other phrases that may not appear in notices for similar positions. These phrases probably refer to matters of special importance to the institution or search committee, and it is wise to speak directly about them in your letter. If you did so in the case of our sample ad, you might observe the following:

- The ad specifically states that the position is available "at the rank of assistant or associate professor." Applicants are thus likely to include, not simply recent graduates, but also those who have already earned promotion and tenure. For this position, it will be even more important than usual for you to demonstrate that you are the "best fit" for this position and have credentials that precisely match what the committee is looking for.

- The ad repeatedly mentions research and graduate teaching as important responsibilities. A letter of application that fails to address these areas in a prominent manner will be less likely to be successful. If the advertisement had said (as many do), "Applicants should have a strong commitment to undergraduate teaching and service to nonmajors," the entire focus of your letter would be different.

- When job responsibilities are mentioned in an advertisement, it can be helpful to the committee reviewing the letter if you tie your experience directly to those duties, rather than forcing readers to make assumptions based on information contained in the curriculum vitae. Ask yourself: What does this reader really want to know and how can I make it easier for the reader to discover it?

- The items that applicants are required to submit can tell you a great deal about what the search committee is expecting of the successful applicant. Almost all searches require a cover letter, résumé, and letters of recommendation. But what additional items are required? In the sample ad, evidence of refereed research is requested. This requirement not only reiterates the research-oriented nature of this position, but also suggests that applicants without strong records of refereed research are highly unlikely to be considered after the initial screening.

- The successful applicant will be expected to seek external funding for professional activities. This statement can mean several things: it could suggest that although research is expected, the required resources are not provided because of funding problems at the school; or it could mean that applicants with grant-writing experience may be preferred. Investigate further, either through the website or people who may know the institution, to discover which of these possibilities is more likely. In either case, if you do have evidence that you can write grants successfully or have engaged in sponsored research, emphasize it in your letter.

How long should your application letter be? Most search firms will tell you that an application letter should fit on a single side of one page or, at most, should extend to the first quarter of a second page. This advice is probably excellent for individuals who are applying for presidencies or other positions where trustees are likely to play a significant role in the selection process; trustees and members of advisory boards tend to come from nonacademic backgrounds where extremely brief application letters are the norm. But this rule can be slightly less rigid for faculty positions. A good letter of application for a faculty position will be roughly two or three pages in length, single-spaced with an additional space between each paragraph. You will need that much space to relate your personal experience and academic preparation to the requirements and preferences of the position. Feel free to quote statements from the advertisement as a way of demonstrating how well you fit the requirements for the position. For instance, you might write:

> Dear Dr. Irvine and Members of the Search Committee,
>
> Please consider my application for the tenure-track position in malingering that was listed in the September 3rd issue of *Careers for Procrastinators*. Your announcement states that the University of Minnesconsin is seeking a scholar with a terminal degree in Procrastination Studies, peer-reviewed articles in a field closely related to vacillation or obstructionism, and a minimum of three years' undergraduate teaching experience in such courses as Introduction to Postponement. I will be receiving my Ph.D. in Procrastination from the University of Southwest North Dakota next May with a dissertation on . . .

To make it easier for members of the search committee to discover your accomplishments as they assess each application, you might even consider placing five or six of your most important achievements in a bulleted list or using boldfaced type to attract attention to one or two extremely important items. Take care not to overuse these devices in a letter, however, as their impact diminishes when they appear too often in the same letter.

Before mailing your application, read it over at least two or three times. If possible, have a friend review it as well. Even a single typographical error may be sufficient to have your application rejected. Particularly annoying to search committee members are errors in which their names or the name of the institution is wrong. (When applying to the University of Minnesconsin, you do not, for instance, want to refer to the institution accidentally as Minnesconsin State University, as the two schools may be bitter rivals. And take care not to refer to "Dr. Irvine" as "Dr. Irwin"; the good doctor has probably had his or her last name misspelled for years and may well be annoyed by it.) Be certain that your letter is free of grammatical errors, that the hard copy is printed on letterhead or plain white paper (which makes better copies if your materials must be reproduced for other members of the search committee), and that your packet of materials includes a current copy of your curriculum vitae in a suitable form for review by individuals outside of your current institution. (On the different forms that your curriculum vitae may take, see Chapter 31, "Creating an Effective Curriculum Vitae.")

When enclosing supporting materials, be sure to submit all items requested by the search committee, and only those items. If you don't include every item requested, your application may be rejected out of hand. At the very least, you'll have made the process harder for those reviewing your application who may need to contact you repeatedly for additional materials or who may assume that you were not interested enough to complete your application. At the same time, be sure to send only the items requested by the committee. Inundating reviewers with books, DVDs, course syllabi, student evaluations, and other items that they do not yet need can create a storage problem for the search, make you seem overeager or unable to follow directions, and do nothing at all to help advance your application. Increasingly, institutions are asking that applications be completed electronically. This process may consist of having to complete an online form (which can require repeating much of the material that is already in your curriculum vitae) or of attaching documents to an email message. If you are sending documents in machine-readable form, make certain that they are in a format that is easily viewed at most institutions. The safest forms to use in most cases are Microsoft Word documents, Rich Text Format (RTF), or Portable Document Format (PDF). Even when using these formats, however, there are certain considerations to keep in mind. If you are using a very new version of Microsoft Word, the document that you create may not be readable by earlier versions of the program. If this is a possibility because you have recently upgraded your software, consider saving your document in an earlier version of Word or converting it to RTF. Also, if your document uses highly unusual fonts, it is best to send it as a PDF file rather than in its original form: if the original document is viewed on a computer that does not have your font installed, your materials could look unattractive or seem scrambled. When in doubt, restrict yourself to fonts in the Times family, Courier, Georgia, Helvetica, Monaco, and Verdana; these fonts come preinstalled on most computers.

Be Distinctive Without Appearing Idiosyncratic

As you review the draft of your application letter, consider the tone of what you have said. Your goal should be to give your potential colleagues as clear as possible an impression of your personality without coming across as either quirky or eccentric. Adopt a formal and polite tone. Eliminate all traces of slang or casual speech. Avoid contractions. Applicants for positions will sometimes attempt to distinguish themselves from other candidates through expressions that are designed to catch the reader's eye, particularly in opening lines. ("Hi! You don't know it yet, but I'm your new organic chemist." Or "If you're like most members of search committees, you're probably pretty bored of reading applications by now. Well, this is one that you'll *want* to read.") Such a strategy is far more likely to backfire than to be successful. The reader will probably assume that you are at best unprofessional, at worst an unstable person of the type that the department definitely does not need and immediately move your application to the bottom of the stack. In a similar way, language that sounds too self-congratulatory, such as "I am highly qualified for this position," often alienates members of the search committee. Reviewers often feel that if an applicant has to state that he or she is highly qualified, then the strength of those credentials must not be immediately apparent from the supporting materials.

Applicants have a very short time to make an impression on a search committee. After all, if a particular position attracts two hundred applicants, it would take each member of the search committee more than sixteen hours to read the applications, even if he or she only spent five minutes on each set of materials. It is not uncommon for members of a very large committee to glance at each packet of materials for less than a minute before deciding whether to give that candidate greater scrutiny. For this reason, you want your application to stand out without coming across as glib, peculiar, or overly egotistical. The best tone to take in an application letter is professional, informative, and accessible. Help the reviewers in any way that you can. For instance, search committees frequently wonder which of their advertising efforts brought them the greatest response, so it is often good to open your letter by mentioning how you learned that the position was available. If you reread the opening to the sample letter of application cited earlier, you'll see that it conveys a great deal of information in a very limited space, demonstrates respect for the reader, and adopts an appropriate tone of professionalism. The audience for your letter is likely to consist primarily of faculty members in your discipline with perhaps a representative or two from outside the department. You can expect your readers to be fairly knowledgeable about your academic area; defining relatively common terms in use by your discipline is thus unnecessary and may even appear condescending to members of the search committee. However, expressions that are likely to be unique to the institution where you are now, such as course numbers, should be explained. You cannot assume that your reader will understand what "PSC 2454" refers to in your current course load unless you also provide the name of the course. Similarly, a reference to your current president, dean, or department chair may not lead to recognition outside of your institution; always identify these individuals both by full name and title.

Because you are talking about yourself and your accomplishments in your letter, you will find that you are using a large number of first-person pronouns. Search committees understand that this practice is inevitable, and they will not regard the number of times you refer to your achievements as a sign of egoism. Even so, you might try varying your sentence structure so that you do not have an overabundance of sentences beginning with "I." For instance, rather than saying:

> I have been successful in increasing the number of majors in our program by working with the departmental curriculum committee to align our courses more closely with industry standards, thus improving our job placement rate. I was also selected by the students as Professor of the Year in [YEAR], and I receive student course evaluations that are regularly either at or near the top of our department.

Consider saying:

> As a member of our departmental curriculum committee, I have been successful in increasing the number of majors in our program by working to align our courses more closely with industry standards, thus improving our job placement rate. The students also selected me as

Professor of the Year in [YEAR], and my student course evaluations are
regularly either at or near the top of our department.

The content is the same in both of these cases, but the more varied
sentence structure causes the second phrasing to seem less pompous or
self-serving.

Use Your Application Letter to Your Benefit

All too often applicants use their cover letters merely to restate the same
information that is already found in their résumés. Doing so wastes a
valuable opportunity to supply additional details and suggests to your
readers that your achievements are so sparse that you can only cite the
same accomplishments over and over. Rather than restating that you
received a nomination for Professor of the Year, use your letter to
expand on why you were nominated. Give your readers insight that
they cannot gain from your curriculum vitae: what are your values,
your plans for the future, and your distinctive qualities? If you already
list the courses that you taught in your résumé, use your letter to discuss your teaching philosophy or how you were able to communicate
effectively in small classes (or large classes, distance learning courses,
seminars, practica, graduate courses, or a combination of teaching environments). If your curriculum vitae already records your presentations,
publications, and grants received, use your letter to discuss why these
were significant accomplishments. What is the best contribution that
you have made thus far to scholarship, and why might that contribution be important to your new institution? If you have postdoctoral or
professional experience, provide some information about how those
opportunities have helped prepare you for the position for which you're
applying. Your curriculum vitae should effectively make the case that
you are a fully qualified candidate for the position. You can use your
letter then to explain what sets you apart from all the other fully qualified candidates and why you would be an interesting, supportive, and
collegial addition to the program.

Be Cautious About Following Up

Once you have submitted your letter of application, your curriculum
vitae, and all the other materials requested in the position announcement,
it is possible that you won't receive a response for quite some time. Most
institutions do acknowledge receipt of applications, and it is not uncommon

for search committees to reply to applicants letting them know the timetable for the search and whether any of the essential pieces of a completed application (such as letters of recommendation) have not yet arrived. Many institutions will also mail you an Affirmative Action or Equal Employment Opportunity (EEO) card, requesting that you self-identify your ethnic and gender information. Responding to these Affirmative Action or EEO requests is strictly voluntary. Doing so helps the institution determine whether their recruitment strategies have been successful in diversifying its applicant pool but it otherwise neither benefits your application to respond to these requests nor disadvantages your application to ignore them.

In certain cases, however, the institution may simply not acknowledge receipt of your application at all. You thus may be left wondering whether your materials arrived or were somehow lost. It could be that the institution is simply waiting until a large enough pool of applications has arrived before responding to all of them. It could be that the school does not acknowledge receipt of applications and only contacts the candidates it wishes to pursue. Or it may be that your materials never arrived. If three weeks or so pass and you still have received no word on your application, it is perfectly acceptable to send a quick and polite email message to the search chair asking whether all of your materials have in fact arrived. Other than this type of message, however, be very cautious about following up with the search committee after you have applied and before the interview process has begun. Acceptable communications with the search committee include:

- Genuine questions that you need to have answered at this stage of the search. "Did my application reach you in time for the deadline?" is an appropriate question. "What sort of start-up package will you be offering the successful candidate?" is not. Never tell a search committee that you will happen to be in their area soon and wonder if you might be able to talk with them about the position. This approach gives the appearance that you are trying to circumvent the regular search process and may well cost you the committee's serious consideration.

- A brief and sincere thank-you note if the search committee has done something exceptional. For instance, you might thank a search committee that has waived its policy of "no electronic submissions" for you because you are out of the country and cannot be assured that an application sent through the mail would arrive by the deadline date.

- Substantive changes to your credentials. For instance, if a
  manuscript that was pending editorial review has now been
  accepted for publication, it is appropriate to send a follow-up note.
  If a grant application that was under review has been funded, bring
  this to the attention of the search committee; note, too, whether
  that project is tied to your current institution or can accompany
  you as the principal investigator. Minor additions to your
  curriculum vitae, such as your service as a guest lecturer in another
  instructor's course or the correction of a typographical error, are not
  important enough to warrant an addition to your application. Small
  changes can make you appear desperate for recognition or unable to
  tell the difference between a major accomplishment and a fairly
  routine activity.

It is important to refrain from contacting the search committee after
you've applied and before it has selected candidates to interview because
the committee is then in the process of selecting its most preferred candidates from what could be a very large pool. In addition to evaluating
your achievements and professional qualifications, the search committee
will also be considering whether you are the sort of person they want to
work with. If you appear to be "nagging" or "greedy for validation" at
an early stage of the search process, the committee may wonder just how
time consuming and demanding you are likely to be after you are hired.
Given the choice between your application and another, they may prefer
the other candidate simply because you have seemed a bit too eager for
their attention.

In general, you should complete the following checklist before sending an
application for a faculty position to any institution:

☐   Am I absolutely certain that all of my application materials are
     completely free of typographical, spelling, and grammatical errors?

☐   Am I submitting all the supporting documents requested in the position
     announcement, and only these?

☐   Is my letter of application tailored specifically to the focus of this
     particular position?

☐   Does my letter convey a sense of my personality without making
     me seem quirky or eccentric?

☐   Does my letter avoid unnecessary repetition of information already
     in my curriculum vitae?

☐ Is my curriculum vitae current?

☐ Have I provided adequate contact information? Remember that you don't want to miss an opportunity for an interview because you are away from your office for a few days. Always provide an email address that you check at least several times each day, as well as a mobile telephone number.

If you follow these guidelines, you will not be guaranteed an interview for the position, but you will have taken all the appropriate steps to increase your likelihood of being favorably noticed by the search committee.

RESOURCES

Adams, K. A. (2002). *What colleges and universities want in new faculty*. Washington, DC: Association of American Colleges and Universities.

Barnes, S. L. (2007). *On the market: Strategies for a successful academic job search*. Boulder, CO: Lynne Rienner.

Darley, J. M., Zanna, M. P., & Roediger, H. L., III. (Eds.). (2003). *The compleat academic: A career guide* (2nd ed.). Washington, DC: American Psychological Association.

Formo, D. M., & Reed, C. (1999). *Job search in academe: Strategic rhetorics for faculty job candidates*. Sterling, VA: Stylus.

Goldsmith, J. A., Komlos, J., & Gold, P. S. (2001). *The Chicago guide to your academic career: A portable mentor for scholars from graduate school through tenure*. Chicago: University of Chicago Press.

Kronenfeld, J. J., & Whicker, M. L. (1997). *Getting an academic job: Strategies for success*. Newbury Park, CA: Sage.

Sowers-Hoag, K., & Harrison, D. F. (1998). *Finding an academic job*. Thousand Oaks, CA: Sage.

Vick, J. M., & Furlong, J. S. (2008). *The academic job search handbook* (4th ed.). Philadelphia: University of Pennsylvania Press.

2

INTERVIEWING FOR
A FACULTY POSITION

Many people approach an academic job interview as though it were an identical process at every institution. Nothing could be further from the truth. Job interviews have many different forms, and your experience at one college or university may be wholly unlike your experience at another. What will interest a research institution is likely to have very little resemblance to what a school with a strong teaching mission will ask you about. A liberal arts college and an institute focused on professional development will evaluate you in very different ways. Moreover, some colleges regard interdisciplinary collaboration as extremely important; others view it as a mere distraction from their core mission. It is vitally important to do your homework, then, on the values that guide the school to which you are applying, the college or division in which the position is located, and the department where your appointment will be made. In addition, the very format that the interview takes could be one of several kinds.

- *Telephone interviews* can occur at any point in the search process. Although they are particularly common near the beginning of a search when the committee is trying to reduce a large pool of semifinalists to a smaller group to be interviewed in person, other scenarios do occur. For instance, some search committees may conduct phone interviews after prescreening applicants at national conferences (see below) in order to give the entire search committee a chance to interact with a few of the candidates who seemed most promising. Some search committees even conduct telephone interviews after an on-campus interview (see below) when they discover that they have follow-up questions or need to make a final decision among two or more candidates, all of whom did extremely well during their campus visits. With the advent of videoconferencing, it is now more possible for the candidate and search committee to see each other during a remote interview. Whether conducted by telephone or videoconferencing, however, these interviews are often awkward because of the artificial environment they create. Speakerphones can make the search committee members seem distant or distort their voices. Without the benefit of visual cues, candidates may not know which of their responses please the committee and which of their responses require more elaboration. Even the best videoconferencing connections sometimes have lags or delays. Good search committees realize the artificial nature of these discussions and do not hold that awkwardness against the candidates. After all, the environment tends to be equally uncomfortable for all candidates alike.

- *Prescreening interviews* are conducted in person, but at far less depth than an on-campus interview. A common location for a prescreening interview is at a meeting of a national or large regional organization in a discipline relevant to the vacant position. Another common type of prescreening interview, although used more frequently in searches for upper administrators than for faculty members, is the so-called airport interview. In an airport interview, numerous applicants are brought in to meet with members of the search committee either at an airport or a nearby hotel. The committee (or sometimes selected representatives of the committee) then conducts short interviews, usually lasting between thirty minutes and two hours, with many different candidates in rapid succession. No matter at which point in the search process the prescreening interview occurs, its purpose is to help the search committee select a smaller subset of candidates from the larger pool that can be given greater attention in a full interview process.

- *On-campus interviews* allow candidates to meet (perhaps several times) with the search committee and other members of the campus community. The campus representatives who are not on the search committee might include the president, provost, dean, or chair of the academic department, as well as a group of students or staff members. On-campus interviews nearly always include some type of "job talk," a formal presentation that may be a summary of the candidate's recent research, a discussion of his or her teaching philosophy in the institution's specific environment, or an extended answer to some question of particular concern to the committee. It is not at all uncommon for candidates to be asked to give several job talks, including one devoted to current research and another with an instructional focus, such as teaching a sample class or demonstrating a particular technique. In certain fields, such as the fine or perform-ing arts, an alternative job talk may take the form of a master class, critique, or coaching session. On-campus interviews may also give candidates the opportunity to explore the local community (either on their own or with a real estate agent) or meet with representatives from human resources to learn more about the institution's benefits plan. Just as the institution is interviewing a candidate, the candidate is interviewing the school, potential colleagues, and the area where he or she would reside. In these situations, ask yourself: Is this a position in which I can easily imagine myself? Are there opportunities to grow there? What will I do when I'm not working? And does this position, as I examine it from every aspect, truly fit my plan for my career?

If you decide to accept an invitation for an on-campus interview, there are several additional considerations to keep in mind.

- *Payment for expenses*. Although your travel expenses and accommodations will almost always be covered by the institution, different schools handle this process in different ways. Some prefer to be billed directly for all expenses, while others prefer you to pay for your travel yourself, with reimbursement coming later. (Sometimes much later.) Be sure you know in advance the school's preference in this regard and bring along enough cash or a credit card to pay for items not directly billed to the institution. Save all receipts and file them promptly after the interview is over. Although not a common practice, colleges and universities will occasionally not reimburse candidates who are offered a position and then decide not to accept it. This is another reason never to apply for any job you would not seriously consider taking.

- *Flexibility*. On-campus searches are very complex to schedule, involving many members of the school's community. Be as flexible as you can in your travel dates, understanding that it may not be possible to honor your first choice. Be flexible, too, in selecting flights: if asked to book your reservation yourself or to explore the availability of flights, try to be considerate of cost. You're trying to make a good first impression, and a candidate who seems indifferent to the high expense of travel is likely to be regarded as someone who would not make a thoughtful colleague once hired.

- *Special needs*. If you have any special needs that must be addressed during the interview, be sure to mention these. Your needs may include accommodations for physical impairments, dietary restrictions, and equipment that you hope to have available during your presentation or job talk. Be flexible and understanding about anything that you can possibly do without, but if meeting a need is essential to your interview, mention it early in the process. If not given sufficient time to meet a need, the search committee may find it impossible to do so or, at the very least, be embarrassed by being caught unawares.

Preparing for the Interview

How you prepare for your interview will depend on the type of interview. For example, if you are preparing for a telephone interview, you might write down a few talking points on several sheets of paper that you can refer to as needed. You can dress however you like because the search committee cannot see you, so consider your best options. Would dressing up put you in a more professional frame of mind? Would dressing casually relax you in a situation that might otherwise make you nervous? And have you practiced thinking quickly when asked a question, as even short pauses can seem distressingly long during a telephone call? Conversely, in an interview where you are meeting with representatives of the institution in person, there are several other ways in which you will need to prepare. Among the most important of these are the following:

- *Do your homework on the institution.* Some candidates pride themselves on learning the institutions attended by everyone from the president to the newest member of the department, their dissertation topics, and their employment history. They consider this type of preparation to be good networking. Although such detailed knowledge can certainly charm some search committees, it is also possible that being prepared to this extent will make a candidate seem insincere and overly eager to please. What you should study is the nature of the curriculum of the institution you are visiting. What are its general education requirements? What are the requirements for a major in the discipline of this position? Are there multiple tracks or concentrations in the major? Does the department have a specific focus within the discipline? Is the mission of the school largely research, largely teaching, or a mixture? What is its vision for the future? Where do its graduate students tend to come from? Where are its alumni hired? How is the school trying to fulfill its most important goals? Knowing the answer to these questions will help you explain why you are interested in this particular position and how you see yourself fitting into the program's specific mission. Understanding the research interests of the department members where you'll work will also tell you something about the program's mission and future direction, as well as indicate whether your scholarly interests are a good "fit" there.

- *Dress professionally.* Even if you know that the department you are visiting has a reputation for informality, you should dress for the interview in good, professional, business attire. Both men and women should wear suits, preferably navy blue or gray rather than in earth tones, which tend to make candidates appear drab. Men should wear attractive but subdued ties; a tie with a simple pattern but without recognizable pictures on it is preferable. Women should wear a modest amount of jewelry (making sure that jewelry won't clink or rattle during a presentation), take steps to keep their hair in place without repeated care throughout the day, and avoid using either too little or too much makeup. No search committee is likely to reject a candidate solely on the basis of his or her appearance. Nevertheless, what you hope to do is to create an environment in which people will focus on the quality of your answers, not become distracted by this or that aspect of your appearance. No member of the search committee will assume that, simply because you dressed in business attire for your interview, you will always dress this way for the job if that is not their custom. Nevertheless, interviews always have a certain degree of formality, a tradition, and a set of expectations that differ from those ordinary workdays. If you are not viewed as having dressed professionally for the interview, the search committee may assume that you are not taking the opportunity seriously enough to warrant further consideration. It may seem disappointing and even hypocritical that certain academic professionals who devote so much energy to defending the rights of individuals to "be themselves" would take a candidate less seriously simply because "he didn't wear a tie" or "she went into her meeting with the president in flip-flops," but these situations do occur, even if no one ever mentions it aloud. Interviews are one of those situations in which, even for academic positions, John T. Molloy's old motto of "dress for success" still applies.

- *Have all the materials you will need ready at hand.* Inevitably during an interview, some issue or question will arise about which you'll want to make a note so that you can return to it later. People may also want to give you a telephone number or email address of someone whom you should contact after the interview. You may even be requested to send back a few additional supporting materials to the committee or be given instructions about how to submit your expenses for reimbursement. For all of these reasons, you should never go to an interview without a notepad and pen. Having to ask for such simple supplies during the interview can make you seem unprepared or insufficiently interested in the position. If you have business cards, bring a large supply and give one to each person at the end of each interview. Similarly, you will want to have a few extra copies of your curriculum vitae handy just in case the person who is speaking to you did not receive a copy or forgot to bring it. Though you will not want to go to an interview burdened with a huge back-pack or an armload of items, if you happen to have an offprint of an article that the search committee has not seen or a particularly inno-vative syllabus or set of course materials, slip a few such items into the back of your notepad. Then, if a question arises for which that item might be particularly relevant, you will have a copy ready at hand. "As a matter of fact," you might say, "I use simulations quite a bit in my upper-level courses. For instance, here's a copy of the syllabus that I designed for this semester and, as you'll see on the second page, we use simulations at the end of each unit to help pull that week's work together."

- *Think through the questions that you are likely to be asked.* You can-not anticipate every question that a search committee might ask, but you can predict the vast majority of the questions likely to be asked during an academic job interview. At the end of this chapter, you'll find a list of many of the most common questions. Think through how you might respond to these questions. Don't practice your answers so much that they come across to the committee as rehearsed. Rather, decide in advance what basic approaches or themes you'll use in answering each question, and then see if you can express those ideas several different ways. Your goal should be to appear knowledgeable of the issues about which you are asked, but not so well prepared for the interview that you follow a set script for each possible question.

During the Interview

Most candidates find that formal on-campus interviews tend to feel a bit awkward or artificial at first but become much more comfortable as the day wears on. The more you learn about the institution and the individuals who compose the search committee, the more relaxed you will feel in your conversations and presentations. Even if you decide early in the process that this position is not right for you, you should always keep doing your best to make a good impression. After all, any interview is good practice, and it is always possible that you will change your mind later. Don't burn your bridges. You want to leave each interview with as many options as possible; never close the door on a search until you have been formally offered the position and have decided not to accept it.

You will do your best in an interview and increase your likelihood of being offered a position if you adhere to the following principles:

- *Moderation in all things.* Answers to questions can be too long, and they can be too short. You want to answer in sufficient length to be clearly understood, to provide at least one appropriate example, and to demonstrate your knowledge of the area. Answers to any one question that go on for ten or fifteen minutes are, however, likely to cause the committee to lose track of your main point in a welter of words. Some candidates "talk themselves right out of the job" by giving the impression that they are too enamored of the sound of their own voice. You will find that you can answer most questions commonly asked at an academic interview in about three or four minutes. This length of answer gives you plenty of opportunity to get your point across, while it allows the other person a chance to ask a follow-up question or proceed to another area of inquiry.

  Be sure to apply this principle of moderation to all aspects of the interview. When going out to dinner with someone during a search, never order the largest or most expensive entrée. (You will probably be asked so many questions during the meal that you wouldn't enjoy it anyway, and certain members of the search committee may be turned off by someone who appears to be improperly taking advantage of the institution's expense account.) Avoid foods with red sauces that can stain your clothing, as well as items that are likely to leave residue in your teeth. Even if other search committee members order alcoholic beverages, you should never order anything more intoxicating than a single glass of wine. Even then, limit yourself to a sip or two, even if it means raising the glass to your lips and pretending to take a drink a few more times. Also, because you are likely to be nervous or excited during an interview, it may be best to refrain from any sort of caffein-ated beverage. Water is always the best thing to drink during a search and, because of the amount of talking you will do, you will find it very appealing.

- *Remember that every comment counts.* If a search committee member picks you up at the airport, your interview begins as soon as you are met beyond the security checkpoint, and it continues until the very instant that you board the airplane back home. In between those two moments, everything you say is an answer to an interview question, even if the search committee alleges otherwise. You cannot afford to let your guard down in social situations or when no member of the search committee is present. Many a candidate has not been offered a position because of an offhand remark made to a faculty spouse or a realtor who was providing a tour of the local community. Comments tend to be reported back to the search committee from all quarters. For instance, a remark that seems unflattering to the institution can put your candidacy in question, even if it is made "only" to a clerk in a local store. After all, you never know who knows whom. In a similar vein, never make disparaging remarks about the institution where you currently work or are completing your degree. A member of the search committee may be among that institution's alumni. In addition, if you don't appear to be loyal to your current institution, the search committee will wonder what you may be saying about them in a year or two.

- *Keep the job talk simple.* Many candidates harm their chances during an interview because they rely on software or other forms of technology that prove unreliable during their job talks. If there are illustrations or other items that you simply must use, prepare several alternatives. If your flash drive fails, you should have your own laptop; if your laptop fails, you should have handouts. Anticipate problems, and develop a plan for dealing with them. Also be sure that you understand precisely what type of presentation is expected and who will be in the audience. What you say to a class of undergraduates may well be different from what you say to a group of senior faculty members. Don't focus on your latest research if you've been asked to teach a sample class in an introductory course.

- *Don't just answer questions; ask questions as well.* A standard final question in any interview is, "Do you have any questions for us?" When this question is asked, you should always have questions ready. Not having a question to ask or saying "All of my questions have been answered" makes you look either superficial or not particularly interested in the position. As you will probably be asked this question repeatedly throughout your visit to a campus, you should prepare an arsenal of "stock questions" to ask just in case nothing else immediately comes to mind. Among these possible stock questions, you might consider these:

  - What, in your opinion, is the single best quality of this program [or department, college, institution]?
  - If you could change any one thing about this program [or department, college, institution], what would it be?
  - By the end of the first year, what would you like the person who fills this position to have accomplished?

- What specific aspects of my background led you to believe that I might be the person you were looking for?
- How would you characterize the morale of the faculty and staff here?
- How would you describe the quality of your students and their level of preparation by the time they reach your courses?
- What have been the recent "hot-button topics" on this campus, or in this program?
- How would you describe the management style of the person to whom I'd be reporting?
- How will the person who receives this position be evaluated for various personnel decisions?
- Are there any likely areas into which the curriculum of this program is expected to grow?
- Which service courses would you like the new faculty member to teach?
- What is the timetable for the rest of the search?

You should carry questions like these around "in your head." If you have to check your notes to think of a question to ask someone, it appears that the question must not involve a particularly pressing issue for you. Always have at least three or four stock questions memorized for every type of interview.

Handling Different Types of Questions

In an academic search, you will be asked many different types of questions. Some inquiries, such as those dealing with your background, experience, and area of specialization, you will find extremely easy to answer. Other types of questions may cause you more difficulty, such as:

- *Hypothetical questions.* One common form of interview question is to present you with the background to a specific situation and ask you how you might handle it. For instance, "Our institutional policy allows students to have excused absences for medical reasons and approved campus events, as long as they make up the work that is missed. One of your students is missing the vast majority of your classes, but always for reasons that the institution regards as excused absences. The student is an athlete, and most of these absences are due to away games and injuries. The student *has* made up the work, but you are still concerned because your course is an important pre-requisite for several other courses in the program. The student is a major in our field, and you have doubts about the student's ability to succeed at upper-level coursework in our discipline because of all these 'excused' absences. What do you do?" Hypothetical questions are frequently asked because the questioner believes that there is no single correct solution to the problem. The person merely wants to see what your thought processes are and to learn a little bit about your values. You should think through the situation carefully, offer the solution that you truly believe to be best, but allow yourself some flexibility just in case you receive the impression that the search committee favors a different type of approach. If this happens, you might continue by saying something like, "Yes, I can see advantages in approaching the situation in that way. I was merely suggesting the solution that I did because . . . " Whenever you are confronted by hypothetical questions in interviews, it is best to keep in mind the following essential principle:

Few, if any, hypothetical questions ever are truly hypothetical.

In other words, search committees frequently construct hypothetical questions about actual situations that have occurred and about which there has been some controversy. They want to determine how you might have handled this problematic situation, and they may even be seeking some advice, almost as though you were an outside consultant. For this reason, you should never provide glib or ill-considered answers to such questions. They are often the most important questions you will be asked during an interview.

- *Litmus test questions.* Certain questions that you will be asked—including certain hypothetical questions—may actually be litmus test questions. These are questions for which there is most definitely a "right answer" that the search committee wishes to hear, and candidates who do not provide that answer may find themselves removed from further consideration. Asking litmus test questions is a poor practice for any search committee; external candidates are not yet aware of the program's entire history and context that may indicate why one answer to the question is preferred. They cause candidates to gamble, perhaps even to make a rash "stab in the dark." But despite these drawbacks, search committees frequently do ask such questions.

Your best course of action is to reflect carefully on the question and provide your best, most well-considered response . . . but not too adamantly. In this way, you can reinforce that position if it appears to be the response that the search committee prefers or revise your opinion if you feel that you have answered incorrectly. "Oh, well," you might say, "I can see now that I didn't understand all the implications of the situation. But you raise a very important point. In light of what you've just told me, I might actually handle the situation somewhat differently. For instance . . ." Certainly, there is no reason to advocate for a solution that you sincerely find unpalatable or morally reprehensible. Nevertheless, you won't have any chance of solving actual problems like the one addressed in the question if you are not offered the position. For this reason, you should always approach litmus test questions with great care and caution.

- *Illegal or inappropriate questions.* Technically, there is no such thing as an illegal question in a job interview. Certain questions are legally inadvisable, however, because they may imply to a candidate that a hiring decision will be made not on the basis of his or her qualifications, but on the basis of rights that are protected under the law. For instance, questions dealing with your religion, ethnicity, sexual orientation, physical challenges, family status, and the like are usually legally inadvisable. Even so, there are exceptions. A private institution with a religious affiliation does have the right to ask you about your religious background if that is integral to its mission. A college or university can speak about your physical limitations to determine whether the institution is capable of offering you reasonable accommodations to fulfill the essential duties of the position. But what do you do in other situations where you are confronted with an inappropriate question? The answer may depend on how egregious the situation is, how uncomfortable it made you feel, and whether you consider it at all likely that your response will be held against you in the search. For example, in a social situation where members of the search committee are talking about coaching their churches' softball teams, someone may slip and ask you about your religious preference. As long as you consider it a bona fide mistake and unlikely to hinder you in the search, you may choose to answer the question or simply say politely, "I'd rather not say." Your response may be quite different if a member of the search committee pulls you aside, mentions that you are not wearing a wedding ring, and appears to be trying to determine your sexual orientation, giving you the impression that you may not be a good fit for the position if you don't answer the question the way the person wants. In cases where you feel that a significant lapse of judgment has occurred, deflect all such questions by saying "That's really not an appropriate topic for a job interview," and bring the matter to the attention of an appropriate campus officer, such as a dean, affirmative action director, or director of human resources.

As a general rule when asked any sort of question, listen carefully to each question, and then answer it fully to the best of your ability. Many candidates fail at interviews because they do not really listen to what is being asked or attempt to convert a question into something that they'd prefer to answer. Although ignoring the question and answering a question you wish you'd been asked is a perfectly good strategy if you are ever confronted by the media, it is a fatal mistake in employment interviews. Always try to answer each question clearly and directly. If you are uncertain that you have fully addressed the issue in the questioner's mind, you can always ask, "Did I answer everything that you were wondering about?" Use this strategy only occasionally, however, since it diminishes in value if a candidate relies on it too frequently.

The following are a few practice questions to review as you prepare to interview for a faculty position:

- Why are you interested in this job?
- How would you describe your teaching philosophy?
- How would you describe your probable research agenda over the next five years?
- How has your background prepared you for helping us fulfill the distinctive mission of our institution?
- How would you go about promoting active learning and a high level of engagement among your students?
- How might you use assessment of student learning as a way to continually improve your courses or our program as a whole?
- What is the most interesting book that you've read in the last six months?
- If there were one book that all first-year college students were required to read, what should it be?
- Have you had any experience teaching subjects from an interdisciplinary perspective?

- How do you tie what you teach to actual, real-world experiences?
- What makes you unique as an individual?
- Which aspect of academic life gives you the most pleasure?
- Which aspect of academic life annoys you the most, exasperates you, or is a pet peeve for you?
- What do you regard as the biggest challenge facing college and university professors today?
- What is the most significant accomplishment you've achieved in your current position?
- What, in your opinion, should be the proper balance between teaching, scholarship, and service for a faculty member?
- What achievement would you like to look back on after your first year as a faculty member here?
- Describe a mistake that you made in your professional life.
- Describe a problem that you have solved in your professional life.
- What is your greatest strength as a faculty member?
- Where do you see yourself in ten years?
- Do you have experience writing grants or securing external funds?
- If I were to speak to those who know you best, what would they describe as your greatest weakness?
- Do you have any suggestions on how our curriculum might be improved? Do you notice any major omissions or redundancies? Is there any way for it to be structured more coherently?
- Do you believe that introductory courses in our discipline should be taught differently to majors than to nonmajors? Why or why not?
- How would you describe yourself? How would those who know you best describe you?
- What do people who don't like you say about you?
- What are some examples of your creativity and innovation as a teacher? As a researcher? As a colleague?
- What three sources do you use most to gain information about recent trends in your field?

Even if you're not asked those specific questions, reflecting on possible answers to them will help you identify how you might respond during an actual interview. Remember that by the time you reach an on-campus interview, the search committee is already satisfied that you're qualified for the position. That decision has been made on the basis of your written materials, transcripts, and letters of recommendation. What the interviewers are most interested in when you meet them face-to-face is whether you are a good fit for their program. Do you seem to share their values? Are you the sort of person with whom they would care to interact on a daily basis? Do you have the stamina to succeed in their challenging environment? Remember that how you present yourself is often equally as important as the content of what you present during an interview.

RESOURCES

Blaxter, L., Hughes, C., & Tight, M. (1998). *The academic career handbook.* Philadelphia: Open University Press.

Gray, P., & Drew, D. E. (2008). *What they didn't teach you in graduate school: 199 helpful hints for success in your academic career.* Sterling, VA: Stylus.

Hume, K. (2004). *Surviving your academic job hunt: Advice for humanities PhDs.* New York: Palgrave Macmillan.

McCabe, L. L., & McCabe, E. R. B. (2000). *How to succeed in academics.* San Diego, CA: Academic Press.

Molloy, J. T. (1988). *John T. Molloy's new dress for success.* New York: Warner Books.

Molloy, J. T. (1996). *New women's dress for success.* New York: Warner Books.

3

WHAT KIND OF
PROFESSOR ARE YOU?

One of the most interesting aspects of culture can be seen when we observe how members of different societies identify themselves. For instance, in response to the request "Tell me a little bit about yourself," many Americans tend to respond in terms of their professions. In other parts of the world, it is more common for people to identify themselves by their heritage, the region in which they live, their religious background, or a few important details about their families. Only secondarily do people in many cultures think that what they do for a living determines who they are. Moreover, as American academics, many of us carry this tendency to view ourselves in terms of our profession even further, identifying ourselves not merely as college professors, but also as historians, American historians, American Civil War historians, or even American Civil War economic historians. In other words, readers of this book may find that their natural tendency is to define themselves wholly in terms of their academic disciplines, overlooking at times many of the other key ingredients that constitute their identities and even their professional lives. This practice can be quite limiting, because knowing who you are outside of your academic field is a critical first step in developing a plan to advance your career. For instance, the strategy that we'll develop in Chapter 4, "Career Planning for College Professors," can be seen as similar to drawing a map that will lead you to a further destination. But for any map to be useful, you have to know where you are starting from. In the same way, if don't understand who you are now, it will be much more difficult for you to become who you want to be five or ten years from now. So, before we begin to develop your career plan, ask yourself: What kind of professor are you? What are your values, hopes, and dreams? What are your strengths and weaknesses? Which activities do you find so unpleasant that you couldn't engage in them regardless of any benefits that may result? What makes you happy? What seems to annoy you more than it does other people? What caused you to seek an academic profession in the first place? What legacy do you hope to leave behind? Keep in mind that there is no one correct answer to any of these questions. The professoriate is a "tent" that is big enough to include people of all types and inclinations. But you need to be honest with yourself about what motivates you in order to pursue your goals most effectively. To do that, it is helpful to conduct a short, informal inventory.

What follows are twenty-six activities that are commonly performed by college professors. Many of them are mundane or routine tasks, but they all relate to the real work that faculty members are expected to perform. You can approach the inventory in several different ways. The easiest way is simply to read over the twenty-six items and to note those activities that interest you more than others or those that you would find particularly unpleasant. A more detailed approach, which can give you more surprising results, is to place the entire list in order of preference. In other words, take a sheet of paper, number it 1 through 26, and then place the items in the order that you find them most interesting, appealing, and exciting (or, if few of them intrigue you, how you find them least *un*interesting, *un*appealing, and *un*exciting). No one else will see your results, so be absolutely candid. Don't respond according to how you think you "should" feel or how others might expect you to feel. If you believe that a particular activity is something that "every good professor is supposed to value highly," but you find it unappealing or dread doing it, then place that activity low on your list. If there is an item that you're afraid most other professors would regard as trivial or a distraction from their "real work," but you enjoy doing it, place it high on your list. You are unlikely to order these items in precisely the same way as any other professor, so don't worry about what others may say or believe. The whole purpose of this inventory is to find out what makes *you* distinctive as a college professor.

The activities that you should rank from 1 ("most appealing or least unappealing") to 26 ("most unappealing or least appealing") are:

A. Receiving a course release to conduct a scholarly project that will cause you to spend much of your time alone in the lab, library, or studio.

B. Answering a telephone call from a parent who is seriously concerned about how his or her child is doing in your course.

C. Being the "point person" selected by your department to present a new and highly controversial curriculum proposal before a meeting of the institution's entire faculty.

D. Meeting one-on-one with a student to conduct an independent study, directed inquiry, or thesis preparation.

E.   Revising a course that you have already taught several times in order to make it more effective.

F.   Completing a report that summarizes assessment data for your entire academic department.

G.   Being appointed to a committee that meets quite often but conducts what you regard as extremely important work for the department and institution.

H.   Being invited at the last minute to answer a few questions about your program's curriculum by the board of trustees. You understand the department's curriculum rather well, but you do not have time to prepare specifically for this meeting.

I.   Devoting a year or more to an interdisciplinary work of scholarship that, although somewhat related to your discipline, does not fall within the traditional confines of that discipline.

J.   Teaching a three-hundred-person introductory course in your discipline.

K.   Serving as the person responsible for planning celebrations whenever a faculty member in your discipline is promoted, receives tenure, or has a major work accepted for publication.

L.   Being listed as third author on a publication for which the first two authors are highly respected members of your discipline.

M.   Coauthoring a work of scholarship or creative activity with a student.

N.   Meeting one-on-one with your dean, provost, or president to discuss a topic that is not revealed to you until the meeting.

O.   Beginning the initial preparation for an innovative curriculum proposal that will not be completed for several years.

P.   Teaching an upper-level seminar or graduate course in your discipline.

Q.   Working on a project that applies your discipline to real-world situations and helps improve the lives of others without cost to them.

R.   Reading an interesting book in your discipline—alone in your office with the door closed.

S.   Giving some quick and spontaneous advice to a colleague who has reached an impasse in his or her own research.

T.   Tutoring a student who is having difficulty in one of your courses.

U.   Being elected to a four-year term on a committee that will radically revise the general education requirements of your institution.

V. Organizing your receipts so that you can be reimbursed for travel expenses related to your scholarship.

W. Serving as the departmental representative on a panel that answers questions parents may have about their children's academic experience at your institution.

X. Writing a solo article that explains a truly innovative idea you have developed in your discipline.

Y. Advising a student regarding which courses to take next term in order to graduate in a timely manner.

Z. Providing an overview of recent developments in your discipline to an alumni gathering.

No matter which method you used to prepare your inventory, you should now have a good idea of your preference regarding certain activities commonly performed by college professors. If you simply noted the ones you particularly like or dislike, go over those two lists. If you ranked all twenty-six activities, focus on the top five and the bottom five. See if your lists run parallel to any of the following. Table 3.1 provides an overview of how the activities sort into different categories.

• Activities related to teaching (items B, C, D, E, J, O, P, and T), scholarship (items A, I, L, M, S, V, and X), or service (items F, G, H, K, Q, U, W, Y, and Z). Nearly all college professors are expected to devote their time to all components of the "academic triad" or "the three legs of the academic stool," as teaching, scholarship, and service are often called. However, it is not at all uncommon for faculty members to have a strong preference for one of these three activities or a relative aversion to one of them. If this is the case for you, then you are in possession of valuable information about yourself. Knowing your preference in this area may help you to tailor a job search more exclusively to your interests: if your top five preferences all included items related to scholarship, for instance, you may well not be happy working at an institution that prides itself on "placing teaching first." Furthermore, if you are an untenured junior faculty member whose top five preferences all were items related to service, you may need to counterbalance this tendency as in matters of tenure and promotion, most institutions weight excellence in teaching and research far more heavily than they do excellence in service. If tenure and promotion are no longer concerns for you, then discovering that you place a strong priority on teaching, scholarship, or service can help define

Table 3.1: College Professor Inventory

	Teaching	Scholarship	Service	Independent Work	Collaborative Work	Student Centered	Faculty Centered
A		•		•			•
B	•			•		•	
C	•			•			
D	•				•	•	
E	•			•		•	
F			•	•			•
G			•		•		•
H			•	•			
I		•					
J	•					•	
K			•				•
L		•			•		•
M		•				•	
N							
O	•				•		
P	•				•	•	
Q			•				
R				•			•
S		•			•		•
T	•					•	
U			•		•	•	
V		•		•			•
W			•		•	•	
X		•		•			•
Y			•				
Z			•	•			

Scholarship of Discovery	Integration	Application	Detail Oriented	Big-Picture Oriented	Large Groups	Small Groups, Individuals	Planning	Improvisation
•							•	
			•			•		•
	•			•	•			•
		•				•		
		•	•				•	
			•				•	
						•	•	
					•			•
	•						•	
			•				•	
•						•		
						•		
						•		•
	•			•			•	
•						•		
		•						
•								
								•
		•	•					
	•			•	•		•	
			•					
			•		•			•
•			•	•				
		•						•
	•				•			

your priorities for the next phase of your career: you can begin to develop an identity as "the program's most highly regarded teacher" or "our area's most widely published scholar." That identity can be extremely useful for establishing new goals—even a wholly new professional reputation—for yourself.

- Activities that involve independent work (items A, B, C, E, F, H, R, V, X, and Z) or collaborative work (items D, G, L, O, P, S, U, and W). Knowing whether you prefer working alone or as a member of a team is an important aspect of determining what kind of professor you are. If you gravitate toward group projects, then you can build on this preference to explore the development of team-taught courses, collaborative research efforts, and group service projects. If you prefer working on your own, then you might seek out such teaching opportunities as online courses and distance learning courses, which may give you greater independence in your instruction. In a similar way, you may wish to identify further examples of research projects and service activities that allow you to work on your own and at your own pace. Even when you are assigned to a committee or task force, you may also wish to explore the type of assignments (such as preparing drafts of proposals or collecting examples of best practices) at which you can excel independently.

- Activities that are student centered (items B, D, E, J, M, P, T, U, W, and Y) or faculty centered (items A, F, G, K, L, R, S, V, and X). Institutions so often state that they are "focused on the needs of the students first" that faculty members frequently adopt this rhetoric regardless of what their actual feelings on the matter may be. When you ask yourself candidly why you are pursuing an academic profession, which takes priority for you: training the next generation of scholars in your discipline or having the privilege of working with the ideas and concepts of your discipline? If you discover that you truly are student centered, then this information will guide you as you seek committee assignments and make requests for the courses that you will teach. If you find that you really focus more on the needs of faculty members in your discipline, such as the ability to conduct innovative research and to develop new theories, then this insight, too, will guide you in the choices you make.

- Activities that involve the scholarship of discovery (items A, L, P, R, and X), integration (items C, I, O, U, and Z), or application (items D, E, Q, T, and Y). In 1990, Ernest Boyer made an important contribution to the way in which research, scholarship, and creative activity were viewed by colleges and universities. In his book *Scholarship Reconsidered*, Boyer concluded that the traditional way in which scholarship had been viewed by the academy (that is, as research) was only one of several legitimate forms that scholarship could take. In addition to this "Scholarship of Discovery," as Boyer called research that introduced new ideas and theories, he also identified what he called the "Scholarship of Integration" (the relationship of existing ideas to one another, including such pursuits as interdisciplinary studies) and the "Scholarship of Application" (through which developments in a discipline are used to solve a practical problem or to produce a tangible benefit). Boyer's fourth category, which he called the "Scholarship of Teaching," where advances are made in the pedagogy of a discipline, will be addressed in Chapter 28, "Alternative Forms of Scholarship." Being conscious of the type of scholarship toward which you gravitate as a college professor will help you both characterize and defend that approach to scholarship more persuasively. For instance, suppose you are performing a new and highly innovative type of scholarship but face tenure, promotion, or post-tenure review by a committee that consists primarily of professors who have been engaged in independent research. Your own thorough understanding of the type of research you do can help you explain it more clearly to committee members who may only be familiar with other forms of the Scholarship of Integration or Application. In addition, reflecting on your research can help you in the future by leading you to new topics, forms, or directions in which to take your ongoing scholarly activity.

- Activities that are detail oriented (items B, E, F, K, T, V, W, and Y) or big-picture oriented (items C, O, U, and X). Some faculty members are more attracted to activities that allow them to take a more global view of their research, curricular development, and the like, while others prefer to work out the details of implementing these ideas. The academic environment is not merely a matter of seeing either the forest or the trees; for any academic unit to function effectively, there is a need for individuals with both of these complementary talents. If you discover that you have a strong preference for either handling the specific facets of a plan that will make it more successful or developing a more visionary and overarching theme, but without much interest in the specific steps leading to implementation, then this is valuable insight into the sort of role that you might seek to play in your discipline. If you find that you are detail oriented, seek out opportunities where you help implement curricular revisions, improve course rotations, gather and analyze data, write budget proposals, and prepare the information needed in departmental reports. If you find that you are more big-picture oriented, become involved in your institution's strategic planning efforts or serve as a faculty representative to your governing board.

- Activities that involve interaction with large groups (items C, H, J, U, W, and Z) or small groups and individuals (items B, D, G, L, M, N, P, S, T, and Y). Some professors feel comfortable working with groups of any size, and they are equally effective no matter how many people are present. Others find that they are more effective in one type of setting or another. For certain professors, addressing large groups is a perfectly comfortable activity; they feel that they are "on stage" in these situations and that a safe distance separates them from the audience. These same people may feel awkward or even tongue-tied when called on to make casual conversation with a small number of people. Other professors are at their best working one-on-one with students or in small seminars, but are far less effective when addressing large numbers of students in an auditorium. You may not always be able to control the environments in which you are called on to speak or teach, but knowing your natural inclination in this regard can aid you in which sorts of courses to request, which types of committee assignments to pursue, and which kinds of venues to present your research.

- Activities that require planning (items A, E, F, G, I, K, O, and U) or improvisation (items B, C, H, N, S, W, and Y). You may prefer to engage in activities in which you spend long periods of time preparing your ideas before you ever "go public" with them. Alternatively, you may enjoy the impromptu give-and-take that occurs in situations requiring more spontaneity. Being conscious of this preference will help you in every aspect of your professional life. It will guide you as you develop your courses (if you crave detailed planning, how can you plan "spontaneous" discussions in your courses, and if you thrive on spontaneity, how do you help the student succeed who requires a great deal of structure and predictability?), and as you conduct your research (if you have a choice between reading a formal paper or participating in a poster session or panel discussion, which would you choose?). It can even assist you with choosing appropriate areas in which to contribute service based on the operating procedures of the various committees available to you.

There are probably as many kinds of college professors as there are kinds of people. Different personalities will flourish in one type of academic environment, but feel frustrated or stifled in another. By knowing the type of professor you are, you stand a much better chance of being satisfied in your professional environment and of serving both your students and colleagues extremely well. It will also provide a wonderful starting point for helping you become the type of professor that you ultimately *want* to be.

REFERENCES

Boyer, E. L. (1990). *Scholarship reconsidered: Priorities of the professoriate.* Princeton, NJ: Carnegie Foundation for the Advancement of Teaching.

RESOURCES

Bassett, R. H. (Ed.). (2005). *Parenting and professing: Balancing family work with an academic career.* Nashville, TN: Vanderbilt University Press.

Boss, J. M., & Eckert, S. H. (2006). *Academic scientists at work: Navigating the biomedical research career* (2nd ed.). New York: Springer.

Coiner, C., & George, D. H. (Eds.). (1998). *The family track: Keeping your faculties while you mentor, nurture, teach, and serve.* Bloomington: University of Illinois Press.

Darley, J. M., Zanna, M. P., & Roediger, H. L., III. (Eds.). (2003). *The compleat academic: A career guide* (2nd ed.). Washington, DC: American Psychological Association.

Frost, P. J., & Taylor, M. S. (Eds.). (1996). *Rhythms of academic life: Personal accounts of careers in academia.* Thousand Oaks, CA: Sage.

Gappa, J. M., Austin, A. E., & Trice, A. G. (2007). *Rethinking faculty work: Higher education's strategic imperative.* San Francisco: Jossey-Bass.

Goldsmith, J. A., Komlos, J., & Gold, P. S. (2001). *The Chicago guide to your academic career: A portable mentor for scholars from graduate school through tenure.* Chicago: University of Chicago Press.

Philipsen, M. I. (2008). *Challenges of the faculty career for women: Success and sacrifice.* San Francisco: Jossey-Bass.

Schuster, J. H., & Finkelstein, M. J. (2005). *The American faculty: The restructuring of academic work and careers.* Baltimore, MD: Johns Hopkins University Press.

Taylor, P. G. (1999). *Making sense of academic life: Academics, universities, and change.* Philadelphia: SRHE/Open University Press.

4

CAREER PLANNING FOR COLLEGE PROFESSORS

Most college professors begin their professional lives with only a vague idea about how their careers may develop. Unless they are familiar with academic life because a member of their family taught at a college or university, they are frequently unaware of the options that are open to them, the choices they'll need to make, and the different directions their professional lives could take. They may see themselves as simply accepting a position that they are offered, moving up through the ranks, and remaining at that same institution for their entire careers. Indeed, many faculty members follow exactly that path, and it can be a very satisfying and rewarding way in which to spend one's professional life. But there are also other opportunities that faculty members may wish to consider—not to mention occasional side routes that deviate from, then reconverge with, their main routes—before they choose any one particular path. All faculty members need, in other words, to do some very basic career planning.

Career planning for college professors involves determining which professional goals are most meaningful to you and then developing a strategy to attain those goals. It does not mean that every detail of your unfolding career will be determined in advance and that you will then be committed to moving lockstep through an inflexible program. On the contrary, a good career plan provides plenty of chances for serendipity. After all, there may be fellowship programs available to you a decade from now that have not even been created yet. Your academic discipline might develop in a dramatic new direction over the course of your career. You may discover new professional interests, or innovations in technology may completely transform the way in which you teach or do research. You can't plan for every eventuality. But what you can do is set yourself some basic career goals and then create an environment in which you will be most likely to fulfill at least some of them. In other words, simply because you can't (and shouldn't) plan for everything, it doesn't mean that you shouldn't plan for anything. Whether you realize it or not, career planning for college professors begins the very moment you have been offered a faculty contract and are considering whether to accept it.

Negotiating a Contract

When an institution offers you a contract as the result of a national search and on-campus interview, the relationship that you have with that institution changes dramatically. Until this moment, you have been trying to persuade them to accept you. During contract negotiations, they are trying to persuade you to accept them. This shift in the relationship is significant, but don't let this altered status go to your head. The institution is likely to have a backup plan with a second- or third-choice candidate already in mind in case you don't accept the position. Moreover, academic institutions rarely have the sort of negotiating flexibility found in large corporations; most of the time, colleges and universities make their first offer very close to the maximum salary they can afford. In other words, if you demand too much, the institution is likely to lose its enthusiasm for you very quickly and rescind their offer. But if you accept the first offer you are made, you may be doing yourself a disservice in terms of your overall career plan. So, before you agree to the contract that has been offered, refuse it, or make a counteroffer, ask yourself the following question: What are the most important things that I want out of my professional life? How you answer that question will help you determine how you can best negotiate the offer you have received. As an illustration, let's consider your possibilities from several different perspectives.

- *Salary.* As we've seen, most colleges and universities tend to make their offers to candidates at near the maximum of what has been budgeted for the position. Though there may be some negotiating room for the chair or dean, it is unlikely to be very much. If you feel that the salary offer is insufficient for your needs, you can always counteroffer, but you should be aware that, if the institution increases its offer at all, it is likely to do so only very slightly. If you are convinced that you need (or are worth) 50 percent more than what the institution has offered, then there is almost certainly no chance that you will reach a salary figure that is acceptable to both of you. Even a counteroffer that is 20 to 25 percent higher than the original offer may well cause the institution to conclude either that you are out of their price range or that you have an inflated sense of your worth. As a general rule of thumb, most successful counteroffers are in the range of roughly 10 percent over what the institution has offered.

In other words, if you are offered a salary of $50,000, a counteroffer of $55,000 would not be viewed as unreasonable by most institutions. For other salary figures, round your counteroffer to a reasonable amount in the range of 10 percent or less. For instance, if you are offered a salary of $60,000, requesting $66,000 might seem like an unusual amount; you could safely request $65,000 or, if the institution seems to be adequately funded, you could possibly stretch your request to $67,500. But going much beyond this figure, such as asking for $70,000, will probably seem far too high to the institution and may cause them to decide not to increase their initial offer at all. In addition, even if you make a counteroffer of 10 percent or less, don't be surprised when the institution tells you that it cannot raise its initial figure at all or can do so by only a very small amount. They may be negotiating in good faith at the very limit of what is available to them.

In making your counteroffer, you must, of course, be cordial and respectful at all times: you don't want your future boss's first impression of you to be that of an egomaniac. Say something like, "Oh. I was hoping for something a little higher than that because of my student loan payments" (or "because my spouse hasn't yet found a job" or "because I need to support my parents" or "because the cost of living is so much higher in your area than what I am used to" or whatever your reason is for needing a higher income). "Did you have a specific figure in mind?" the chair or dean might ask. That's when you can say, "Well, I was thinking something more along the lines of . . . " and state your counteroffer. The person's response may be, "I'm sorry, but the figure I mentioned is the best we can do" or the person may immediately either meet your figure or suggest an amount somewhere between the two figures. More commonly, however, the person will say that he or she needs to determine whether the offer can be revised and that you'll receive another call later. All this means is that the caller needs to check with someone, either his or her supervisor or a budget director, to see whether it is financially possible to make an increase to the offer and if so, by how much. If the institution meets your counteroffer, it is *never* acceptable to try to negotiate for a still higher salary. When your counteroffer is met, you really only have two options: either accept the offer that is now on the table or refuse it on grounds other than salary. ("I've been talking this matter over with my spouse, and we've decided that, despite your very generous offer, we simply don't wish to relocate at this time. I'm going to focus on positions closer to my home.") Being professional and responsible while negotiating a contract is an important part of your career planning. After all, even if you decide to reject an offer, you don't want to leave the institution with a bad impression of you. As we've seen, higher education is a very small world, and how you treat one institution can easily come back to haunt you later. For this reason, individuals who sign contracts and then fail to honor them often discover that this action hurts their careers when they least expect it.

- *Start-up funds.* Start-up funds are the one-time investment that an institution makes in order to assist you with the continued progress of your scholarship and teaching. In such fields as the natural sciences, engineering, and health care, start-up funds can be substantial, possibly involving, at larger research institutions, the creation of a full laboratory or another facility. In many fields, however, start-up funds consist of nothing more than the purchase of a computer or the reallocation of existing equipment and the assignment of an office. What you should ask yourself before signing a contract is, "What sort of initial investment will I absolutely need to continue my work as effectively as possible from the starting date of the position?" State your needs as a request to be added to the original contract. Again, don't be surprised if your request cannot be met or can only be addressed in part. Certain schools, particularly smaller private colleges, do not have the budgetary flexibility needed to provide significant start-up funds to new faculty members. But even if your request cannot be granted, stating your needs could cause the institution to explore whether they might address your concerns in some other fashion. For instance, the institution might allow you to begin applying for access to its internal research funds even before the starting date of your contract. It could lend the support of its Office of Research and Sponsored Programs in helping you apply for external funding. It could partner with other institutions in a consortium to provide you with access to necessary equipment at a nearby campus. Be flexible in considering the institution's response to your request. It is almost certainly trying to find a way to meet your needs while working within the constraints of its fiscal reality.

- *Moving expenses.* Some institutions always allocate a certain amount to new faculty members for moving expenses. Other institutions are prohibited from funding moving expenses at all. Still others will only cover a portion of moving expenses if you negotiate it into your original contract. It is always appropriate to ask what the institution's policy on moving expenses happens to be. Try to be precise in your questions: In addition to the costs associated with the transportation of furniture, can the institution also cover the costs of packing and unpacking? Can they reimburse you for meals and mileage expenses while you are in transit? Can they cover the cost of transporting office equipment and laboratory items in addition to your household furnishings? Even in cases where the institution is prohibited by its policies from covering your relocation costs directly, they may be able to compensate you for an expensive move in some other way. For example, they may be willing to increase their salary offer slightly so that your moving expenses are covered within your first three years. Or they may be able to hire you for a consultancy, bringing you in for a few days before the start of the official contract and paying you a stipend sufficiently large to defray at least part of your moving expenses. If no other alternative is possible, either the institution or its foundation may be able to loan you the cost of your move, which you will then repay—at low or perhaps even no interest—over an extended period via payroll deduction. Finally, if the institution is private, they may even have access to vehicles and employees who can assist with your move. Here again, the institution's response to your need may well be creative, but it is unlikely to explore these possibilities if you do not inquire about them.

- *Special benefits.* At times the most important thing to you might be not an increase in salary per se, but some less tangible factor that will make your life better. Institutionally subsidized day-care centers, flexible working hours, the ability to continue your education, assistance with spousal employment, tuition remission for dependents, workload adjustments, opportunities for advancement, and help in securing affordable housing are all special benefits that may matter more to you than salary alone. Be clear about indicating the challenges that you face because of your special circumstances and allow the institution to develop creative ways of meeting your needs. Remember that a salary that is $5,000 lower than what is offered by another institution may be worth far more in the long run if it includes the equivalent of $30,000 a year in tuition remission to one of your dependents, a lighter teaching load, and a less stressful pathway to promotion and tenure. If your family is reluctant to make the move, inquire about a second visit to the institution—this time including your spouse and children—so that they may all experience where their new home will be. Each prospective faculty member has an individual set of needs and personal circumstances; institutions can often be quite flexible in addressing those needs.

Plotting a Career Trajectory

Once you have accepted a contract and are working at an institution, it is time to begin plotting the future course of your professional life. If you don't occasionally give some thought to where you may be going, you could easily look backwards in ten to twenty years and discover that you have not gone anywhere at all. For some people, that type of stability and predictability is a wonderful thing. For others, it can lead to frustration and burnout. The only way to determine which of these possibilities is more likely to be true in your case is to give the matter some serious thought.

Begin by preparing an updated version of your curriculum vitae. This may be a copy of the one that you sent the institution when applying for your current job. It may be a version that you revised after reading Chapter 31, "Creating an Effective Curriculum Vitae." Or it may simply be the résumé that you submit as part of your annual performance review. No matter which version it is that you use, sit down with it and begin to change it using a red pen (or, if you prefer to perform this exercise electronically, save your résumé under a different name and make changes to the new file). First, choose an appropriate date in the future. If you are a relatively senior faculty member, a date five years from today will be appropriate. If you are an associate professor, choose a date ten or fifteen years from now. If you are relatively new to the profession, try to look ahead fifteen or twenty years. Then, rewrite your curriculum vitae from the perspective of what you would like to have attained by that date. In conducting this exercise, try to achieve a balance between being unreasonably optimistic and excessively cautious. Try to stretch your goals a little. It is appropriate to reach a little bit beyond your grasp, but the exercise will not be valuable if you do not balance your dreams with some practicality. (For instance, many of us would like to serve as endowed distinguished professors at Harvard University, but this should only be your goal if that vision seems attainable in light of your current circumstances.)

As you draft your visionary curriculum vitae, ask yourself the following questions:

- Will my profession still be in the area of higher education? If not, what other career path might I find more satisfying?
- If I remain in higher education, do I see myself continuing largely as a faculty member or will I pursue administration or some other role within the academy?
- If I decide to continue my progress as a faculty member, what rank will I have at that time?
- If I choose to pursue administration or some other role, what position do I wish to have at that time?
- What salary level do I hope to achieve?
- Will I still be at my current institution or will I have used my experience here to pursue an opportunity elsewhere? (Be absolutely honest about

all of these questions. Although you may never say to your colleagues, "I see my position here as simply a springboard for something better," the current exercise is for your eyes only and requires absolute candor.)

- How many products of scholarship (as appropriate to my discipline) will I have produced? What form (that is, books, refereed articles, conference presentations, poster sessions, recitals, exhibits, reviews, productions, patents) will this scholarship assume?

- For what may I be recognized through awards and honors? You do not have to specify the particular awards, because you have no control over their selection, but think in terms of general categories such as "Campuswide Teacher of the Year," "Outstanding Scholar in the Department of X," "National Distinguished Service Award," and the like. In what time frame might you hope to be recognized for these achievements?

- In which professional organizations do you hope to hold office or serve on committees?

- On which institutional committees do you hope to serve?

- Which new courses will you have developed? For which courses will you be particularly well known?

- What will your median scores on student course evaluations look like? What types of comments will students be making about your classes?

- Will your course load be primarily at the undergraduate level, graduate level, or some combination of the two? Will you be supervising theses? If so, what might some of those thesis topics be?

- How will your teaching philosophy have developed? Your scholarship philosophy? Your service philosophy?

- What will be your single greatest accomplishment, the achievement of which you will be the most proud?

In Chapter 3, "What Kind of Professor Are You?" we saw that your responses to an inventory of common activities performed by faculty members helped clarify where you are now in terms of your values, interests, and priorities. Your visionary curriculum vitae is an indication of where you hope to go. The next step is to outline a career plan that will help carry you from where you are now to where you want to be. For instance, in order to produce the number of scholarly products that are listed in your visionary vita, how many will you need to start creating each year? Will you need to write book reviews or volunteer for editorial boards of prestigious journals so as to increase your chances of being published there? If you see yourself as having made your future reputation as a stellar teacher or distinguished scholar or solid campus citizen, how does that desire guide the decisions you make over the next few years? Do your priorities suitably complement the goals that you hope to achieve?

Your career plan plots the distance from your current professional position and your ultimate professional goals and breaks it into a number of manageable steps. In the jargon of strategic planning, your career plan operationalizes your goals; it takes your dreams and creates a series of concrete, feasible actions to help you achieve them. It outlines for you the types of experience you will need to obtain in order to be ready when opportunities arise. A good career plan can help you think practically about which journals should receive your submissions, which committees deserve your most active participation, which organizations you need to become involved in, and which activities should matter most to you.

As you create your career plan, develop it to the level where you can say, "Over the course of the coming year, I need to do the following five things . . ." and then make those five things your highest priorities. At the end of each academic year, review both your career plan and your visionary curriculum vitae. How have you fared in attaining the goals you set out to achieve? Which goals no longer seem desirable or realistic to you? Are there new goals to take their place? Even though you may have developed a visionary curriculum vitae for fifteen or twenty years in the future, you will find that it is most helpful with planning strategies for the next five years. Both your visionary vita and the career plan that you development from it will need to be updated frequently. Moreover, developing, implementing, and reviewing a career plan is no guarantee that you will achieve all the goals that you have established for your career, but it will increase the likelihood that you will achieve at least some of them. It will also ensure that you have done as much as you can to be in the best possible position when that unexpected and highly desirable opportunity comes your way.

RESOURCES

Bataille, G. M., & Brown, B. E. (2006). *Faculty career paths: Multiple routes to academic success and satisfaction.* Westport, CT: American Council on Education/Praeger.

Berberet, J., Bland, C. J., Brown, B. E., & Risbey, K. R. (2005). Late career faculty perceptions: Implications for retirement planning and policymaking. *Research Dialogue, 84,* 1–12.

Gappa, J. M., Austin, A. E., & Trice, A. G. (2007). *Rethinking faculty work: Higher education's strategic imperative.* San Francisco: Jossey-Bass.

O'Meara, K., & Rice, R. E. (2005). *Faculty priorities reconsidered: Rewarding multiple forms of scholarship.* San Francisco: Jossey-Bass.

Schuster, J. H., & Finkelstein, M. J. (2005). *The American faculty: The restructuring of academic work and careers.* Baltimore, MD: Johns Hopkins University Press.

5

THE TENURE AND PROMOTION PROCESS

Few academic processes cause faculty members as much anxiety as being reviewed for tenure or promotion. Not only are matters of reputation and livelihood at stake, but the very process of having your materials reviewed by a committee and the administration can make you feel as though your fate is in the hands of other people, including those who barely know you and may not appreciate the way your discipline works. In this chapter, we'll explore strategies for placing yourself in the best possible position for a favorable promotion and tenure decision. Of course, no advice from this book or from anyone can guarantee a positive result, but there are still plenty of steps you can take to help make the process as smooth and fair as possible. Let's begin with the most basic.

Prepare for Your Review Now

The day to begin preparing for your tenure review is the day you are hired. The day to begin preparing for your promotion to full professor is the day you're promoted to associate professor. If you think that these statements are exaggerated, consider the following essential principle:

> Consider each aspect of the promotion and tenure process, not from your own perspective, but from that of the people who will be reviewing your application. What will they be looking for and what will they need in order to say "yes" to your request?

When you approach the process in this way, it becomes apparent that the people who will be considering your application will be taking a long view. Even as they're considering your record of progress (what did all of your efforts add up to?), they'll also be considering your record of consistency (have you sustained your efforts since your last evaluation either for hiring or promotion?). It is important to begin both earning your promotion and tenure and documenting how you've earned them at the earliest possible date. Keep in mind, however, that we are speaking of achievements at your current job and in your current rank. On how your earlier accomplishments before you were hired or last promoted relate to this process, see the very end of this chapter.

If you're reading this section and it is already well after the day you signed your contract or received your last promotion, don't despair. Unless you've made almost no preparations for this process and are on the verge of being reviewed, you can still do everything you need to do in order to receive fair and thorough consideration. But you'll need to act immediately. Begin by thinking about how you will gather and organize the documents you will need to support your application. Many faculty members find it useful to set up three files for this purpose.

- *A hard copy file*, which will probably be a file drawer or even an entire cabinet. In this file, keep all printed materials relevant to your accomplishments as a college professor. These materials may include publications, grant applications and award letters, correspondence from publishers about books and articles in press, syllabi and course materials that do not exist in electronic form (see below), letters of support or commendation, materials relating to recognitions, peer review reports, records of student achievements related to your work as a teacher or mentor, printed copies of student ratings of instruction, products resulting from committee work and other service, and any other item that could help you demonstrate your success in any aspect of your career.

- *An email file*, which may exist as a folder within your email program or may be printed and included as part of your hard copy file. Because so much academic communication occurs through email, these messages will be an essential part of your documentation. Every time you receive a message thanking you for doing a good job, praising your work, asking you for an offprint of an article, describing the influence that you've had on other scholars, or noting in any way the exceptional work that you've done, save a copy of that message in this file. Doing so will prevent you from having to recall who wrote you about what issue at what date when you are under time constraints to assemble your materials for review. If you find that your email file becomes too large and cumbersome, subdivide it into sections relating to teaching, scholarship, and service or any other subdivision that makes sense for your discipline and institution.

- *An electronic file*, which consists of word processing documents, PDFs, videos, Web files, recordings, and any other type of material that either exists in or can be converted to machine-readable form. Some faculty members will prefer to maintain only a single tenure and promotion file, scanning all hard copies into electronic versions and storing emails alongside other files on their computers. This approach can be very useful, as all of your materials are in one location, searchable electronically, and stored in a manner that is environmentally friendly. If your hard copy documentation is extensive, however, you may find that the time required to scan it can be considerable. Moreover, if you choose to track all of your documentation electronically, be sure to keep multiple backups, because machine-readable files are vulnerable to computer theft and hardware disasters.

You can find excellent guidelines on the types of materials that best document success in teaching, advising, research, and service in Diamond (2004).

Distinguish Between Necessary Levels of Documentation

Simply because you have a piece of documentation, you don't have to provide it to the review committee as part of your application. Some items are worth keeping because you'll need to refer to their contents in order to summarize information. Others will provide you with useful quotations that you can include in your application. Still others will help remind you of activities you may otherwise have overlooked. Many others end up being saved "just in case." In short, the purpose of keeping tenure and promotion files is not to inundate the search committee with all of their contents. Rather, it is important to keep these files so that you can easily locate particular items you may need and have access to other information when you wish to consult it. Your institution is likely to have clear guidelines on the types of items you must include as part of a tenure or promotion application. Regardless of whether these documents are sufficiently specified, consult the chair of your school's promotion and tenure committee, your department chair or mentor, or a colleague who has recently gone through the process for some guidance. Colleges and universities vary considerably in the amount of materials they wish to receive from applicants, so advice from colleagues who work at other institutions may be of limited value. Some schools encourage applicants to assemble several large binders that include all of the faculty member's course syllabi, teaching evaluations, minutes from committee work, and letters of appreciation submitted by students. Other schools would regard many of these items as "padding" or evidence that the applicant was unable to determine what is truly important. It is vital, therefore, to learn from well-informed people at your own institution precisely how much documentation the review committees will want to receive and in what form. Also keep in mind that what your department may want to review could well be different from what a college- or university-level committee may wish to consult, so revising these materials at various stages of the process may well be inevitable.

Create an Academic Portfolio

Seldin and Miller (2008) propose a useful alternative to the bulging binders of material that so many committees claim they need (but which probably go unread or, at best, are quickly scanned): an academic portfolio that, in conjunction with a well-prepared curriculum vitae (see Chapter 31, "Creating an Effective Curriculum Vitae"), more clearly documents what a faculty member has done in a manner that is less onerous for the applicant to prepare and the reviewers to analyze. The key feature of an academic portfolio is that it is simultaneously selective and reflective. Rather than providing numerous offprints that a review committee is unlikely to read (or to understand if read), the academic portfolio forces the faculty member to select representative examples of his or her most important scholarly achievements and to indicate why these works are important in the discipline, innovative, and regarded by qualified reviewers as superior in quality. Rather than containing the syllabi of perhaps a dozen courses, the academic portfolio requires the faculty member to select a few of his or her best syllabi and to describe how each course's design and methods relate a personal philosophy of teaching, how each course is structured both to increase student learning and to adapt to individual needs, and how each course has evolved over time in response to new perspectives in the discipline, best practices elsewhere, and the faculty member's own growth in the profession. Rather than repeating information already contained in a faculty member's résumé about committee memberships or the offices held, the academic portfolio encourages the applicant to provide evidence of the benefits that resulted from this service and the value that it provided to the discipline, institution, or community. By requiring applicants to identify their best work in each area and the reasons why that work was superior, the academic portfolio helps the review committee use their time more effectively, giving them only and precisely what they need. Moreover, because applicants do not have to assemble a large amount of material, the tenure and promotion process becomes more meaningful and less time-consuming for them as well. Seldin and Miller also present a large number of sample academic portfolios from a wide range of disciplines, including biomedical engineering, child and family studies, education, foreign languages and literature, jazz and contemporary music, nutritional sciences, political science, and psychology. These sample portfolios are a valuable resource in how to document success in teaching, scholarship, and service, particularly when there may be little supporting evidence that lends itself to quantification or quick summaries.

But what can you do if your institution already has very specific requirements about the type of documents you must submit and the format in which you submit them? How can you prepare an academic portfolio when your college or university *insists* that you assemble huge binders of supporting material? To be sure, you do not want to create a situation where the members of the promotion and tenure committee are expecting one type of documentation but you have provided another. Their reaction is likely to be very similar to what yours would be if you had assigned a twelve-page research paper but received a five-page autobiographical essay instead. So, if you're in an institution that insists you supply vast amounts of documentation in support of your tenure or promotion application, by all means provide it—but once you are tenured or promoted, try to get appointed to the body that can get those procedures changed. In the meantime, borrow a few elements from the academic portfolio approach and combine them with the type of documentation your institution requires. For example, rather than merely providing copies of syllabi from all of your courses, prepare annotated copies in which you relate what occurs in the course to your philosophy of teaching, the course's objectives, your ongoing strategies for promoting student engagement, and current developments in your field; illustrate how your approach to each course has evolved in light of your own growth as a college professor. Rather than simply including copies of your books, articles, and other scholarly achievements, accompany them with commentary regarding what these works have added to your discipline, how they have influenced other scholars, what further research has been made possible by your own work, and so on. In this way, even as you supply the items that your institution requires, you can place those items into a clearer context, helping to make the case of why your work was important, of high quality, and influential. In keeping with the essential principle introduced earlier in this chapter, you are viewing your application from the perspective of the committee, making it easier for those who review your application to support your request and, by so doing, increasing the likelihood of a favorable result.

Have Your Materials Reviewed Early

The advice of a chair, mentor, or trusted colleague is invaluable when preparing for a promotion and tenure review. Most faculty members understand that this advice is important, but many of them seek it too late in the process. They ask someone to review their materials shortly before they must be submitted to the review committee, making substantive revision all but impossible. Certainly, we've seen that many institutions require so much documentation that it is all but impossible for faculty members to assemble it long before the deadline. But there are undoubtedly other cases where the applicant is not looking for genuine advice about what can be done differently, but validation that the materials are indeed well prepared and that success will be inevitable. Whatever the reason for the delay, it is never in the faculty member's interest.

Advice about what you should be doing as you proceed toward promotion and tenure should be requested early and often. A good mentor can tell you if the activities at which you are spending most of your time are truly those that can pay off in the long run. He or she may dissuade you from agreeing to serve on this or that committee, may recommend publishing fewer articles in first-tier journals rather than a number of short pieces in relatively unimportant publications, or may take a completely different approach. If the advice you receive from your mentor doesn't seem right to you, you can always consult a few other people, particularly those who have recently been promoted or who have served on a review committee. If you find yourself eventually agreeing with the advice you've received, you'll then have enough time to take corrective action. If, on the other hand, you seek advice too late in the process, you may already be on a path that will prove less successful for you.

The need for sound advice increases dramatically if you are submitting an application for review before it is required, such as for an early promotion. Although it can be very disappointing to be told, "I don't think you're ready yet," it is far preferable to receive this news from a mentor or chair who is simply trying to help you than from a committee that has been appointed to evaluate you. Remember to seek advice early in order to have time for an additional review.

Address All the Review Criteria

Once you have decided to apply for tenure, promotion, or both—or once your institution's timetable requires you to undergo a review—it becomes your responsibility to make the case that you deserve the committee's approval. No matter how distinguished your career or how celebrated you are in your field, no review committee is going to grant you tenure or promotion if you are not effective in demonstrating that you have earned it. And to make your strongest possible case, you will need to address all the criteria relevant to the decision being made, not simply the criteria that you happen to believe in, regard as relevant to your situation, or think may be unclear from your curriculum vitae. When committees review applications, they are charged with deciding whether an applicant has adequately demonstrated that he or she has met the criteria, not with debating the merits of the criteria themselves or with extracting information that a candidate has neglected to supply. The process of applying for promotion or tenure is not the time to argue that your school is placing too much emphasis on research or that it fails to value service sufficiently. Nor is it the time to assume that your accomplishments are so "obvious" that everyone should already know them. Read carefully the criteria that your institution has established, address each criterion as completely as you can, and supply the documentation your institution requires. No one will be able to determine whether you fulfill the requirements unless you do everything you can to make your best case, and you cannot count on anyone else to make that case for you.

One important element in preparing the strongest possible application is to organize your materials in such a way that those who review it can readily find all the answers they are seeking. We've already discussed the advisability of supplying annotated copies of your materials in order to place your achievements in their proper context. In addition, good organization of your materials is also a matter of clearly labeling and arranging everything you submit. Documents that appear simply to have been "dumped" into a binder, folder, or envelope create the impression that the applicant has not taken the process very seriously, and thus the review committee may end up not taking that application very seriously. As you organize the documentation that supports your application, it is good practice to ask yourself these questions:

- Other than the fact that these items were required parts of my application, will it be clear to a reviewer why I have included each of them?

- Can a reviewer quickly find evidence in support of my success as a teacher, advisor, researcher, academic citizen, or any other role that is relevant to my application?

- What message am I trying to convey with each item that I have included? If someone doesn't know me or my discipline very well, is that message clear? If your scholarship has occurred in a highly innovative or nontraditional field, be sure to consider the advice on documenting these achievements that appears in Chapter 28, "Alternative Forms of Scholarship."

To help reviewers find the information they need, you might also consider including the following among your documentation:

- *A table of contents*, which indicates where each section of your documentation begins and where all particularly important materials may be found.

- *Section dividers*, which make it easy for the reader to locate all the major parts of your documentation. If you are submitting hard copies of materials in binders, it is a good idea to have dividers with tabs keyed to your table of contents. If you are submitting your materials electronically, hyperlinks should take the reader directly from the table of contents to the beginning of each section.

- *Section guides*, which enumerate for readers all the specific items that can be found in each section and, wherever possible, make it clear what insights you hope the reviewers will gain from those items. Once again, if you're submitting your materials in electronic form, hyperlinks make it extremely easy to jump from the section guide to the specific item.

Your department, college, and institution may have additional rules for how tenure and promotion materials must be organized as part of your application. If these rules exist, follow them as carefully as possible. As you'll discover when you serve on a review committee, it is far easier to evaluate applicants' materials when everyone has followed the same basic format and procedures.

The Politics of Promotion and Tenure Review

Faculty members sometimes worry about the "politics" of promotion and tenure. Will my record be evaluated fairly? Will the review committee and upper administration regard this process merely as a means of exerting authority rather than rewarding quality? Should I be concerned that someone on the committee might just "have it in for me"? Will I be the victim of retribution for something I've said or a position I've taken? It would be misleading merely to dismiss these concerns and say that the problems they allude to never occur. It is undeniable that certain campuses seem perpetually torn by conflict. Power struggles can sometimes exist between presidents or provosts and rank-and-file faculty members, grievances can be filed, and members of the institutions' governing boards can declare that they are opposed to the very idea of academic tenure, arguing that it protects the unproductive and is irrelevant to academic freedom. These are the situations that cause the American Association of University Professors (AAUP) to censure the institutional leaders for violating academic freedom and tenure (see www.aaup.org/AAUP/about/censuredadmins/) and that appear occasionally as stories in the *Chronicle of Higher Education*. But remember that these situations are far from the norm and that when they occur, internal grievance procedures almost always protect the faculty member's rights. Compare, for instance, the number of schools that appear on the AAUP's watch list to the nearly three thousand colleges and universities in the United States, and you'll see that truly egregious cases of political interference in promotion and tenure decisions are extremely rare. The vast majority of institutional review committees take their responsibilities very seriously when they evaluate the performance and credentials of faculty members. One reason for this care is that these committees tend to be composed largely of faculty members. A second reason is that administrators—who often rise from the ranks of the faculty and still see themselves primarily in this role—have very little to gain by not setting high standards and rewarding those college professors who achieve them. For this reason, if you enter a promotion and tenure process expecting it to be highly confrontational and tense, it may very well turn out to be exactly what you expect; the attitude that you yourself bring to the process can end up being contagious. But if you approach your review with the understanding that people at all levels of the institution will usually do their best to be fair in what is inevitably an imperfect process, you are likely to find the entire experience far less antagonistic than you had feared. It can thus make a palpable difference if you treat a review committee as a group of potential allies in support of your cause rather than as potential obstacles who simply stand in the way of what you are trying to achieve. Even more surprising, if you approach your review in this way, the committee's own attitude toward their work may also change, and you may discover that what you had thought would be a conflict was simply yet another collaborative academic process, shared governance at its best.

We began this chapter by saying that it's never too early to begin preparing for a promotion or tenure review because committees and administrators will be evaluating everything you have done since you were hired or last promoted. Faculty members sometimes wonder, therefore, whether the review process will also place a great deal of emphasis on the work they completed *before* they reached their current institutions or ranks. The general rule of thumb is that although no professional achievement is irrelevant to a major performance review, most of the committee's attention will focus on your achievements since you began your present position or earned your last promotion. In other words, from a reviewer's perspective, your earlier accomplishments have already been evaluated and rewarded: they are what earned your current job or your present rank. So, present your entire record to the committee, but don't be surprised if their questions are primarily about your more recent accomplishments.

REFERENCES

Diamond, R. M. (2004). *Preparing for promotion, tenure, and annual review: A faculty guide* (2nd ed.). Bolton, MA: Anker.

Seldin, P., & Miller, J. E. (2008). *The academic portfolio: A practical guide to documenting teaching, research, and service.* San Francisco: Jossey-Bass.

RESOURCES

Buller, J. L. (2007). Improving documentation for promotion and tenure. *Academic Leader, 23*(11), 8–9.

Chism, N. V. N. (2007). *Peer review of teaching: A sourcebook* (2nd ed.). Bolton, MA: Anker.

Diamond, R. M. (2002). *Serving on promotion, tenure, and faculty review committees: A faculty guide* (2nd ed.). Bolton, MA: Anker.

Sawyer, R. M., Prichard, K. W., & Hostetler, K. D. (Eds.). (2001). *The art and politics of college teaching: A practical guide for the beginning professor* (2nd ed.). New York: Peter Lang.

Seldin, P., & Associates. (1999). *Changing practices in evaluating teaching: A practical guide to improved faculty performance and promotion/tenure decisions.* Bolton, MA: Anker.

Whicker, M. L., Kronenfeld, J. J., & Strickland, R. A. (1993). *Getting tenure.* Thousand Oaks, CA: Sage.

6

SPECIAL CHALLENGES FOR JUNIOR FACULTY

Each stage of a faculty member's career involves its own challenges and opportunities. For example, if you are relatively close to the beginning of your academic career, you are much more likely than your senior colleagues to:

- Be untenured
- Have multiple promotions still ahead of you
- Be repaying student loans
- Have young children at home
- Be in the process of finding your own "niche" within your discipline or at your institution

You are also probably facing these challenges while living on a fairly modest salary and dealing with expectations that can seem at times excessively high. While it may provide some comfort to know that you are not alone in this situation, is there any way in which your path can be made easier for you? What advice can senior faculty members give their junior colleagues about strategies that really work and can lead them to success in their fields? This chapter contains some very candid advice and recommendations for newer faculty members. Even if you decide that much of this advice is irrelevant to your situation, you would be well advised to reflect on it carefully. The guidelines that follow have helped many college professors who were just starting their careers and may well assist you in avoiding difficulties as you proceed toward tenure and promotion.

Select Your Service Commitments Carefully

One of the mistakes that junior faculty members occasionally make is agreeing to serve on too many committees or task forces. Committee appointments may be attractive because they seem easy goals to achieve, fill a line on a résumé, and provide contact with other members of the

57

department or institution. Sometimes junior faculty members are flattered to be asked to serve on a committee or, not wishing to make a bad first impression, are reluctant to say no when asked. Moreover, it can appear ungrateful to refuse a request for help from an institution that so recently had been generous enough to offer a full-time contract. Finally, because junior faculty members often bring a great deal of energy to their positions, they may be eager to form student clubs, lead field trips, and help select computer software or resources for the library. The impulse behind these activities is commendable, but this can lead to a situation that will harm the faculty member in the long run. If there is an essential principle that every junior faculty member needs to know, it is this:

Few faculty members, if any, ever earn tenure and promotion primarily through service.

Certainly, every faculty member should engage in service. It is also certain that when you are evaluated for tenure and promotion, you will need to demonstrate a successful record as a citizen of your department and institution. But most tenure and promotion systems place far less emphasis on service than they do on the quality of instruction and on scholarship. In fact, in systems where each component of the "academic triad" is given a percentage weighting, service may contribute as little as 5 to 10 percent of a faculty member's evaluation. Teaching and research account for the other 90 to 95 percent. So, what is the most important direction in which you should channel your energy?

Talk to your department chair or a trusted faculty mentor about developing a realistic plan for your service and related activities. Explore the possibility of choosing one truly significant area of service each year until you are granted tenure, and use the remaining time to enhance the quality of your teaching and to complete additional works of scholarship. The service activity that you choose to complete might well be something that has high visibility and importance to your community. Perhaps you can serve as the untenured faculty representative on a department- or institution-wide promotion and tenure committee; this type of activity is a valuable source of information to you about how best to present your own materials when it is time to do so, the standards by which faculty members are evaluated, and the pitfalls that you will want to avoid. Perhaps you can serve as the secretary to the faculty senate or at meetings of the full faculty; working in this capacity will introduce you to numerous issues that are vital to your institution, make you highly visible to other members of the faculty, and train you for your own eventual role as a faculty senator. Of course, no single service assignment is appropriate for every faculty member; the important thing is for you to find an activity that suits your talent and has the greatest amount of impact for the least investment of your time.

If possible, have your department chair record as part of your annual written evaluation the agreement that the two of you make about pursuing only a single major service activity per year. This practice will be helpful in the unlikely event that someone later challenges your level of service as having been too small when compared with that of other junior faculty members. If your chair has recorded that this single assignment was in accordance with the instructions you were given—particularly if the chair reports that you have performed this major assignment extremely well— then you should be able to deflect any potential criticism. In a similar way, try to focus your other volunteer activities on those that will make the biggest impact. Rather than taking time away from publication to revise or develop course proposals, work out with your chair which new courses or revisions to existing classes constitute the department's highest priority, and attend to those first. Rather than serving as a moderator for several student organizations, put your energy into one, using the time you save to keep abreast of innovative teaching techniques or new technologies that you can introduce into the classroom. As a basic rule of thumb, therefore, be very practical—almost calculating—about the tradeoff between your time and its long-term benefit to you. Remember that you only have a limited amount of time to earn tenure and promotion, and you want to use that time to your best advantage.

Balance Your Activities

It is easy when your salary is still very modest to look for a short-term increase in income even if what you end up doing has little long-term value. For instance, junior faculty members may seek out opportunities to teach overloads, summer classes, and expanded course sections because these activities provide a temporary boost in salary. This temptation is very great when you're still paying off student loans and trying to start a family. Nevertheless, the time that you spend teaching the overload or summer school course or grading the papers of your larger course section is time that could have been devoted to scholarship or discovering new ways of teaching your existing courses. More than one junior faculty member has been caught in this trap when evaluated for promotion and tenure: "But you needed those overload sections taught, and I did you a favor by teaching them. Now you tell me that they don't count for anything in my evaluation and that I should have spent more time on my scholarship?" That predicament does seem extremely unfair, but remember this inconvenient truth: there's a *reason* why people are paid for teaching overloads, summer courses, and large sections—the extra money they receive is the sum total of their reward for that activity. What tenure and promotion committees want to see is that you have excelled in your duties, that you went above and beyond what was required, not merely that you performed the tasks you were paid for. This is why taking on too many additional paid assignments as a junior faculty member may end up being a bad bargain in the long run.

The key consideration should be balance. If you truly need extra income (and few junior faculty members don't), then an occasional overload, summer course, or expanded section may be perfectly fine. But to keep both your short-term and long-term goals in balance, it may be advisable to incorporate that occasional opportunity for extra income into a larger work plan. For most junior faculty members, a well-designed work plan should include everything they feel they need to do in the years before they are evaluated for promotion and tenure, with target dates for all of their goals. For example, if you conclude that you must have one refereed article accepted for publication each year in order to be tenured, what type of schedule will best permit you to do that? Perhaps you are better off teaching an overload during the academic year (when it is difficult to devote a large amount of time to scholarship anyway) and keeping your summers free. Perhaps it makes more sense for you to teach a double- or triple-sized section of a course (which at least limits your number of preparations and the hours that you must spend in the classroom) rather than to accept an overload or summer contract. Work out the precise details of your plan with your chair. In most cases, your supervisor will be highly sympathetic to your need to balance income-producing activities with sufficient time to enhance your teaching and advance your scholarship. He or she may even have some creative suggestions on how best to achieve this goal.

Create a Career Plan

As we saw in Chapter 4, "Career Planning for College Professors," every faculty member can benefit from a career plan that provides guidance about choosing the most appropriate activities to pursue over the course of the next five, ten, or twenty years. For a junior faculty member, however, such a career plan can be indispensable. The plan can guide you in establishing a clear identity within your department or within your discipline outside your institution. For instance, you might be the new assistant professor of environmental economics with a secondary specialty in forecasting international financial trends, but who are you *really*? What will your legacy be? How will you help shape your institution, discipline, and higher education in general? Will you be most noted as an innovative teacher, a world-class scholar, or an astute participant in campus politics? Are there aspects of higher education policy and practice about which you might like to become an expert, such as assessment, budgeting, faculty development, post-tenure review, course evaluation, strategic planning, hiring practices, diversity development, legal issues, or curricular development? Make no mistake about it: any of these areas can become an important basis for establishing a faculty niche. Learn to be an expert in any one of them, and you could easily make yourself irreplaceable. By developing your career plan, therefore, you will be well on your way to determining not only *where* you want to be, but also *who* you want to be in your campus community. Do you see yourself as the wise counselor whom every student comes to see when they have a problem, or as the office gadfly, the departmental wit, the heart and soul of the community, or something else? As you're still relatively new in your career, any of these identities is possible. Consider whether one of them appears to be particularly well suited to your goals and temperament.

You may also decide that after a number of years as a faculty member, you may want to explore a potential role in administration, perhaps serving as a department chair, dean, provost, or university president. Deciding early in your career that this goal may be a possibility for you will assist you in making some of the choices that lie ahead. You might begin seeking a broader range of institutional assignments, some experience in development (which is increasingly expected in every administrative role), and supervisory roles where you chair a committee or evaluate someone's performance. But remember that becoming involved in administration too early can also take valuable time away from your scholarship and creative activities. If you were to decide later that working full time as a college professor is a far better route for you to take than being an administrator, you may realize that others have easily surpassed you in research. So, give very serious consideration to whether you ought to defer any administrative ambitions you may have, at least until you have been tenured and received your first promotion.

Select Your Scholarly and Creative Projects Carefully

Significant scholarly projects require a great deal of time, even after you've "completed" them. Manuscripts may have to be revised several times on the basis of referees' comments. Rehearsals for performances that will be recorded may require months of work, followed by additional coaching and revisions. Experiments may need to run for weeks or months even before the lengthy process of data analysis can begin. Applied projects in the community may need to be preceded by permits and hearings before local commissions. Even consideration of an initial proposal by an institutional review board or institutional animal care and use committee may require a great deal of time for first review, revision, subsequent reviews, and then approval. Then, once all the referees, reviewers, editors, and boards are satisfied with a work of scholarship, there may be a lag time in excess of a year before the final product is available. With a tenure clock running, these prolonged schedules become more than a mere nuisance; they can derail a career. It's often not possible to postpone scholarly achievement for a year or two as you focus on preparing new courses and adjust to a new environment. Most new college professors are expected to proceed very quickly to an extremely high level of scholarly achievement, so you can't afford to spend time on works that don't matter very much when others review them. Sit down now with your chair or mentor and gain a clear sense of those products of scholarship that people really care about in your program and at your school. Naturally, if your job happens to involve research alone without any teaching responsibilities, or if you are working at a school that prides itself on the importance of its teaching mission, your plan will end up being very different from that of a college professor who has major responsibilities in both areas. But if you fail to ask about the precise nature of your area's expectations, it is very easy to make a false assumption about what they may be.

Remember that even though at times it may feel like it, you're not starting from scratch. Take stock of the scholarly accomplishments you already have. Has your research consisted largely of minor articles, reviews, conference presentations, local performances, and poster sessions or have you already received major grants, placed refereed articles in top-tier journals, had a research monograph accepted for publication, placed works in international juried competitions, and had abstracts accepted at prestigious conferences? Ask your chair or mentor very precisely which of these achievements your institution and your discipline expect you to have completed by the time you have been reviewed for tenure, and you'll gain a good sense of how to build on what you've already done.

- For information on how to apply for grants, see Chapter 23, "Writing a Grant Proposal."

- For advice on how to secure a book contract, see Chapter 24, "Writing a Book Proposal."

- If your field tends to produce scholarship in nontraditional forms (for example, in forms other than conference presentations, poster sessions, and refereed publications), see Chapter 28, "Alternative Forms of Scholarship."

Moreover, if your discipline is one in which it is customary for graduate students to work as part of a research team, participate in writing a grant proposal, and prepare articles for publication, you already have a good understanding of where you need to begin. But what do you do if you don't have this advantage? To begin with, don't panic: there are several steps you can take and, unless you're already up against a deadline for tenure and promotion, you still have time to take them. If your institution offers small, internally funded grants for research, start applying for them. Treat this opportunity as seed money for a project that can then lead to a larger, external grant proposal or provide the basis for a sponsored program. Starter grants help you demonstrate that you are a careful steward of resources, generate some initial results that you can cite in a larger proposal, and introduce you to the style of writing and system of accountability that you will need to win larger grants.

Also remember that not every external grant has to be extremely large. If your field of study is the humanities, consider applying for one of the summer seminars or institutes sponsored by the National Endowment for the Humanities (www.neh.gov). The summer seminars tend to be somewhat smaller than the institutes and focus more on the enhancement of the participants' scholarship rather than on ways of incorporating new ideas into teaching. However, both the seminars and institutes can play an important role in helping you get new research projects under way and in introducing you to sources of funding for larger projects. If your field is in the arts, state arts councils frequently have small grant programs that faculty members can use to initiate or expand creative projects. The National Endowment for the Arts (http://arts.endow.gov) funds projects that deal, not only with visual and performing arts, but also literary arts, such as poetry and translation. The National Science Foundation (www.nsf.gov) oversees a vast array of funding opportunities that can be used to support research, equipment, and course improvement. Also remember that NSF does not fund projects in the *natural* sciences alone; many NSF programs are targeted at research in the social sciences, such as anthropology, and several are even intended for writers and artists who are involved in creative works that relate to some aspect of the natural world. Certain NSF projects overlap with research into the humanities and social sciences, such as those that fund opportunities to document endangered languages or to explore the relationship between science and society. The Alden B. Dow Creativity Center (www.northwood.edu/creativitycenter) offers a number of fellowships each summer to faculty members in any field who wish to pursue an innovative project or creative idea. In general, there is no area of academic research or field of study for which there are not some small grants for which scholars are eligible, regardless of their institution's size or focus. Although all grants are competitive by nature, many of these minor grants are readily accessible to individuals who do not have significant grant experience or the support of a large institutional Office of Research and Sponsored Programs.

Use Mentors and Peers for Support

Finally, don't forget that you have many resources at your disposal! Your department chair or assigned faculty mentor can provide you with plenty of advice on how to navigate the shoals of your department's and institution's political processes. In addition to any formal mentor you may have, you might consider establishing an informal mentoring relationship with a senior faculty member, inside or outside your discipline, with whom you've developed a good rapport. A mentor can be an important confidant (which is why you may sometimes prefer to discuss sensitive issues with someone who will not be participating in personnel decisions about you), a source of wisdom and institutional history, and a sounding board for your plans and goals. Though you should never feel that you must take a mentor's advice, you should carefully consider whatever you are told, weigh its value, and reject it only after giving the matter sufficient thought. Particularly if you select a mentor who is the type of person you admire or aspire to be, that person's advice can often be invaluable (see Chapter 35, "Serving as a Mentor").

Another important resource may be found in your junior faculty peers, both within your department and across the university. Coalitions of junior faculty members can become important networks of information, support groups, and sources of mutual assistance. One valuable way in which junior faculty can assist one another is through the creation of scholarship networks, small groups of individuals who meet on a set schedule to report progress on scholarly projects, discuss concerns, and critique one another's work. (For more on scholarship networks, see Chapter 27, "Seeking and Providing Peer Support for Scholarship.")

A scholarship network that brings together related academic disciplines—the social and behavioral sciences, the fine arts, the performing arts, the natural sciences, and the like—can lead to an increase in scholarly productivity and forge the basis for a number of innovative, collaborative projects. In addition, you are likely to produce stronger presentations and more compelling publications as a result of the criticism that you receive from your peers. By practicing your presentations before you go to a conference, you will have the opportunity to improve any sections that did not work effectively, and your delivery will be more confident. Your peers will constructively critique your articles to make them tighter, less prone to jargon, and more persuasive. Because the audience for your scholarly works will be perceptive and intelligent, but perhaps not completely familiar with the specific area of your research, you will quickly come to realize where your argument is clear and where the evidence is muddier than you had initially believed.

Perhaps some of the most sound advice for junior faculty members comes from John N. McDaniel, dean of the College of Liberal Arts at Middle Tennessee State University:

> The successful faculty member knows the importance of the "grand triad" of teaching, research, and service for advancing in the professoriate. Even more to the point, successful faculty members will know the *relative* importance of each of these three components at the institution at which they are working or to which they aspire. The span in expectations between two-year community colleges and the elite public or private research universities—with a host of four-year liberal arts colleges and comprehensive universities in between—is vast, with extraordinarily different expectations for excellence in teaching, research, and service. Beginning professors would do a great service to themselves and their institutions by determining the relative importance of teaching, research, and service, a determination that can best be arrived at by reading such pertinent material as mission statements, tenure and promotion policies, and department guidelines and by consulting with senior faculty either in a formal mentoring program or informally with conferences with the chair and others "in the know." The old maxim that knowledge is power applies with full force for the professor desiring a long and happy career. (Personal communication, November 15, 2007)

RESOURCES

Adams, K. A. (2002). *What colleges and universities want in new faculty.* Washington, DC: Association of American Colleges and Universities.

Boice, R. (2000). *Advice for new faculty members.* Needham Heights, MA: Allyn & Bacon.

Gibson, G. W. (1992). *Good start: A guidebook for new faculty in liberal arts colleges.* Bolton, MA: Anker.

Lang, J. M. (2008). *On course: A week-by-week guide to your first semester of college teaching.* Cambridge, MA: Harvard University Press.

Lucas, C. J., & Murry, J. W., Jr. (2002). *New faculty: A practical guide for academic beginners.* New York: Palgrave Macmillan.

Marcinkiewicz, H., & Doyle, T. (2004). *New faculty professional development: Planning an ideal program.* Stillwater, OK: New Forums Press.

Menges, R. J., & Associates. (1999). *Faculty in new jobs: A guide to settling in, becoming established, and building institutional support.* San Francisco: Jossey-Bass.

Sawyer, R. M., Prichard, K. W., & Hostetler, K. D. (Eds.). (2001). *The art and politics of college teaching: A practical guide for the beginning professor* (2nd ed.). New York: Peter Lang.

7

SPECIAL CHALLENGES FOR MIDCAREER FACULTY

The midcareer faculty members we consider in this chapter are people who are tenured and well established in their careers, but who still have at least one more promotion to earn. Most individuals who fall into this category hold the rank of associate professor, because institutions usually tie this rank to the tenure process. If you're an associate professor, you have probably demonstrated a great deal of success in teaching, research, or both, depending on the nature of your position and the focus of your institution; otherwise you would not have been granted tenure. You are also more likely than other faculty members to be coping with challenging personal circumstances (such as the birth of a child, the entry of your children into a new level of schooling, a divorce, aging parents, or a family member with a serious illness) at the same time that you are still trying to advance your career. The pressure of these competing priorities may, at least for some midcareer faculty members, cause a temporary decline in productivity. The good news, however, is that the strict timetable of your tenure evaluation is behind you. You've already accomplished many of the career goals that you set out to achieve, and other priorities may start to appear more pressing. The goal of this chapter is to explore ways in which you can keep making progress toward your next promotion, set new career goals, and still maintain a sense of balance in achieving your highest priorities. That may be a tough agenda, but you've already proven that you're up to it.

Reconsider Your Priorities

When faculty members reach midcareer, it is time to reorder the ways in which they direct their energy. For many people, this means moving from a framework in which teaching and research are their first priorities to a framework in which research and service are their first priorities. This advice is bound to elicit cries of outrage at many institutions, particularly those that pride themselves on their quality of their instruction. "Teaching must *always* remain the highest priority," some schools will claim, "and midcareer faculty members should be demonstrating excellence in all three areas, not limiting their concerns to only two." But there are reasons for placing more emphasis on service and less on developing new instructional strategies at this point in your career. After all, it's highly unlikely that you would have been granted tenure (and probably promotion to the rank of associate professor) if there were serious reservations about the quality of your teaching. In other words, you're in an excellent position to let your record of superb teaching stand while you devote your energies to the type of scholarship and service that will get you promoted to the rank of full professor. Taking your scholarship to the next level will benefit your institution in many different ways.

- It will ensure that you stay on the cutting edge of your field.
- It will help you continue to model effective scholarly techniques to your students.
- And it will provide you with any number of exciting new ideas that you can use to help realign your field's curriculum during the *next* stage of your career.

In a similar way, emphasis on your service contributions will help you build the institution-wide reputation that you need for your next promotion and allow you to use the institutional knowledge you've gained over the last several years for the good of others.

Scholarship

A good place to begin the process of carrying your scholarship to the next level is to reread the last chapter and make certain you've taken all the advice there that is relevant to your discipline, position, and institution. Focus on these questions:

- Have you used small grants available from either your own school or external sources as seed money for larger scholarly projects?
- Have you submitted a book proposal, if that's an appropriate work of research for your discipline?
- Have you explored the possibility of a scholarship network to enhance your research productivity?

If you've done all of these things, the next step is to identify the pinnacle research activity appropriate to your discipline and begin taking steps to achieve that goal. The precise nature of this pinnacle research activity will vary by discipline. In many areas, it will be the externally refereed book of research. In others, it will be a paper in a top-tier journal, a large research grant, a patent, a presentation at a highly competitive international conference, a performance of new works that receive critical acclaim, a solo exhibition at a prized venue, or any number of other possibilities. No matter what the appropriate activity may be for your field, your goal will be the same: to identify the goal, plan the steps that will be necessary to achieve that goal, and then carry out the plan, preferably in time for your next promotion. If you find that you've already achieved what many would regard as the pinnacle goal for scholarship in your field, identify ways in which you could set the bar even higher. Thus, if you've already published a book of research, select a more prestigious press or a more ambitious topic. If you've already received several large grants, start imagining what your dream project would be and use your success in grant writing to help fund it. If your performances or compositions have been of high enough quality to earn you tenure, what sort of international awards or recognitions could you receive to carry this success even further?

Second, midcareer faculty members should consider opportunities to conduct research or engage in creative activities abroad, such as those sponsored by the programs known collectively as Fulbright Fellowships (www.fulbrightonline.org). Faculty Fulbright Fellowships are awarded in many different categories—research only, teaching only, combined research and teaching, and short-term seminars—that can make them suitable for nearly any type of personal situation. Many faculty members find it convenient to apply for Fulbright grants after a major life change, such as a divorce or the departure of children for college, using these awards to help transform what could be a bleak period in their lives into an exceptionally positive experience. Many Fulbright awards require proficiency in a language other than English, although others do not. Regardless of the type of grant received, however, most scholars return from a Fulbright program with renewed energy and commitment to a significant scholarly project. Receiving a Fulbright can also be a significant factor when midcareer faculty members apply for promotion to the rank of full professor.

Third, midcareer faculty members should take a moment to pause and reconsider their entire career agendas. It may well be that the topics that carried you through graduate school and your first few years as a college professor now hold slightly less interest or don't seem sufficient to sustain you through the rest of your career. Many midcareer faculty members will be active in their professions for more than twenty years and may need to refocus their research several more times to maintain their enthusiasm and keep their approaches sharp. If you begin the process of "reinventing yourself" in midcareer, you'll find it easier to continue refining your identity periodically in the years to come. Wait too long, however, and your identity may become so established in your discipline or at your institution that later change is much more difficult. As you set what you hope to be your research agenda for the next five to seven years, you may find that you are perfectly comfortable continuing a path that you have already taken. If that is the case, you're very fortunate, and many of your colleagues should envy you. But if you don't stop for a midcareer reflection, you might never realize how many other paths were once open to you.

Service

As preparation for your eventual promotion to full professor—and as recognition of your increasing experience as a faculty member at your institution—it is appropriate for you now to assume a greater role in the area of service. On the campus level, you should begin seeking service opportunities where you can have a significant impact and become known by a large cross section of your institution. For example, it may now be an appropriate time to seek election to the faculty senate, an institution-wide curricular committee, a search committee for an upper administrator, a planning group for an important event, a major task force, a committee preparing for the reaccreditation of a program or the institution as a whole, or a council that reports to the institution's governing board. Discuss with your chair and fellow faculty members whether it might be effective for the discipline to adopt a "block voting" system that would increase the likelihood that at least one member of your department who needs a major service assignment would be successful in an election. Presenting your campaign as a matter of ensuring that departmental interests are furthered at the institutional level may also reinforce to your colleagues that you are a strong advocate for your discipline and a good "departmental citizen."

Now may also be an appropriate time for you to seek office in a national or large regional professional association, if you haven't already done so. Holding office as a president or vice president of an important organization in your discipline, getting your name known throughout your academic area as you help plan conferences and chair committee meetings, evaluating sites for future conventions (perhaps even having your own institution host some type of conference), and serving on the editorial board for journals all help to make you known more broadly throughout your academic area. If your institution permits or requires letters by external peer reviewers when you are considered for promotion, establishing this reputation can play a very helpful role. Also, by exposing yourself to a wide variety of programs in your discipline nationwide, you will find yourself developing new and creative ideas about how your department's curriculum can be improved, where its alumni can be placed in graduate programs, and which programs are producing large numbers of minority doctorates as your institution continues its efforts to diversify the faculty.

Refocusing Your Career and Setting Transformational Goals

Above all, midcareer faculty members should do a candid assessment of where they are in their professional lives and what steps they may wish to consider next. After all, the more senior your rank, the less easy it can be to relocate if you wish to do so. The vast majority of academic positions that are advertised each year are designed to be entry-level positions. Though institutions will often consider faculty members holding the rank of associate professor for these lower-level positions, they are far less likely to consider an applicant who has already reached the rank of professor. To be sure, positions for experienced, even distinguished senior faculty members certainly exist, but they appear far less often than do positions for assistant or associate professors. For this reason, it may be time to start asking yourself such questions as:

- Do I see myself remaining at my current institution for the rest of my career?

- If there were a very attractive position elsewhere—but one that would require me to start over again from the point of view of earning tenure—would I consider such a position?

- Which factors (salary, job security, research opportunities, collegiality, location, placement for my spouse, greater challenge, more prestige) would make me consider relocating?

- If I could design a position that I would find irresistible, what would that be?

By considering questions such as these, you can help determine whether you are at all likely to wish someday that you were working at a different institution. If such a plan seems likely, you may well be at the point in your career when you should begin planning for this type of change.

Midcareer faculty members might also wish to consider whether they are interested in a different sort of work assignment, such as an administrative role as a department chair or dean. In the last chapter junior faculty were cautioned away from making such a decision too soon, but you may be at the perfect place in your career to consider this option.

So, if you believe you might consider an administrative position within the next five to ten years, one way to begin this process is by reflecting on the following questions:

[handwritten margin note: Great questions for emerging K–12 leaders (adapted)]

- What is it that attracts me to college administration? If my honest answer is that it is largely a matter of increased salary or prestige, might there be other ways to obtain this goal that make better use of my individual strengths?

- When I have chaired committees, written reports, or planned events, did I find these activities satisfying or did I feel that they took time away from my more "important" work?

- Can I handle opposition? Distrust? Animosity? Can I do what needs to be done in tough situations without taking criticism personally?

- Do people who know me well tend to believe that I achieve a desirable balance between standing for something and keeping my mind open to other perspectives?

- If I had a choice between publishing a book and significantly improving a degree program, which would I truly prefer?

- Am I a good listener?

- Am I a caregiver? How do I feel when I'm called on to counsel people who have problems that I can't solve for them?

- Do I enjoy fixing things that are "broken"?

- Do I conduct meetings that are as efficient and pleasant as possible for those who attend?

- Do I resent paperwork or having to devote a large amount of time to details?

- Can I achieve satisfaction by helping others achieve their goals even if it means that I will not be receiving the acclaim myself?

- Do I find it satisfying to develop a vision for an academic program? Am I the sort of person who can inspire others through my vision?

- When I think of the most important things that my institution does, what immediately comes to mind? Do I only think of faculty concerns and academic issues or do I also think more broadly in terms of student development and student life issues, the overall strategic direction of the institution, the institution's relationship with external constituencies (trustees, legislators, advisory groups, donors), staff needs and concerns, and other such matters?

- Can I easily let things go when a decision is finally made and it hasn't gone my way? Do I need to revisit issues continually and to justify my perspectives repeatedly?
- Can I keep information confidential? If I could not discuss a matter even with my spouse or closest friend, would I find that situation endurable?
- Do I handle pressure well?

These questions are not intended to discourage you from thinking about administration as an appropriate next step, but rather to point out some of the realities that are faced every day by chairs, deans, provosts, and presidents. For the right sort of person, an administrative assignment can offer challenges that are personally satisfying and result in important improvements to the institution. Administration is not, however, an appropriate answer to everyone's "midcareer crisis," and no faculty member should pursue this type of position simply because he or she is dissatisfied with teaching and research. Moreover, one aspect of the caution given to junior faculty members may still apply to you: because many administrative appointments can leave you with less time for research and fewer opportunities to build a record as an effective teacher, accepting an administrative appointment can delay your promotion to the rank of full professor if you should decide to return to the classroom at a later date. To learn more about the precise responsibilities of chairs and deans, see Bright and Richards (2001), Buller (2006, 2007), Chu (2006), Gmelch and Miskin (2004), Gunsalus (2006), Henry (2006), and Lucas and Associates (2000).

———————

It is natural for faculty members at midcareer to ask themselves "What's next?" but there is no single answer that applies to every individual. Setting transformational goals as part of a career plan is a highly individualized activity. In many cases, by devoting as much energy as possible to truly significant scholarly works and major service opportunities both at the institution and within their area of academic specialty, midcareer faculty members will help keep their options open, position themselves effectively for their next promotion, and discover whether they have the sort of attributes that may make an administrative position appropriate for their personalities and career goals. For more on setting transformational goals, see Chapter 8, "Taking the Next Step in Your Career."

REFERENCES

Bright, D. F., & Richards, M. P. (2001). *The academic deanship: Individual careers and institutional roles.* San Francisco: Jossey-Bass.

Buller, J. L. (2006). *The essential department chair: A practical guide to college administration.* Bolton, MA: Anker.

Buller, J. L. (2007). *The essential academic dean: A practical guide to college leadership.* San Francisco: Jossey-Bass.

Chu, D. (2006). *The department chair primer: Leading and managing academic departments.* Bolton, MA: Anker.

Gmelch, W. H., & Miskin, V. D. (2004). *Chairing an academic department* (2nd ed.). Madison, WI: Atwood.

Gunsalus, C. K. (2006). *The college administrator's survival guide.* Cambridge, MA: Harvard University Press.

Henry, R. J. (Ed.). (2006). *New directions for higher education: No. 134. Transitions between faculty and administrative careers.* San Francisco: Jossey-Bass.

Lucas, A. F., & Associates. (2000). *Leading academic change: Essential roles for department chairs.* San Francisco: Jossey-Bass.

RESOURCES

Baldwin, R. G., Lunceford, C. J., & Vanderlinden, K. E. (2005). Faculty in the middle years: Illuminating an overlooked phase of academic life. *Review of Higher Education, 29*(1), 97–118.

Caffarella, R. S., & Zinn, L. F. (1999). Professional development for faculty: A conceptual framework of barriers and supports. *Innovative Higher Education, 23*(4), 241–254.

Gillespie, K. H., Hilsen, L. R., & Wadsworth, E. C. (Eds.). (2002). *A guide to faculty development: Practical advice, examples, and resources.* Bolton, MA: Anker.

Kalivoda, P., Sorrell, G. R., & Simpson, R. D. (1994). Nurturing faculty vitality by matching institutional interventions with career-stage needs. *Innovative Higher Education, 18*(4), 255–272.

Karpiak, I. E. (1996). Ghosts in a wilderness: Problems and priorities of faculty at mid-career and mid-life. *Canadian Journal of Higher Education, 26*(3), 49–77.

Romano, J. L., Hoesing, R., O'Donovan, K., & Weinsheimer, J. (2004). Faculty at mid-career: A program to enhance teaching and learning. *Innovative Higher Education, 29*(1), 21–48.

8

SPECIAL CHALLENGES FOR SENIOR FACULTY

Reaching the level of a senior faculty member brings with it an entirely new set of opportunities and challenges. Although junior faculty members may sometimes believe that tenured full professors have finally "made it" and face no more serious obstacles to their careers, senior faculty members may view their situation quite differently. For some full professors, the very fact that there are no more promotions to earn can in itself be unsettling. After a career spent in pursuit of one academic degree after another, followed by progressions up the various faculty ranks, reaching a point in one's career where there are no more levels of recognition to seek can be disconcerting. Moreover, with increasing numbers of institutions promoting professors after twelve or fewer years of full-time service, many faculty members find that they face more than half of their careers with few opportunities for upward advancement, validation of their accomplishments by peers, or chances to increase their incomes significantly without changing institutions. Certainly, post-tenure review procedures were adopted to help institutions keep their most highly paid senior faculty members as active and productive as possible. Properly constructed, systems of post-tenure review accomplish far more than simply penalizing deadwood by rewarding and celebrating the accomplishments of truly outstanding senior faculty members. Nevertheless, it can be a real challenge for college professors to stay motivated and preserve the energy of their early years when they realize the opportunities for reward are few, they have taught the same courses more than a dozen times, and they find themselves asking that nagging question—"And just why am I still doing this?"—with increasing frequency. Fortunately, many senior professors still find a great deal of excitement in helping to shape young minds, associating with other members of the academy, engaging in new approaches to research, and serving as a leader in an institution that has been such an important part of their lives. But if you do feel as though you'd like new opportunities or are simply looking for a change, what can you do?

Institutional Approaches

One approach is for institutions to recognize that there are limitations in the traditional system of rank and promotion and that senior faculty members need new kinds of incentive and acknowledgment. Designations such as distinguished professor or eminent scholar can serve as a significant recognition for those who have devoted their lives to an institution and left a remarkable legacy. At times, too, these titles can be further refined, resulting in such honors as distinguished teaching professor or eminent research scholar, with the expectation that individuals who hold these positions will serve as mentors to their junior colleagues. Fully or partially endowed chairs can also serve as a highly sought-after distinction for those who have already completed the full promotion process. A fully endowed chair is tied to a financial corpus large enough that its annual "draw" (the amount of interest, usually 4 to 5 percent, that the institution receives each year from the endowment, reinvesting any interest in excess of that amount so that the corpus will grow over time) fully supports the faculty member's salary, benefits, and research expenses. The difficulty for most institutions is that it takes an exceptionally large gift to support a fully endowed chair. To fund a chair that initially pays a faculty member $100,000 in salary with a 30 percent rate for benefits, and that also supplies an additional $25,000 in research funding, the institution would need to receive a gift of $3,875,000 if its institutional draw is 4 percent. Gifts of that magnitude occur only rarely at most institutions. Some colleges and universities have thus begun experimenting with partially endowed chairs, where the institution continues to pay a faculty member's salary and benefits out of its regular budget but provides the faculty member with access to an endowed fund for travel and research. In this way, a gift of a million dollars could result in a faculty member's access to a tax-free fund of $40,000 in support of scholarship. Such a fund is a significant reward and, though million-dollar gifts are not common, they are far more attainable than the truly massive contributions required to support a fully endowed chair.

What can you do if your institution does not offer special designations or lacks the resources to support endowed chairs? Your legacy could be to change this situation. Discuss with your institution's development office your willingness to meet with potential donors who could provide the funds for your school's first fully or partially endowed chair. Make a presentation to your president and governing board on the merits of expanding your institution's promotion structure to include eminent scholars and distinguished professors. Remind administrators that these titles can serve as a powerful motivating factor, reward the truly deserving for their important contributions to the institution, and help retain the very individuals the institution would most like to retain. Particularly if your college or university has a post-tenure review process already in place, you can present your proposal as the carrot that corresponds to post-tenure review's implied stick. Distinctions for full professors can even transform post-tenure review from something that all too frequently becomes highly politicized into a more equitable and palatable process. Distinctions for senior faculty members could become just the "cause" you need if you are seeking to become reenergized. So, if your institution already has these distinctions, continue the process of earning one. And if your institution has not yet created these titles, make it your mission to develop them.

Develop a New Focus

Sometimes the key to rediscovering the passion and energy that we once brought to our professional lives is in developing a new project about which we can become excited. For instance, if professors find that they are no longer challenged by teaching a course they have already taught numerous times, they can often regain their interest by teaching it in a new format or at a new level. Having to rethink how concepts are best explained to others can assume an entirely new dimension when a classroom course is converted to an online course, a regular section to an honors course, or a graduate class to an undergraduate course. If none of these options is available, perhaps you can propose teaching a few special topics or directed inquiry courses on material not currently part of your department's curriculum. For example, you might volunteer to teach a freshman seminar on a book or idea that is of particular interest to you, but which you have never had time to address in your other courses. Apply to your chair or dean for special funding that will allow you to take the technology that you use in the classroom to an entirely new level. In fact, your institution may already have sufficient technology available to convert one of your courses, units, or lessons to a new format.

- If you teach in an area such as history, foreign languages, or world cultures, you could create a project in which some unit that is difficult to teach in a traditional classroom setting is taught by video, complete with musical soundtrack and an opportunity to replay critical scenes. In other words, rather than showing your students static, two-dimensional images of a sculpture that you talk about in class, have yourself filmed explaining the work right beside it, with the camera following you as you discuss the piece from each side. Or, rather than simply talking about a historical document, create a montage that students can watch with images of the document itself, portraits of the major figures involved in its creation, and "subtitles" with key terms spelled correctly for them.

• Consider the possibility of revising your courses so that they can be more discussion-oriented and seminar-like. Record the lectures in which you are essentially presenting factual information and distribute them to your students via podcasts, streaming audio, files that they can download through course management software such as Blackboard, or on CD-ROM. Students can then listen to your lectures at their own pace as part of their homework, and you can reserve a greater portion of class time for discussing their reactions to the ideas you presented in your recorded lectures.

• Other online software allows you to create simulations, self-correcting exercises, or course reviews. For instance, instead of describing for students what it is like to participate on the trading floor of a stock exchange or place an order with a waiter in another language, you can create electronic lessons in which students actually engage in these activities.

If technology is not an area that holds much attraction for you, there are still other ways in which you can refocus your instruction as a senior faculty member. You can offer to serve as a mentor to a newer instructor who could benefit from the experience you have gained from teaching several generations of students. You can develop a new course guide for a class that you teach particularly well. Or you can take the course that was always your most challenging or least successful class and revise it thoroughly to discover whether there is a better way of presenting the material. The experience that you've amassed as a senior faculty member has probably exposed you to several dozen strategies that have worked successfully for your peers, role models, and colleagues. You've earned the right to "borrow" some of them. Best of all, these are not strategies that faculty members need to wait until they're senior professors to implement. If you're still a new or midcareer faculty member, consider taking some of these steps both now and periodically in the years ahead to keep your engagement in your courses high and to promote the most effective environment for enhanced student learning.

This same approach of refocusing your efforts can be applied to other areas of your professional life as well. For example, take some time to map out the next big scholarly project or research question that will occupy you for at least several years. Think in terms of not just traditional research in the form of Ernest Boyer's Scholarship of Discovery, but of the full range of scholarly possibility, including integration, application, and pedagogy. (Regarding these terms, see Chapters 3, "What Kind of Professor Are You?" and 28, "Alternative Forms of Scholarship.") If you have not already completed a Fulbright Fellowship or other international opportunity as recommended in the last chapter, start preparing an application. The insights that you will gain from exposure to different cultures and ideas will almost certainly lead you to new, exciting ideas for research. Similarly, in the area of service, try to discover some ways to make creative contributions that do not have the feeling of "just serving on another committee." Is there some aspect of your department's policies and procedures that is inadequate, badly out of date, or nonexistent? Why not offer your chair or dean an opportunity to have these critical areas updated and improved at your own initiative? Or is there some faculty development planning that could genuinely help your department improve its research record or quality of instruction? Offer to serve as an unofficial assistant department chair with the responsibility of improving your discipline's faculty development efforts. Could your department benefit from a grant proposal that no one has yet had time to develop or that the staff in the research office lacks the discipline-specific knowledge to pursue effectively? Providing your services as the one who prepares this grant proposal, works with a program officer at the funding agency to marshal it through the process, and serves as principal investigator once the grant is awarded can help to transform your department and bring you a level of excitement that you may not have felt about your work in some time.

Finally, nearly every academic department has some important responsibilities that remain unassigned because none of the existing committees sees it as their responsibility. For instance, many departments find that there is a perceived inequity in advisement loads but no established mechanism for addressing the problem. Junior faculty members may be hesitant to broach this issue because they are afraid of alienating peers who will be voting on their eventual promotion and tenure applications. As a senior faculty member, you can feel liberated from these concerns and raise the questions that need to be asked for the good of your discipline as a whole. Discuss with your chair the possibility of being appointed (even unofficially) as your area's ad hoc Czar of Advising, charged with examining the entire approach toward advising students. How are students assigned to individual faculty advisors? How does advising count into faculty load? How is it evaluated for the purposes of merit increases, promotion decisions, tenure considerations, and post-tenure review? Should student advising be limited to guiding students in course selection, or can it include a larger role as mentor, internship coordinator, or graduate school counselor? (For more ideas, see Chapter 34, "Serving as an Academic Advisor," and Chapter 35, "Serving as a Mentor.") Alternatively, if advising is already well handled in your department, find some other area in which you can make a difference. There is bound to be a connection between your interests and an existing need in your department, college, or institution. Decide how you'd prefer to make a difference, and then set out to focus your energy on that issue.

Develop an Area of Interest Outside of Academic Life

At times, the area of greatest interest that you will discover involves some pursuit not directly related to your professional work. While we are establishing ourselves in our careers, we may be unwilling to "divert" time from professional activities to hobbies, civic groups, religious organizations, book clubs, political campaigns, and other outside interests. Now that you are a senior member of the faculty, however, there is no time like the present. You don't need anyone's permission to invest your time in a cause or activity that is truly meaningful to you. Nevertheless, if you do feel that you need a professional justification for an outside interest, you should know that faculty members frequently discover unexpected connections between their avocations and their teaching or research. Outside interests can offer us new metaphors for explaining difficult concepts in our disciplines. These activities also inspire us to pursue research projects in new areas. Developing a new interest can, in other words, often be good for your work. Yet, even if it does not improve your productivity in any way whatsoever, it is undeniably beneficial for you and for the satisfaction that you derive from all that you have achieved in your life.

Of course, not all senior faculty members need to receive official "validation" for their work from their institutions, reenergize themselves by finding a new professional focus, or expand their perspectives by developing new interests outside of work. Many senior faculty members receive all the energy they need from the successes of their students, the challenges of their ongoing scholarship, and the support of their colleagues.

If you find, however, that you are not approaching your job with the same level of enthusiasm that you once did, it is important that you not regard this situation as inevitable or as a sign of defeat. As we grow and develop, our interests change. Your key task is to discover what it is that still excites and motivates you *now* and then to develop a plan that can help you direct your energy and experience in that direction.

RESOURCES

Alstete, J. W. (2000). *Post-tenure faculty development: Building a system for faculty improvement and appreciation.* San Francisco: Jossey-Bass.

Bland, C. J., & Bergquist, W. H. (1997). *The vitality of senior faculty members: Snow on the roof—fire in the furnace.* San Francisco: Jossey-Bass.

Bonk, C. J., & Zhang, K. (2008). *Empowering online learning: 1001 activities for reading, reflecting, displaying, and doing.* San Francisco: Jossey-Bass.

Bonzi, S. (1992). Trends in research productivity among senior faculty. *Information Processing and Management, 28*(1), 111–120.

Epper, R. M., & Bates, A. W. (2001). *Teaching faculty how to use technology: Best practices from leading institutions.* Phoenix, AZ: American Council on Education/Oryx Press.

Ferren, A. S. (1998). *Senior faculty considering retirement: A developmental and policy issue.* Sterling, VA: Stylus.

Finkelstein, M. J., & LaCelle-Peterson, M. W. (Eds.). (1993). *New directions for teaching and learning: No. 55. Developing senior faculty as teachers.* San Francisco: Jossey-Bass.

Licata, C. M., & Brown, B. E. (Eds.). (2004). *Post-tenure faculty review and renewal II: Reporting results and shaping policy.* Bolton, MA: Anker.

Licata, C. M., & Morreale, J. C. (Eds.). (2002). *Post-tenure faculty review and renewal: Experienced voices.* Bolton, MA: Anker.

Licata, C. M., & Morreale, J. C. (2006). *Post-tenure faculty review and renewal III: Outcomes and impact.* Bolton, MA: Anker.

9

TAKING THE NEXT STEP
IN YOUR CAREER

At the end of each of this book's four sections, you'll find a chapter that deals with the topic of taking the next step. The purpose of these chapters is to help you pull together material found in each of the chapters of that section, develop a plan of action for making the best use of the topics that have been covered, and then start using these concepts to make a substantive difference in your career, teaching, scholarship, and service. In this chapter we'll explore how you can incorporate your career plan, knowledge of your professional strengths and challenges, the stage where you are in your career, and the other information covered in this section as part of a strategy to carry your career to the next level.

Identifying a Transformational Change

In Chapter 4, "Career Planning for College Professors," we discussed the technique of taking your curriculum vitae, imagining a point somewhere between five and twenty years in the future, and developing a visionary résumé outlining where you'd like to be at that point in your career. Then, after setting those future goals, we explored ways of identifying intermediate steps that will help place you in the best possible position to achieve the objectives you've created. In this chapter, we'll conduct a similar exercise, but in a more focused way, tailored specifically to who you are right now and who you'd most like to be as an academic professional.

To begin this exercise, review what you discovered in Chapter 3, "What Kind of Professor Are You?" What did you learn about your priorities, professional strengths, and individual perspectives? With that information in mind, conduct the following exercise:

- Imagine that it is seven years from now. (If you will be retiring in fewer than seven years, imagine that it is your last year of full-time teaching.)

- Imagine that since the time you conducted this exercise, you have experienced a single, overwhelmingly positive change that has utterly transformed your career.
- What type of change would you most like to have occurred?
- How did it enhance your life and improve your work as a college professor?

Depending on where you are in your career and what you have learned about your professional values, your answers to these questions are likely to be quite different from those of someone else in your field. For instance, the following are common responses made by faculty members who have participated in this exercise in the past. Notice how broad a spectrum of activities they represent. Do any of these responses reflect the future you envisioned? Do any of these visions seem to be more appealing than the one you chose? (If so, feel free to revise your answer.)

- Obtain a full-time, tenure-track position in my discipline.
- Publish a book of my research through a well-respected university press.
- Receive a large grant for a project that will fund my ongoing research.
- Be honored with a university-level award for the quality of my teaching.
- Relocate to a more selective institution with a larger number of highly qualified students in my discipline.
- Become a full-time administrator.
- Be elected president of my professional association.
- Receive a major fellowship that will allow me to take a leave of absence and pursue my research extensively for a full year.
- Be promoted to the rank of full professor.
- Retrain by redirecting my academic focus to a new area of specialty that has arisen in my discipline.
- Shift my teaching load away from introductory courses to upper-level and graduate courses exclusively.
- Release a well-reviewed CD of my performances.
- Move to a different institution where I will find more supportive and collegial faculty members in my discipline.
- Become sufficiently fluent in a foreign language to enable me to conduct research abroad, perhaps through a Fulbright Fellowship.
- Publish several articles in the first-tier journals of my discipline.

- Be acknowledged by the students of my institution as Professor of the Year.
- Develop a national reputation as an expert in my field who is consulted by the media when stories arise related to my discipline.
- Expand my research team to include a larger number of graduate students who are qualified in my area of specialty.
- Be granted a sabbatical.
- Publish a bestselling textbook in my field.
- Update all my courses to make the best use of new technology.
- Be recognized with a highly prestigious, international award for my scholarship.
- Increase the number of full-time faculty lines in my discipline so that we can better serve our students.
- Receive my institution's award for excellence in service.
- Have one of my creative works favorably reviewed in the *New York Times Review of Books*.
- Earn tenure.

As you can see from this list, the ways in which our careers can be transformed vary considerably. But if each of us reflects on our careers candidly and creatively, we inevitably discover that there is at least one transformational change that could radically improve our professional lives in the relatively near future. So, the first step in advancing your career comes when you identify what will be the appropriate transformational change for you.

Planning for Your Transformational Change

The second step comes when you identify the intermediate goals that will make it possible for you to undergo the change you have envisioned. For example, suppose that you have identified your seven-year goal as having several of your articles accepted by a first-tier journal in your discipline. There are a number of intermediate actions you can take to place yourself in a better position to achieve that goal. You might start by carefully examining articles that have appeared in that journal for the past several years to see if you can determine a particular focus, methodology, or writing style that appears to characterize successful submissions. Especially consider the types of citations that occur in articles that are most similar to what you hope to write: What sources have those scholars used and how have the authors incorporated earlier research into their own works? As you prepare your own submissions, you will want to do similar citations to the same kinds of sources and publications.

As a next step toward your eventual publication, you might bring your name to the attention of the journal's editors by offering to review books or to serve as a referee for potential articles. Serving as a referee can be particularly valuable because you will get an insight into the editor's instructions for the scholars who will eventually be considering *your* article for publication. On what basis are articles accepted or rejected? What are referees asked to examine and what type of response are they asked to provide? Be sure to construct your own submission so that it can pass the standards given to the referees.

As a third step in your preparation, submit a nearly complete draft of an article to several colleagues who have been successful in placing their scholarship either in your target journal or in similar publications. Pay very close attention to their suggestions, particularly when it comes to the strength of your documentation, the flow of your argument, and the appropriateness of your style to the publication you have in mind (see Chapter 27, "Seeking and Providing Peer Support for Scholarship"). Use these suggestions to create a polished submission that you can then send to the editor of the journal. Don't get discouraged if your first attempt is not accepted. If the referees' comments are not provided to you automatically, ask to see them, read them dispassionately (remember that a rejection of your article is never a rejection of you), and then revise your work accordingly. It is not at all uncommon for an article that has been submitted to a first-tier journal to go through three or more revisions before it is finally accepted. With each revision, you will learn a bit more about how to make your next article even more appropriate for the journal. If you keep at it, this process eventually becomes easier. In certain disciplines, you may reach the point where many of your contributions are accepted on their first submission. That level of success, however, does not often happen immediately. Like most other aspects of our professional lives, writing for first-tier journals can require something of a learning curve and, in many cases, this process can become quite extended.

This example is one that is probably most appropriate for a faculty member relatively new in his or her career who is working in a discipline in which publication is not a regular part of graduate training or postdoctoral experience. But you can use a similar approach no matter where you are in your career and no matter what your transformational goal may be. By their nature, visionary goals are quite difficult to achieve. Keep in mind, though, that they can be achieved if you break down large, possibly intimidating projects into a number of discrete, intermediate goals that position you for reaching your overall objective. Many of the chapters in this book are designed to assist you with these intermediate goals. For instance, if your transformational goal is to:

- *Obtain a full-time, tenure track position in your discipline,* begin by preparing your application according to the principles outlined in Chapter 1, "Applying for a Faculty Position," and update your résumé according to the principles outlined in Chapter 31, "Creating an Effective Curriculum Vitae."

- *Receive a large grant for a scholarly project,* start by reading Chapter 23, "Writing a Grant Proposal," enlist the support of your colleagues as outlined in Chapter 27, "Seeking and Providing Peer Support for Scholarship," and plan for how you will incorporate the grant project into your overall responsibilities as outlined in Chapter 26, "Balancing Scholarship with Other Duties."

- *Increase your effectiveness as a teacher,* start with the general information that appears in Chapter 18, "Promoting Student Engagement" and then select among the various topics related to instruction that are discussed in Chapters 10 through 22.

No matter what the next step in your career may be, there are small, easily attainable goals that you can start achieving now in order to help you realize your visionary goal later. Too often we find ourselves frozen into inaction because the obstacles in our path seem insurmountable or because the results we desire seem so distant. Nevertheless, the vast majority of any college professor's career goals can be obtained by taking small, manageable steps along the way. Becoming president of a highly prestigious university may seem impossible now, but you can bring yourself closer to fulfilling that dream if you start by asking, "How can I best position myself to become an extremely successful chair of my own department?" or "How can I go about being elected chair of the faculty senate?"

10

ASSESSING STUDENT LEARNING

Beginning a discussion of teaching with a chapter on assessment will strike some readers as backwards: what sense does it make to talk about the final exam before you even begin to introduce the topic itself? Though this may be a common reaction, it's important to understand how thoroughly integrated assessment has become with effective teaching at the college or university level. Instead of pausing at the end of a process and asking, "How did we do?" assessment in higher education today occurs throughout the entire learning process and asks, "How can we do even better than we are doing now?" To see how assessment has become one of the foundations of effective college-level learning, it is useful to begin with a few definitions.

A Brief Primer on Assessment

Assessment is a process that measures the degree to which some action appears to be leading to a specific set of goals. In this way, assessment can be distinguished from evaluation, the process that measures the degree to which a particular standard has been reached. See Table 10.1 for the important distinctions between the two.

College professors perform both assessment and evaluation all the time. If you have ever read a set of research papers written by seniors in your program and found yourself thinking, "The grammar and argumentation in these papers are terrible! We need to place more emphasis on how to write a proper research paper in our lower level courses," you were engaging in assessment. You thought about how to improve a process based on your review of how a group has performed in achieving an objective (writing well). However, if you have ever read a set of research papers written by seniors in your program and found yourself thinking, "This student deserves a failing grade. The form, content, and reasoning of this particular paper all fail to reach acceptable standards for our program," you were engaging in evaluation. You made a judgment about a level of quality in an individual case, leading to a specific action (failure

Table 10.1: Differences Between Assessment and Evaluation

Assessment Is	Evaluation Is
Formative; provides constructive advice on how an activity can be improved.	Summative; renders a judgment as to whether a specific action is warranted.
Process oriented; looks for ways to improve the activity itself.	Goal oriented; determines whether a particular level of quality has been reached.
Deals with larger or collective entities, such as an entire group of students in a course, courses in a curriculum, or departments in a college.	Deals with individual entities, such as a single person, course, or program.

in the course). We evaluate students when we grade their work; we're evaluated by our supervisors during an annual review. When we assess our courses, we think about ways we can improve them; our programs are assessed whenever our institutions prepare for reaccreditation.

Although you engage in assessment every time you try to improve a course based on past experience, assessment can be much more effective if you go about it in a systematic and intentional manner. To do so, it is necessary to identify student learning outcomes: clear expressions of what you intend students to know or to be able to do at a specific point in your curriculum. The outcome you seek may involve learning on a wide variety of levels. For instance, it could relate to mastery of information, development of skills, attainment of performance standards, demonstration of attributes, or any sort of learning that researchers in the field of cognition have identified in their taxonomies of understanding (taxonomies and their importance to assessment are discussed later in this chapter). To help identify an appropriate student learning outcome for one of your courses, begin by asking the following questions:

- What specifically do I want all the students in a course or program to know or be able to do?
- At what point in the course or program should this objective be achieved?
- How will I be able to recognize whether my students in fact know, or are able to reach, the objective I have identified?
- What minimum acceptable success rate will make it clear that I am achieving my goal?

- How will I determine what went wrong if that success rate is not reached?
- How will I develop a plan to improve that success rate in the future?

For example, let's suppose that you're teaching a lab for an introductory course in biology. In this course, you will provide students with their first exposure to sterile technique, an important process that they will need in their upper-level courses in microbiology, biotechnology, and similar subjects. Although you always strive for every student in the class to master this technique, experience has taught you that this goal is simply not feasible at this point in the curriculum and that students will have several other chances to perfect their technique in later courses. You might develop an outcome that looks like this:

> By the tenth week of the laboratory portion of Principles of Biology, 80 percent of the class should have demonstrated its competence at sterile technique by successfully transferring an uncontaminated specimen between media through the use of either the dry heat or flame sterilization procedures. If that rate of success is not achieved, laboratory assistants will carefully observe the students who are not performing the transfer successfully, and a review session will be offered that focuses on the precise steps that appear to cause students the greatest difficulties. In addition, the way in which this procedure is taught in the future will be revised in order to direct more attention to the specific problems that students are most likely to have.

In this way, you have a very clear idea of the goal you are trying to achieve, an immediate plan of action if that goal is not achieved, and a long-range plan for ongoing improvement (for more on the most meaningful and beneficial way to express student learning outcomes, see Diamond, 2008, and Wiggins & McTighe, 2006). By adopting a similar approach, you can also develop student learning outcomes and assess the effectiveness of entire degree programs, particular tracks or emphases within degree programs, specific degree requirements (such as general education requirements, writing-across-the-curriculum requirements, or service-learning requirements), and any other aspect of the students' experience at your institution (on these broader assessment processes, see Banta, 2003, 2007, and Buller, 2006). In this chapter, we'll focus on the type of assessment that has the most immediate impact on what college professors do in their capacity as teachers: course assessment techniques for continuous improvement of student learning.

Using Assessment for Continuous Improvement

Using assessment techniques for continuous improvement of instruction involves the creation of a feedback loop that (1) tells the instructor whether adequate progress toward an objective is being achieved; (2) provides this information in a timely manner so that adjustments to the course can be made while it is still in progress; and (3) measures the effectiveness of those adjustments, thus beginning the process all over again. Without this type of loop, we might discover—only while grading a final exam or a research paper—that a significant number of the students did not understand a major concept or know how to apply a certain technique that we could easily have clarified earlier. By the end of the course it is too late to remedy the situation; any changes will have to wait until the next time that class is offered. That new group of students, however, may have an entirely different set of needs or may already have mastered these concepts and techniques in an earlier course. The goal, therefore, should be not just evaluation of each student's performance, but ongoing assessment of how effectively students are learning. Assessment is such an important topic in higher education that there are many excellent resources on this subject. The best place to begin is with the three classics in the area of continuous assessment in the classroom, studio, lab, or experiential activity: Angelo and Cross (1993); Banta, Lund, Black, and Oblander (1996); and Palomba and Banta (1999). As but one example, Angelo and Cross provide detailed information on fifty different kinds of classroom assessment techniques that can be used in nearly every discipline. A few of these techniques are:

- *One-sentence summaries.* Students summarize their understanding of an idea through a single sentence that answers the question "Who does what to whom, when, where, how, and why?"

- *Approximate analogies.* Students relate a new concept or process to something they already understand, using the standard formula A: B:: C: D.

- *Annotated portfolios.* Students comment on and perform a self-assessment of a limited number of their projects, papers, or creative works.

- *Documented problem solutions.* Students identify all the steps they took in reaching a particular conclusion or solution.

- *Classroom assessment quality circles.* A subset of the class is responsible for consulting with their colleagues about which issues are still confusing, which classroom techniques are more effective, and which strategies should be adopted to enhance their learning.

- *Group work evaluations.* The process and dynamics involved in group projects are examined while the work is still under way, so procedures may yet be improved.

All these techniques provide the instructor with valuable information about whether a particular learning outcome is being achieved. More important, they do so without taking a great deal of time away from the process of learning itself.

The Microtheme or One-Minute Essay

One of the most widely used and flexible types of classroom assessment is the microtheme, also known as the one-minute essay (see Angelo & Cross, 1993; Bean, 1996; Davis, 2009; Diamond, 2008; Palomba & Banta, 1999). Microthemes are extremely short essays, usually under two hundred words and occasionally as brief as a single sentence, and may be adapted to any type or level of course. Requiring very little time to prepare, administer, or review, they encourage student writing even in large lecture or online courses and provide convenient midcourse assessment. They may be introduced at any moment in a class when the instructor tells the students to take out a piece of paper and restate, in their own words, the key concept that has just been described for them, the three issues that the last student who spoke regarded as most important, or the most significant aspect of the unit about which they are still uncertain. Microthemes may also be completed outside of class through an assignment that asks students to identify the thesis statement in an article they are reading, the most influential principle they have learned in the course so far, or the technique they used to learn the material that would be on that day's quiz. The last question is particularly useful as it encourages reflective learning and lets the teacher know whether the class tends to be engaging in effective study techniques.

Microthemes are also valuable because they force students to write repeatedly and consistently throughout a course, require them to verbalize ideas that may not otherwise have reached full formation, and provide the instructor with insights that can be used to enhance the learning process. It is not necessary to spend a great deal of time grading a microtheme. These assignments may simply be checked off as completed, or they may be given a small amount of credit (0 points for not completed, 1 point for completed, 2 points for completed in an extremely thoughtful manner). As a form of ongoing assessment, microthemes help you take the pulse of your class on a daily basis. A quick glance at them will tell you who is understanding the material immediately, who is being left behind, what has captured the students' interest the most, and what is causing the class the greatest frustration.

Technology and Assessment

Other types of assessment for continuous improvement are extremely easy to implement through various forms of classroom technology. Short questions that test student understanding of a new idea, surveys or opinion polls that provide insight into students' perceptions and values, or midcourse ratings of instructional techniques can all be tabulated automatically using various means. For instance, in Chapter 14, "Teaching Large Classes," we'll discuss the use of electronic student response systems, also known as "clickers," for obtaining instant feedback from large numbers of students. Class management software, such as Blackboard, Moodle, and Angel Learning, automatically tabulates certain types of exam questions or survey formats, including calculated numerics, either-or and true-false questions, ordering of lists, matching, short answer questions, multiple choice, opinion scale-Likert questions, fill-in-the-blank, and others. These techniques can quickly provide instructors with information about:

- What students in the class already understand about a topic.
- Students' current conceptions and misconceptions about a subject.
- Whether sufficient numbers of students have mastered a concept or process before the course moves on to the next topic.
- The students' preferred methods of learning.
- Issues that, unless addressed early in the course, could cause negative responses on student ratings of instruction.
- How the range of opinions reflected among students in the course relates to those of the general population.
- Which perspectives that tend to be found among the general population are missing among the students enrolled in the course.

All of these areas provide the instructor with valuable information and can lead to enhanced student learning. For instance, if you discover that students in a particular course have already covered a certain topic thoroughly in other courses, this knowledge frees you to spend more time on areas that will be more valuable to that particular class, reduces the risk that students will become bored by excessive repetition, and allows you to build on a class's existing knowledge in a way that can make their understanding of an area deeper and more meaningful. In a similar way, if you learn that a particular simulation, assignment, or instructional technique was not effective for many students in the course, you can explore other ways of teaching that concept or information more successfully while the course is still under way.

Bloom's Taxonomy

In 1956, the cognitive psychologist Benjamin S. Bloom suggested that learning and knowing were highly complex processes that could be organized into a taxonomy of six activities. Although often presented as a wheel of interconnected processes, Bloom's taxonomy can also be viewed as a progression from simple memorization to higher-order understanding:

- *Knowledge*. The ability to recall information.
- *Comprehension*. The ability to restate information in one's own words.
- *Application*. The ability to use information in specific practical situations.
- *Analysis*. The ability to separate information into its component parts.
- *Synthesis*. The ability to assemble new types of information from bits of data or observation.
- *Evaluation*. The ability to appraise information for its strengths and weaknesses and to estimate the further implications of that information.

Although Bloom's original taxonomy remains extremely influential, later researchers sought to refine or expand it.

Gardner's Multiple Intelligences

Gardner did not set out to revise Bloom's taxonomy per se, but to suggest that intelligence should be regarded as a complex phenomenon consisting of many different *kinds* of intelligence. In so doing, Gardner developed a taxonomy of intelligence that provides an important complement to Bloom's taxonomy of learning. The original seven types of intelligence that were identified in Gardner (1983) included:

- *Musical intelligence*, often demonstrated by performers and composers.
- *Bodily-kinesthetic intelligence*, often demonstrated by athletes and dancers.
- *Logical-mathematical intelligence*, often demonstrated by philosophers, scientists, and mathematicians.
- *Linguistic intelligence*, often demonstrated by authors, poets, and orators.
- *Spatial intelligence*, often demonstrated by navigators, artists, and architects.
- *Interpersonal intelligence*, often demonstrated by teachers, counselors, and diplomats.
- *Intrapersonal intelligence*, often demonstrated by people commonly regarded as well balanced or self-actualized.

In addition to these original seven types of intelligence, Gardner (2006) later suggested that there may be one or two others:

- *Naturalist intelligence*, often demonstrated by biologists, farmers, and ecologists.
- *Spiritual intelligence*, often demonstrated by mystics, members of the clergy, and the devout. (Although Gardner seriously considered this kind of intelligence as parallel to the other eight, he ultimately rejected it as not sufficiently comparable to them.)

Anderson and Krathwohl's Response to Bloom

In 2001, Anderson and Krathwohl suggested that Bloom's original taxonomy, while more helpful than earlier models of learning, did not sufficiently embrace the full complexity of human cognition. They suggested that, for each of six different types of cognitive processes, there were four different types of knowledge. The six types of cognitive processes identified by Anderson and Krathwohl are:

- *Remembering*. Recognizing, recalling, and retrieving relevant knowledge from long-term memory.
- *Understanding*. Constructing meaning from instructional messages, including oral, written, and graphic communication. This includes interpreting, exemplifying, classifying, summarizing, inferring, comparing, and explaining.
- *Applying*. Carrying out or using a procedure in a given situation; executing and implementing.

- *Analyzing.* Breaking material into constituent parts and determining how these parts relate to one another and to an overall structure or purpose. This includes differentiating, organizing, and attributing.

- *Evaluating.* Making judgments based on criteria and standards; checking and critiquing.

- *Creating.* Putting elements together to form a coherent or functional whole; reorganizing elements into a new pattern or structure. This includes generating, planning, and producing.

Each of these six cognitive processes may be used to address four different kinds of knowledge (Anderson & Krathwohl, 2001):

- *Factual knowledge.* The basic elements students must know to be acquainted with a discipline or solve problems in it: knowledge of terminology, specific details, and elements.

- *Conceptual knowledge.* The interrelationships among the basic elements within a larger structure that enable them to function together: knowledge of classifications, categories, principles, generalizations, theories, models, and structures.

- *Procedural knowledge.* How to do something: knowledge of methods of inquiry, of subject-specific skills, algorithms, techniques, and methods, and criteria for determining when to use appropriate procedures.

- *Metacognitive knowledge.* Knowledge of cognition in general as well as awareness and knowledge of one's own cognition: strategic knowledge, knowledge about cognitive tasks, and self-knowledge.

Within this framework, it is thus possible to speak very precisely about specific types of learning, clearly distinguishing the process of remembering factual knowledge from applying procedural knowledge, and so on.

Fink's Taxonomy of Significant Learning

Working at about the same time as Anderson and Krathwohl, Fink explicitly sought to revise Bloom's taxonomy, making it less restrictive or unnecessarily narrow. By recognizing such types of cognition as caring and learning about the human dimension, Fink (2003) developed an important synthesis of Bloom's taxonomy and Gardner's multiple intelligences:

- *Foundational knowledge.* Understanding and remembering:
  - Information
  - Ideas

- *Application*. Utilizing:
  - Skills
  - Thinking: critical, creative, and practical thinking
  - Managing projects
- *Integration*. Connecting:
  - Ideas
  - People
  - Realms of life
- *Human dimension*. Learning about:
  - Oneself
  - Others
- *Caring*. Developing new:
  - Feelings
  - Interests
  - Values
- Learning how to learn by:
  - Becoming a better student
  - Inquiring about a subject
  - Improving as a self-directed learner

The Relationship of These Taxonomies to Assessment

The approaches to intelligence and learning posited by Bloom, Gardner, Krathwohl and Anderson, Fink, and others provide an important context for the development of a truly effective approach to assessment. For one thing, they demonstrate the care that must be used when forming outcomes that include such words as *know, learn*, and *understand*. The type of understanding that enables students to use a formula properly is not at all identical to the type of understanding that allows them to derive a formula from the data. The level of learning that permits a student to recognize a specific work of art is quite different from that which permits a student to discuss the significance of that work within its cultural setting, compare it to others by different artists or entirely different cultures, or create an entirely new work of art on his or her own. Without considering these taxonomies, it can be extremely difficult for college professors to be clear about what they are trying to assess in their classroom assessment plans. As every researcher knows, if you do not understand what precisely you are trying to conclude or measure, your ultimate results are likely to be absolutely meaningless (see Wiggins & McTighe, 2006).

These taxonomies also remind us that different assessment strategies must be in place for different disciplines and for institutions with different instructional missions. We can't expect how and what students learn to be identical at such diverse institutions as St. John's College with its "Great Books" curriculum; New College of Florida with its individualized and highly flexible curriculum; Northwood University with its exclusive focus on business education and leadership development; California State University, Monterey Bay with its competency-based curriculum that transcends all majors and programs; Hampshire College with its inherently interdisciplinary curriculum; and so on. One of the great strengths of American higher education is the sheer diversity in how college students are taught, what they are taught, and why they are taught it. There will never be a standardized test that captures the full benefit of the college experience at every type of school and in every subject. Nevertheless, college professors at all institutions are constantly assessing whether their instructional techniques are effective and how they can be made better. Even professors who do not realize that they are engaging in assessment are doing so constantly. The important goal for accreditation bodies and university administrations should not be, therefore, to insist that the same methods of assessment be used in every discipline or at every school, but rather that techniques be appropriate for the educational goals of each individual class. College professors can help achieve this goal by reflecting carefully on their individual teaching philosophies and the types of learning that best suit the different missions of different units in different courses. Educational outcomes will thus *always* be a fusion of the instructor's own learning philosophy, broadly accepted objectives of the academic discipline, and the college's or university's distinct mission within higher education. Where you as a college professor fit into the educational goals of your discipline, your institution, and of American higher education in general can become clearer after serious consideration of how your teaching objectives relate to the taxonomies of learning and intelligence developed by Bloom and his successors.

The topic of assessment in higher education has developed a huge literature, and the college professor who wishes to learn more will find numerous resources readily available. Nevertheless, college professors who are relatively new to the concept of using assessment for continual improvement of instruction can achieve a great deal simply by following this formula:

- *Identify goals.* What are you trying to achieve with a particular exercise, class period, unit, or course? What should students be able to know or do by a particular point in that activity? Be as specific as possible in setting your goals. Make them easy to determine whether they have been met. "To understand *Hamlet*" may be a commendable life goal, but it is extremely difficult to ascertain when and if it has been achieved. Select instead a goal that makes it easy for you to determine whether or not a student has reached it.

- *Measure progress.* To what extent has the class as a whole met the goals you have set out? Is this an acceptable success rate? For certain concepts and processes, you will need 100 percent of the class to reach the goals that you have set. For other learning objectives, it will simply not be possible to avoid moving on even if a small number of students are still having difficulties. Balance your idealism with the practical realities of the type of students who enroll in your program. Establish a success rate that you can defend, based on the mission of your institution and program, as well as the actual student population you serve.

- *Develop plans.* What will you do if your minimum acceptable rate of success is not achieved? What steps will you take in the short term to help this class and in the long term to improve the level of student learning for future classes? Failing to meet your anticipated level of success is a good indication that action must be taken. Good teachers learn from unsuccessful efforts to avoid problems in the future. Excellent teachers both revise their approaches for the future and take steps now to help current students reach their full potential.

- *Implement well-considered strategies.* What does your ongoing assessment reveal about the needs of each class you teach? How can you adopt strategies that help you meet those individual needs? No two classes you teach will ever be alike. What works for one group of students may well be completely unsuccessful with others. Assessment helps you select those learning strategies that are best tailored for each individual class you encounter. As Bain (2004) suggests,

> To make learning-based assessment work, the best teachers try to find out as much as possible about their students, "not so I can make judgments about them," one instructor explained, "but so that I can help

them learn." He and others began early in the term to collect information about their students. They explored their ambitions, their approaches to and conceptions of learning, the ways they reasoned, the mental models they brought with them, their temperaments, their habits of the heart and mind, and the daily matters that occupied their attention. (p. 157)

By basing your assessment process on this philosophy, you are adhering to the following essential principle, the foundation for all successful college teaching:

Truly effective instruction is not measured by how much college professors teach, but by how much college students learn.

We'll encounter several important applications of this essential principle, as well as the landmark essay that inspired it, in Chapter 18, "Promoting Student Engagement."

REFERENCES

Anderson, L. W., & Krathwohl, D. R. (Eds.). (2001). *A taxonomy for learning, teaching, and assessing: A revision of Bloom's taxonomy of educational objectives.* Needham Heights, MA: Allyn & Bacon.

Angelo, T. A., & Cross, K. P. (1993). *Classroom assessment techniques: A handbook for college teachers* (2nd ed.). San Francisco: Jossey-Bass.

Bain, K. (2004). *What the best college teachers do.* Cambridge, MA: Harvard University Press.

Banta, T. W. (Ed.). (2003). *Portfolio assessment: Uses, cases, scoring, and impact.* San Francisco: Jossey-Bass.

Banta, T. W. (Ed.). (2007). *Assessing student achievement in general education.* San Francisco: Jossey-Bass.

Banta, T. W., Lund, J. P., Black, K. E., & Oblander, F. W. (1996). *Assessment in practice: Putting principles to work on college campuses.* San Francisco: Jossey-Bass.

Bean, J. C. (1996). *Engaging ideas: The professor's guide to integrating writing, critical thinking, and active learning in the classroom.* San Francisco: Jossey-Bass.

Bloom, B. S. (1956). *Taxonomy of educational objectives: The classification of educational goals, by a committee of college and university examiners. Handbook 1: Cognitive domain.* New York: Longman.

Buller, J. L. (2006). The department chair's role in assessment. In J. L. Buller, *The essential department chair: A practical guide to college administration* (pp. 94–104). Bolton, MA: Anker.

Davis, B. G. (2009). *Tools for teaching* (2nd ed.). San Francisco: Jossey-Bass.

Diamond, R. M. (2008). *Designing and assessing courses and curricula: A practical guide* (3rd ed.). San Francisco: Jossey-Bass.

Fink, D. L. (2003). *Creating significant learning experiences: An integrated approach to designing college courses*. San Francisco: Jossey-Bass.

Gardner, H. (1983). *Frames of mind: The theory of multiple intelligences*. New York: Basic Books.

Gardner, H. (2006). *Multiple intelligences: New horizons*. New York: Basic Books.

Palomba, C. A., & Banta, T. W. (1999). *Assessment essentials: Planning, implementing, and improving assessment in higher education*. San Francisco: Jossey-Bass.

Wiggins, G., & McTighe, J. (2006). *Understanding by design* (2nd ed.). New York: Prentice Hall.

RESOURCES

Banta, T. W. (Ed.). (2004). *Hallmarks of effective outcomes assessment*. San Francisco: Jossey-Bass.

Barr, R. B., & Tagg, J. (1995). From teaching to learning—A new paradigm for undergraduate education. *Change, 27*(6), 12–25.

Bryan, C., & Clegg, K. (Eds.). (2006). *Innovative assessment in higher education*. New York: Routledge.

Butler, S. M., & McMunn, N. D. (2006). *A teacher's guide to classroom assessment: Understanding and using assessment to improve student learning*. San Francisco: Jossey-Bass.

Fox, M. A., & Hackerman, N. (Eds.). (2001). *Evaluating and improving undergraduate teaching in science, technology, engineering, and mathematics*. Washington, DC: National Academies Press.

Haswell, R. H. (Ed.). (2001). *Beyond outcomes: Assessment and instruction within a university writing program*. Westport, CT: Ablex.

Huba, M. E., & Freed, J. E. (1999). *Learner-centered assessment on college campuses: Shifting the focus from teaching to learning*. Boston, MA: Allyn & Bacon.

McKeachie, W. J., & Svinicki, M. (2006). Assessing, testing, and evaluating: Grading is not the most important function. In W. J. McKeachie & M. Svinicki, *McKeachie's teaching tips: Strategies, research, and theory for college and university teachers* (12th ed., pp. 74–86). New York: Houghton Mifflin.

Mezeske, R. J., & Mezeske, B. A. (Eds.). (2008). *Beyond tests and quizzes: Creative assessments in the college classroom.* San Francisco: Jossey-Bass.

Myers, C. B. (2008). Divergence in learning goal priorities between college students and their faculty: Implications for teaching and learning. *College Teaching, 56*(1), 53–58.

Wehlburg, C. M. (2008). *Promoting integrated and transformative assessment: A deeper focus on student learning.* San Francisco: Jossey-Bass.

Weimer, M. (2002). *Learner-centered teaching: Five key changes to practice.* San Francisco: Jossey-Bass.

11

WRITING AN EFFECTIVE COURSE SYLLABUS

Our English word *syllabus* comes to us, via Latin, from the Greek word *sillubos*, the term used for papyrus labels at the end of scrolls that identified the text inside. From an etymological perspective then, a syllabus was originally a table of contents, and that is how many college professors think of syllabi today: outlines of the content that students will find in their courses. Syllabi usually tell students the topics that a course will cover, the readings that will be assigned, the projects that must be completed, the dates of exams and other requirements that will come due, and other basic course information. From a syllabus, an observer can quickly gain a sense of what will be covered in your course, at what rate, and with what expectations. Yet some faculty members, after they have developed a course syllabus, give relatively little thought to ways in which it can be revised or improved. It is not uncommon for college professors who have already taught a course to update their syllabi only a day or two before the term begins, merely adjusting the dates from a previous version to correspond with the current calendar. This is a bad practice, because developing better syllabi can often lead to increased student learning. Moreover, syllabi have lots of important dimensions:

- *Legal.* As Parkes and Harris (2002) state in their influential survey of course syllabi, "The first purpose of a syllabus—either explicitly or implicitly—is to serve as a contract between the instructor and the student" (p. 59). Because the syllabus is an implied contract, faculty members either win or lose grade appeals based on whether they have followed the evaluation system they themselves outlined in their syllabi. College professors who flagrantly disregard their own syllabi may find themselves subject to grievances or even legal challenges by students. Of course, a syllabus's status as a legal document does not mean that, once that it is issued, a syllabus can never be altered. What it does mean is that substantive changes must be made with adequate advance notice given to the students and for justifiable reasons.

- *Evaluative.* Even long after a course has ended, syllabi may be used when making personnel decisions about a faculty member. For instance, it is not at all uncommon for course syllabi to be included in the supporting material for tenure and promotion decisions (see Chapter 5, "The Tenure and Promotion Process"). In addition, awards for excellence in teaching, certain grant applications, and other types of evaluations may require a faculty member to submit sample course syllabi from current or past semesters. Syllabi thus become one of the most important ways in which your supervisors and colleagues form an impression about the quality of your instruction.

- *Programmatic.* Syllabi are often examined after a course is completed for various programmatic purposes. For instance, syllabi may be consulted if a student transfers between institutions (to determine whether courses are comparable to one another), when the institution is being considered for accreditation (to determine whether certain standards are in effect), or during an institutional program review (to determine whether a program remains viable, of high quality, and central to the institution's mission).

- *Practical.* One of the first impressions that prospective students may have of you can come from your syllabus. Students often choose courses on the basis of experiences that their friends have had at the institution, and they may ask to see the syllabi of their friends' courses before deciding on a schedule. A well-constructed syllabus may thus actually attract larger numbers of more highly motivated students to enroll in your course. An increasing number of institutions are requiring that syllabi be posted several months before courses begin as an aid to advising and so that students have an option of buying books and materials from less-expensive sources.

- *Pedagogical.* A syllabus serves one obvious pedagogical purpose by ensuring that students are aware of pending deadlines far enough in advance to prepare for them adequately. But a syllabus can serve other pedagogical purposes by clarifying to students the proper approach, content, and methods of a discipline.

Moreover, in addition to all of these different roles that syllabi play, it is also the case that people use the term *syllabus* in different ways that can sometimes be confusing. So let's begin our consideration of how to design an effective syllabus by distinguishing the most important ways in which the word *syllabus* is used at colleges and universities.

Different Types of Syllabi

Although they are rarely differentiated, we sometimes find the term *syllabus* applied to any one of three different types of documents.

- *The course syllabus* is an outline of goals and requirements that remain consistent from term to term regardless of who the instructor may be. When a curriculum committee "approves" a syllabus for a new class, it is this type of syllabus that it is approving. A different instructor may be assigned to the course, and in many cases, the textbook, deadlines for assignments, and even the assignments themselves may change, but the essential focus of the course, the topics that will be covered, and the primary pedagogical methods will remain the same. The course syllabus is also what the registrar or department chair examines when attempting to determine whether a course taken by a student at another institution is comparable to one of your department's own courses. Ideally, course syllabi should not contain the instructor's name, dates for specific class periods, or textbooks that may vary from one offering of the course to the next, as these items are not essential to the nature of the course itself. Some institutions are very clear in distinguishing a course syllabus from what teachers actually distribute in class; most are not. But this practice can lead to clear inconsistencies: if the curriculum committee approved the syllabus for a specific instructor, textbook, and set of assignments, does it have to reconsider the course any time one of these items changes?

- *The section syllabus* is an outline of an individual professor's plans and requirements for a specific section of a course. If a course syllabus tells us what students will learn and how they will learn it in, for instance, general chemistry, a section syllabus will specify how that basic plan will be applied in, say, Dr. Smith's fall semester section of general chemistry that meets Mondays, Wednesdays, and Fridays at 11:00 AM. It is the section syllabus that professors distribute to students on the first day of a course and that outlines when exams will occur and when various requirements are due. Inevitably, this form of the syllabus will be different even for the same faculty member during different terms or when offering the course in different ways. Thus, Dr. Smith may have a substantially different section syllabus for the section of general chemistry that meets on Tuesday and Thursday afternoons at 2:00 and for the additional section that is taught online.

- *The policies and procedures syllabus* may be included as part of a section syllabus or may exist as a separate document (at times, even as several documents). Whichever form it takes, this is where the professor outlines policies and procedures specific to the courses that he or she teaches. For instance, one professor's attendance policy may be quite different from another's. Different professors may also impose different rules about whether students may bring food or drink into the classroom, whether late assignments or missed exams may be made up, whether caps and sunglasses may be worn during exams, whether cell phones and other electronic devices may be brought to class, whether the professor may be contacted at home, and so on. In most cases, a particular professor's policies and procedures will apply to all of the courses that he or she teaches, and they thus may be addressed independently of either the course syllabus or section syllabus.

In the discussion that follows, we will focus on the section syllabus and the policies and procedures syllabus, as these are the documents that individual professors tend to develop most frequently and which can play an important role in the success of their courses.

The Basics of Good Syllabus Design

When developing a section syllabus, it is often helpful to start with the following considerations.

- *What information does my institution and program require for my syllabus?* Almost every school will have a list of items that are mandatory for every section syllabus. A list of these requirements is often found in the faculty handbook, faculty resource manual, or online and may include such matters as the institution's plagiarism policy, procedures for requesting accommodations for disabilities, and the last date to withdraw from a course without academic penalty. These items will certainly not be the only things you will want to include in your syllabus, but they often provide a clear framework that you can expand to suit your course's individual needs.

- *What is my ultimate goal in this course?* As we saw in Chapter 10, "Assessing Student Learning," having a clear sense of the goal or objective you have for a course can be essential for many reasons. First, knowing what you want students to be able to understand and do by the end of the course helps you plan the logic and progression of the units that will reach that goal. Second, the goal gives you a way of periodically assessing whether students are making adequate progress and, if not, how you can remedy the situation. Third, knowing your ultimate goal from the beginning allows you to break that task down into achievable objectives—milestones along the journey, so to speak—that can form the basis for individual units or exercises. These intermediate objectives are often best phrased in the form of student learning outcomes, which makes it easier to perform ongoing assessment for continual improvement, and enables you to document your successes for your own personnel evaluations, your program's reaccreditation, and your department's academic program review. Moreover, some college professors find that if they establish their ultimate goals and secondary objectives with sufficient specificity, the rest of the syllabus almost writes itself.

• *What means will I use to determine whether my course is on track at any particular moment or whether it needs midcourse modification?* College professors regularly evaluate their students through assignments, quizzes, exercises, projects, papers, and exams. But do these techniques tell you everything that you need to know to increase the likelihood of student success? For example, if 80 percent of your students fail your first test, does the test alone tell you *why* the success rate on this exam was so low? Perhaps this is a particularly weak class. Perhaps the students were ill prepared by an introductory course, or the new textbook you adopted is less effective than the old one, or perhaps there is a particular concept or method that needs to be reexplained. Without a strategy for ascertaining the reasons for these scores and a plan for remedying the situation, you cannot do much to improve your students' level of learning . . . and your own reputation as an excellent instructor.

• *What other information is typically contained in any well-written syllabus?* Your own institution may have guidelines requiring you to include some of the following items in your syllabi. But whether this information is required by your school or not, a well-written syllabus should contain:

  • Your full name
  • Your title or information about how you wish to be addressed
    • Some students will worry excessively about addressing you with the title "Mr." or "Ms." if you would prefer to be called "Dr." or "Prof."
    • Other students may be uncertain as to whether you would like to be addressed by your first name.
    • The easiest solution to this problem is simply to include the information on the syllabus; for example, "Joan Anderson, Ph.D. [Dr. Anderson]" or "Dr. Timothy [Tim] Jones."

- The location of your office (and where to leave messages or assignments if you have a mailbox in a different location)
- Your office phone number
- The best times to call you in your office
- Your email address
- Your office hours
- A statement of your teaching philosophy
- A statement of your specific goals and philosophy for this particular course
- The course title, prefix, and number, and the number of credits students will earn on completing the course successfully
- The topics you will cover
- Essential dates and deadlines for all requirements
- How the student's final grade will be calculated
- Any criteria that you will use to evaluate all assignments
- Information about the types of exams you will give

Many faculty members create a syllabus that is too large and unwieldy because they attempt to include in it every single course policy they have. For this reason, unless your institution specifies otherwise, it is probably best to produce two separate documents: a section syllabus (that includes information specific to that section, such as dates when certain topics will be discussed or when certain assignments are due) and a policies and procedures syllabus (that includes your attendance policy, grading policy, extra credit policy, and the like). Together, these two documents constitute *the* syllabus for your course, but they divide information in a manner that makes it easier for your students to find and easier for you to discuss with them. As an added advantage, you may even find that you can use the same policy and procedures syllabus in every course that you teach. A well-designed policy and procedures syllabus should contain:

- Instructions about calling you at home
  - If you don't mind students calling you at home, you should say so.
  - Nevertheless, it is also perfectly acceptable to say, "I'd prefer not to receive calls at home. If you need to reach me and I'm not in my office, please send me an email message or leave a

voice mail at my office and I will return your call as soon as I can."

- You can also say something like "You may reach me at home by calling ###-#### but please do not call between 10:30 PM and 8:30 AM" or "Calls to my home should only be made between 6:00 PM and 9:00 PM."

- The last date to add a course
- The last date to drop a course
- The last date to change grading systems (such as from traditional letter grades to pass-fail)
- The last date to withdraw from all courses
- Your attendance policy
- How your course relates to the institution's honor or academic dishonesty policy, if applicable
- How you will address instances of disruptive student behavior (see Chapter 21, "Dealing with Student Problems and Problem Students")
- Your policy on allowing students to retake an exam
  - Do you allow exams to be retaken at all?
  - If so, how many times can a student retake each exam?
  - How does a student go about requesting to retake an exam?
  - Do you allow students to take the final exam at times other than the regularly scheduled time?
- Your policy on extra credit assignments
  - Do you allow extra credit at all? If not, it is best to explain why you don't. Include a statement like "Because I want each student to focus on doing his or her best work on each assignment or test and not to assume that poor preparation can be compensated for later, I do not offer any possibilities for extra credit in this class."
  - Is there a maximum amount of extra credit that a student can earn?
  - How are extra credit points applied? Do you apply these points to the next exam, to the final grade, or in some other manner? (If you do not specify how extra credit points will be used, students will be likely to dispute any system that you devise later.)

The Tone of Effective Syllabi

Adopting a tone in your syllabus that is helpful and supportive, while still insisting that certain standards must be met, is far more effective than adopting a tone that students may regard as suspicious, punitive, or hypercritical. Faculty members frequently revise their syllabi in response to single instances where someone abused the system because there was no specific rule forbidding the infraction. Poor policies are then made out of efforts to avoid repetition of single acts of misconduct that are unlikely to recur anyway. If you fill your syllabus with <u>underlining</u>, *italics*, CAPITALIZATION, **bold face type**, exclamation points!!!—or, even worse, <u>***ALL OF THESE AT ONCE!!!!***</u>—it will look to students like a censorious catalog of "Thou shalt nots!" rather than as a constructive guide to help them learn the most they can from you. The University of Minnesota's Center for Teaching and Learning maintains an excellent website (www1.umn.edu/ohr/teachlearn/tutorials/syllabus) that provides numerous examples of various components of section syllabi, all written with an appropriate focus and tone. Buller (2006) contains an example of how to write and how not to write a statement of attendance requirements, and why the tone can matter when outlining classroom policies.

One way to achieve the appropriate tone in a syllabus is to include a brief biographical statement that will allow the students to understand you a bit better as a person. Information about how you first became interested in the subject that you are teaching might awaken a similar interest in many students. Other biographical information might allow students to feel more comfortable in your class because they already know someone who seems somewhat like you. Even such background information as the ages of your children will make you appear more accessible and help explain why you may have imposed limits on when you can be reached at home. You might conclude your biographical statement with a summary of "What you can expect from me," followed by a summary of "What I expect from you" as a way of making it clear that the expectations in your course are not simply one-sided and that you have reasons for the policies that you have adopted. For an example of such summaries, see www1.umn.edu/ohr/teachlearn/tutorials/syllabus/expectations/student/index.html.

Another useful way to set an appropriate tone for your syllabus is to include a relevant quotation or epigram that you can refer to periodically throughout the semester. For example, the following might be an effective opening for a course on mythology or folklore:

*If only I could never open my mouth, I thought, until the abstract
idea had reached its highest point—and had become a story! But only
the great poets reach a point like that, or a people, after
centuries of silent effort.*

—NIKOS KAZANTZAKIS, ZORBA THE GREEK,
TRANSLATED BY CARL WILDMAN (NEW YORK, 1952), p. 279.

By selecting a quotation that helps summarize your approach or an
important theme of·your course, you send a message to your students
that the material you will cover has broad applicability, that you care
enough about their mastery of this material to have given this matter
considerable thought, and that your course will consist not simply of a
series of unrelated classes, but of a well-organized progression, a journey
that is intended to carry the students toward a specific destination.

The Appearance of Effective Syllabi

The appearance of a syllabus is quite different from its tone. For instance,
if the tone of your syllabus includes the manner in which you will phrase
your requirements, philosophy, and expectations, its style or appearance
will be expressed by the way in which that information is organized,
designed, and graphically conveyed. With the flexibility of word processing and publishing programs now available, it is extremely easy for a faculty member to develop a syllabus style that expresses something
important about the nature of the course through the document's design
and structure. With a little bit of creativity, you can design a truly distinctive syllabus that helps you reinforce for students the focus of your individual course.

- *Fonts.* Many different fonts are now available, and the creative selection of a font can be extremely desirable for your syllabus. The title
  of the course, for instance, might be written in a font appropriate for
  your material. Courses dealing with particular periods of histories
  or cultures could have the course title and topic headings presented
  in a font that captures the spirit of that period or society. Courses in
  the natural sciences might take a similar approach with any of the
  numerous fonts available that have a design associated with technology or even science fiction. Courses in the performing arts might
  incorporate the style of font commonly used on marquees, in
  playbills, or on posters.

- *Colors.* A judicious use of color can make a syllabus more striking and can even encourage students to pay closer attention to it. With color printers now widely available at a relatively low cost, it is possible to produce syllabi in full color that would have been prohibitively expensive in the past. While you may still not want to incur the expense of printing full color syllabi for extremely large sections, it is always possible to distribute paper copies of your syllabus in black and white and then make the color version available electronically through a course management system such as Blackboard. Color can be used for text, graphics, or even to provide a background for the entire document.

- *Graphics.* Instructors should avoid burying important information in the fine print. Including several graphics along with a certain amount of blank space makes a syllabus more inviting and easier to read. Photographs can help reinforce particular themes of the course, depict earlier classes in some of the activities you will be providing, and get students thinking from the very start of the course about the material they will be learning throughout the semester.

- *Themes.* You and your students will think differently about your course if you adopt a creative theme or metaphor for the class. For example, we might regard any individual class we teach as something similar to a play, a pilgrimage, a banquet or feast, an excavation, an investigation, a conversation, an experiment, a session of psychoanalysis, a saga, military basic training, or as any number of things (see Buller, 2006). The metaphor that you choose for the experience that you'll share with your students can begin to take shape through the appearance you give your syllabus. You could design this document in the form of a menu, map, travel brochure, owner's manual, police report, newspaper, or any other type of document that suits the material you will cover. Even if you do not have a particular metaphor in mind that can characterize your entire course, you can still establish a compelling sense of style by combining the right fonts, colors, and graphics. You might create syllabi that are art nouveau, neoclassical, baroque, art deco, Egyptian revival, Old West, or any other type of design that suits your personality and helps engage your students with the material.

Once you begin to realize that effective syllabi don't have to look anything like the ones you may have received as a student, even more creative possibilities begin to arise. For instance, Nilson (2007) proposes completely rethinking a syllabus to make it not a text-bound litany of policies and rules, but a more fluid graphic syllabus, outcomes map, or flow chart. Using a number of examples drawn from a wide variety of disciplines, Nilson demonstrates that through the use of a graphic syllabus, visual learners can more easily comprehend how a course is intended to progress, instructors can become more creative in their course design or organization, a desirable amount of flexibility can be incorporated into the structure of a class, and course goals can be more effectively integrated into student learning activities.

———————————

Your syllabus should always contain the critical information your students need to succeed in your course. Effective syllabi achieve this goal while conveying a tone that seems supportive of student success and in a style that reflects both the instructor's personality and the course material. The best syllabi are never those that are quickly written shortly before a course begins, but those that are well integrated into the instructor's overall concept of and goals for that particular course.

REFERENCES

Buller, J. L. (2006). *The essential department chair: A practical guide to college administration*. Bolton, MA: Anker.

Nilson, L. B. (2007). *The graphic syllabus and the outcomes map: Communicating your course*. San Francisco: Jossey-Bass.

Parkes, J., & Harris, M. B. (2002). The purposes of a syllabus. *College Teaching, 50*(2), 55–61.

RESOURCES

Colins, T. (1997). For openers . . . an inclusive syllabus. In W. E. Campbell & K. A. Smith (Eds.), *New paradigms for college teaching* (pp. 79–102). Edina, MN: Interaction.

Garavalia, L. S., Hummel, J. H., Wiley, L. P., & Huitt, W. G. (1999). Constructing the course syllabus: Faculty and student perceptions of important syllabus components. *Journal on Excellence in College Teaching, 10*(1), 5–21.

Grunert O'Brien, J., Millis, B. J., & Cohen, M. W. (2008). *The course syllabus: A learning-centered approach* (2nd ed.). San Francisco: Jossey-Bass.

Lowther, M. A., Stark, J. S., & Martens, G. G. (1989). *Preparing course syllabi for improved communication.* Ann Arbor, MI: University of Michigan, National Center for Research to Improve Postsecondary Teaching and Learning.

Prégent, R. (2000). *Charting your course: How to prepare to teach more effectively.* Madison, WI: Atwood.

12

DEVELOPING CREATIVE
COURSE MATERIALS

Included within the general category of course materials are such items as syllabi, handouts, assignment sheets, quizzes, exams, review summaries, and a wide range of other documents that supplement the coursework and textbook(s) that students will use throughout the class. Chapter 11, "Writing an Effective Course Syllabus," considered several principles college professors might adopt when designing syllabi; in this chapter we'll focus on those other documents. Certainly, however, a number of principles that we examined with regard to syllabi also apply to many different types of course materials. For instance:

- Adopting a tone that is supportive and that anticipates student success will help students learn better than a set of instructions saying "Don't do *this*!" and "Don't do *that*!" If you design your course materials, including quizzes and exams, with the expectation that students will do well, they are far more likely to do so than if your materials convey a tone that they are likely to fail or do poorly.

- Like syllabi, other kinds of academic course materials do not have to be dull or consist solely of text. A creative use of fonts, color, illustrations, and other design elements will make supplementary material more interesting for you and the students.

- If you have experimented with a theme or metaphor for your course, giving your syllabus the form of a menu, newspaper, travel brochure, or some other type of document, you can continue this theme as you create other course materials. We'll explore some additional ways of incorporating themes into materials below.

Every faculty member's personal style is different, and you will want to design course materials that reflect your own individual personality and approach to teaching. Remember, too, that the course materials you create may well have an impact beyond your individual class. Along with syllabi and evaluations from your peers and students, these are the items that you will submit for various personnel reviews. People will make decisions about the quality and creativity of your teaching based at least in part on these materials, so it is extremely important to design them well.

Aligning Materials with Course Goals

In Chapter 10, "Assessing Student Learning," we saw the importance of establishing clear goals both for your course as a whole and for each individual unit or exercise within that course. As you begin to develop your course materials, therefore, the most important questions to ask are:

- How does this set of course materials relate to my overall goals for the course?
- How will I determine whether I have been successful in moving closer to these goals?
- What will I do if I discover that I haven't been as successful as I had planned? How do I get back on track toward helping my students achieve the overall purpose of this course?

In order to see how these questions can help you develop truly effective course materials, let's take the hypothetical case of an introductory course in music appreciation for which the instructor has set the following goals:

- To introduce students to some of the basic forms and genres of world music
- To encourage students to listen more carefully to all forms of music
- To expose students to types of music with which they may not already be familiar
- To enhance students' vocabulary for talking about all types of music
- To increase students' musical literacy
- To complement the information that students may also encounter in such courses as world literature, world civilizations, survey of theatre, and introduction to art appreciation

For several semesters now, this instructor has been giving the class a handout that explores the concept of a musical cadence: the formula that provides listeners with a sense of finality, completion, and (at least momentary) rest. The handout defined the differences between authentic and plagal cadences (that is, progressions from either the dominant or subdominant chord to the tonic) and directed students to a website with several recorded examples, but this approach has not been very successful.

Although the class as a whole mastered the concept for the sake of the exercise, few in the course could apply it to new examples later on or easily relate it to popular or non-Western music.

The instructor decides to start from scratch, rethinking the entire exercise. Tying the assignment more closely to the goals of the course, the instructor tries to determine the best way to make this handout encourage students to listen to music more carefully, help the class develop a new musical vocabulary, and relate the experience to the type of music students are likely to hear every day. Because of these goals, the instructor abandons the handout for a new type of assignment that is posted as an announcement on the course management system, shown on the screen of the classroom as the students enter the auditorium, and sent to every member of the class via email. What was once a handout is now a simple instruction of where students can find five brief recordings on the class website, each of which presents the last few minutes of a work:

- A performance by Famoudou Konaté on a West African djembe
- Act I of Giacomo Puccini's *Tosca*
- Francis Poulenc's *Dialogues of the Carmelites*
- Gurdas Maan performing *Nach Ni*, an example of Punjabi Bhangra
- A Joruri puppet play from Japan

While they are listening to these selections, the students are then asked to reflect on how each piece provides the listener with a sense of finality or conclusion. The website includes simple checkboxes to make providing and collecting this information as easy as possible.

- At the end of the selection, does the music become faster? Or slower?
- Does it become louder? Or softer?
- Does the rhythm change (note: not the speed or tempo, but the rhythm itself)?
- Is there a change in the melody that signals the end of the piece?
- Is there an obvious change in harmony?
- Does the music simply stop without any sense of completion?
- Does something else happen that is not listed above?

Once the students have identified the ways in which these five pieces of music draw to a close, an open-ended response instructs them to identify a song or some other piece of music, in any style and from any genre, that they particularly like. They are instructed to listen to that piece again very carefully and to come to class next time ready to discuss the way in which the performer or composer achieves a cadence in that work. The instructor reminds the students that they are welcome to ask questions about these concepts on the discussion board of the course management system.

The use of checkboxes that are automatically tabulated tells the instructor very quickly how well students have identified the various techniques for achieving a cadence. If the responses do not meet an acceptable standard of accuracy, the instructor can revisit the issue in the next class, perhaps using as examples some of the works that the students themselves have identified as their favorites. The concept can also be reviewed more carefully before the next test and as other clear examples are encountered in the course. However, if the vast majority of the class seems to have understood the concept immediately, the instructor can go on to other material or reinforce the students' understanding by expanding their vocabulary to speak about the phenomena they experienced. Merely by reexamining a course document through the lens of the course's overall goals, the professor has transformed what was once an unsuccessful assignment into one that students can more easily relate to, producing deeper levels of understanding and opening the possibility for better integration of current material into what students will encounter later in the course.

All of this sounds easy enough. In actual practice, our own attempts to design effective materials can fail if we don't identify our goals with sufficient clarity. For instance, in our hypothetical music appreciation course, one of the instructor's goals was "to expose students to types of music with which they may not already be familiar." But what does it mean to *expose* students to something? And is that a worthy enough goal for a college-level course? On the one hand, we might say that the instructor has obviously achieved this goal because, in this exercise, students were required to listen to several types of music they may not have heard before. But on the other hand, it seems fair to ask why this exposure mattered. What is the instructor really hoping that students will gain from this activity? How can we improve the course materials even more in order to demonstrate that the students have, in fact, gained what the instructor intended? One way of answering these questions is to recall what we saw in Chapter 10, "Assessing Student Learning": that higher-level learning is not a single activity, but a complex of many different types of processes. In other words, we should realize that if the instructor's intention is for students simply to be able to recognize and identify the sound of a djembe when they hear it, that goal will produce one type of course material. But if the goal is for students to generalize about the ways in which cadences are made in world music, a different type of material would be more appropriate. If the instructor expects students to identify the type of cadence that occurs in a piece of music they never heard before, then a third type of course material would be needed. And if the purpose of the exercise is for students to determine the type of cadence that would be most effective in achieving a given effect in a given culture, still another type of assignment would be required. As was the case in drafting student learning outcomes, it is not enough for college professors to say that they want their students to know or understand something; they also have to be clear in their own minds what knowing or understanding means in this particular case. Until that level of clarity is reached, it is extraordinarily difficult to design course materials that effectively engage students and promote the highest level of learning.

Making Learning Goals Transparent

Once you take the time to identify precisely what your goals are for a particular handout, assignment, quiz, or test (and how those goals are related to those you've set for the course as a whole), one of the best things you can do is to state those goals clearly and boldly right on the course materials themselves. For instance, in a course in probability, a handout that contains exercises dealing with matrices might begin with a statement like this:

Inverse of a Matrix

Purpose: This exercise will help students determine whether any given matrix is nonsingular and thus has a unique inverse. This material will be essential in order for us to calculate probability through the use of Markov Chains, the next topic we're going to encounter. We'll be using Markov Chains to discuss probability patterns for voting, predicting various meteorological events, and critiquing several gambling "systems."

There are several advantages to including a brief purpose statement like this on all course materials. First, such a statement helps to reinforce for the instructors themselves exactly what they are trying to achieve. Every now and then, purpose statements will indicate to teachers that the test or assignment they've prepared really will not achieve the goals they had in mind. If it seems that these course materials aren't really necessary, they can simply be omitted, and attention can be redirected to more productive activities. If it seems that the item is truly necessary but poorly designed, it can be revised to achieve the purpose the instructor had in mind. Second, the reason for the assignment will become transparent to the students. People in general are less likely to complain about having to do work when they understand its value. They may even complete the task more successfully because they're now given a context for the assignment and can prepare to apply the knowledge they gain to other relevant contexts. Third, purpose statements can be very beneficial when an instructor is evaluated for annual review, peer assessment, or promotion and tenure consideration. Purpose statements illustrate that tests and assignments have been thoughtfully and systematically constructed. They help underscore a teacher's pedagogical approaches, allowing reviewers (who may be from other disciplines) to understand the professor's philosophy of instruction.

There is also another way in which it is important to make your purposes clear in all of your course materials: students can often misunderstand what we want them to do. For instance, suppose we are teaching a large lecture course in European civilization, and the time has come for a brief quiz. To keep our example simple, let's assume that what we're looking for at the moment is nothing more complex than the Knowledge level of Bloom's taxonomy. We've even made this goal clear in a purpose statement at the top of the quiz:

Purpose

This test will evaluate the degree to which students have mastered basic factual information about the religious wars in Europe by having them reproduce, from memory, several key names, terms, and concepts that were discussed in class and reviewed in the textbook.

What we haven't done in the following imaginary example is to write the document itself in a clear and ambiguous style. What is the problem, for instance, with the following fill-in-the-blank question?

Henry III of England was originally _____. After becoming king, he stopped being a _____ and became a _____. In 1598 he signed _____, which _____.

A central problem with this question is that our intentions are unlikely to be easily understood by a student in the course. For instance, what we were probably looking for was something like this: Henry III of England was originally *Henry of Navarre*. After becoming king, he stopped being a *Protestant* and became a *Catholic*. In 1598 he signed *the Edict of Nantes*, which *provided a certain amount of religious freedom*. What we are likely to receive may be something more like this: Henry III of England was originally *not a king*. After becoming king, he stopped being a *noble* and became a *king*. In 1598 he signed *many different documents*, which *have not all survived*. Even though these answers are trivial, tautological, and ultimately meaningless, they might be regarded as "correct" since our phrasing of the question itself was so vague. Is the student's hypothetical answer so ridiculous that you'll never see anything like it on one of your exams or assignments? Not at all. Nearly every college professor can recall at least one student essay or answer to an exam question that went in a completely unexpected direction because a student legitimately misinterpreted a question. The essential principle at work here is the following:

If it is at all possible for your students to misunderstand a question or a set of instructions on an assignment or exam, at least one of your students is guaranteed to do so.

It's always a good idea to review all your course materials, including policies and procedures, to identify areas where misunderstandings are likely to arise. Even better, have a colleague review your materials with you and alert you to areas where misinterpretation seems most probable. Even the best proofreading will not eliminate every miscommunication, but multiple reviews can be important. This is one area where your computer's spelling and grammar capabilities cannot help you at all; only the human mind can imagine how another mind can become misled by a seemingly straightforward assignment.

Using Metaphors or Themes with Course Materials

We noted in our discussion of syllabi that one way of adding creativity to a course is to approach your class in terms of a metaphor (such as a pilgrimage, banquet, talk show, or a mystery to be solved) and then to design all of your course materials based on that metaphor. But how can you develop one of these themes if you don't consider yourself a particularly creative person, have relatively little time available, or do not have much experience in layout or design? One useful approach is to keep in mind that almost all word processors come with document templates that you can easily adapt for any course. For instance, users of Microsoft Office have access to a website (http://office.microsoft.com/en-us/templates/default.aspx) that is filled with templates for all kinds of documents, including award certificates, brochures, flyers, greeting cards, newsletters, postcards, and stationery. Users of iWork for Macintosh computers will find that Pages comes with many templates, including brochures, flyers, journals, newsletters, menus, posters, screenplays, and scrapbooks. There is therefore no need to start from scratch when creating most types of course materials; if you find yourself out of ideas for innovative approaches to designing documents, you can refresh your creativity by simply browsing through the various templates available to your word processor, choosing one, and then adapting your materials to that format. Once you've been inspired by a format for your documents, you'll find it easier to develop additional ideas to enhance your basic concept.

As but one example, suppose that you were designing an exam, and the material of your course inspired you to design this test in the form of a menu. Different questions could be organized under different "courses." The students might select one short initial question as an "appetizer," two longer essays as their "first course" and "second course," a shorter essay as a "side dish," and a shorter, perhaps even humorous question as a "dessert." Or you could organize your questions into the type of menu that has "Column A," "Column B," and so on, instructing students that they must sample at least one "dish" from each column. If you have sufficient preparation time and begin feeling truly inspired, you could insert the "dessert" questions into fortune cookie shells and "serve" them to your class on trays. That approach will certainly not fit every faculty member's personal style but, if a little levity is right for you, creative design of course materials can help diffuse tension during an exam, allowing students to relax and do their best. Even if you're not the sort of college professor to "serve" your students with "menus," you should be able to think of some appropriate theme or metaphor that fits both your personality and the nature of the class.

Indeed, certain types of documents seem almost irresistible as course materials in certain subjects. A course in biography, for instance, might include course materials that are formatted like letters. A sales course might have documents that take the form of catalogues, advertisements, and order forms. A history course might include handouts that are made to look like ancient documents. A laboratory course can have materials that are designed with images and fonts that students will recognize from science fiction films. A criminal justice course might include materials that look like police reports or pieces of evidence. A drama course might have materials that look like scripts and playbills. With a little bit of creativity, therefore, the style of your course materials does not have to be some extraneous element simply added on for its visual effect. It can actually enhance the overall tone of your course and help you achieve your goals.

Using Technology with Course Materials

In most of the examples we just considered, it is easy to think of course materials only in terms of documents that are printed and distributed in hard copy. As our discussion of the music appreciation course makes clear, however, technology has made it possible for course materials to assume an almost unlimited number of forms. Graphs and other illustrations that used to be printed on paper can now be made available via websites and updated or revised as often as desired. At their own convenience, students can review podcasts, which can include sound files of lectures, interviews, musical examples, photographs, images, and video files, and the like. The software that enables an instructor to edit video clips, add titles, and include multiple tracks for music and other sound effects has become exceedingly easy to use; with a little bit of practice, most college professors will find that they can create rather advanced movie clips and DVDs in less than the time it would take to develop a printed handout. The new technology thus allows the college professor to create course materials that take students into the laboratory, to a foreign country, into a legislative session, and so on, tailor-made for the needs of that particular class or the instructor's own pedagogical goals. Rather than telling students *about* an activity, course materials can now be developed that allow students to participate in that activity, either directly or virtually. Moreover, with websites that include hyperlinks, students do not need to progress in a strictly linear manner through a set of course materials, unless that is the instructor's desire. It is possible to create electronic course materials that allow students to explore several different paths through a unit, receiving additional help in mastering certain concepts if they need it and branching out into secondary areas of research if a topic catches their interest. With course management software such as Blackboard, a calculated formula function allows students to encounter problems based on different data sets each time they attempt the question. A "hot-spot" problem can present students with a map, chart, or diagram on which the student must identify a particular point, area, or region that best answers the question or solves the problem. Opinion scales can be used to poll students for their views on particular issues, automatically tabulating the results. There are even electronic games that the instructor can develop through a Quiz Bowl function that is similar to the game show *Jeopardy!*: students are given answers for which they must develop a suitable question. For more on electronic alternatives to distributing hard copies of course materials, see Chapter 16, "Teaching with Technology."

Effective course materials should engage the students in the learning process, relate closely to the overall goals of the course, and have objectives that are clear to the instructor and the student alike. Many textbook series come with websites, handouts, exam sets, and lesson outlines already prepared. Many of these materials are extremely attractive and, with all the time constraints facing college professors today, it can be tempting simply to use them without modification. After all, why reinvent the wheel? But if these prepackaged course materials do not relate well to your individual course goals or to the needs of the students who actually enroll at your institution, they are ultimately of very little benefit to you. With a bit of planning and creativity, you can easily develop your own materials—or adapt (with permission) those provided by textbook companies—in such a way as to greatly enhance the level of instruction that occurs in your courses.

RESOURCES

Davis, B. G. (2009). *Tools for teaching* (2nd ed.). San Francisco: Jossey-Bass.

McKeachie, W. J., & Svinicki, M. (2006). *McKeachie's teaching tips: Strategies, research, and theory for college and university teachers* (12th ed.). New York: Houghton Mifflin.

Walvoord, B. E., & Anderson, V. J. (1998). *Effective grading: A tool for learning and assessment*. San Francisco: Jossey-Bass.

13

TEACHING SMALL CLASSES

Most college professors regard the opportunity to work with a small class as the best of all possible teaching situations. With fewer students in the course, it is possible to assign certain types of written work that would be impossible to grade effectively in larger sections. Discussions can involve every member of the class simultaneously. The strengths and weaknesses of individual students become readily apparent, allowing the instructor to adapt the material so as to capitalize on each student's strengths and help them overcome their weaknesses. Frequent studies suggest that students at all levels perform better on exams at the end of classes with few students than they do in larger sections (see Blatchford, 2003). Given all these advantages, it may appear that faculty members don't need the sort of training in teaching small classes that they do in larger classes. Perhaps for this reason, although there is a substantial literature on techniques college professors can use to improve their teaching of large sections, relatively little has been written that specifically addresses the strategies for teaching smaller classes. Does this lack of resources occur because teaching small classes is easy or because it is intuitively obvious how teachers should relate to small sections?

In fact, neither one of these assumptions is true. Teaching small classes provides its own type of instructional challenges. It is simply not the case that you can take any technique that is effective in a large section, modify it slightly or ratchet it down, and have an effective method for teaching a small class. Each type of instructional environment offers its own opportunities and challenges. So, if you have been fortunate enough to have been assigned one or more small sections, it is important for you to consider the principles that will be discussed next.

How Small Is Small?

Large and *small* are, of course, relative terms, and a section that may be considered minuscule at a large state university may well be regarded as unacceptably huge at a private college. For the purpose of our discussion, however, we'll consider a section small if it enrolls fewer than forty students. In a section of that size, certain types of written assignments and discussion become possible that are much more difficult to conduct in larger sections. This general principle does not mean, however, that it is impossible for students to improve their written or oral communication skills in large courses, as we shall see in Chapter 14, "Teaching Large Classes." Nevertheless, we should recognize at once that the entire concept of section size can vary dramatically according to the institution, and the principles that will be discussed in this chapter can be important to you if you are assigned any course that would be regarded as small for your institution and discipline, regardless of how that course might be perceived elsewhere.

The Challenges of Small Classes

Some instructors assume that those who teach small classes have all the advantages and those who teach large sections have all the obstacles, but this is not necessarily the case. Larger classes are more likely to include people who represent a broader variety of opinions, experiences, and approaches to your course material. In an introductory-level class of three hundred, you might be able to conduct an opinion poll on various subjects and achieve results that closely mirror the national average; you are unlikely to achieve the same result in an upper-level seminar of eight, where the sample size is simply too small to be representative even of your entire school. You may find in a small class that you lack the critical mass to produce a diversity of opinions in discussions or that the students' greater familiarity with one another results in a type of "groupthink" or unwillingness to challenge one another's ideas. The three or four students who come to class unprepared or in a bad mood may have no effect whatsoever on the course you teach in the auditorium; they can bring the entire learning process to a grinding halt when they constitute half, or even a fifth, of all the students in a course.

Successful Teaching Strategies for Small Classes

It should come as no surprise to anyone that excessive use of lecture in a small class is ineffective and squanders one of the real advantages these sections have: the greater ability of students to interact with one another. Occasionally, of course, lecturing—"teaching by telling"—can be the most efficient way to convey a great deal of information quickly. But when you wish to move beyond simply providing information and to encourage students to apply, evaluate, or add to existing sources of information, other teaching strategies can be far more successful. As we review the strategies that follow, keep in mind that none of these approaches is mutually exclusive. You can, for example, use simulations as well as the Socratic method in a seminar setting. You can combine case studies with coteaching in a laboratory. Nevertheless, for ease of consideration, let's divide the five most common strategies for teaching small classes into separate categories. They are all ways to complement "teaching by telling" with learning by discussing, asking, examining, showing, and doing.

- A *seminar* is a style of teaching that places a great deal of emphasis on discussion and on responding to the perspectives of others. In most seminars, students sit not in rows and columns facing the instructor, but in a circle or around a table to facilitate discussion in all directions. For a seminar to be effective, the students must arrive with some thoughts about that day's topic already developed. Usually this goal is accomplished through a common reading assignment, often accompanied by questions on which the students are instructed to reflect before class. The seminar begins with someone, usually the instructor but possibly another member of the class (see section on "coteaching" below), posing a question or making a statement to which other members of the seminar then respond. Seminars tend to be most interesting when participants bring different perspectives, experiences, or interpretations from which other members of the course may learn.

- In the *Socratic method*, teachers cause students to probe into a subject deeper and deeper by posing a series of questions that cause the students to clarify or advance their approaches to an issue. The Socratic method may be used to address puzzles (questions for which there is at least one correct answer or problems that can be "solved") and conundrums (questions for which no single correct answer exists or problems that must be addressed through several alternative approaches). Using the process known by the Greek term *elenchos* (or its Latinized form *elenchus*), the instructor and other members of the class cross-examine one another, leading each person to defend positions or perceive the flaws in his or her reasoning. In the case of puzzles, the *elenchos* may be a series of questions that suggest a way in which the speaker's solution, model, or hypothesis fails to solve the problem under consideration. In the case of conundrums, the *elenchos* may be a series of questions that lead the speaker to understand the ways in which an alternative approach or solution could be effective.

- In the *case study* method, course participants consider either an actual or hypothetical situation that explores the issues to be addressed in class that day. All the students read over the case in advance, sometimes as part of their homework for that day and sometimes in class itself. Analysis of a case study usually begins with one member of the class summarizing the case in his or her own words. Other members of the class may then fill in additional relevant features of the case that the first speaker has omitted. The instructor then begins a critique of the case: Was the situation handled appropriately by the participants described by the study? What alternative approaches could have been taken? Are there any generalizations that can be drawn from the case? Frequently, an instructor will suggest additional considerations once the class has thoroughly discussed the case as originally presented. If this or that factor had been different in the case, how might that change the way in which we should handle the situation? Case studies have the advantage of actively engaging students in direct consideration of a complex question and encouraging them to combine theory with practicality in their approach to a situation.

- In a *simulation*, students learn by role playing or by engaging in a situation that, although realistic, is free from the possibility of dangerous consequences for wrong decisions. Simulations can be conducted for a wide variety of situations that college students might study, including court cases ("moot court"), the buying and selling of securities on trading floors, negotiations for treaties, medical procedures (for which highly sophisticated mannequins and artificial organs exist), historical events, interviews, or investigations, and the like. Simulations can be valuable for the students who participate directly in them and for other students who act as observers, critiquing the decisions made by their colleagues.

- In *coteaching*, the instructor shares responsibilities for conducting lessons with the students in the course. In the simplest form of coteaching, the instructor assigns each student to be in charge of teaching a lesson or a day in turn. The students may be given some freedom in selecting the best method they can devise for teaching that set of material. Some students will lecture. Others will conduct discussions. Some will use one or more of the methods that we are considering now. The class as a whole then assesses each day or lesson. What worked well? What approach was not as effective as it could have been? How can these lessons become more useful in the future? As every instructor comes to realize, one of the most effective ways to learn material is to teach it yourself. Coteaching arises out of this observation, and many students will find that they best understand those units they needed to explain to others in the course.

In all of these strategies, the goal is to change the role of the instructor from being, as the common expression goes, a "sage on the stage" to a "guide on the side." One of the advantages of small classes is that the instructor need not be seen as the purveyor of all information. Teachers can adopt a role more like that of a personal trainer than that of an all-knowing guru. They can assist students with making their own personal discoveries in a subject, discoveries that will be all the more memorable to them as a result. The Center for Critical Thinking (www.criticalthinking .org) offers a wide variety of workshops and materials that instructors can use in conjunction with any of the strategies just outlined.

Increasing the Diversity of Perspectives in a Small Class

As we saw earlier, one of the problems that can occur in a small class is that with relatively few students enrolled, a limited number of different opinions or perspectives may be introduced during class discussions. Moreover, because students get to know one another rather well in a small class, they may be reluctant to contradict a fellow student whom they have come to regard as more of a friend than a colleague. To encourage the freer exchange of views in a small class, there are several options that you might consider.

- *Open up the class discussion to students who are not regularly involved in the course.* If you establish a course website with an option for threaded discussions, bring that resource to the attention of other students who can be invited to participate in your class electronically. Students on your own campus can be alerted to the website's existence through a campus announcement or email system. Students at other institutions could be invited to participate in your course's virtual discussion through notices that your own students place on their pages at such sites as Facebook, MySpace, LiveJournal, Friendster, Classmates.com, Twitter, LinkedIn, and so on. If you have a colleague at another institution who is teaching a similar course, explore the possibility of linking your sections electronically, either through a shared website or through occasional videoconferencing. If you discover that a few students at your own institution or in a nearby area are bringing some well-considered alternative points of view to the electronic discussion, you could even invite them to a discussion in person as a way of expanding the number of viewpoints shared in your course.

- *As a class assignment, give different students specific perspectives to research and defend.* Students may also be assigned specific perspectives that they are to introduce and defend in a discussion, regardless of whether they personally support such a position. At times, this approach can be adopted as part of a formal debate:

> If your last name begins with the letters A through M, you are going to be responsible for the concept of approaching illegal immigration through tighter border security and stiffer penalties. If your last name begins with the letters N through Z, you're going to be responsible for the concept of the guest-worker program and limited amnesty for undocumented workers. Research these positions carefully. Find out the arguments that proponents of these positions advance in favor of their own approach and the limitations they see with alternative approaches. On Friday we're going to have a formal debate in which you to defend the position you've been assigned and refute the alternative position.

At other times, you may prefer to assign students to research particular perspectives, but to have those perspectives addressed in an informal discussion rather than in a formal debate.

- *Encourage students to see an issue from different perspectives through role playing.* As a refinement to simply assigning students to research and present different perspectives, you might assign students a role to play as part of a discussion. When we pretend to be someone else, we often find ourselves far freer to say things and to explore ideas that we would never say or explore as ourselves. For instance, imagine that you are teaching a unit on the French Revolution. You find that all twelve students who are enrolled in your course are so persuaded of the arguments advanced by the *sans-culottes* that they have a hard time understanding other perspectives found at that time, such as those of the National Assembly, the aristocracy, the clergy, and the upper middle class. When assigned historical identities of individuals from each of these groups and then facilitating an organized discussion, students may find themselves far more able to view a question from a different perspective simply by imagining the mindset of people who are quite different from them.

It is undeniable that small classes offer many advantages over larger sections. In them, you will have more time to spend interacting with each student. The class will be able to write more, speak more, and receive from you more detailed critiques of their writing and speaking. Your role in the course may shift from that of "star performer" to that of "party planner"; your primary task will be to plan and manage the experiences that will best suit your pedagogical goals. Quieter students may need to be urged to have greater confidence in their own views. More dominating students may need to be restrained. In the end, however, the class is likely to find the activities that you create for it to be engaging, and thus the students will develop a mastery of the material that would not have been possible for them in a large lecture course.

REFERENCES

Blatchford, P. (2003). *The class size debate: Is small better?* Philadelphia: Open University Press.

RESOURCES

Barnes, L. B., Christensen, C. R., & Hansen, A. J. (1994). *Teaching and the case method: Text, cases, and readings* (3rd ed.). Boston: Harvard Business School Press.

Brookfield, S. D. (1987). *Developing critical thinkers: Challenging adults to explore alternative ways of thinking and acting.* San Francisco: Jossey-Bass.

Brookfield, S. D., & Preskill, S. (2005). *Discussion as a way of teaching: Tools and techniques for democratic classrooms* (2nd ed.). San Francisco: Jossey-Bass.

Christensen, C. R., Garvin, D. A., & Sweet, A. (1991). *Education for judgment: The artistry of discussion leadership.* Boston: Harvard Business School Press.

Davis, B. G. (2009). *Tools for teaching* (2nd ed.). San Francisco: Jossey-Bass.

Exley, K., & Dennick, R. (2004). *Small group teaching: Tutorials, seminars, and beyond.* New York: RoutledgeFalmer.

Miller, J. E., Groccia, J. E., & Miller, M. S. (Eds.). (2001). *Student-assisted teaching: A guide to faculty-student teamwork.* Bolton, MA: Anker.

Naumes, W., & Naumes, M. J. (1999). *The art and craft of case writing.* Thousand Oaks, CA: Sage.

Nilson, L. B. (2003). *Teaching at its best: A research-based resource for college instructors* (2nd ed.). Bolton, MA: Anker.

14

TEACHING LARGE CLASSES

Assigning students to large classes has become so common in higher education that there is now an extensive body of literature on the topic of how to teach these massive sections effectively. Many academic conferences even include pedagogical panels devoted to the challenge of teaching auditorium-style classes. With a clear tension between the increased costs of operating a college or university and the belief that the tuition charged to students is already too high, many administrators feel compelled to increase the size of course sections for the sake of greater "efficiency." Many state legislatures, too, have become actively involved in managing the costs of higher education and have placed an emphasis on credit hour production that all but mandates larger sections for certain courses. To the surprise of many professors, certain students even *prefer* larger classes, enjoying the anonymity and decreased pressure of a class where they are unlikely to be called on or put on the spot during any given period. In this chapter we'll discuss approaches that you can adopt to use class time more effectively and to help your students learn better, if you have been assigned to teach a large section of a college course. We'll also explore ways in which you can help make an anonymous megaclass feel a little less anonymous.

How Large Is Large?

Just as we discovered with small sections (see Chapter 13, "Teaching Small Classes"), the definition of a large class is relative, changing quite a bit depending on the type of institution at which one teaches, the instructor's discipline, and the goals for the course. A writing-intensive course on nineteenth-century literature may be unmanageably large if it enrolls fifty students. A lecture course on music appreciation may be regarded by another professor as attractively small if it enrolls only eighty. A laboratory course becomes too large if it is difficult for the instructor and lab assistants to provide adequate supervision. A foreign language course may be too small if students do not have the number of colleagues they need for diversity in conversations, simulations, and break-out discussions. As a general rule, a class should be regarded as large if it is significantly bigger than the norm in your discipline and at your institution. Beyond this very flexible definition, most would consider a section to be large if it meets one or more of the following criteria:

- Because of its size, it must be taught in a room that is configured as an auditorium, rather than a traditional classroom or seminar room.
- It enrolls more than one hundred students.
- Due to the number of enrolled students, it "counts more" when the instructor's workload is calculated.
- The size of the section would limit the amount of discussion, number of oral presentations, or amount of writing that the instructor would ordinarily assign the students in a course on this topic.

If you have been assigned a course that fits this description, you are likely to notice that the atmosphere of the course will be distinctly different from what you would experience in a seminar or even in a traditional lecture-and-discussion course.

The Challenges of Large Classes

In large classes you are less likely to know your students well than you are in smaller classes. Though some professors make valiant efforts to learn the name of every single student even in sections with scores of students, it is impossible to learn enough about each student in these situations to understand his or her individual strengths and weaknesses, plans for the future, idiosyncrasies, and special needs. In addition, many students find it difficult to develop a sense of rapport with a teacher in a very large class. The structure of an auditorium can exacerbate this sense of distance, particularly when the professor is isolated on a stage or platform while the students are in fixed rows of seats some distance away. The sheer physical symbolism of a professor facing in one direction with the students facing the other can create a sense of "us versus them" that we don't find in a seminar or even an ordinary classroom where the chairs are more easily moved. Moreover, regardless of how the room is organized, certain students will simply be too intimidated to ask a question or make an observation before two or three hundred other students, whereas they may have no difficulty whatsoever speaking in front of only ten or fifteen of their peers.

The difficulty of discussion in a large section may mean that students in the course become overly passive or cease to pay attention. Even when the professor makes an effort to encourage questions and discussion, most of the students must remain silent while one of their colleagues is speaking, making it difficult to engage them as fully in the learning process as one might like. Less frequent oral and written contributions from the students may distort the degree of progress that students are making. You could easily spend several days covering what you believe to be a difficult concept, only to learn later that most of the students had already learned the material in a previous course. Conversely (and far more common), you may receive an impression that the class is following you closely and learning quite well everything you are presenting, only to discover that nearly everyone in the course fails the next exam, misunderstanding even the most basic material that you have tried to teach them. Furthermore, attendance policies can be difficult to enforce in large courses. Unless you are adequately staffed with teaching assistants who spend most of the class period taking attendance and making certain that no one leaves the class early, you are faced with a dilemma: do you waste a great deal of valuable time taking attendance, allow students to come only when they wish to do so, or have students sign attendance rosters (and trust them not to sign in their friends)? Most professors discover that the greater anonymity students have in a large course is detrimental to attendance. It is harder to miss a small class where one's absence is immediately obvious, but easy to go AWOL from a large class, even for extended periods.

Faced with all of these challenges, teaching successfully in a large course can sometimes seem a daunting task. Nevertheless, there are several proven strategies that you can use to make your teaching in a large course as effective as possible.

Successful Teaching Strategies for Large Classes

Let's begin our discussion of effective strategies when teaching large classes with the following essential principle:

In any teaching situation, students tend to learn more when the instructor capitalizes on opportunities that are characteristic or unique to that particular learning environment while also using creative means to compensate for the specific disadvantages of that environment.

For instance, in discussing the best way to teach small classes, we saw that college professors should make full use of what that particular environment made easy—such as the opportunities it gave for the students to engage more frequently in oral and written communication and the greater knowledge the professor would have of each student's unique talents and limitations—while seeking innovative ways to compensate for the problems caused by having a small number of students, such as encountering a limited range of perspectives offered during class discussions. In a similar way, when seeking strategies to use in a large class, the instructor is well advised to exploit the unique characteristics of that learning environment—the greater breadth of student talent, experience, and perspectives present in each class—while compensating for the challenges we saw arising from teaching this type of course.

If we view the problem in this way, we can see why the following strategies can be particularly important in the teaching of large classes.

- *Take steps to become less anonymous yourself.* In large classes it may be even more important than in other teaching environments for your students to see you as a real person rather than as a remote and possibly aloof figure. Consider telling your class a little bit about yourself, what first got you interested in the subject that you are teaching, and perhaps a defining moment you had in your own academic career when you were about the average age of the students in your course. If you don't feel comfortable relating this information orally on the first day of class, consider including it on a website for the course, as part of the "instructor information" in a course management system such as Blackboard, or in a section on your syllabus (see Chapter 11, "Writing an Effective Course Syllabus"). By opening up more to your students, you will discover that they are more likely to open up to you in return.

- *Use course management systems to encourage discussions outside of class.* Course management systems, such as Blackboard, CourseWork, eCollege, Angel, and Moodle can be used to supplement traditional courses, just as they can be used to teach online or distance learning courses. You can post outlines of material that you have covered, review exercises, audio or video clips (including recordings of entire lectures, if you wish), photographs and other graphic materials, and the like. One of the most beneficial features of course management systems is that they often allow for live "chats" and asynchronous threaded discussions where students can ask and answer questions, make observations, and share perspectives that may be difficult to introduce in the setting of a large class. You can use these discussions to get to know your students a bit better, and to allow them to get to know you. A student who may be far too reserved to speak up before more than a hundred other students may prove to be quite eloquent in an electronic discussion. By supplementing your class with electronic resources, therefore, you can get to know your students in a way that may not otherwise be possible. You might consider having an assignment in which students are required to make an observation or ask a question online after each of the first few classes. This type of assignment gets the students familiar with the technology and makes it much more likely that they will continue to participate voluntarily in online course discussions later on.

- *Don't let the organization of the room dictate your teaching style.* Although many large classes are taught in auditoriums and other rooms that tend to intensify the distance between the professor and the student, you can take steps to minimize that distance. Simply because there is a stage or lectern, for instance, you should not feel obliged to use it for every moment of every class. Getting away from the front of the classroom to stroll among the students as you talk to them immediately breaks the boundary between "us" and "them." It also encourages students to pay closer attention, stop listening to music through their earphones, and develop greater eye contact with the instructor. If your classroom situation is such that you need a microphone, request a lapel microphone or headset rather than a microphone that is handheld or fixed to a stand. Moving among the students in this way both develops a more flexible teaching style for you as an instructor—it's hard to remain tied to your outline when it's up on the lectern, and you're fifty feet away—and establishes a better rapport with your students.

- *Have the students themselves lead certain units.* Coteaching, one of the strategies that we discussed in Chapter 13, "Teaching Small Classes," can be adapted for large classroom use as well. By appointing certain students as team leaders for particular concepts or days, and then allowing those students to teach their peers about a specific set of material, you are accomplishing several goals simultaneously. First, you are making the material more memorable for the team leaders because, as we have seen, the best way to learn material is to teach it to someone else. Second, you are breaking down the boundary between teacher and student by demonstrating that these roles are flexible: the person who teaches one day is the person who is taught the next. Third, you will gain some insight into how your current students learn material best by observing how they choose to relate concepts, which metaphors they use, and which terms you may have taken for granted but they choose to explain in class. Classroom quality circles, one of the assessment techniques we explored in Chapter 10, "Assessing Student Learning," can easily be incorporated into the team leader approach to coteaching in large course sections.

- *When you lecture, encourage active rather than passive listening.* It is easy, when teaching a large class, for the instructor to become overly dependent on his or her lecture notes or on presentation software such as PowerPoint or Keynote. A lecture outline is fine if you use it as a guide to the points that you wish to address; it can become overly restrictive if an instructor never feels free to deviate from it to pursue a topic of interest to the students, to seize the teachable moment, or to abandon it when it's just not working. Presentation software can be pedagogically valuable when it is used to its fullest potential, including graphics, video clips, and audio selections that create experiences far superior to those of an "ordinary" lecture. That same type of software becomes a burden, however, when instructors use it merely to show students how to spell key terms, as an electronic form of their lecture notes, and (worst of all) to read to the students what has been projected onto the screen. Ask yourself what benefit you hope to gain in any given class period from the presentation software. Unless you clearly need the combination of text, sound, video, and graphics at which this type of software excels, you are better off not using it. Adopt instead more active teaching techniques (see Chapter 18, "Promoting Student Engagement") or simply converse with the class. Your goal, after all, is to wake your students up to new ways of seeing the world, not put them to sleep through rigid adherence to a lecture outline or piece of software.

- *Assign break-out groups to transform one large class into numerous small classes that happen to meet simultaneously in the same room.* Break-out strategies such as jigsaw groups (www.jigsaw.org) promote collaborative learning at the same time that they help students analyze issues into manageable parts, master those parts, and then synthesize these small pieces of information back into a larger picture. Like a classic jigsaw puzzle, jigsaw groups involve a number of interlocking units. For example, in a college-level history course, each student might be assigned (1) a specific city, region, or nation; (2) a specific era; (3) a specific topic (art, literature, warfare, politics, or architecture); and (4) a specific resource (a book, website, collection of essays, or CD-ROM). On any particular day, you can have the class reorganize itself according to one of these preestablished categories. You can say something like, "Let's have all the Paris people over here, Rome over there, London in that corner, and Madrid across from them. The issue that I want you to talk about today is . . ."). After twenty minutes or so of this discussion, the students might be asked to leave their "city groups" and reorganize according to their "era groups"; they would then address the same issue, but from a different perspective and with a different group of peers. The advantage of this approach is that students tend to be more productive when given frequent opportunities to work with other students, modifying and improving their ideas based on the suggestions of their classmates. The usual disadvantages to a team-based approach are that groups all too often move no faster than the level of the least productive member, share work assignments inequitably, and receive grades that are not reflective of individual effort or learning. You can minimize the effect of these disadvantages by constant reconfiguration of break-out groups according to the jigsaw method and then by encouraging group critique and improvement of assignments that are ultimately the responsibility of each individual student (see Buller, 2006).

- *Use short written assignments to determine what students know and where they are having the most difficulty.* It is difficult in large classes to assign a great deal of writing because grading papers and essays with any degree of care is extremely time consuming. One alternative to long written assignments is the use of the microtheme or one-minute essay that we discussed in Chapter 10, "Assessing Student Learning." These are short written assignments that need not be graded and that will tell you a great deal about the progress students are making in the course. At the beginning of a class, for instance, students might be asked to write on the topic of "The Three Most Important Points Raised in the Reading Assignment for Today" or "The Concept That Is the Least Clear to Me from the Assignment for Today." These topics will let you know immediately who has been doing their assignments and who has not, which points students feel they have mastered, and which concepts you will still need to review. A short written assignment at the end of a class might be "Today's Most Important Principle, Expressed in My Own Words" or "The Two Issues That I Wish We'd Spend More Class Time On." Because students have only a minute or so to write these essays, you can read several hundred of them in far less than an hour. You'll have included a writing component in your large class, given your students a chance to express where they still need help (an opportunity that could improve your course evaluations at the end of the term), and learned a great deal about the progress they are making.

- *Use written or electronic surveys to gauge student progress.* Another way of determining student progress is the use of noncredit surveys. A survey could be any type of question but as it is conveyed to students as a desire for their opinion, they will approach it without the sort of anxiety that they might bring to a test or pop quiz. For instance, in an algebra course, you might pose a survey as follows: "Our college's policy says that there must be one faculty member along on each study-abroad trip for every eight students. If we were pricing packages where there were *exactly* one faculty member for every eight students, which of the following group sizes would we not have to inquire about:

  a. 63
  b. 57
  c. 18
  d. 108
  e. 99

If your class by an overwhelming majority provides you with the correct answer to this survey ("b," because 57 is the only number offered that is not evenly divisible by 9; which is 8 students + 1 faculty member), you will know that they understand this concept, and you can move on. You could even give anonymous advice to the few students who answered incorrectly about where they might receive help in reviewing this concept. However, if most of your class gets the survey wrong, you will immediately know what you need to review in class before you can continue.

- *Electronic student response systems, commonly known as "clickers," are mechanical devices that allow you to ask a survey question, receive student responses instantly, and learn how many correct and incorrect answers have been made.* Clickers can be used for everything from taking attendance to formal quizzes or tests, but their most interesting use is when instructors use them to take the pulse of a class in midunit, learning whether students are making adequate progress in the lesson or being left behind. The instructor can then easily make a midcourse correction based on how well the students have done with the sample question. For more on this idea, see Chapter 10, "Assessing Student Learning," and Chapter 16, "Teaching with Technology."

- *Take roll with clickers or tickets.* Clickers can also be used to improve course attendance. Because each device is coded to a particular student, you can know who is present and who is missing on any given day. By having a general question posted as students enter the classroom, they can respond while they are waiting for the class to begin, effectively taking attendance for you with no effort from you or your teaching assistants. Another effective means of taking attendance in large classes is the use of entry and exit tickets. The "tickets" can be either actual paper tickets that students receive on arrival and turn in when class is over (thus encouraging students both to show up on time and to remain for the entire class period) or they can be variations on the microthemes discussed earlier. "Bonnie Kendall of Indiana University in Bloomington takes attendance with entry or exit tickets. These tickets are questions or comments on the course material written by students before they enter or leave the classroom. In this way, attendance can be taken simply by tallying the slips with the further benefit that the instructor receives student feedback regarding the course" (University of Maryland, 2008).

- *The best strategy to improve attendance is to make students want to come to your class* by teaching in such a way that they will not want to miss a single class. Every professor's personality is different, and what works for one of your colleagues may not be appropriate for you. Nevertheless, the use of humor, surprise, cliffhangers at the end of each class (an approach that we might call "The Scheherazade Method"), innovative class themes or metaphors (see Chapter 11, "Writing an Effective Course Syllabus," and Chapter 12, "Developing Creative Course Materials"), and other means designed to get students excited about your course will help your class become "must-see" material. Teaching, whether we agree with this principle or not, always involves being a bit of a performer. In large classes, you can often use this performance element to your advantage and introduce an element of excitement into your course that will make students look forward to your class, even if they do not receive credit for attendance.

———————————

Every environment for teaching and learning poses its own opportunities and challenges. Though certain types of learning activities are difficult or even impossible in large classes, other types of activities that would not be possible in a tutorial or small class can *only* be conducted in a large section. If you find yourself assigned a large section of a course, focus on the new possibilities that this larger canvas creates for you instead of despairing about the types of classroom activities you will not be able to conduct. Seen from the right perspective, you will discover that teaching a large course is not an inferior instructional assignment to teaching a small course. It is simply a different teaching environment, and it can enable you to think about your subject in creative and unexpected ways.

REFERENCES

Buller, J. L. (2006). *The essential department chair: A practical guide to college administration*. Bolton, MA: Anker.

University of Maryland, Center for Teaching Excellence. (2008). *Large classes: A teaching guide: Establishing ground rules*. Retrieved July 8, 2007, from www.cte.umd.edu/library/teachingLargeClass/guide/ch3.html

RESOURCES

Carbone, E. (1998). *Teaching large classes: Tools and strategies*. Thousand Oaks, CA: Sage.

Gibbs, G., & Jenkins, A. (Eds.). (1992). *Teaching large classes in higher education: How to maintain quality with reduced resources*. London: Kogan Page.

Edwards, H., Smith, B., & Webb, G. (2001). *Lecturing: Case studies, experience, and practice*. Sterling, VA: Stylus.

Heppner, F. (2007). *Teaching the large college class: A guidebook for instructors with multitudes*. San Francisco: Jossey-Bass.

MacGregor, J., Cooper, J. L., Smith, K. A., & Robinson, P. (Eds.). (2000). *New directions for teaching and learning: No. 81. Strategies for energizing large classes: From small groups to learning communities*: San Francisco: Jossey-Bass.

McKeachie, W. J., & Svinicki, M. (2006). Teaching large classes (you can still get active learning!). In W. J. McKeachie & M. Svinicki, *McKeachie's teaching tips: Strategies, research, and theory for college and university teachers* (12th ed., pp. 254–266). New York: Houghton Mifflin.

Stanley, C. A., & Porter, M. E. (Eds.). (2002). *Engaging large classes: Strategies and techniques for college faculty*. Bolton, MA: Anker.

15

TEACHING ONE-ON-ONE

There are many situations in which college professors may need to instruct or supervise students individually outside of the traditional classroom setting. For instance, music lessons are frequently taught privately. Theses are often directed through individual meetings. Papers are sometimes best reviewed in private conferences. Internships and service-learning activities are frequently supervised one-on-one. Moreover, students may also be offered tutorials if they need a class that is not otherwise offered that term, if they are able to work far faster or need to work much more slowly than the rest of a class, or if they are interested in pursuing a topic that is not otherwise covered in the curriculum. The last of these types of tutorial is frequently known as directed readings, directed inquiry, or an independent study course. Coaching of various kinds (athletic, musical, professional) must be conducted independently, and there are numerous other circumstances under which students may need to work directly with a professor. Each of these situations brings with it its own possibilities, challenges, and limitations, and these are the issues that we'll be exploring in this chapter.

Special Considerations for One-on-One Teaching

The dynamic that you will have working one-on-one with a student is necessarily different from any other teaching situation. It is even unlike what you would experience if you were tutoring two students simultaneously. Barriers that often exist between professor and student tend to be lowered. This different relationship can be a good thing, and many students later say that their most rewarding educational experiences occurred when they were working independently with a professor. On the other hand, problems can also occur, and you can best prevent difficulties by being aware of these challenges from the start. Unfortunately, students will sometimes assume that the greater intimacy resulting from one-on-one sessions with a professor implies that the relationship is becoming based more on friendship than on professional standing. In fact, it can be quite easy at times to begin treating a student whom you are tutoring or whose internship you are supervising a bit differently because you know that student better, perhaps see a bit of yourself in the student, and are aware of what is going on in that student's life in a way that is not possible with other students. Problems sometimes arise when you return assignments to the student or assign a final grade only to be met by surprise that a "friend" could have regarded the student's work as anything less than perfect.

At times, the student's misperceptions about the faculty member will go even further. Just as therapists become familiar with the phenomenon of patients who mistake the professional relationship for the beginnings of a romance, students who work closely with a professor can sometimes confuse professional interest for personal involvement. Usually, a student crush is not particularly dangerous and fades quickly after the end of a term. Occasionally, however, students can become fixated on a professor, causing difficulties when the instructor is compelled to correct the student's false impression or when the student even shares with friends the stories of his or her new "love." Finally, it is possible that even if the student and faculty member do not misunderstand the nature of their relationship, other observers might. Students and faculty colleagues who see the same student entering or leaving a professor's office repeatedly may assume that the relationship is inappropriate, even when nothing improper has occurred. For all of their worldliness, college and university campuses still function in many ways as extremely small communities. Rumor and innuendo abound and, when there is no accurate gossip to spread about, people will frequently allow their speculations to become confused with the truth.

For all of these reasons, keep the following guidelines in mind whenever you are meeting with a student:

- *Avoid meeting alone with students individually behind closed doors as much as possible.* One-on-one meetings with particular students may convey false impressions to the student and to outside observers alike. Though occasionally it may be necessary to discuss confidential information with a student in private, these sessions should be kept to a minimum and should be conducted in such a way as to reduce the likelihood of false impressions. Frequently campus libraries have rooms for small groups that isolate sound but include plenty of windows so that others can see in. Office doors, particularly those that are opaque, should be kept open as much as possible when meeting alone with a student. Meeting in a public space, such as a library or busy coffee shop, can also be beneficial. Always ask yourself how a situation might be misinterpreted by others, including the student with whom you are meeting.

- *Never meet with a student alone at either your home or the student's residence.* Although it can often create an improved rapport with students to have them to one's house for a meal, this should only be done in large groups. Moreover, if the student meets your family or significant other in such a setting, such a meeting may dispel any romantic illusions the student may be harboring.

- *Be careful with how much personal information you share with students.* We have seen in Chapter 14, "Teaching Large Classes," that telling students a bit about yourself can help decrease the artificial amount of distance that tends to occur in big lecture courses. In some ways, the opposite principle should be considered when directing students independently. In these cases, you may need to create a bit *more* distance from the student to be effective as an instructor. If you are in the habit of dressing in a particular way when you teach a regular course, you should not dress any differently on a day when you are meeting individually with a student. Don't share as many private details of your life as you might share with an entire class of students, and certainly do not tell a student anything individually that you would not share with a class as a whole. Preserving a certain amount of distance helps you maintain your professional standing with the student and reduces the likelihood of misunderstandings.

- *Whenever possible, avoid providing only a single grade to the student at the end of the tutorial, internship, or other independent study.* Assign as many grades throughout the term as possible. You will find that doing so both reinforces your professional relationship in the student's mind and reduces the likelihood that the student will be surprised by his or her grade at the end of the course. In addition, many professors find that they tend to grade students with whom they work independently higher than they would grade similar work in an ordinary classroom setting. In part, this grade inflation may be due to the greater intimacy that teaching one-on-one creates; in part, it may be due to the fact that better students tend to take more tutorials, become involved in internships, seek out coaching, and the like. One solution to this problem is to conduct the tutorial on a pass-fail basis. Alternatively, you will find that you are more likely to grade with consistent standards if you give grades routinely throughout your work with a student than if you assign only a single grade at the end of the term.

Special Opportunities for One-on-One Teaching

Reading about all of the challenges that can arise from teaching students one-on-one, you may think that the risks are far greater than the rewards. Properly done, however, independent work can be extraordinarily valuable for the student and can even help you to begin to see certain aspects of your field in new and important ways. Let's consider next the various opportunities that can be found in direct supervision of individual students.

- Direct supervision allows individual students to pursue topics of special interest in far greater depth than would be possible in a traditional course. Working independently with a student, it is possible to take several "side trips" to explore topics of special interest. One way of conducting an independent study, for instance, is to run it as a formal tutorial in the Oxford manner. Each week the student is instructed to complete a required set of readings and then to complete a writing assignment on a topic related to those readings. The length of the writing assignment you choose can vary a great deal depending on the level of the course and the type of material you are covering. You could assign as little as a single, well-crafted paragraph that you can use to launch your exploration in your next tutorial session. Alternatively, you could assign a full five- to ten-page paper that the student is to complete in a week and that you will grade and return. (Long assignments such as this may initially seem intimidating to the student and to you as the instructor. Nevertheless, you'll soon find the student will become much faster and better at writing the assigned papers, and you'll become much more efficient at reviewing them.) This type of directed inquiry gives the student a great deal of freedom in exploring issues of individual interest at the same time that it develops critical thinking skills and improves the student's expository style. You would begin the tutorial session by having the student read or summarize the writing assignment from the past week, refining the issues addressed in it (possibly by use of the Socratic method as discussed in Chapter 13, "Teaching Small Classes"), and introducing issues that will lead to the next week's assignment.
- Direct supervision of individual students allows them to be more reflective about their learning than would be possible in a traditional course. Particularly when students are involved in internships, service-learning projects, private lessons, and coaching sessions, it can be extremely important for them to write essays reflecting on their experience.

For instance, a short essay at the beginning of the process on the topic of "What I Hope to Gain from This Experience" can inform you of potential directions in which you might like to guide the student, possible misconceptions the student might have about what is reasonable to accomplish during your time together, and how much the student already knows about what he or she is likely to experience during the activity. For the student, the assignment causes the learning process to become more intentional from the very beginning; as in most efforts, students in an independent learning experience are more likely to attain their goals if they articulate those goals early in the process. As the activity continues, the student should then be asked to reflect on progress that is being made: is it proceeding as he or she envisioned it or have there been surprises and unexpected challenges or opportunities along the way? Finally, at the end of the process, the student should engage in a significant reflection on the entire activity: What did the student realize about his or her individual learning style? What worked particularly well? What might he or she do differently if the process were to start all over again? What lessons about how to learn on one's own can the student transfer to other experiences? Though it is certainly possible to pose questions like this in a traditional class, the independent learning experience is so personal and individually tailored to the needs of each student that it lends itself particularly well to this type of introspective analysis. The process of reflection thus both enhances the student's own experience and provides the instructor with a useful means of assessment for improving such learning opportunities in the future (see Chapter 10, "Assessing Student Learning").

• Direct supervision of individual students provides the instructor with opportunities for writing far more specific letters of recommendation than are possible for students who are only encountered in a traditional course. One of the challenges that faculty members face when asked by a student for letters of recommendation to graduate school, professional school, or employment is making these letters sound anything but generic. For students who major in our disciplines and with whom we've worked in several different courses, it is usually possible to come up with a few specific anecdotes that provide insight into the student's ability and character. For students in large lecture classes or even introductory courses of forty to eighty students, it can be difficult to write a compelling letter, having only grades and possibly attendance records at our disposal. Few of these problems exist, however, for the students whom we've tutored, coached, or supervised independently. There are usually memorable instances of the student's willingness to go beyond the bare minimum or the student's failure to do so. We often know a great deal about the challenges that these students have had to overcome and their degree of success in adhering to high standards. As a result, one-on-one meetings tend to do the students a great deal of good because they receive far more specific, personally written letters of recommendation from the professor. They also help the instructor because, unlike many such letters, they tend to be extremely easy and pleasant to write. For more on this topic, see Buller (2006).

One drawback to courses taught one-on-one is that the student tends to be exposed to only two perspectives: yours and his or her own. To compensate for this limitation, you may wish to review some of the strategies that were discussed in Chapter 13, "Teaching Small Classes," including using websites and other technological approaches to gaining alternative points of view, assigning the student to present as objectively as possible the major arguments antithetical to his or her own perspective, having the student engage in role playing, and so on. Despite this limitation and the need always to be cautious when meeting one-on-one with students, independent learning experiences can be some of the most stimulating, creative, and enjoyable academic activities for the student and faculty member alike.

REFERENCES

Buller, J. L. (2006). How to write outstanding letters of recommendation. In J. L. Buller, *The essential department chair: A practical guide to college administration* (pp. 33–40). Bolton, MA: Anker.

RESOURCES

Boylan, J. C., & Scott, J. (2009). *Practicum and internship: Textbook and resource guide for counseling and psychotherapy* (4th ed.). New York: Routledge.

Capasso, R. L., & Daresh, J. C. (2001). *The school administrator internship handbook: Leading, mentoring, and participating in the internship program.* Thousand Oaks, CA: Corwin Press.

Coats, M. (1992). *Effective tutorials*. London: Open University Press.

Exley, K., & Dennick, R. (2004). *Small group teaching: Tutorials, seminars, and beyond*. New York: RoutledgeFalmer.

Kreber, C. (Ed.). (2006). *New directions for teaching and learning: No. 107. Exploring research-based teaching*. San Francisco: Jossey-Bass.

Munson, C. E. (Ed.). (1984). *Supervising student internships in human services*. New York: Haworth Press.

Podsen, I. J., & Denmark, V. (2007). *Coaching and mentoring first-year and student teachers*. Larchmont, NY: Eye on Education.

Quinn, P. O., Ratey, N. A., & Maitland, T. L. (2000). *Coaching college students with AD/HD: Issues and answers*. Silver Spring, MD: Advantage Books.

16

TEACHING WITH TECHNOLOGY

Any resource that discusses technology is outdated before it can be read. The lag inherent in publishing—even the very short lag between when something is written and when it can be posted electronically—is time enough for major new developments to occur. Moreover, the very concept of what teaching with technology means can change quite rapidly. Each new wave of faculty members and students largely takes for granted technologies that their predecessors adopted only after extensive training. Computer scientists are familiar with the notion that what was recently a cutting-edge innovation in artificial intelligence can be found in today's appliance, already reduced for clearance at a local discount store. For this reason, even though this book explores elsewhere how specific technologies may be used to meet specific opportunities in college-level courses, in this chapter we'll focus more on the issue of teaching with technology in a general or theoretical sense. What are the basic principles that lead to effective use of technology in the classroom regardless of recent developments in the field? What are some of the guidelines for how technology should or should not be used in college courses? What factors should be noted in considering whether a new piece of hardware or software has strong educational potential? We can begin to answer these questions by considering several important guidelines for the instructional use of technology at the college level.

Take Advantage of Technology Training and Resources

Most major colleges and universities have a center for teaching excellence that offers workshops on various pedagogical issues. A large portion of the training that these centers offer tends to deal with teaching with technology, precisely because technology changes so rapidly. It's a good practice to participate in as many of these workshops as possible, even if they don't seem immediately relevant to your academic field or the way in which you teach. After all, it's always possible that a connection will arise later. For instance, much of the early training in course management software, such as Blackboard and eCollege, focused on the use of this technology in distance learning courses. Faculty members may have elected not to learn how to use these applications because they thought that they were unlikely to teach in anything other than a traditional campus setting. It quickly became clear, however, that course management systems were valuable resources for *any* type of class because they allowed students to have access to material "on reserve" electronically, engage in threaded discussions about course material outside of class, and take quizzes and tests whenever they liked, thus freeing class time for additional material or review. It is even possible that certain faculty members who swore they would never teach an online class will eventually begin offering courses through distance learning as the mission of their schools or the nature of their student populations evolve. There are also additional benefits to participating in a wide variety of technological workshops. Any type of training in how to teach causes an instructor to reflect on the methods he or she uses to help students learn and on how those methods might be improved. Even if you find yourself concluding, "Well, I'd never have a use for *that*," this thought is likely to be followed by inspiration of a different kind: "But what I could do is *this*." In addition, even if you don't adopt a new form of technology, your students will be encountering it in their other courses. They may well ask you why you aren't using a particular type of hardware or a software application and, if you are unfamiliar with it, it can be difficult to explain why it doesn't fit the subject you are teaching or your instructional approach. Finally, participation in technological workshops puts you in touch with a community of scholars at your institution, all of whom are devoted to excellence in instruction. These peers can be good role models for you— as you can be for them—and you might even discover the basis for a teaching circle, regardless of whether its focus is on technology in the classroom. For more on teaching circles, see Chapter 27, "Seeking and Providing Peer Support for Scholarship."

Many centers for teaching excellence offer additional forms of training that you may find even more useful than workshops. Individual tutorials allow you to focus on problems that you are having with a particular application or type of hardware or on how to integrate technology directly into your individual academic discipline and the courses you are likely to teach. Online guides make it possible for you to move at your own pace, skipping over sections that you already understand and reviewing several times material that you find particularly challenging. Centers may also maintain libraries of books and journals dedicated to using technology in college-level courses. If you're relatively new to using technology in the classroom, good places to begin are Bates and Poole (2003) and Clyde and Delohery (2005).

If you're more comfortable with instructional technology—if you already know how to operate presentation hardware and software in a smart classroom, use course management software either to conduct an online course or enhance a classroom course, and are familiar with the application packages that are most relevant to your discipline—a useful resource to take advantage of is the organization EDUCAUSE (www .educause.edu) and its journals, *EDUCAUSE Review* and *EDUCAUSE Quarterly*. EDUCAUSE is the premier national organization dealing with issues of technology and higher education, sponsoring national and regional conferences, supporting major initiatives to improve the educational use of technology, providing a wide variety of printed and electronic resources (including selected content from its publications and an excellent *Student Guide to Evaluating Information Technology on Campus*, 2006), and offering access to blogs, podcasts, wikis, and feeds dealing with technological issues. Although many EDUCAUSE resources are written more for the information technology professional than the teaching professor, these materials do provide advance notice of trends long before they are discussed in other professional journals. Of the association's two journals, *EDUCAUSE Review* is more topic oriented and *EDUCAUSE Quarterly* provides more detailed technical information. Both journals offer plenty of ideas for the college professor who has already mastered all the technology on campus and is eager to learn what may be coming next. Moreover, if your interests in instructional technology lead you to a more advanced level of proficiency, the group known as Campus Technology (www.campustechnology.com) offers Webinars, newsletters, and events that can keep you up to date on the latest developments and issues in the field of educational technology.

Some Common Approaches to Teaching with Technology

Although instructional technology will continue to change rapidly over time, there remains a certain degree of continuity about the benefits technology can provide to the instructional mission of a college or university. The following are among the most common approaches to technology in higher education that are likely to persist even as new developments occur:

- *Technology can provide students with educational opportunities that would not otherwise be available to them.* We saw in Chapter 8, "Special Challenges for Senior Faculty," that computer simulations make it possible for students to gain hands-on experience in situations that would otherwise be too dangerous, remote, or expensive for them to engage in personally. Moreover, in Chapter 12, "Developing Creative Course Materials," we saw that technology enables students to "visit" virtually an almost unlimited range of locations and periods of history that they could not actually visit. In a similar way, computer software allows instructors in science classes to model structures far too distant or small to be seen by the human eye; architects and engineers to demonstrate the effects of using materials in specific designs; musicians to modify the entire orchestration or harmony of compositions; literary scholars to search entire libraries of text for parallel passages; and mathematicians to develop virtual universes where various mathematical laws or principles are altered.

- *Technology can help students and professors alike overcome challenges that occur in specific learning environments.* In Chapter 13, "Teaching Small Classes," we saw how social networking websites can help expand the limited range of perspectives and opinions that may occur if a course does not enroll a broad cross-section of students. In a similar way, presentation technologies make it possible for students even in the back or corners of a classroom—not to mention those miles away who are taking the course via distance learning—to see and hear with perfect clarity everything that occurs in the class. For students who have specific learning disabilities or challenges, technology can help level the playing field. Technology can thus help compensate for the challenges that arise because a learning environment is too large or too small, too far from the instructor, or because a course is compressed into too short a time. Though not a panacea for every type of educational challenge, technology certainly makes possible a high level of learning in environments where instruction would have been extremely difficult a generation or two earlier.

- *Technology helps address the needs of students with different kinds of learning styles.* Everyone learns best in his or her own way. In addition to auditory, visual, and experiential learners, some students learn better when information is text based, others if it is quantitative or symbolic, and still others if course material combines all of these approaches. Certain students flourish when a course progresses in a very structured and orderly manner; others learn better when they can move at their own pace or explore material nonsequentially. Some students learn best on their own, while others require the support of a group to perform their best work. Technology allows instructors to address many more of these learning styles in a single course than ever before possible. Presentation software such as PowerPoint and Keynote allows college professors to combine text, graphics, video clips, sound, and hyperlinks all within the same class session. Course management systems can provide students with access to a wide range of resources in any medium. "Smartpen" technologies like Livescribe allow students to replay audio recordings of whatever was being said in class at the precise moment that they were writing a specific item in their notebooks, search electronically for a particular word or page, and share their notes electronically with classmates. Tablet PCs allow for the quick integration of electronic and handwritten material. Mind-mapping software, such as Inspiration, MindManager, and ConceptDraw, permit students to move quickly from brainstorming, through the organization of ideas, to a finished document, spread-sheet, or presentation. Electronic gaming systems can provide an experiential element to courses in nearly any discipline. In addition, the use of wikis—collaborative websites that can be expanded and edited by any member of the class—allows for experiential or group activities even in courses that would not ordinarily lend themselves to this type of approach. For online courses, Bonk and Zhang (2008) and Conrad and Donaldson (2004) offer many innovative activities, exercises, and techniques to engage distance learning students, regardless of their learning style.

- *Technology makes it possible for learning to occur anywhere and at any time.* In addition to providing entire courses to remote sites through distance learning, technology also makes it possible for learning to occur long after a course is over. With course management systems, students can continue talking about course material online either in live chat rooms or through threaded discussions. They can have access to a wealth of course materials, including graphics and video, through course websites. They can review course material by listening to academic podcasts. Through iTunes U (www.apple.com/education/itunesu), many colleges and universities are making enhanced podcasts that include course materials, recorded lectures and discussions, and other supplementary learning aids available for download. The Teaching Company (www.teach12.com) offers a wide range of courses in a variety of audio and video formats; these courses provide a convenient way for students to supplement traditional instruction and for professors to offer prerequisite or corequisite courses to students who need additional preparation in a given academic area. Through videoconferencing services such as Skype or iChat, or computer screen sharing tools such as Yugma or WiZiQ, college professors can work computer-to-computer with students at any time of the day or night; this technology makes it possible to construct a virtual classroom or to conduct online office hours right from your home or office. Smartboards, electronic copy boards, and interactive screens allow students to download after class anything that was written or drawn on the board. Even in classrooms not yet equipped with this technology, it is easy for college professors to snap a digital photo of important diagrams or other items on whiteboards for later posting through a class management system or website. Presentations prepared through PowerPoint or Keynote are also easily disseminated in this way.

- *Technology can make assessment both easier and more meaningful.* As we saw in Chapter 10, "Assessing Student Learning," and Chapter 14, "Teaching Large Classes," technology makes it very easy for faculty members to assess whether specific student learning outcomes are being met while there is still time to take corrective action, if necessary. Student response systems ("clickers"), course management systems, and optical character or mark recognition software all make collection and processing of information extremely quick. Instructors can determine instantly what portion of the class understands a term, concept, or process, and thus rapidly adapt teaching to suit the changing needs of different groups of students. Moreover, for learning outcomes that do not readily lend themselves to quantification, e-portfolios permit students to assemble electronically a representative sample of their progress in writing, performing public service, demonstrating leadership, engaging in cultural activities, developing creativity, working well collaboratively, and so on. A student's e-portfolio can then provide supporting material to an application for a job or further educational opportunity. Unlike paper portfolios, e-portfolios do not require extensive shelf space, can be evaluated quickly (and at times even automatically), and can remain accessible long after a student graduates.

Other approaches to technology in education will certainly emerge, but the five just described provide a convenient place to begin when considering whether a new piece of software or hardware is worth incorporating into your teaching. Cost limitations and the time it takes to learn new applications mean that not every college professor will find it productive to adopt every new technology in every course. Based on the approaches just discussed, it may be useful to ask yourself the following questions when considering whether a technological innovation is suitable for one of your courses:

- Will this new technology help students gain access to an experience they would not otherwise have?
- Will it help overcome the challenge of learning in a specific type of environment?
- Will it help address the different learning styles of the students in my courses?
- Will it extend the learning experience outside the classroom in a significant way?
- Will it help assess whether the educational objectives of my courses are being met?

In addition, it can always be helpful to ask whether the new technology is cost effective. Certain technologies *save* money. On the one hand, it costs less to distribute material electronically than to print it, to make contact through audio- and videoconferencing than to travel, and to offer courses online than to hire faculty members (or teaching assistants) in several different locations. On the other hand, many types of new instructional technology are more expensive than the methods that may currently be in place at your school. A useful question, therefore, is: to what extent is this added expense worthwhile, given the quality of education that I'll be able to provide? If investing in this technology means that I needed to forgo a raise, see fewer student scholarships next year, have less travel and research funding, or be unable to take advantage of other opportunities in my discipline, would I still think that this expenditure is the best use of this money? Institutional budgets may be large or small, but they are never unlimited. Spending more in one area almost always means spending less in another. For this reason, one consideration when adopting new technology is what you are willing to do less in order to do more in the area of the new hardware or software.

Instructional technology has so many advantages that some college professors may wonder, "Is there ever a reason for *not* adopting a new technology into my instruction?" The answer is that there are many good reasons why incorporating new technology may not be in the best interests of either you or your students. We've already seen, for instance, that the high cost of certain technologies may not make them cost effective because resources may need to be reallocated from other, more critical areas. But your time is a critical resource as well. For a junior faculty member who must still earn promotion and tenure at an institution where evaluation of research plays an important role, spending many hours to learn a new application or to revise course materials in light of new technology may simply not be the best investment of limited time. In addition, it is inadvisable to adopt technology that requires students to spend significant time to learn that might be better spent learning the material of the course or engaged in other activities. Having students spend a great deal of time learning a new technology that they are unlikely to encounter elsewhere in their education or careers is also an inefficient use of class or study time. Moreover, adopting a technology that provides no advantages over traditional methods of instruction is simply wasteful. Nevertheless, even with all of these provisos, college professors need to become technologically proficient regardless of their disciplines. Administrators demand technological proficiency from faculty, and students increasingly expect it. Saying "I'm just not good at technology" has become roughly akin to stating that one is "just not good at" reading, understanding difficult ideas, or communicating with others. Technology has become part of the tools of the trade for college professors, and the more training faculty members can get in new instructional technologies, the better their students are likely to learn in the years to come.

REFERENCES

Bates, A. W., & Poole, G. (2003). *Effective teaching with technology in higher education: Foundations for success*. San Francisco: Jossey-Bass.

Bonk, C. J., & Zhang, K. (2008). *Empowering online learning: 1001 activities for reading, reflecting, displaying, and doing*. San Francisco: Jossey-Bass.

Clyde, W., & Delohery, A. (2005). *Using technology in teaching*. New Haven, CT: Yale University Press.

Conrad, R.-M., & Donaldson, J. A. (2004). *Engaging the online learner: Activities and resources for creative instruction*. San Francisco: Jossey-Bass.

EDUCAUSE. (2006). *Student guide to evaluating information technology on campus*. Boulder, CO: Author.

RESOURCES

Davis, B. G. (2009). *Tools for teaching* (2nd ed.). San Francisco: Jossey-Bass.

Garrison, D. R., & Vaughan, N. D. (2008). *Blended learning in higher education: Framework, principles, and guidelines*. San Francisco: Jossey-Bass.

Iiyoshi, T., & Kumar, M. S. V. (Eds.). (2008). *Opening up education: The collective advancement of education through open technology, open content, and open knowledge.* Cambridge, MA: MIT Press.

Inoue, Y. (Ed.). (2007). *Technology and diversity in higher education: New challenges.* Hershey, PA: Information Science.

Laurillard, D. (2002). *Rethinking university teaching: A conversational framework for the effective use of learning technologies* (2nd ed.). New York: RoutledgeFalmer.

Maeroff, G. I. (2003). *A classroom of one: How online learning is changing our schools and colleges.* New York: Palgrave Macmillan.

Slator, B. M., & Associates. (2006). *Electric worlds in the classroom: Teaching and learning with role-based computer games.* New York: Teachers College Press.

West, J. A., & West, M. L. (2009). *Using wikis for online collaboration: The power of the read-write web.* San Francisco: Jossey-Bass.

Zhu, E., & Kaplan, M. (2006). Technology and teaching. In W. J. McKeachie & M. Svinicki, *McKeachie's teaching tips: Strategies, research, and theory for college and university teachers* (12th ed., pp. 229–252). New York: Houghton Mifflin.

Zumbach, J., Schwartz, N., Seufert, T., & Kester, L. (Eds.). (2008). *Beyond knowledge: The legacy of competence.* New York: Springer.

17

REDUCING GRADE ANXIETY

Students exhibit grade anxiety when concern about their performance in a course stops being a healthy desire for excellence and starts to be a paralyzing fixation on the grade itself. Some professors say things like, "I don't regard grade anxiety as a problem. I *want* my students to feel anxious about their grades. If they're worried about how they'll perform, they're more likely to work hard." But statements like this miss the point. Actual grade anxiety does not spur students on to outstanding work; it immobilizes them because they become so afraid of failure that they are unwilling to attempt anything new or at least unwilling to try anything that ventures beyond a narrowly defined comfort zone. The premed student with grade anxiety will balk at the possibility of taking a poetry course because "I might not be good at that, and a B would ruin my chances of getting into Johns Hopkins." The art student with grade anxiety will avoid completing a math assignment, assuming that you can't fail at what you don't even try. Grade anxiety may be found among students in all majors, among honors students as well as students who are just getting by academically, among athletes as well as "mathletes," and among students who went to highly selective private schools as well as those who attended open admission public schools. If you teach long enough, sooner or later you will encounter a student who appears to be ruining his or her own chances at a genuine education largely because of grade anxiety.

The grade anxiety that we discuss in this chapter is a condition that is not so severe that it requires professional counseling. Such extreme cases of grade anxiety certainly exist and, if you suspect that a student has become so fixated on grades that the situation is truly debilitating, you should refer the student to your campus counseling center or a private therapist (see Chapter 21, "Dealing with Student Problems and Problem Students"). The cases that we'll discuss in this chapter are not of a very extreme nature but are serious enough that they are having at least some negative effect on the student's education or breadth of academic choices. In these instances, there are steps you can take as an instructor that may help the student better cope with his or her anxiety and perform better in your course.

coping strategies

Strat. #1

To begin, let's explore a few of the causes that may be responsible for a student's grade anxiety. Psychologists distinguish between coping strategies that are problem focused and those that are emotion focused. For instance, if someone walks out into a parking lot and cannot find his or her car, a problem-focused strategy would consist of trying to recall precisely which entrance to the store was used when leaving the parking lot, whether the car may accidentally have been left in a no parking zone and thus may have been towed, whether it is at all possible that the car was stolen and thus the incident should be reported to the police, whether the store provides any assistance that could help locate the car, and so on. The person may also develop a plan of walking up and down the various rows of the parking lot, just in case the car happened to be left in a different location from where he or she remembered parking it. If a person in a similar situation happens to use an emotion-focused strategy, however, the person may devote time to worrying what his or her spouse might say because of this act of carelessness, become nervous because the police might have to get involved with the car's recovery, engage in self-recrimination for "being so stupid to shop in a dangerous neighborhood," and so on.

Many students with grade anxiety tend to employ an emotion-focused coping strategy. Rather than applying problem-focused strategies and breaking the task of earning a good grade into manageable parts, they focus on the negative emotions of failure, disappointment, and embarrassment that may occur if they do not succeed. In these cases, it can be helpful to redirect the student's strategy for coping with the challenge of earning a good grade. When you sense that a student has become inappropriately caught up in the negative emotions associated with the possibility of receiving a bad grade, help the student develop a more constructive approach to the challenge. "Let's look at the issue in a different light," you might say. "Have you taken good notes on each of the units that we discussed in class? Have you carefully reviewed those notes several times? Did you complete all of the assigned reading in the textbook? Did you highlight or take notes on important points while you were doing that reading? Did you review those key sections? Are you working as part of a study group?" If the student finds that he or she has taken all of the steps that you suggest, then you can discuss with the student how he or she has already done the right things and thus should feel a sense of accomplishment from these activities. If the student has been so caught up in worrying about the assignment that he or she has omitted some of the steps that you suggest, then you can formulate a concrete plan to begin making progress. In either case, you're doing the student a tremendous service by demonstrating how problem-focused strategies can be particularly productive in academic situations and can divert attention from negative emotions such as anxiety and fear of failure.

Another psychological principle that can be useful when dealing with cases of grade anxiety is the notion of one's optimal level of arousal. The basic idea is this: for every activity that we wish to perform, there is a degree of excitement that can help us to make our best effort. If we are too blasé, we may be inattentive or indifferent to our unsatisfactory results; if too anxious, we can become preoccupied with the anxiety itself and not with the quality of our performance. When we bring the proper level of excitement to a task, however, our strong energy and attentiveness allows us to make our best effort. But there is also an important corollary to this observation: people who are extroverted often require additional external stimulation to achieve their best energy level; people who are introverted more often need to be calmed in order to achieve their optimal level. Being aware of this general principle, you can adapt the way in which you approach a case of grade anxiety based on what you know about the student. If the student is extroverted, a pep talk may well be your best strategy. Get him or her excited about the positive challenges of the exam or assignment. Demonstrate that you have confidence in the student. Provide a great deal of active encouragement. However, if the student is more introverted, seek a soothing approach. Reassure the student that the situation is not as onerous as it may seem, that many other students, including some who have not worked as hard, have undergone similar experiences before, and they have successfully graduated and gone on to careers in their chosen field. Seek to settle the student's anxiety and overstimulation, doing the opposite of what you might attempt with an extroverted student where you are hoping to increase the person's level of stimulation.

In addition to these general strategies for helping students cope with their grade anxiety, there are also several other techniques that you can use, depending on the specifics of the situation.

Discover the Fear Behind the Grade Anxiety

Aristotle said that we engage in each action for the sake of some good. Most of these goods are only intermediary in nature; they are designed to achieve some higher good. But when we reach the good of "happiness," we can't go any further. We don't seek happiness as a means to attaining any other good. Happiness, in other words, is an end in itself, what the Romans would later call a *summum bonum*, a "highest good." The inverse of this principle tends to be less universal, however. The ultimate evil—what we might call the *pessimum malum*—is not the same for everyone. Consider the case of why different people may resist entering a burning building. One person may not wish to do so because he or she is afraid of being burned; burning is painful, and that person regards pain as the ultimate evil. Another person may be willing to endure pain, but is still reluctant to enter the building because a severe enough burn could lead to death, and that person regards death as the *pessimum malum*. A third person may not fear death, but believes in an afterlife where there may be an eternal condemnation, which for this person would be the ultimate evil. Moreover, we can think of numerous cases in which, despite a natural reluctance to enter a burning building, someone may actually do so. The person may be a firefighter for whom dereliction of duty is a greater evil than pain or death. The person may be the parent of a child trapped in the building, and abandoning one's child would constitute the *pessimum malum* for that person. It is even possible that someone draws a perverse pleasure from pain or injury and does not regard such experiences as evil at all. The fact of the matter is that although happiness is a universally shared concept of the highest good, the worst evil that each of us faces can be a very personal and individual matter.

This concept is important to understand because most students with grade anxiety will assume that the poor grade itself is the *pessimum malum*, although it rarely if ever is. If you probe the matter a bit further with the student, you may end up with a dialogue that goes something like this:

Professor: But what's the worst possible thing that could happen if you get a C on this paper?

Student: It would ruin my chances of getting an A in the course.

Professor: And what's the worst possible thing that could happen if you didn't get an A in the course?

Student: It would blow my whole GPA.

Professor: Why does that matter?

Student: Because then I couldn't get into my first-choice graduate school.

Professor: And if you didn't make it in, what would happen then?

Student: But that's been my dream my whole life! I couldn't *bear* that!

Professor: What do you mean when you say it's been your dream for your whole life?

Student: Well, my dad went there, and I just know that if I don't get in, I'll have let him down in a major way.

Finally you have reached the level of the student's greatest fear. The precise nature of that fear will vary from student to student; one student may be afraid of disappointing his or her parents, another may be worried about not achieving some major goal in life, being embarrassed by not being able to fulfill a commitment, not following the example of a friend or sibling, or something utterly unique.

For some students, simply identifying what they *really* fear can be liberating. For others, knowing what they are trying to avoid can be a path toward developing a more constructive strategy for dealing with the challenges of earning a good grade. For instance, it may be possible for the student to discover that he or she doesn't need a perfect 4.0 GPA to get into that "dream" graduate program. The student's conversation with a parent or sibling might reveal that the standards of perfection that he or she was attributing to others were really misunderstandings or self-imposed. Asking one's friends whether they would feel the student had let them down if he or she received grades that were less than perfect might reveal that those friends are far more accepting of imperfections than the student had believed. Even in cases far more complicated than these, it can be highly beneficial for the student to understand that "It's not the low grade itself that I fear. It's that a low grade will lead to X." With that awareness, he or she can start taking more constructive steps to avoid X.

Even honors students—perhaps *particularly* honors students—seem prone to confusing a low grade with what they actually fear most. In a significant number of cases, when the students identify that fear, they can also discover that it is illusory. As Guzy (2007) has noted:

> Honors students also experience difficulties learning to separate the grade from what they have actually learned in a course. I share with them that I learned and retained more information from some courses in which I earned a hard B than from some "blow-off" classes in which I received an easy A, all while still earning a 3.79 GPA and graduating from my own undergraduate honors program. Shifting their focus to life after college, I ask whether they have ever queried professionals in their prospective fields regarding GPAs. For example, our campus has a medical school with an early admissions program, and at least fifty percent of our incoming honors freshmen are planning to attend medical school, so I ask them whether they have ever asked their own physicians about their undergraduate GPAs, transcripts, test scores, and such. None ever has. We then discuss why pre-med students believe that they must maintain a 4.0 GPA to be admitted to medical school and whether grades can predict such

intrinsic characteristics as good bedside manner. For some students, separating learning from grades can be a painful revelation, and not all are successful at it. (p. 34)

When college professors approach their role as not simply the students' instructor but also as their mentor, they can ease the difficulty of this sometimes painful revelation, performing a valuable lifelong service for the students in the process.

Explain the Benefits to Being Corrected

Another cause of grade anxiety can be a student's inability to separate "My work could have been improved in this course" from "I am flawed as a person." Certain students, in other words, take grades personally, or at least more personally than they should in order to make their best progress in the subject. They regard every grade lower than a full A (or even an A+) as a statement by a professor that they themselves are being rejected or insulted. In these cases, you may be able to help the student by discussing why a grade is not the same thing as a personal validation and why receiving constructive criticism is actually an essential part of the learning process.

If the student happens to be involved in athletics or dance, sings or plays a musical instrument, skates or enjoys skateboarding, surfs, writes poetry or short stories, is a member of the debate or chess team, and so on, you may be able to make a useful comparison between these activities and the student's coursework. Rarely do individuals excel at any of these activities the first few times they try them. In fact, beginning an activity is often extremely difficult, and we stay with it only because we know that persistence along with hard work are needed to attain a high level of skill. Moreover, these activities are ones in which there are frequently plateaus in the course of our progress. We feel that we're doing well, but then a new coach or a friend says, "Now if you *really* want to be good, you need to . . ." and we feel almost as though we are starting over again. This type of advice is given to us not out of a desire to make us feel bad, but out of a recognition that we are good and are capable of doing even better. In this way, when an instructor or coach points out things that can be improved, it is really a compliment to us, as the person is expressing confidence that we are capable of excelling even further.

You may be able to share a personal experience in which you learned from making a mistake and from receiving someone else's advice. You may also have had a situation in which you missed an opportunity because you didn't think you'd be good enough or could not accept being anything less than perfect, only to discover later that you had deprived yourself of a chance to learn something new or to grow as a person. The student may need reassurance that even people whom he or she respects have made mistakes . . . and have learned from them and triumphed. An error, possibly even a significant failure, can be overcome as long as one approaches it from the perspective of "What can I learn from this situation? How can I now proceed to do even better next time?"

Provide Opportunities for Risk Taking

When a student is extremely reluctant to explore new academic areas because "I may not be good at that, and I can't afford to ruin my GPA," we can sometimes assist by providing the entire class with low-risk opportunities to branch out. Giving an assignment that cannot lower a student's grade if it is not well done but can only raise a grade if well done may encourage the student to try something that he or she would never have attempted otherwise. When reviewing what the student turns in, it is rarely the case that *nothing* about the project can be praised. For example, if a student who is highly science oriented is reluctant to write a poem in your class, giving the student a low-risk opportunity to test the waters can sometimes lead to a great deal of self-discovery. Even if the poem that results is nowhere near the quality of the work submitted by students who have been writing their own poetry for years, you will almost always find something that the student can build on. Perhaps there was an innovative use of language, an unexpected metaphor, a creative adaptation of an archaic poetic form to a modern situation, or some other novelty of this sort. At the very least, the student will have made an attempt in an area that he or she would never have considered earlier.

In a similar manner, if you are the advisor of a student who will not consider taking a course in an area where he or she may not do well— despite how personally beneficial that area of study may be—you may be able to create a low-risk opportunity for the student to take a chance. Offer to place the student in the course that you highly recommend, and then to schedule a joint conference with the student, the instructor, and you as the student's advisor on the day before the last day to drop the course. If, at that time, the instructor feels that the student is still unlikely to do well or if the student still wishes to drop, say that you will agree to sign the drop form. Of course, this solution is only possible at institutions where the advisor's signature is required on such a document. If this opportunity is open to you, however, then make no mistake about it: if you make this offer, you will end up signing a substantial number of these drop forms. Particularly at institutions where the last day to drop a course comes as early as the first or second week of class, the student may not have had sufficient time to develop a level of comfort with the material, and the instructor may not yet have had enough time to develop an informed opinion of the student's likelihood to succeed. Nevertheless, you will still have exposed the student, however briefly, to a new way of experiencing the world. And in a surprising number of instances, your advice and assurances will persuade the student to stick it out, creating a wonderful learning opportunity that the student would otherwise have missed.

Explain the Purpose for an Assignment

It is easy to fear an evaluation when you don't understand its purpose except to denote your success or failure. Students tend to become less anxious about their grades when their attention is focused on what they're supposed to be gaining from an exercise. We saw in Chapter 12, "Developing Creative Course Materials," that stating your goals on every assignment, handout, Web page, or test can motivate students to do their best: they know what benefit they'll receive from this activity, so they're more likely to engage in it willingly and well. But the inverse of this statement is also true: if students do not understand the goals of an assignment, they are likely to become preoccupied with the *wrong* things, such as grades merely for the sake of grades. It is easier to state clear purposes when you have numerous assignments and evaluation opportunities in a course. A class that is graded only on the basis of a midterm and a final is one in which the instructor is trying to accomplish so many things on each of those tests that it is difficult to identify all the goals involved. These relatively few grading opportunities can exacerbate student anxiety in and of itself. "I only get two chances to make an A in this class, and I just *have* to get a high score on the midterm." But this problem becomes even worse when those limited chances to earn a grade have so many different objectives that the only goal a student can understand is success or failure in terms of a letter grade. Numerous grading opportunities, with frequent status reports of how each student is progressing, can themselves allay a great deal of grade anxiety.

Grade anxiety arises in students for a variety of reasons. In certain cases, it is symptomatic of a deeper personal problem and should be addressed only by a professional counselor. Often, however, grade anxiety is an extension of the very natural desire to succeed at everything we do, to be well liked, and to avoid letting our family and friends down. In these situations, instructors and advisors can help students either overcome or learn to cope with their grade anxiety, thus providing them with important lessons about life and the true meaning of the word *success*. For an excellent website that can help students overcome a quest for perfectionism that is ultimately destructive and self-limiting, see www.utexas .edu/student/cmhc/booklets/perfection/perfect.html.

REFERENCES

Guzy, A. (2007). Evaluation vs. grading in honors composition or how I learned to stop worrying about grades and love teaching. *Journal of the National Collegiate Honors Council, 8*(1), 31–36.

RESOURCES

Antony, M. M., & Swinson, R. P. (1998). *When perfect isn't good enough: Strategies for coping with perfectionism.* Oakland, CA: New Harbinger.
Basco, M. R. (1999). *Never good enough: How to use perfectionism to your advantage without letting it ruin your life.* New York: Touchstone.
Galbraith, J., & Delisle, J. (1996). *The gifted kids' survival guide: A teen handbook.* Minneapolis, MN: Free Spirit.

18

PROMOTING STUDENT ENGAGEMENT

Student engagement refers to the degree to which students learn the material in courses actively rather than passively, relate it to their lives and what they are learning in other courses, and are effectively challenged by their coursework. Since 1998, Indiana University, supported by a grant from the Pew Charitable Trusts, has been working with a national inventory of best practices in this area known as the College Student Report or, more commonly, as the National Survey of Student Engagement, or NSSE (http://nsse.iub.edu/html/origins.cfm.). In addition, a project for the American Association for Higher Education, the Education Commission of the States, and the Johnson Foundation produced Chickering and Gamson's *Seven Principles for Good Practice in Undergraduate Education* (1987) and a faculty inventory based on those principles (Chickering, Gamson, & Barsi, 1989). Chickering and Gamson later expanded on these ideas in *Applying the Seven Principles for Good Practice in Undergraduate Education* (1991). Probably one of the best ways in which college professors can begin enhancing the level of student engagement in their classes is to get copies of both the NSSE (current versions can be found on the survey's homepage), and the faculty inventory, complete these instruments with information relating to their courses, and then begin revising their courses according to what they learn from this exercise.

Normally, of course, college professors resist the entire idea of "teaching to the test." In the case of the NSSE and the *Seven Principles*, however, what instructors are really learning is the degree to which their own teaching techniques reflect best practices in promoting active learning and increasing student engagement with the material of their courses. Adapting your teaching strategies so that your courses would "do better" on these tests is not such a bad thing. With this idea in mind, if you were to take this approach, what are some of the strategies you might consider adopting in your courses?

Learn Students' Names Whenever Possible   *Participant Profiles*

One of the best ways in which you can increase student engagement is also the most obvious: get to know your students. People tend to invest more attention and energy in projects where they are not anonymous, where they know that people are concerned about how well they do. In a class with forty or fewer students, it is not particularly difficult to learn students' names so that you can acknowledge them individually, particularly if your course involves more than lecture alone. In large courses, which can easily enroll far more than a hundred students, this task can be extremely challenging for most of us. But even if you despair of learning every student's name, by learning as many names as you can you make the course far less impersonal for students, increasing the likelihood that they will engage actively with your material.

There are various devices you can use to help you learn students' names. If you have assignments to return, arrive in class a bit early, call out names, and pass back some of the student papers yourself rather than leave this task to a teaching assistant or telling students to come to the front of the room to find their own papers. Even occasionally connecting a name with a face will help you learn a surprising number of names. (Calling out the names yourself seems to work better for most people than having the students come up to you, tell you their names, and have you look for their papers.) In addition, you can make it a class policy that unless you call on a student specifically by name, each student should begin any class comment or question with his or her name. The practice would then mean that students would begin their remarks by saying things like, "Yes, my name's Lorraine Albertson, and I thought that the author was actually making a very different point here, specifically . . ." In extremely large lecture classes, you might even come into each class with five or six names memorized and call on those students for comment. "Is Arthur Baumgartner here today? Good! Arthur, would you please recap for us in your own words . . ." By calling on students in this way, you will find that you begin to know several of their names after a few days. In addition, students are likely to come to the class better prepared because they never know when it will be "their day" to be called on by name. *online*

 Learning students' names and calling on them individually, rather than waiting for them to volunteer a response, can be particularly important when you are teaching a distance learning course, either through videoconferencing or online. The physical separation that is involved in these instructional platforms frequently causes students to become more disengaged

In synchronous activities, keep the pace brisk and unpredictable. Spontaneously call on students to reply in some way,

or inattentive than they would be if the instructor were standing a few feet away from them in a classroom. It is not uncommon for students who are taking certain online courses to stroll away from their computers for long stretches, assuming that their "presence" will not be missed. The dynamic of the course changes entirely, and students are far more likely to become actively engaged with the material, when the instructor occasionally calls on individual students by name. Whether it occurs during a videoconference or online chat, it can focus students' attention extremely well if you ask, "Mark, there was a passage in yesterday's reading that related very closely to this point. Why don't you summarize for us what Thompson said about . . . ?"

Include Opportunities for Students to Speak in Class

When students listen to a lecture or read a text, they are largely passive. By giving students abundant opportunities to speak in class, their style of learning becomes far more active and engaged. But giving students an opportunity to speak involves far more than asking a few discussion questions or taking the last five minutes of the class to see if any of the students have an issue that needs clarification. Students may be reluctant to ask questions because they are afraid that they would look stupid or because they don't want to be embarrassed in front of their friends. For this reason, you may have to take a very aggressive role in getting your students to speak in class. In Chapter 14, "Teaching Large Classes," we saw how break-out opportunities such as jigsaw groups can help encourage students to speak and evaluate one another's perspectives in smaller groups before reassembling the class as a whole. In addition, you might introduce other techniques to prime the pump for more active classroom discussion. Among these techniques are:

- The *Send-a-Problem* technique involves students interacting with each other in a variety of ways that help them simultaneously learn new material, become comfortable speaking before one another, develop their skills at teamwork, and enhance their approach to critical thinking. Break the class into groups of five to ten students each. The first task for each group is to develop a significant question or problem based on the material they have just read or learned in class. Depending on the type of course you are teaching, the problem that the students create could be either a puzzle or a conundrum. (On the difference between these two terms, see Chapter 13, "Teaching Small Classes.") The problem is then written on a sheet of paper and clipped to a folder. The groups then exchange folders and try to answer the problem created by another group. If the problem is a puzzle, the new group attempts to solve it. If the problem is a conundrum, the group tries to think of as many appropriate solutions as it can. A sheet of paper containing the answer(s) is then placed inside the folder. When this stage of the process is complete, groups exchange folders again, and a third group, one that has neither developed the problem nor formulated the answer(s), receives the folder. If the problem is a puzzle, this group again attempts to solve it and then compares its answer to the one in the folder. If the problem is a conundrum, the instructor has a choice. The third group could develop its own list of possible solutions and then compare its answers to those of the second group. Alternatively, the third group could be asked to look at all of the possible solutions developed by the second group and place them in priority order, indicating what it believes to be the three "best" answers. For further discussion of the Send-a-Problem technique see Millis and Cottell (1998).

- The *top-ten list* was made popular by the comedian David Letterman. The basic idea is to perform a countdown of the ten most important ideas on a particular topic, with the most important and climactic idea as number one, the last item. Because students tend to be extremely familiar with this format, they take to the idea very easily and will often try to compete with one another for clever, humorous answers. Break the students into groups of four or five, have each group come up with its own top-ten list, and then have the members of that group take turns presenting their conclusions. To get students talking on the first day of a chemistry course, for instance, an instructor might make the following assignment: "The Top Ten Things You Should *Never* Do in a Chemistry Lab." The exercise thus helps review lab safety procedures in an amusing way at the same time that it gets everyone in the class speaking from the very beginning of the course.

- A *"whip"* is a good icebreaker, as it gets students talking and raises the energy level of a class, thus encouraging further conversation. In a whip, the instructor leaves a sentence unfinished and then goes around the class, having each student in turn supply an appropriate conclusion. For instance, a history instructor might start a whip in this way: "In the 1770s, one of the biggest problems facing France was . . ." A large number of appropriate answers are correct, and students will begin to feel more comfortable expressing opinions before their peers once they have participated in a whip.

Evaluate Students Through Written Work

Written assignments of a paragraph or longer dramatically change the type of learning that occurs from what may be found in a course where tests are largely multiple choice, fill-in-the-blank, matching, or short answer. By having students write, instructors encourage them to proceed from being able to *recognize* a correct answer to being able to *generate* a correct answer. Moreover, the skills needed to structure even a single well-constructed paragraph require a level of logical analysis that is difficult or impossible to reproduce in other types of assignments. In very large classes, it may be impossible to grade all of this writing, but that does not mean that students should never be asked to write in these classes. Assignments can be quickly checked as complete or incomplete, and course management systems can even perform this step automatically. Microthemes, discussed in Chapter 10, "Assessing Student Learning," encourage students to articulate their thoughts in ways that do not require a great deal of class time or instructor grading. Journals or course blogs compel students to write on a certain topic daily and to engage with the course material outside of class. But whenever possible, the best writing experiences are those when students craft a paper through several drafts, responding to the comments of their instructor and peers, gradually refining their thoughts with each iteration. Repeated drafts of a paper can cause students to feel that they "own" a specific topic, and that very sense of ownership and increasing mastery can lead to greater engagement with the topic. Elbow and Sorcinelli (2006) provide some excellent advice on how to work with students through multiple drafts of papers.

progressive assignments

Attend Events Where Students Are Likely to Be Present

Most students are more likely to become engaged with material in a course where they feel that they have a good rapport with their professor. If students feel that there is a great deal of "distance" between themselves and the instructor, they often have difficulty visualizing themselves mastering the course material and succeeding in the class as the instructor has done. At one time students may have wanted their college professors to seem almost superhuman with lofty eminence, but today's college student is more likely to regard a professor who does not seem to be a "real person" as phony, pretentious, or simply not the type of person who should be emulated. When a student gets to know an instructor through encounters outside of class at campus events, student life activities, book discussions, and the like, the student is more likely to be able to visualize

Ideas for an online environment?

himself or herself in a similar role—as a person who is successful in a chosen field—and to engage more actively in your courses. For this reason, consider participating in activities that are likely to attract students for positive, academic purposes. Getting to know students at a local bar, for instance, may end up sending precisely the opposite message from the one that you need to send. Offering to serve as a club advisor, to speak at a residence hall meeting, or to serve alongside students on a campus committee, however, can help reinforce the positive relationship that you wish to develop with students. You will expand your image as a role model, and you may even end up recruiting some good students to your discipline whom you would not have met otherwise.

Promote Student Interaction on Class Projects

Having students work together on projects or as part of group assignments can have many benefits. Through group projects, students can develop techniques of effective teamwork and cooperation, learn from positive and negative examples of their peers' work, and be exposed to more perspectives on an issue than can be introduced by the professor alone. Group projects also produce a high level of engagement as they are by their very nature a highly active form of learning. Nevertheless, instructors frequently are reluctant to assign group projects because they also can have numerous limitations. All too frequently work is performed very unevenly in group projects, with one or two students doing the majority of the work while the rest of the group contributes very little. Highly motivated students dislike situations where part of their grade may be dependent on the performance of peers over whom they exert little or no control. At times, assignments become group projects in name only, with little interaction among the students outside of class; what was supposed to be a panel discussion, in these situations, turns out to be little more than five largely independent reports.

Instructors can avoid these difficulties by the way in which they assign the group project and calculate each student's grade. Most group projects should involve both an individual grade and a group grade. The group grade should be able to enhance any individual's score as a reward for a demonstration of good teamwork. However, the group grade should probably not detract from any individual's score, because the individual may have ended up with a group that, for reasons completely beyond his or her control, was somehow dysfunctional. Alternatively, each member of the group can be asked to assess the perceived level of contribution by each member; students who are clearly recognized as having done more can be rewarded as a result. Also, specifying the *way* in which the group must interact can minimize many of the inequities that arise during group projects. For instance, the groups can be assigned to switch roles throughout the project. The student who one day acts as an interviewer or who poses the review questions for a study group may be instructed on the next day to act as the interviewee or part of the panel that answers the questions. Required midproject progress reports can alert you to inequities in group assignments that you can correct. Each member of the group could be required to critique every other member as an additional way to illustrate to you and to the students themselves where extra effort was contributed or where inequities occurred.

Encourage Students to Analyze or Synthesize Information

Bloom's Taxonomy

As we saw in Chapter 10, "Assessing Student Learning," tests that are largely multiple choice, fill-in-the-blank, matching, or short answer tend to reinforce passive learning skills. In order to involve students in a higher level of learning, assignments should encourage students to:

- Restate a position or perspective in their own words
- Relate a concept discussed in the course to an event in their own lives or to material encountered in their other courses
- Identify an author's or speaker's assumptions; the ideas or facts that the person has taken for granted
- Spot a deficiency in an author's argument
- Determine what type of audience an author assumed that he or she was addressing
- Suggest an alternative title for a work
- Highlight an author's primary thesis
- State the methods by which an author or speaker reached a conclusion

Maintain High Standards

"Patriotism," Samuel Johnson said, "is the last refuge of a scoundrel." In academic life, maintaining high standards is frequently the ineffective teacher's last refuge. Certain professors use it to justify why students refuse to enroll in their courses (although some might suspect that poor teaching and an unpleasant demeanor in the classroom could potentially play some role as well), why numerous students fail a course (even if the instructor was teaching in a manner that tended not to promote much learning), and why colleagues tend to avoid them (though a lack of collegiality could potentially also come into play). "I have high standards of teaching," we might hear one of our colleagues state from time to time, "but my students have low standards of learning." *ouch*

It is not this use of the term *high standards* that can lead to highly engaged and motivated students. Students tend to perform at their highest level when an instructor makes it clear that much will be expected of them and that the instructor is confident that they are up to the challenge. Positive ways in which you can set high standards for college students include the following:

- Revise your courses regularly to ensure that you are incorporating recent developments in your discipline and maintaining a level of expectation for your students that continually challenges them without being so far beyond their reach as to frustrate them.

- *midpoint check — this can be dif. online* Don't be afraid of midcourse corrections. For example, if you discover after the first several assignments that students are not being sufficiently challenged by the material, consider ways in which you can aim the assignments at a slightly higher level. Similarly, if the class as a whole does not do as well as you had thought they might, consider ways that you could develop different types of assignments or greater frequency of assignments so that your students will build to the level of expertise you expect.

- Consider involving the students themselves in setting some of the course's goals and timetable. People tend to participate far more eagerly and work more diligently at processes in which they have "buy in." By involving the students in deciding when certain projects are due, whether there will be an additional exam between units, where the cumulative assessments will occur, and so on, you may discover that the students both set and meet far higher standards than you may have set on your own. As you are not only teaching students about your discipline but also about how to continue learning actively throughout their lives, guiding them toward setting challenging goals and then meeting those goals should be an important lesson in every course. See Hofer (2006) for additional suggestions on this topic.

- One final approach to attaining high standards is to include multiple perspectives in as many of your units as possible. On the 2007 NSSE, for instance, students were asked to report how often they had "included diverse perspectives (different races, religions, genders, political beliefs, etc.) in class discussions or writing assignments" (see http://nsse.iub.edu/pdf/NSSE2007_US_English_paper.pdf). Part of meeting high standards thus involves an understanding that many topics can be approached from multiple points of view. Even where students cannot agree with certain points of view, it can enhance their engagement with a subject to explore it from the perspective of other people who bring very different experiences and assumptions to the discussion.

Return Assignments Promptly

As we discussed in Chapter 17, "Reducing Grade Anxiety," students sometimes need to be reminded that growth and improvement arise from correction and constructive criticism. If a coach or personal trainer never identified flaws in a person's performance, that person might be unable to overcome those flaws simply because there was no awareness that they existed. So it is with the criticism that we provide students regarding their work. To be effective, however, criticism needs to be promptly given, constructive in its nature, and clear in indicating how improvements could be made.

When assignments are not returned for several classes after they were turned in, students cannot benefit from the advice they contain in order to improve on their future work. When corrections on assignments are not constructive, they leave the reader only with a feeling that he or she has performed unsatisfactorily without gaining a sense that you believe the student can do better and, in fact, have so much confidence in the person that you are sharing a few helpful suggestions. When corrections only point out a student's errors without providing any clear guidance about how to improve, it is similar to telling a person that he or she is lost without giving any sense of which direction the person should now take. The identification of mistakes without constructive guidance tends to cause students to become more disengaged with a subject, not to embrace it and to learn more actively.

Encourage Student Discussion

Engaged students realize that learning does not end with the granting of a degree but is an important part of a person's entire life. You can reinforce this perspective by encouraging students to relate what they do in your course to activities elsewhere in their lives, such as material encountered in other courses, books or articles they have read, experiences they have had, and even songs, television shows, and movies with which they are familiar. Engaged students tend not to view information in compartments that are completely isolated from one another. Moreover, as students understand the application of material in one field to another and the relevance of what they learn in one discipline to other aspects of their lives, their learning ceases to be merely for the sake of the test and becomes a positive and highly desirable activity in which they engage for the personal benefits to their lives.

Support Student Involvement in Extracurricular Activities and Service Projects

A college student's learning is not limited to the classroom, studio, and laboratory. Students also gain a significant amount from their college experience through conversations in the residence hall, intramural and intercollegiate athletics, Greek life, participation in musical ensembles, performance in campus plays, leadership positions in clubs, service-learning projects, and a variety of other experiences. Because students vary widely in their learning styles, it is even possible that certain students gain more from participatory or experiential learning activities than they do from reading textbooks or listening to lectures. To the extent that such an approach is possible in your courses, therefore, active learning is promoted when you encourage students to participate in constructive activities outside of class. You can do so by demonstrating interest when students speak of such activities, going to student events whenever possible, or being flexible with course deadlines when they conflict with official sanctioned school activities.

———————

In a landmark essay from 1995, Robert Barr and John Tagg discussed the need for undergraduate education to move to a new paradigm that deemphasizes the amount that instructors *teach* and reemphasizes the extent to which students *learn*. Many aspects of administrative philosophy in higher education—from outcomes assessment to shared governance—have originated directly or indirectly from the paradigm change proposed by Barr and Tagg. Most important, the whole focus that colleges and universities have on student engagement is an outgrowth of the greater emphasis placed on active student learning encouraged by Barr, Tagg, and their successors. Academic initiatives as different as complete revisions of graduate school curricula and the across-the-curriculum movement at undergraduate institutions have resulted from a significant new commitment by college professors to enhancing learning through increased student engagement.

REFERENCES

Barr, R. B., & Tagg, J. (1995). From teaching to learning—A new paradigm for undergraduate education. *Change, 27*(6), 12–25.

Chickering, A. W., & Gamson, Z. F. (1987). Seven principles for good practice in undergraduate education. *AAHE Bulletin, 39*(7), 3–7.

Chickering, A. W., & Gamson, Z. F. (Eds.). (1991). *New directions for teaching and learning: No. 47. Applying the seven principles for good practice in undergraduate education.* San Francisco: Jossey-Bass.

Chickering, A. W., Gamson, Z. F., & Barsi, L. M. (1989). *Seven principles for good practice in undergraduate education: Faculty inventory.* Milwaukee, WI: Johnson Foundation.

Elbow, P., & Sorcinelli, M. D. (2006). How to enhance learning by using high-stakes and low-stakes writing. In W. J. McKeachie & M. Svinicki, *McKeachie's teaching tips: Strategies, research, and theory for college and university teachers* (12th ed., pp. 192–212). New York: Houghton Mifflin.

Hofer, B. K. (2006). Motivation in the college classroom. In W. J. McKeachie & M. Svinicki, *McKeachie's teaching tips: Strategies, research, and theory for college and university teachers* (12th ed., pp. 140–150). New York: Houghton Mifflin.

Millis, B. J., & Cottell, P. G., Jr. (1998). *Cooperative learning for higher education faculty.* Phoenix, AZ: American Council on Education/Oryx Press.

RESOURCES

Bonwell, C. C., & Eison, J. A. (1991). *Active learning: Creating excitement in the classroom.* San Francisco: Jossey-Bass.

Fink, L. D. (2003). *Creating significant learning experiences: An integrated approach to designing college courses.* San Francisco: Jossey-Bass.

Johnson, D. W., Johnson, R. T., & Smith, K. A. (1991). *Active learning in the college classroom.* Edina, MN: Interaction.

Kuh, G. D., Kinzie, J., Schuh, J. H., & Whitt, E. J. (2005). *Assessing conditions to enhance educational effectiveness: The inventory for student engagement and success.* San Francisco: Jossey-Bass.

Kuh, G. D., Kinzie, J., Schuh, J. H., Whitt, E. J., & Associates. (2005). *Student success in college: Creating conditions that matter.* San Francisco: Jossey-Bass.

Leamnson, R. (1999). *Thinking about teaching and learning: Developing habits of learning with first year college and university students.* Sterling, VA: Stylus.

Meyers, C., & Jones, T. B. (1993). *Promoting active learning: Strategies for the college classroom.* San Francisco: Jossey-Bass.

Sandeen, A. (2003). *Enhancing student engagement on campus*. Lanham, MD: University Press of America.

Silberman, M. (1996). *Active learning: 101 strategies to teach any subject*. Boston: Allyn & Bacon.

Sutherland, T. E., & Bonwell, C. C. (Eds.). (1996). *New directions for teaching and learning: No. 67. Using active learning in college classes: A range of options for faculty*. San Francisco: Jossey-Bass.

Svinicki, M. D. (2004). *Learning and motivation in the postsecondary classroom*. Bolton, MA: Anker.

Weimer, M. (2002). *Learning-centered teaching: Five key changes to practice*. San Francisco: Jossey-Bass.

19

ADDRESSING ACADEMIC MISCONDUCT

Student academic misconduct covers a broad range of unacceptable behaviors that can occur on research projects, in coursework, and elsewhere within academic programs. At most institutions, definitions of student academic misconduct include but are not limited to the following:

- Plagiarism
- Cheating on assignments and tests
- Submission of the same paper or product of research in multiple courses without permission (that is, self-plagiarism)
- Theft of an examination
- Misrepresentation of identity (for instance, taking a test on behalf of another student or assuming a false identity to gain access to a restricted facility)
- Unauthorized altering of a grade
- Falsifying the results of research, scholarship, or creative activities
- Improper treatment of animals while conducting research
- Improper treatment of human subjects while conducting research
- Failure to follow institutional procedures when engaged in a project that involves human or animal subjects
- Conflict of interest (such as engaging in a research project that results in inappropriate personal financial gain)
- Academic sabotage that interferes with the scholarship of another individual
- Abetting the attempts of other students to perform any of the above actions

Almost certainly your college or university already has a policy in place that addresses most, if not all, of these activities. In cases of academic misconduct, it is important to know this policy well and to understand how you are required to handle each specific situation *before* it occurs. The reason why a full understanding of the policy is so important is that the policies of different institutions can vary dramatically due to different philosophies about the best approach to academic misconduct and, if you are unaware of your own institution's views on these matters, you could inadvertently proceed in a way that greatly compounds the problem, possibly even turning it into your problem rather than the student's problem. How could this happen? Well, some institutions place their pedagogical mission above all other concerns and require first offenses to be treated as an opportunity to instruct the student about proper academic practice rather than as a situation calling for punitive action. Other institutions see their primary duty as upholding high academic standards, and so they adopt a zero-tolerance policy toward academic misconduct, imposing stiff penalties even for a first offense. In addition, some schools—particularly those placing a great deal of emphasis on an honor code—require a faculty member to refrain from intervening directly in a case of suspected academic misconduct. The faculty member is directed to file a report about the incident and to allow a committee, often a committee of the student's peers, to investigate. This approach is felt to be much fairer by some institutions as it accords rights to both the accuser and the accused, frees students from the possibility of unfair treatment by an individual professor, and frees the professor from allegations of defaming the student's character. (The incident report is, in these cases, merely a request to investigate a situation, not a formal accusation.) At other institutions, however, the professor is required to intervene directly in cases of suspected academic misconduct. In these situations, it is felt that no one knows the source material and methods of the subject as well as the professor, and outsiders would complicate rather than improve an initial investigation. The professor is thus instructed to meet individually with the student, discuss the alleged misconduct, and give the student an opportunity to admit wrongdoing, declare his or her innocence, or provide a clearer context for the situation. Only after this informal discussion takes place between the professor and the student is the matter then referred elsewhere on campus, such as to the office of the dean of students.

Whatever your institution's policy about how to handle academic misconduct, it is important to realize that some of the expectations we take for granted as faculty members are actually quite confusing to many college students. For instance, students may have been rewarded throughout much of their earlier education for their ability to absorb and repeat the insights of others, and suddenly they find themselves expected to provide citations for information that they earlier "just assumed that everyone knew." As a result, until students understand proper practices at the college level, they are likely to err either on the side of overcitation, including a footnote after every single sentence regardless of whether it simply contains common knowledge, or undercitation, believing that including a work in their bibliography is sufficient to indicate that it was consulted unless they directly quote the author. In a similar way, students may be confused when we expect them to apply to one course what they have learned in another but not to reuse the products of that learning, such as papers or creative works, in more than one class without permission. For this reason, it can be extremely important for college professors not to assume that students already know the "obvious" about matters of academic misconduct. Rather, we should always consider it part of our teaching role to help train the next generation of conscientious scholars. Most orientation and first-year experience programs do, it is true, include a session on the institution's honor code or plagiarism policy, but a single discussion of this highly complex issue is rarely sufficient. The standards of good academic conduct are important enough to be clarified and reinforced frequently, just as it is important to help students develop their abilities to conduct research according to accepted methods and policies.

Some of the ways in which college professors can help reinforce good standards of academic practice include:

- *Modeling desirable practices yourself.* You would not, of course, submit an article for publication that does not adequately cite its sources or largely duplicates what you have stated in other publications. But what about your standards in developing syllabi and other course materials? What about PowerPoint or Keynote presentations that you use in class? Do you include images that are under copyright but that have been downloaded from the Internet? Do you properly cite these sources? By following good practices in these cases you will have an excellent opportunity to explain to your students the differences between use of an item that is in the public domain and one that is subject to protection and citation. You will also have the added advantage of avoiding the accusation, if you ever allege that a student is guilty of academic misconduct, that your class was merely following the example you set in your own materials.

- *Referring students to sources that can clarify matters of appropriate academic standards for them.* There are numerous websites and books available that can help students identify behaviors that might constitute academic misconduct and thus avoid these actions or activities. Works such as Lipson (2004), Menager-Beeley and Paulos (2006), and Stern (2006) can be useful as ancillary materials in courses where students are either studying composition or making their first significant efforts at independent research papers. In addition, so many faculty members and writers have already developed websites dealing with plagiarism and proper citation that most faculty members will not need to create their own handouts on these subjects (just be sure to cite the original source!). For instance, you might wish to include a reference on a syllabus that refers your students to such sites as http://nutsandbolts.washcoll.edu/plagiarism .html, http://owl.english.purdue.edu/owl/resource/589/01, or www .winthrop.edu/english/plagiarism.htm. Indiana University Blooming-ton's School of Education (www.indiana.edu/~istd/plagiarism_test .html) offers an excellent online quiz dealing with plagiarism; students can check their answers to see whether they can identify what constitutes proper use of information that is common knowledge, what constitutes word-for-word plagiarism, and what constitutes paraphrasing plagiarism. In addition, a website at George Mason University (http://wac.gmu.edu/supporting/plagiarism.php) provides links to numerous additional sites that help faculty members address this important issue. With the availability of these well-developed materials on avoiding plagiarism and academic misconduct, you'll certainly find at least one that suits the needs of your courses without having to reinvent the wheel.

- *Taking full advantage of on-campus resources.* Most colleges and universities have a writing center, research office, and student affairs office, all of which tend to be quite familiar with effective ways of explaining what plagiarism is, when citations are needed, what protocols are expected for scholarly projects, and the like. Partnering with these offices can be an extremely effective way to help students in your courses understand what is expected of scholars in their research and reinforce the idea that academic misconduct is not just your personal pet peeve, but a serious concern throughout colleges and universities everywhere. Frequently those who work in these campus offices wonder why they are so rarely asked to lend their expertise until after a problem has already been identified. It is to your students' benefit to take full advantage of these campus resources as you teach your classes not just the material of the course, but also how to conduct research honorably and effectively.

Use of Human or Animal Subjects

Special procedures come into play whenever a researcher is planning to work on a project that involves human or animal subjects. Care must be taken to ensure that sentient creatures are not treated cruelly, that any sacrifice they make is warranted by the significance of the project, and that any lasting effects of the research are either eliminated or absolutely essential due to the important nature of the work. Federal law requires that any institution in the United States that makes use of animals for research or instructional purposes must establish an institutional animal care and use committee (IACUC). This committee is intended to supervise all aspects of the institution's procedures with animals, evaluate their appropriateness, and make recommendations for improvement. If your institution does not yet have an IACUC, a variety of resources on establishing such a committee are available at www.iacuc.org/index.htm. An institution's IACUC will usually work in cooperation with an institutional review board (IRB) that reviews and approves either all proposals for research projects or at least those that deal with human or animal subjects. IRBs are an institution's first line of defense in ensuring that research projects adhere to accepted standards and protocols, including all policies on acceptable academic conduct. In addition, an IRB will review research protocols to make certain that proposed projects do not unduly put at risk those who participate in the project and that all who do take part are aware of their rights. Some changes in evolving standards for research have made it even more important for proposed projects to be examined by a review board that is aware of these changes. In the past, scholars in the natural sciences were accustomed to submitting research proposals to an IRB, whereas those who worked in the humanities and the social or behavioral sciences did so far less frequently. But it has now become a requirement for all types of research involving human subjects, including the collection of oral histories and the distribution of most types of surveys, to be reviewed by an institutional panel before the project is approved. Students (and even on occasion faculty members) who completed large research projects that relied on, for instance, oral histories have had their findings invalidated or their work rendered unpublishable because they did not obtain prior approval from an IRB. For this reason, having students develop a proposal, submitting it to an IRB, and then modifying the research protocol based on this institutional review is not only a good pedagogical practice for instructors and advisors, but it can also prevent the student from receiving an unwelcome surprise late in his or her academic career.

Use Multiple Drafts to Promote Honesty and Originality

One of the most effective ways of promoting academic honesty and good research strategies is to require students to turn in their papers in multiple drafts. Not only does this approach make it much more difficult for students to purchase completed term papers from unscrupulous vendors of so-called research services, but it also gives you an opportunity to spot weak documentation or logic before a student's final draft is due. For instance, if you suspect that a student has simply used "cut and paste" to insert a sentence or more from a website into a work in progress, you will have an opportunity to address the problem with a note like the following:

> This sentence has been taken, without attribution, from the article on Werner Heisenberg that appears at www.wikipedia.org. Not only is Wikipedia an inappropriate source for a college-level paper (please go over the information I distributed earlier this term on the importance of using peer-reviewed sources for scholarly research), but the lack of appropriate citation here would be regarded as serious academic misconduct in your final draft. I think you should go through your entire draft, find all other instances of unattributed material taken from any source, and meet with me to review the differences between word-for-word plagiarism, paraphrasing plagiarism, and material that is safely regarded as common knowledge or in the public domain.

As we saw in Chapter 18, "Promoting Student Engagement," asking students to submit multiple drafts of a paper can also cause them to become more involved with a topic and increase their mastery of the material.

Use Electronic Resources to Reinforce Good Academic Conduct

Just as technology provides students with new opportunities to "cut and paste" material from websites and previously written papers into research projects and give the impression that these plagiarized passages are their own work, so does technology give faculty members new protection from such deception. Websites such as turnitin.com and catchitfirst.com, as well as classroom grading systems such as Scriptum, compare student work to millions of online pages, reporting passages where similarities appear to be more than coincidental. In addition, turnitin.com also compares the student's paper to all of the other student papers in its database to report occasions where one member of your course may have "recycled" material from a colleague, scans for similar passages in thousands of newspapers, books, and scholarly journals, and (if you choose) can allow other members of the class to offer peer review of a student's work in progress. Faculty members can choose to grade and comment on student work electronically through turnitin.com, and the website has been fully integrated into such course management software as Blackboard, Moodle, and Angel. These electronic solutions can be used not only to detect plagiarism but also to point out citation problems before students have completed their papers. As a result, they not only help teach appropriate research strategies, but they can also penalize academic misconduct at the same time.

Use Courses to Promote Responsible Research

One other approach you can take to avoid academic misconduct is to offer a course on appropriate documentation, determining proper research protocols, and other aspects of good scholarly practices that students are required to complete before engaging in a significant research project. The course may be offered in either a traditional classroom format or as an electronic tutorial. Examples of online tutorials focusing on academic integrity and avoiding plagiarism may be found at York University of Canada (www.yorku.ca/tutorial/academic_integrity/index .html) and at Idaho State University (www.isu.edu/library/research/ait/ aitintropage.html). A more comprehensive tutorial, including a focus on ethical issues in research, health and safety concerns, philosophical implications of advanced research, and how to follow institutional protocols, is offered by the University of Sunderland (www.grs.sund.ac.uk/grssite/ database/students/Induction/PGR_ONLINEMATERIALSv4.htm). Having such a training program in place is often a requirement for eligibility imposed by certain foundations and grants agencies; it may also be a requirement for accreditation by a discipline-specific accrediting body. Even if such requirements do not apply to your discipline or institution, however, requiring all majors or graduate students to undergo a comprehensive tutorial in the ethical standards for research is appropriate to our pedagogical mission in higher education, and this may be an idea that you wish to discuss with your colleagues to see whether it can be initiated or enhanced as part of your department's curriculum.

Academic misconduct has been a perennial challenge ever since colleges and universities first existed. As new technologies appear, new opportunities arise for students to cheat on exams and plagiarize the ideas of others, but new techniques for detection of these practices also appear. An appropriate response to academic misconduct should not only be to penalize it when it occurs but also to teach and reinforce *appropriate* academic procedures as part of our central mission at all institutions of higher education.

REFERENCES

Lipson, C. (2004). *Doing honest work in college: How to prepare citations, avoid plagiarism, and achieve real academic success.* Chicago: University of Chicago Press.

Menager-Beeley, R., & Paulos, L. (2006). *Understanding plagiarism: A student guide to writing your own work.* New York: Houghton Mifflin.

Stern, L. (2006). *What every student should know about avoiding plagiarism.* New York: Longman.

RESOURCES

Decoo, W. (2002). *Crisis on campus: Confronting academic misconduct.* Cambridge, MA: MIT Press.

Hamilton, N. W. (2002). *Academic ethics: Problems and materials on professional conduct and shared governance.* Westport, CT: American Council on Education/Praeger.

Lathrop, A., & Foss, K. (2005). *Guiding students from cheating and plagiarism to honesty and integrity: Strategies for change.* Portsmouth, NH: Libraries Unlimited.

Marsh, B. (2007). *Plagiarism: Alchemy and remedy in higher education.* Albany, NY: State University of New York Press.

McKeachie, W. J., & Svinicki, M. (2006). What to do about cheating. In W. J. McKeachie & M. Svinicki, *McKeachie's teaching tips: Strategies, research, and theory for college and university teachers* (12th ed., pp. 113–122). New York: Houghton Mifflin.

Whitley, B. E., Jr., & Keith-Spiegel, P. (2002). *Academic dishonesty: An educator's guide.* Mahwah, NJ: Erlbaum.

20

MAINTAINING APPROPRIATE FACULTY-STUDENT RELATIONS

The relationship that students have with faculty members is different from most other types of working relationships we encounter. Colleges and universities spend a great deal of energy debating whether students should be regarded as "customers." Those who are horrified by such a notion—including, it seems, the vast majority of faculty members—believe that the-customer-is-always-right mentality degrades the academic enterprise, encourages institutions to pander to their students' basest motives, and makes it increasingly difficult to achieve high academic standards. But those who advocate in favor of this idea—including, it seems, a large number of administrators—point out that students pay for and receive a service, have an increasing array of options in higher education, and deserve to be treated with the consideration that is implied by the phrase *customer service*. Aspects found in both these perspectives have some merit, but the difficulty is that the simple equation "the students are our customers" creates an ambiguous metaphor. "What *type* of customer and what *type* of business do you have in mind?" we might ask. "Are you thinking of a customer in a restaurant or department store who expects to be served, to have his or her desires met to the last degree, and to be treated with a great deal of deference? Or are you thinking more of the customer with a health club membership who cannot reach the level of fitness and weight loss that he or she wants without a great deal of personal effort, hard work, and sacrifice?" There are, in other words, many different kinds of customer relationships, and our response to the idea that students should be seen as customers is likely to depend on the sort of customer we tend to think of first.

Perhaps a better way of viewing the relationship that a student has with a professor is to approach it, not in terms of the customer-business relationship, but in terms of the client-profession relationship. The expectations that we have and the ways that we behave are different when we are in a restaurant, department store, or service station from what they are when we are meeting with a doctor, lawyer, or accountant. In a business relationship, it is our *desires* that are of paramount importance; in a professional relationship, it is our *needs* that take precedence. Consider the following two scenarios. In the first, a customer enters a restaurant. That customer is then free to order whatever he or she would like, even if the order would seem to many people to be irrational or not in the customer's best interest. For instance, if the customer decides to forgo the entrée and eat five desserts instead, it is the rare server who will suggest that this meal might be detrimental to the customer's waistline. Even if the customer's order appears to be wholly idiosyncratic—"I'm on a diet where I only eat foods that begin with the letter 'p', so bring me the pepperoni pizza, a pair of pears, and a pint of Pepsi."—any server who wishes to remain employed will honor these strange requests with grace, good will, and efficiency. That result will be quite different, however, if the customer exhibits the same behavior with his or her physician. In our second scenario, the same individual enters a doctor's office and says to the physician, "I'm interested only in medications beginning with the letter 'z' today, so I'd like a prescription for Zoloft, Zocor, and Zyrtec, and then please bring me a sample of Zantac." The doctor's response will be completely different from that of the server in the restaurant. The doctor is far more likely to say something like, "Let's just hold on a minute. First, I need to diagnose what your problem is, and then I'll determine what I believe you *need*."

Client-profession relationships involve a set of rights and responsibilities that can overlap with those that we find in a customer-business relationship, but at times are quite distinct. For example, in a client-profession relationship, the client has the right to:

- Be treated with professionalism and courtesy
- Have his or her needs understood and addressed in an appropriate and professional manner
- Receive reasonable accommodation based on his or her personal situation
- Suffer no harm through abuse of the professional relationship
- End the professional relationship if the client so chooses

In return, however, the client also has certain responsibilities in this relationship, such as the responsibility to:

- Follow the instructions or advice of the professional as closely as possible
- Refrain from insisting that the professional pursue a course of action that conflicts with his or her professional judgment or standards
- Expect only that a high level of professional effort will be exerted, not that a particular result will be guaranteed

We can see how these rights and responsibilities come into play if we return to our example of the relationship between a patient and a physician. In this situation, the patient has the right to be treated in a polite and professional manner. Each doctor will differ in his or her bedside manner, but it is no longer regarded as acceptable for physicians to be surly, demeaning to their patients, or indifferent to their suffering. The physician is expected to listen to the patient's account of his or her symptoms, perform appropriate tests when they are necessary, and use his or her training and experience to determine the best course of action, depending on the patient's individual challenges (such as an inability to swallow large pills or difficulty in understanding complex instructions). One of the statements found in the Hippocratic oath is usually paraphrased as "First, do no harm," and so the physician should refrain from any action that is not in the best interests of the patient, including abuse of their professional relationship for personal pleasure or profit. Finally, the client always has the right to a second opinion or even to select a new doctor if the patient feels that his or her care has not been adequate.

At the same time that the patient has these rights, however, certain responsibilities also come into play. The patient must follow the prescribed treatment, taking his or her medication as directed, altering diet or lifestyle where necessary, and keeping appointments for follow-up. The patient mustn't pressure the physician to prescribe a medication or treatment that the physician regards as inappropriate or attempt to recast the professional relationship as a friendship, romance, or business partnership when it is not. Finally, the patient should expect to be *treated*, not necessarily *cured*. No physician can claim to cure 100 percent of the illnesses or conditions presented by his or her patients. The patient's own behavior, the nature of the illness or condition, and sheer chance all play a role in whether the patient's situation will improve. These rights and responsibilities have parallels in other professional relationships as well. For instance, a lawyer can work on a client's behalf but cannot promise acquittal or success in a civil suit. An architect should be expected to use professional training and judgment but cannot overcome the force of gravity or the limitations of certain materials. And a student's relationship with a college professor involves the same types of rights and responsibilities, each of which we'll now consider in turn.

Treat Students with Professionalism and Courtesy

Your manner of interacting with other people is likely to be quite different from that of other faculty members in your department. You may be a natural introvert, a natural extrovert, a learned extrovert, or some combination that is hard to classify. You may find it easy or difficult to strike up a conversation with a stranger. You may have been attracted to higher education as a profession because you like working closely with colleagues and meeting large numbers of new students each year or you may have chosen this career because it was the chance to pursue important ideas, not to interact with people, that you saw as appealing. You may be impressed by how quickly students learn or be put off with how little they already know. No matter who you are, there is a way for you to be the person you are naturally and without affectation in your relationship with students. Nevertheless, as an academic professional, your academic freedom and your right to be yourself do not allow you to treat your students rudely, with contempt, or indifferently. Your right to "be who you are" ends, in other words, when it comes in conflict with a student's client-profession rights to learn in an environment that encourages his or her own development.

Striking the precisely appropriate relationship with students can be challenging for college professors. If you are naturally gregarious, you may find yourself erring too far in the direction of allowing your students to view you as a friend. The problem with developing too close a relationship with students is that ultimately you must make serious, professional judgments about them. As we've already seen, the time for an exam arrives or an important grade must be assigned, and the college professor who has tried to be a "buddy" with students is likely to hear, "But I thought you were my friend." Young faculty members, who may not be much older than the students they teach, often find it particularly challenging to maintain appropriate professional boundaries. After all, it wasn't that long ago that they themselves were in a situation very similar to their students, and they may sympathize with the difficulties the students are facing. Despite this temptation, however, it is extremely inadvisable to allow that line of professionalism to be crossed. Once a position of authority is surrendered, it is almost impossible to reestablish it if it becomes necessary to do so because, for instance, there is a lack of discipline in the class or the quality of the students' work declines. Younger faculty members may wish to consider ways in which they can establish quite clearly the level of the professional relationship they have with their students. Dressing in a manner appropriate to a business or professional setting rather than in the casual manner quite common at colleges and universities can help younger faculty members clarify their professorial identity in the eyes of their students. Moreover, meeting with students one-on-one or in small groups for class discussions is best done in your office or at the library rather than at a pub or at a private residence. (For more information on maintaining proper relationships in individual meetings with students, see Chapter 15, "Teaching One-on-One.") At campus events, students may want professors to dance with them or engage in games and activities that may, either to an observer or to the students themselves, distort the student-teacher relationship. Each instructor should consider very carefully whether agreeing to these requests is advisable. Professors who find themselves wondering, "But what harm can it really do?" often end up learning the answer to this question through unpleasant experiences. A good rule of thumb is to remember what we explored earlier: Your role with your students is similar to that which your doctor, lawyer, or architect plays with respect to you. Is the activity in which you are asked to engage one in which you would think it was appropriate for your doctor to engage in with you while still maintaining your professional relationship? Is the activity one in which you would be perfectly comfortable for your supervisor(s), your colleagues, and the members of your family to witness or learn about? If your answer to either of these questions is no, it is probably an activity that you should avoid. The essential principle to keep in mind in these situations is:

When dealing with students, your goal as a professor should always be to adopt a tone that is friendly, not familiar.

Another important part of establishing a good professional relationship with your students is getting to know them for who they are and for what they need. A first-generation college student may have substantially different expectations about what college will be like from a student whose parents are themselves college professors. A student with a diagnosed and certified learning disability will have significantly different needs from a student who learns quickly and easily in a wide variety of environments. The greater diversity of the student body today means that many students have challenges—the need to work full-time while going to school part-time, for instance—that require special attention and, at times, appropriate accommodations. Just as not all college professors are alike, so is it important not to assume that all students are cast from the same mold. It is part of our professional responsibility as college professors to acknowledge these differences and, to the extent possible, help meet students' needs so that they might learn to the best of their potential.

Address Student Needs in an Appropriate Manner

Every faculty member is familiar with the common student practice of presenting excuses about why an assignment is not complete, a class was missed, or a test must be postponed. It is a natural impulse for people to attribute their own failures and irresponsibility to situations beyond their control. Faculty members also tend to be quite familiar with the type of student who admits being unprepared but then assumes that his or her honesty will earn an extension. To be sure, professors are entitled to impose whatever standards they regard as professionally appropriate, to enforce deadlines, and to hold students to the terms outlined in the syllabus (see Chapter 11, "Writing an Effective Course Syllabus"). Nevertheless, faculty members should also remember that students will always be diverse in their talents and their prior knowledge of the material they encounter in any given course. For this reason, there is one other essential principle that can be important for college professors to consider:

The job of the college professor is to teach those who do not yet understand, not simply to enjoy the company of those who already know. For this reason, it is no more appropriate for a faculty member to be judgmental and dismissive of a student's lack of knowledge than it is for a physician to blame patients for their illnesses or for attorneys to disparage clients for their problems.

When you discover a student whom you are tempted to dismiss as woefully underprepared in your discipline, it can make all the difference in the world if you regard the situation as an opportunity to serve rather than as an imposition on your time. Many college professors would gladly mentor the brilliant students for free; it is with the struggling student that we earn our salaries.

Provide Reasonable Accommodation Based on Students' Personal Situations

No two people have identical learning styles. The student who learns best in a traditional lecture where there is ample time to think about and digest the points raised is likely to feel frustrated by a large number of break-out sessions and hands-on activities. Conversely, the student who learns best by experience may feel poorly served by having to endure too many lectures. Because of this difference, varying the teaching technique that you use in a course—providing opportunities for auditory, visual, and experiential learners all to succeed—is a perfectly reasonable accommodation that excellent teachers gladly embrace. Moreover, with the passage of the Americans with Disabilities Act in 1990, college professors have been called on to make accommodations for a variety of student challenges, from physical impairments to a wide range of learning disorders. Faculty members are sometimes reluctant to undertake the extra work required to provide an alternative form of examination for a student who is diagnosed as unable to take multiple-choice tests effectively or to write essays under time constraints, regarding these abilities as essential to success in the discipline. Almost every college or university has an office that handles issues relating to student disabilities that can ensure that each disability is appropriately documented and that clear guidance is provided about the types of accommodations instructors should make. Despite these measures, however, some college professors remain unconvinced that learning disabilities are problems worthy of their respect and attention. "I've just been informed that one of my students has a learning disability that prevents the student from being able to write long and coherent essays," you might hear a professor say. "Isn't that the condition that we used to call 'stupid'?" Although these attitudes are diminishing, they still pose impediments for students at all too many colleges and universities. The key issue is this: is the learning disorder a condition that prevents the student from mastering the material at all or from demonstrating mastery in one manner but not in every manner? In other words, no one would feel that a student who was blind was "stupid" simply because the student could not read a standard text; the student may well be perfectly capable of learning the material through recordings, electronic text readers, or other accommodations. In a similar manner, a student who is prone to anxiety attacks in crowded or stressful situations may not be able to complete a final exam under ordinary test conditions but may be perfectly capable of demonstrating that he or she has learned the material under other conditions. Certainly, there are courses of study that cannot be open to a blind student because technology has not yet been developed that allows them to perform some task essential to that field. Flight programs, for instance, usually have mandatory vision standards, and certain health fields require their members to have an adequate level of sight. In the same way, there are some disciplines for which the student who is prone to anxiety in stressful, crowded conditions may not be suited, such as emergency health care management. The key issue must always be to distinguish *essential* abilities from *desirable* abilities. If a student is documented with a severe inability to understand quantitative concepts, certain disciplines may be unable to make adequate accommodations, while others may find it relatively easy to teach their methods, principles, and information using nonquantitative methods.

Do Not Abuse the Professor-Student Relationship

It is unethical for a therapist to develop a romantic relationship with a patient. The patient has placed a high degree of trust in the therapist, and that trust is violated when the professional relationship becomes transformed into a personal liaison. Because, as we have seen, a client always has the right to end the professional relationship if it is no longer serving his or her needs, romantic entanglements can infringe on that right or ability. Moreover, even if the patient does not view it in this way immediately, there is an implicit "power differential" between the therapist and the patient: the therapist has a skill the patient needs, and the patient may later begin to feel that the therapist has used this unequal footing to his or her advantage. Finally, people are apt to reveal information in a romantic situation or in a professional situation that is not suitable for the other type of environment; having your therapist and your lover be the same person means that the individual in either of those roles has access to information that you may not want someone in that role to have.

Substitute the word *professor* for *therapist* and the word *student* for *patient* in the above paragraph, and you encounter many of the difficulties that arise through abuse of the professor-student relationship. Of course, institutions of higher education vary widely in their tolerance of amorous or sexual contact between students and professors. Some colleges and universities ban all non-professional relations entirely; they consider it a violation of an instructor's professional ethics to fraternize with any student at the institution, even if the student is not now and has never been in the professor's own courses or otherwise under the professor's supervision. At the other extreme, some colleges and universities regard the right of personal association to be paramount and point to case law striking down many institutions' bans on faculty-student relations. Most institutions fall somewhere in the middle. Either they prohibit liaisons with students who are directly under the professor's supervision, require that these relationships be reported to a central office, or strongly discourage but do not officially ban such relationships. At the very least, you will want to follow your institution's policies in these matters. Even beyond what is required, however, as a professional you should always regard what is in your students' best interests as your overarching concern. Those interests are rarely served in the long run by amorous or sexual relations with a faculty member.

In a similar way, it is inappropriate for faculty members to abuse the relationship that they have with students through other unsuitable affiliations. For instance, it is never acceptable to profit from your own students by abusing your professional standing with them. Requiring students in your class to purchase a textbook that you have written, entering into business relations with current students, or serving as an advisor for a club that buys items from a firm in which you have a financial interest are all practices that are banned at some schools and inadvisable at any school. Even if you have written the best possible textbook (perhaps the *only* textbook) in a discipline, you should avoid profiting directly from your students through sales of this work. As the author, you may be able to provide free copies of the book to those who are enrolled in your class. You may be able to donate back to the institution any proceeds that you made from sale of this work. Or you may be able to find some other alternative that frees students from even the perception that you have used your professional role to pressure them into increasing your income.

Understand the Students' Right to Switch Advisors, Major Professors, or Instructors

Every now and then a student, possibly even someone with whom you believe that you have an excellent relationship, will choose to drop your course, choose a different advisor, or select someone else to supervise his or her thesis. It may be hard to avoid taking this rejection personally, but the best professors accept the situation professionally and with good grace. All of us have been in situations where we believe our needs may be addressed better elsewhere. Our doctor may be perfectly competent and excellently trained, but we may feel that our personalities are not properly suited. Our attorney may be extremely professional, but it is difficult to travel to that person's office on a workday because it is across town. Our architect may have won a large number of prestigious awards, but the style of the homes he or she designs no longer suits us. In each of these cases, we feel free to terminate the professional relationship for any reason, or for no reason at all other than our personal preference. Our students have that same right. When they bring us a form to drop one of our courses or to switch advisors, it is inappropriate to use our professional positions to try pressuring them to change their minds or to feel bad about their decisions. If dropping the class means that the student will not be able to graduate on time or if changing advisors means that the student will have to switch major programs, it is our professional duty to mention this fact. But demeaning the student's choice or responding to it as though it were a personal insult rather than a professional matter is never acceptable.

Students Are Obligated to Follow Their Professors' Instructions

Just as students have a number of rights in their relationship with a professor, so do they have certain important responsibilities. One of a client's primary responsibilities is to follow the instructions of a professional if he or she hopes to be successful in reaching a goal. A patient who refuses to take a prescribed medication should not expect to get well. A client who does not follow the attorney's advice is unlikely to have the sentence reduced. In the same way, a student who does not adhere to the course of study designed by the professor is unlikely to learn very much. Required assignments should not be regarded by students merely as optional or to be completed only at their convenience. Attendance policies are usually created for a very good reason. Just as the person who joins a health club but who never attends or does not follow the advice of the trainer is unlikely to lose weight, so too do students learn not by *enrolling* in college but by following their professors' instructions.

Students Are Obligated to Refrain from Engaging Their Professors in Inappropriate Activity

Just as college teachers have an obligation to avoid abusing their professional relationship with their students, so do students have an obligation not to put their teachers into situations that could compromise their professional ethics. Make no mistake about it: there is no justification in a faculty member's saying, "But it was the student who initiated the relationship, not me!" As professionals (and, in the vast majority of cases, as adults who are older and thus should be more mature than our students), it is our responsibility to say no and to prevent a relationship from veering too far into inappropriate territory. Nevertheless, despite the greater responsibility that a faculty member has, both sides in a client-profession relationship have an obligation to preserve the primary nature of the relationship and not to coerce or tempt the other party into inappropriate activity. Students should understand that many of the activities that they consider to be sheer harmless fun could jeopardize the career of the professor. There is a certain line in a professional relationship that neither party should ever cross.

Students Are Obligated to Expect Their Professors' Best Efforts, Not a Guaranteed Result

Students have a right to expect us to make our best efforts on their behalf. Nevertheless, whether a student succeeds in our courses is at least as much dependent on his or her own efforts as it is on the quality of our instruction. Your students, therefore, have the right to expect you to remain current in your field and to understand the pedagogical techniques that are most conducive to learning in your courses; they do not have a right to an A in the course. Your students have the right to expect that their advisors will work on their behalf to recommend courses best suited to each student's individual needs and academic program; they do not have the right to expect you to waive requirements for them, get them into courses that are already enrolled to capacity, or negotiate on their behalf with other professors (see Chapter 34, "Serving as an Academic Advisor"). Your students have the right to expect their mentors to make the best possible efforts to identify and help seek the students' admission to suitable opportunities for employment, graduate school, professional school, and the like; they do not have the right to expect you to guarantee their employment or admission to the graduate program of their dreams (see Chapter 35, "Serving as a Mentor"). Your students have the right to expect you to offer them a learning environment in which their motivation is encouraged and to not burden them with impediments or disincentives to excellent performance; they do not have a right to expect you to motivate them without any effort on their part or to reward or "stroke" them for every exertion, no matter how minor. The doctor does not give the patient a trophy simply for showing up for an appointment, and the attorney is unlikely to praise the client who makes occasional efforts to avoid breaking the law. Just as our obligations are similar to those of such other professionals, so should our expectations be from the clients we serve: our students.

Viewing the relationship between students and professors as more similar to a client-profession relationship than to a customer-business relationship serves as a constructive guide in how best to develop those relationships. Your own interpersonal style will affect exactly how you relate to those whom you teach. It is perfectly acceptable to be perceived as the faculty member who is friendly, engaging, and approachable, as long as you are not perceived as being the friend of one particular student or a small group that does not include every student you meet. It is perfectly acceptable to be perceived as a somewhat intimidating eminence, as long as you do not appear to be so intimidating that you are completely unapproachable or that you seek to preserve your eminence through the disdain that you show to "mere students." No matter how skilled the physician or attorney, the doctor is irrelevant without patients, as is the lawyer without clients. The brilliant researcher who ends up without students because of having been too close to some or too condescending to others will in the end prove to be a professor who no longer has a profession.

RESOURCES

Aguinis, H., Nesler, M. S., Quigley, B. M., Lee, S.-J., & Tedeschi, J. T. (1996). Power bases of faculty supervisors and educational outcomes for graduate students. *Journal of Higher Education, 67*(3), 267–297.

Deresiewicz, W. (2007). Love on campus: Why we should understand and even encourage a certain sort of erotic intensity between student and professor. *American Scholar, 76,* 36–46.

Grauerholz, E. (1989). Sexual harassment of women professors by students: Exploring the dynamics of power, authority, and gender in a university setting. *Sex Roles, 21*(11–12), 789–801.

Pascarella, E. T., & Terenzini, P. T. (2005). *How college affects students: A third decade of research* (Vol. 2). San Francisco: Jossey-Bass.

Plaut, S. M. (1993). Boundary issues in teacher-student relationships. *Journal of Sex and Marital Therapy, 19*(3), 210–219.

Wilson, P. (1994). The professor/student relationship: Key factors in minority student performance and achievement. *Canadian Journal of Native Studies, 14*(2), 305–317.

Zachary, L. J. (2000). *The mentor's guide: Facilitating effective learning relationships.* San Francisco: Jossey-Bass.

21

DEALING WITH STUDENT PROBLEMS AND PROBLEM STUDENTS

Throughout our careers as college professors, students may confront us with all kinds of challenges and difficulties. Some will not complete their work when it is due. Others will have excuses about why they cannot fulfill the various requirements of our courses. Some will have their parents intervene when they feel that a grade is too low or an exception needs to be made. Still others will cut class repeatedly and then show up at our offices asking, "Did I miss anything important?" These are the perennial and relatively insignificant problems that all college teachers encounter from time to time. Human nature being what it is, there is unlikely to be any scarcity of sick grandparents, missed emails, malfunctioning alarm clocks, and any of the myriad other justifications we receive for late or inadequate work. Yesterday's dog that ate the homework has become today's hard drive that mysteriously crashes every time a major assignment is due. Usually we simply point to the policies outlined on our syllabi, send a sympathy card or note of concern to the student's parents whenever we've been told that a grandparent is seriously ill (which prompts a reply of "I have no idea what you're talking about" in a surprising number of cases), and consider such challenges to be a regular part of our work. In this chapter, we're going to explore a range of more serious challenges when stronger intervention is necessary and which may tax our resources as college professors.

A *student problem* is a nonacademic difficulty that becomes serious enough to threaten a student's academic performance, health, or well-being. A *problem student* is someone whose inappropriate behavior threatens, not just his or her own chances of success, but also the academic performance, health, or well-being of other members of the college community. For instance, a student whose excessive drinking makes it impossible to take the final exam and complete the course is an example of a student problem. The student who comes to the test so inebriated that his or her boisterous behavior prevents the other students from doing their best on the final exam constitutes a problem student. Often a student problem will evoke our sympathy and compassion. In the case of problem students, however, it is important to balance our sympathy and compassion for the students creating the difficulty with our obligations to other people who may be adversely affected by it.

Problems Stemming from Controllable Behavior

When faced with particularly challenging student behavior, we must first ask: is the student exhibiting a behavior that is within his or her power to control? For instance, a student who appears at your home without a very good reason is demonstrating inappropriate behavior that is probably within that person's control. Your expectations need to be outlined, boundaries between public and private life need to be set and, in the most serious of cases, sanctions or even restraining orders may need to be imposed. In most situations, the student has a great deal of control over whether he or she engages in this particular type of inappropriate behavior. But problems relating to addiction—such as excessive drinking, use of illegal drugs, misuse of prescription drugs, or compulsive gambling— are likely to involve behaviors that the student *cannot* control without professional help. The difficulty we face as college professors is that the distinction between what is controllable and noncontrollable is not always clear or easy to make. For example, the student who regularly interrupts your class with rude remarks may simply be illustrating extremely poor social skills (which could be improved through guidance and mentoring) or may be suffering from a specific condition, such as Tourette's or Asperger's Syndrome. In the latter cases, professional intervention is necessary and, in accordance with the Americans with Disabilities Act, reasonable accommodation would have to be made in the classroom. There will then need to be a distinction between what constitutes a reasonable accommodation (perhaps including some inconvenience for the other students or occasional discomfort) and what must be regarded as unreasonable expectations (such as seriously infringing on the rights of the other students to learn effectively).

Your first line of defense regarding students who exhibit controllable problems is a statement of behavioral expectations that applies either to your individual courses, laboratory, studio, office, and other learning environments or that constitutes an institution-wide policy on acceptable student behavior. You may not need to develop your own statement from scratch. Many colleges and universities already have policies in place that provide rights for both students and faculty members in situations where someone's behavior becomes detrimental to the learning process. Some good models to consider as you prepare your own policy include:

- DePauw University

  www.depauw.edu/univ/handbooks/dpuhandbooks
  .asp?ID=117&parentid=518

- Georgia State University

  www2.gsu.edu/~wwwsen/minutes/2002–2003/disrupt.html

- Brigham Young University

  http://honorcode.byu.edu/index.php?option=com_content&task=
  view&id=3592

- James Madison University

  www.jmu.edu/counselingctr/Resources/fac_disruptive_students
  .html

As you develop your own policy, you may wish to keep in mind these common practices.

- *Many policies on student behavior begin with an explanation of why these expectations exist in an academic setting.* Without this context, restrictions can appear to be imposed simply for their own sake rather than to improve the academic environment. Good policies make it clear that they do not intend to limit free speech but to create a collegial environment so that genuine academic discourse is possible.

- *In situations where unacceptable behavior occurs, problems should first be addressed at the most direct level possible, through a discussion with the student.* As college professors we always want to seize the teachable moment and provide instruction whenever possible. It may be the case that the student is unaware of the negative effect that he or she is having on the class. The student may believe that freedom of speech entitles people to do or say whatever they wish, without regard for restricting these remarks to the appropriate time, place, or manner. By beginning the process as a conversation, it avoids the need for making what could be easily remedied problems into far more serious issues.

- *Many policies recommend getting advice from others who may have faced similar challenges.* Each instance of disruptive behavior in an educational setting is likely to be somewhat complex, and an overarching one-size-fits-all policy is unlikely to cover every contingency. By speaking to a mentor or senior colleague, an instructor may gain insight into effective ways of handling the situation that restore a desirable amount of order and are not unduly punitive to the student involved.

- *Some policies also address disruptive student behavior outside the classroom.* We can't assume that the only environment in which problems are likely to occur is during a class itself. Students may be disruptive during conferences in faculty offices. They may confront teachers in an inappropriate manner while the instructors are walking to their cars. They may harass their fellow students or the teacher through email barrages or threaten them in their blogs. They may interfere with the experience of others during their internships or field trips, or during the meetings of academic clubs. It is useful for institutions to consider the implications of enforcing their policies in all of the learning environments they support. For instance, at Mary Baldwin College (2004), where a majority of the students study abroad at some point in their programs, the institution's "Policy on Responding to Disruptive Student Behavior" includes the following proviso: "If the course occurs abroad or at some other location away from the home campus, the [student who is removed from the course] will be responsible for all expenses incurred, including transportation home."

- *Good policies provide a structure for due process to ensure that the student who is accused of disruptive behavior and the faculty member who is making the accusation have their rights protected.* Policies that do not provide for appeal or due process run the risk of creating situations in which a student may be removed from a course by a professor without adequate reason or branded without warrant as a "troublemaker" in a manner than can harm his or her future prospects. On the other hand, policies that do not allow the professor to act quickly in truly severe situations may put the faculty member and other students at risk or at least infringe on the quality of the educational experience. For this reason, attention must be given to the rights of both parties in matters of disruptive student behavior.

- *Good policies place a primary emphasis on safety.* Higher education is sometimes a dangerous environment. We don't always have the luxury of following a policy lockstep through multiple levels and multiple appeals when the safety of the faculty member and others may be in jeopardy. Therefore, good policies also contain emergency mechanisms that may be invoked after even a single incident if faculty members feel that a student is providing a substantive risk to the college or university environment.

If your institution does not already have a policy in place that addresses disruptive behavior in an academic setting, you may wish to include a section in your syllabus that addresses how you will handle instances of students who disrupt your class (see Chapter 11, "Writing an Effective Course Syllabus"). One way of drafting such a section would be to create a statement such as the following:

As a community of scholars, we owe one another respect for our individuality and right to learn. For this reason, expressions of racism, sexism, homophobia, or any other form of bigotry are unacceptable in this class, even if you are only "expressing your opinion." The use of such statements interferes with the learning of other students in the course; your right to free speech stops where another student's right to learn begins. Other types of disruptive behavior—such as inappropriate talking, use of electronic devices to check email or play games, listening to music, reading material unrelated to the course, use of cell phones, the failure to silence electronic devices, use of profanity or threatening language, and the like—will also not be allowed. On the first occurrence of such behavior, you will receive an oral warning. On the second occurrence, you will receive a written warning, and your highest exam grade will be reduced by 10 percent. On the third occurrence (or after three unexcused absences), I reserve the right either to have you removed from the course or to reduce your final grade in the course by a full letter grade. Actions that I regard as particularly egregious disruptions or poor behavior may cause you to be removed from the course after only a single occurrence.

Of course, you should always check in advance with your chair or dean to see how much leeway your institutional policy allows you in ejecting students from the classroom. At some schools, this matter is entirely at the instructor's prerogative. At others, students are accorded greater individual rights. It is important, therefore, that your classroom policy does not contradict any limitations imposed on you by your institution.

In situations where your institution either does not have a specific policy on disruptive students or does not provide you with sufficient guidance in the current situation, keep the following guidelines in mind:

- Try not to confront the student in a public setting as this reaction may well aggravate the problem. Though you do not want to meet alone with the student if you believe there is a risk to your personal safety, a student whose behavior is simply disruptive but not threatening may be best counseled one-on-one in your office or another quiet setting (see Chapter 15, "Teaching One-on-One").

- When speaking to a student who has caused disruptive behavior, don't allow your voice to rise in either volume or pitch, even if the student becomes excited. A calm, assertive, and level tone is more likely to diffuse anger or anxiety.

- Do not allow yourself to be sworn to a level of secrecy that you may not be able to keep. Many students will say, "Okay, I'll tell you about what's bothering me, but you have to promise that you won't share it with anyone." In certain cases, however, you may be required to report what you hear from the student or it may be in the student's best interests for you to make a report. Answer the student by saying, "I can't promise you that I won't report or act on the information. As an employee of this institution, there are certain things I'm required to report. Also, as your professor, there are certain things that may be in your best educational interests for me to report. So, tell me the issue first, and then let me discuss with you how it may be best to proceed."

- Focus on the problematic behavior itself; don't be judgmental of the student as a person. You are entitled to define the behavior that you find unacceptable and to provide a clear indication of the consequences that will result if the behavior occurs again in the future. If, however, you cause the student to trust you less by appearing to disapprove of the student as a person, you can exacerbate the problem rather than solve it.

- Intervene as soon as you feel that the unacceptable behavior has become an issue. If you ignore the problem, it is unlikely to go away; your failure to intervene may even be viewed as acceptance or encouragement. As difficult as these discussions often are, they are easier when they are begun early before the situation has grown out of hand.

- Ascertain which resources the student has available and is using. Is there family support? An appropriate group of friends? Is the student a member of a fraternity, sorority, club, or social group? Has the student sought professional counseling? It can be a clear warning sign that the student has a serious problem if he or she lacks—or *claims* to lack—any of these standard support mechanisms. Urge such a student to visit the institution's counseling center for at least a preliminary conversation and to learn about available resources.

Maintaining a Focus on the Positive

One disadvantage to policies on disruptive student behavior, regardless of whether these policies are institution-wide or only in a professor's own syllabus, is that they tend to be extremely negative. They tell students what they must *not* do, rather than emphasizing the type of behavior that we expect in an academic setting. One solution to this problem is to create a code of conduct that emphasizes the positive behavior you expect rather than the troublesome actions you are seeking to prohibit. An example of a code of conduct that sets a constructive tone would be the following (see also Buller, 2006):

> We communicate with others, both orally and in writing, in a polite, respectful, and courteous manner. Whenever we disagree with someone, we restrict our differences to the subject at hand while continuing to value the individual with whom we disagree. Our discourse, including discussion and argumentation, is always conducted in a polite, courteous, and dignified manner that respects as well as values the other members of our community. We are sensitive to the needs of our colleagues for expression as well as for quiet reflection, conducting ourselves at all times in a manner that does not infringe on the rights of others. In public settings where others must concentrate, we make certain that electronic devices are silenced and that our actions do not distract those around us from the focus of their attention.

You might even consider having students sign this code of conduct and turn it in to you on the first day of class. Then, if a student fails to live up to these expectations, you have a convenient way of discussing why the person's lapse of behavior violated the terms of the code and how you expect improved conduct in the future.

Positive approaches are often more effective than relying on punishments alone because a negative approach may induce students to become defensive simply to protect their egos. Nevertheless, just as negative approaches may be ineffective, it is also probably futile to ignore the problem and hope that it will resolve itself. Faculty members at times believe that the student is merely trying to get attention and that, by refusing to acknowledge the poor behavior, it will not be reinforced. This strategy is rarely successful. If the student is indeed seeking attention, the object of that attention is more likely his or her fellow students, not you. By failing to acknowledge the inappropriate behavior, you may be sending an implicit message, both to that individual student and (even more troubling) to his or her colleagues, that you condone such behavior or are too meek to intervene. For this reason, you should acknowledge the behavior, doing so firmly but with the courtesy that you are trying to encourage, and point out that the action fails to live up to the classroom code of conduct because it interferes with the learning of the other students. State that you know that the person is capable of better behavior. Do not ridicule the student or use abusive language yourself. Rather, keep your tone positive and constructive even as you are firm in stating your expectations. If at all possible, try not to let the situation make you angry. Your response is far more effective if you are calm but assertive.

Problems Stemming from Noncontrollable Behavior

Not every behavior problem is the result of a student's conscious choice. Students may suffer from disorders that cause them to act inappropriately in social settings. They may be taking prescribed medications that have side effects or unintended consequences. Other factors may have occurred in their lives or experience that render the situation far more complicated than it first appears. The important thing to realize is that there may be situations in which students whom you encounter are simply unable to control actions or utterances that you or the other students find unpleasant, distracting, or unusual. In these situations, the student is in need of professional help, either from the institution's medical and counseling staff or from his or her own physician or counselor. Don't be tempted into thinking that this is a situation that you can remedy simply by lending a sympathetic ear or offering advice. To the contrary, you may complicate a course of treatment that is already under way. It can be tempting to diagnose the problem yourself, particularly if you believe that you've encountered similar issues in the past, but you should never assume the role of professional counselor or therapist. Direct these situations to the people at your college or university who are professionally trained to handle such problems. At many institutions, it is possible to refer a student to a counseling center based on the behavior that you have observed. Other institutions regard formal referrals as a violation of the student's right to privacy and so have chosen not to create specific referral mechanisms. Nevertheless, even in these cases, it is frequently possible to speak confidentially to one of the counselors, describe the situation, and allow the counselor to use his or her professional judgment to decide whether it is appropriate to invite the student in for a conversation. The counselor may already be familiar with the student because of earlier problems or previous consultations. Most important, in any case where you believe that your personal safety or the safety of other members of the community may be at risk, you should notify the campus police or security office. There are times when concern for safety takes precedence even over such cherished rights as privacy and individual freedom. Finally, if the student is clearly at the point of having a crisis, do not leave the student alone to deal with the problem. Walk the student to the counseling center yourself if you can or call your school's counselor with the student still in your office. A student who is having a serious problem may well promise you that he or she will go directly to seek help, but it is possible that the student will not follow through on that promise, causing either self-harm or posing a danger to other students.

The following are some warning signs that indicate a student may have a serious problem:

- Sudden gain or loss of weight
- Noticeable decline in personal hygiene
- Repeated sleeping in class
- Erratic attendance at required activities
- Written or spoken remarks indicating despair such as "It all seems so hopeless"
- Written or spoken remarks indicating a clear inability to empathize with the suffering of others
- Speech that is excessively rapid or slow, slurred, or garbled
- Sudden outbursts, particularly if they seem violent or aggressive
- A tendency to become increasingly withdrawn or isolated
- Excessive, unreasonable, and increasing demands for special consideration or attention

---

Even in cases where the student's disruptive behavior results from a condition beyond his or her control, it is clear that the rights of other students to learn in an acceptable environment may also be affected. As academic professionals, we are expected to make *reasonable* accommodations based on the individual needs of a student who faces certain psychological or behavioral challenges. We are not required, however, to put ourselves or our students at risk or harm or to condone situations that have a significantly negative effect on our ability to teach and our students' ability to learn. Being inconvenienced and making reasonable modifications to what we do is one thing; allowing any individual's behavior to make learning difficult or impossible is quite another.

Note: Dr. Philip Cromer, assistant director of counseling for the MacArthur campus of Florida Atlantic University, provided valuable insights for this chapter.

REFERENCES

Buller, J. L. (2006). *The essential department chair: A practical guide to college administration*. Bolton, MA: Anker.

Mary Baldwin College. (2004). *Disruptive student behavior: Policies and procedures*. Retrieved April 7, 2009, from www.mbc.edu/docs/admin_docs/ DisruptiveStudentBehavior.doc

RESOURCES

Kadison, R., & DiGeronimo, T. F. (2004). *College of the overwhelmed: The campus mental health crisis and what to do about it*. San Francisco: Jossey-Bass.

McKeachie, W. J., & Svinicki, M. (2006). Dealing with student problems and problem students (There's almost always at least one!). In W. J. McKeachie & M. Svinicki, *McKeachie's teaching tips: Strategies, research, and theory for college and university teachers* (12th ed., pp. 172–190). New York: Houghton Mifflin.

Noonan-Day, H. L., & Jennings, M. M. (2007). Disruptive students: A liability, policy, and ethical overview. *Journal of Legal Studies, 24*(2), 291–324.

Servaty-Seib, H. L., & Taub, D. J. (Eds.). (2008). *New directions for student services: No. 121. Assisting bereaved college students*. San Francisco: Jossey-Bass.

22

TAKING THE NEXT STEP
IN YOUR TEACHING

In this chapter we'll explore three approaches that college professors might consider to help transform their teaching from good and effective to excellent and exemplary. No matter whether you are just beginning your career or already an experienced instructor, these strategies can assist you in promoting your quality of teaching to the next level of excellence while simultaneously enhancing the learning of your students. We'll assume that you've already mastered all the basics required for good teaching at the college level; the plan that we'll consider is appropriate for teachers who are already regarded as highly capable and who find themselves wondering, "What else can I do to help my students learn even more?"

Step One: Select a Course for a Complete Makeover

Begin by examining all the courses that you teach and then selecting one for closer scrutiny. If you're a relatively new instructor, choose any course that you are likely to be assigned a great deal. If you're more experienced as a college professor, you may prefer to choose a course that doesn't receive student ratings quite as high as the others you teach. Or perhaps there is a course with which you've never been quite satisfied, even if you can't quite put your finger on why. You could choose a course in which you feel you must lecture extensively because otherwise you couldn't cover all of the material. You could focus on a course where you're not quite certain what advantages technology might bring to student learning, or whether there are any alternatives to structuring it in the way it has always been, or how the methods used in the course could possibly be improved. Or you may prefer to focus on a course that you feel other faculty members have taught even more successfully than you have. Whichever course you choose, this is the one that we will subject to an "extreme makeover." In this chapter, we're not simply going to tweak the course and make a few improvements; we're going to rethink it entirely.

So, set your old syllabus and textbooks aside, and prepare to approach this course as though you had never taught it before.

The first thing we're going to do is to select an entirely new focus or approach for the course. For example, suppose that you're a professor of engineering and that the course you've decided to revise is your under-graduate, junior-level course in statics. Approach this course not by thinking "I'm going to teach my students statics," but rather "I'm going to help my students develop their skills in _____ while teaching them statics." What you use to fill in that blank is entirely up to you, but here are some suggestions that you may find useful:

- Written communication
- Oral communication
- Critical thinking
- Creativity and innovation
- Leadership
- Entrepreneurship
- Quantitative literacy
- How to conduct original research
- Global awareness
- Appreciating diversity
- Learning through service
- Learning through direct experience
- Communicating in non-English languages
- Promoting sustainability and good stewardship of resources
- Understanding the distinctive features of and opportunities provided by our institution's setting

Depending on the precise subject matter covered in the course you have selected, several of these possibilities may seem far more likely to be productive than others. The only guidelines for selecting one of these course enhancements are:

- For the purposes of this exercise, select only one of these course enhancements. It can be very attractive to think, "I want to improve my students' writing and their speaking and their critical thinking and their creativity. In fact, I'm trying to do a lot of that already." Certainly, most good professors probably are already trying to achieve many of these goals in their courses. In this exercise, though, we're not going to be looking at all the diverse objectives you may have in any one class; we're going to focus on one and truly develop it until it becomes a significant and noticeable part of what makes that particular course excellent. So keep refining your list until you have identified the one special focus that excites you the most and that can motivate you to reconsider every aspect of how the course is taught.

- Don't choose an approach that is likely to be inherent in the course material. For instance, don't choose oral communication skills for a course in speech, communicating in non-English languages for a course in Spanish, or appreciating diversity for a course in multiculturalism. Choose an approach that harmonizes well with the subject at hand but also enhances or extends your course in some significant way.

- Similarly, don't choose an approach simply because it looks as though it might be easier than the others to adopt or because you were thinking about moving in that direction anyway. Our goal in this exercise is to explore possibilities for improvement that you are unlikely to have considered, not to validate the choices you would have already made. Although you wouldn't want to adopt an approach that causes your course to move in an entirely different direction from its primary subject, the approach that you adopt should seem to be a bit of a stretch, even a challenge.

Once you have decided on your approach, incorporate it into a statement that describes the purpose of your course. For instance, you might write, "The purpose of this course is for students to develop their skills in creativity and innovation while they learn the basics of statics" or "The purpose of this course is for students to learn how to conduct original research in biology while they master the principles of biodiversity."

With this purpose firmly in mind, try to envision a semester in which everything seems to have come together. The students are all interested in the subject and highly engaged with all the activities of the course. You have been at your best consistently throughout the course, responding creatively and effectively to each opportunity that has come your way. The class as a whole has succeeded in doing everything that you could possibly have hoped. Now, freeze that moment in your mind and ask, "What do the students know and what are they able to do at the end of the course that makes me so convinced the course went as well as it could?" Don't just say, "They all got As on the final exam." Remember: The final exam would need to be entirely different from those you've given in the past because the course is now about your major new theme or approach. What would this new sort of creative and highly challenging final exam be like? Or perhaps a traditional final exam is no longer suitable. What type of final project would students complete if they were the best class you've ever taught and learned everything that you had hoped, both about the primary material of the course and the additional theme or approach you have taken? Be as innovative as you can. Try to imagine the perfect scenario with the most exciting and interesting final exam or project you could possibly devise. Take notes and try to describe that test or assignment. If you can imagine particularly creative or challenging questions, topics, or activities, write them all down. Don't stop until you've developed the sort of final exam or project that makes you say, "If my students could do that, I'd know that they really had learned in the best possible way in this course."

Once you've fixed this image firmly in your mind or on paper, go about designing the type of course that would make this final exam or project possible.

The approach that we're adopting here was pioneered by Walvoord and Anderson (1998) and further enhanced by Wiggins and McTighe (2006): backwards course design. With your overall course goal in mind, begin building your course backwards in small stages. If you've envisioned having all your students achieve at least a certain score on a nationally normed test in your discipline, what is the material that the students will need to have mastered by the date of that test? When will you provide your class with practice tests so that when they take the national exam, students will be comfortable with the format and expectations? How can you subdivide the material into manageable units? Alternatively, if the capstone project that you have proposed requires students to make a formal, public lecture, prepare an article that could be submitted to a national journal, or develop a poster presentation for consideration at a regional conference, how will you help them prepare for these activities along the way? Far too frequently, a professor will spend all semester lecturing, require a research paper at the end of the course, and then be disappointed at the results. If the instructor is asked what steps prepared the students to succeed at the research project, he or she may well answer, "Well, they should have learned how to do that in their other courses." Excellent and exemplary teachers—those who carry their instruction to the next level of excellence—are not satisfied with such an answer and will give students the experiences they need to be successful.

They consider it an essential part of their job to create an environment in which the best kind of learning can occur and where most (perhaps not all, but certainly most) of the students will feel motivated to do their best. Excellent instructors will even review material and provide training in skills that students "should have learned" in other courses because they understand that, for all of us, practice makes perfect. In this way, if you are teaching history, try not to become preoccupied with the events, perspectives, and later interpretations of a period, assuming that a brilliant product of historical analysis will "emerge" from each student's efforts by the end of the semester. Rather, reimagine your course as a way for students to learn how historical research and analysis is done—in a course that just happens to focus on a certain period. Be as intentional as possible, therefore, in designing a course that will attain the goal that you have identified as important.

In so doing, consider whether it may be useful to give your syllabus and course materials a distinctive new look, as we explored in Chapter 11, "Writing an Effective Course Syllabus," and Chapter 12, "Developing Creative Course Materials." Does it suit your individual teaching style and the course as you've now reconceived it, to incorporate a particular theme or metaphor that will help your students maintain a central focus? After all, if you provide your students with access to a truly distinctive syllabus and set of course materials, they will begin thinking differently about your course from the very first day. Your students will be more creative in their work because you have been more creative in the way the course is designed and in how you present the material. Even more important, you'll feel differently about your course because everything about the class now has a wholly new look. Even if you were a superb teacher before, you are likely to approach the course with greater enthusiasm. Activities in which you may have found yourself simply going through the motions will now seem new and innovative. Thus, by giving your course its "extreme makeover," you have taken your first step toward enhancing your own effectiveness as an instructor. The second step can then be taken as the course proceeds.

Step Two: Revitalize Your Teaching by Discovering a New Technology or Teaching Technique

In Chapter 14, "Teaching Large Classes," and Chapter 16, "Teaching with Technology," we explored some of the possibilities of enhancing learning through course management software, podcasts, presentation software, electronic student response systems, smart boards, smart pens, and other types of instructional technology. Other software applications allow college professors to create videos, DVDs, movies, elaborate Web pages, and multimedia presentations after only a small amount of training or experimentation. In addition, print-on-demand publishers, such as Xlibris, iUniverse, and Lulu, give instructors the option of creating textbooks that can be used for a single course and then revised each semester as your students' needs change or your approach to the material develops. In Chapter 18, "Promoting Student Engagement," we explored class exercises such as Send-a-Problem, the Top-Ten List, and the Whip that can help make students more active learners. Find one of these approaches that appeals to you and explore ways of incorporating it into the course that you completely redesigned. This new pedagogical approach could be highly technological or it could be simply a new technique for promoting class discussion. Whatever it is, it should be something that you personally find engaging, can easily explain the value of to your students, and compels you to rethink the way in which you explain concepts and course information to your class.

For instance, let's suppose that you decide to incorporate an electronic student response system ("clickers") into one of your courses because you find this technology relatively easy to use and, of all the options that we have outlined, you are most intrigued by its possibilities. Even though clickers were discussed in this book primarily with regard to their value in large classes, you have decided to test their applicability to a 3000-level course that usually enrolls only twenty to twenty-four students. On the first day of class, rather than the typical "forced march" through the syllabus, classroom procedure, and course goals, you take advantage of your course innovation immediately. Since the course has no prerequisite, you start with a simple yes-no question: Have you ever taken a course in this discipline before? With their clickers, the students anonymously answer that eight of them had already taken a course in your field, but fourteen students are wholly new to the subject. You generate a simple pie chart from these results, illustrating to the "beginners" that they're in the majority in this course; they shouldn't feel intimidated if other students seem to be more familiar with some of the material at first, because the numbers are clearly on their side. You tell your students, "Now remember what you just saw. If you don't understand a term or a concept that we're discussing, be sure to ask about it. Keep in mind that there are thirteen other people in this class who are probably wishing that you would." Then you go on to introduce the first key concept you'll be addressing that semester. Ordinarily this idea would not be presented until the second day of the course because the first day would have been devoted solely to reviewing the syllabus and other logistical matters. But because you've completely redesigned the course, you explain the concept in ten minutes or so, present the students with a problem related to the concept, and have them use their clickers to reply anonymously. Immediately both you and your students realize that 100 percent of them have already grasped the concept. In earlier courses, as you would have had no way of knowing that your students understood the idea so quickly, you would have spent the entire class period clarifying and illustrating the idea, probably boring a large percentage in the class as a result. Now, armed with the knowledge that the students are "with" you in terms of what they've understood, you congratulate them on their rapid progress, give them a sense of pride that they have earned, and feel free to move on. You introduce a few key terms, again check the class's progress with the clickers, and devote the last twenty minutes of the class to a discussion of real-life examples the students can think of that incorporate the concept you have introduced or the key terms you have defined. In other semesters, the first few discussions in this class were awkward and tentative as students gradually got to know each other and felt more comfortable with the material, but now you find that the class has an excellent discussion on the very first day. For one thing, the students began to feel more comfortable with the material almost immediately through the technology that you have adopted; for another, since they have already been participating at one level through their use of clickers, elevating that participation into active discussion seems a natural development. This single use of technology, therefore, has already begun to transform the way in which you teach.

Alternatively, perhaps you feel less comfortable introducing a new technology into your course but have decided to experiment with the jigsaw groups that were discussed in Chapter 14, "Teaching Large Classes." In this case, let's imagine that you are teaching a music appreciation course. Using the jigsaw method, you assign each student to one of five groups first by musical elements (pitch, dynamics, timbre, rhythm, and harmony), then by genre (concerto, symphony, opera, ballet, and art song), and finally by period (early music, Baroque, Classical, Romantic, and Twentieth- and Twenty-first-Century Music). Each student is thus a member of three different groups—for instance, one student may be a member of the Timbre, Opera, and Early Music groups, and another might be assigned to the Harmony, Symphony, and Romantic groups—causing them all to meet and interact with different students at different times. Then, you decide that you will abandon your previous practice of devoting the first three weeks of the course to an extended discussion of musical elements, based on the first half dozen chapters in the textbook. Instead, you'll try a more innovative approach. You tell the students that they will first meet in their music elements group, master what that concept is as it appears in their textbook, and formulate a clear, inventive, and possibly humorous way of explaining and demonstrating that element to the class as a whole. The students break into these groups and immediately become engaged in the material. You notice that they are having great fun thinking of a way that they'll present the concept to the class so that the "skit" will be both memorable and enjoyable. You end class that day with each of the five element groups teaching their concept to the others. In the next class, you break the students into their period groups and have the students use their textbooks or a simple Internet search to find five interesting observations to make about that particular musical period, one for each of the five musical elements they discussed in the previous class. After each group presents its "top-five" list to the entire class, you break them into subgroups again, this time by genre, and have them speculate as to how they imagine each one of the five musical elements may be important to or demonstrated in that particular genre. Rather than have the entire class discuss all twenty-five speculations from the subgroups, you have the students record them on large flip charts. Your course, you tell the students, has now become a music appreciation laboratory, and the five flip charts contain twenty-five hypotheses that you will now be testing along with them throughout the semester. As you verify or disprove each hypothesis, you will place a green checkmark or a black X before it, and part of their final "lab report"—that is, the take-home section of the final exam—will be to discuss at least six of those hypotheses and why they are important to our understanding of music. As a result, with the single course modification of incorporating jigsaw groups into your course, you've covered in only two periods material that used to take you three weeks, given your students an active learning experience from the very beginning of the course, provided them with an opportunity to get to know and interact with their colleagues, and adopted a metaphor—the music appreciation course as research lab—that will cause the students to see the material in a different light from what they expected to encounter. You will be more creative in your teaching because your teaching strategy has been more creative. In all probability, you will observe a demonstrable increase in the ratings that you receive from your student course evaluations, and your students will receive higher grades because they will have learned the material more thoroughly.

Step Three: Set a Goal of Being Recognized as a Star Teacher

Finally, when you have given at least one of your courses a complete makeover and incorporated a new teaching technique that revitalizes your approach to your material, set yourself the explicit goal of being recognized as a master teacher. Many faculty members know that they teach extremely well and secretly hope that their effectiveness in the classroom will someday be recognized by their colleagues. At many institutions, however, a professor's peers rarely if ever experience what occurs in that teacher's classroom. Perhaps while an individual is being considered for promotion or tenure, a few members of an evaluation committee may sit in on a class session or two. Perhaps, too, the professor's department chair may visit a class as part of the department's plan to maintain a high level of teaching. More commonly we learn about our colleague's success (or lack thereof) in the classroom through "rumor and innuendo," the periodic comment made by this or that student, the formal course evaluations we may review if we serve on a committee that receives them, or the sheer reputation that an instructor develops over time. For the most part, however, you will have little opportunity to be widely recognized for excellence in classroom instruction unless you make that recognition a specific goal. It may seem presumptuous to put yourself forward as a "master" teacher, but you should set these concerns aside. Our scholarship is easily recognized because our peers see the books we publish, the performances we provide, and the grants we receive. Our service is widely known because, as an act that by definition affects a larger community, it is witnessed and continually appraised. Setting yourself the goal of being recognized for your quality of instruction is simply a matter of leveling the playing field so that excellence in teaching receives the same public acknowledgment as excellence in scholarship and service. Indeed, if you are trying to improve a record in teaching that in the past has been less than stellar, you may need to set a clear goal of public recognition for the high quality of your teaching in order to change the impressions of you that others have already formed.

How do you go about being more intentional in your pursuit of recognition for your quality in teaching?

- *State your intention to a supervisor.* Meet with your chair, director, or dean and make it clear that you are pursuing the goal of recognition for teaching excellence. If your institution uses an evaluation system that places different emphasis on various criteria depending on whether you are on a teaching track, research track, or service track, state that for the next several years you wish to be placed on the teaching track. Show your supervisor the innovative syllabi and course materials that you have developed. Mention the creative teaching techniques that you have adopted to promote active student engagement and increased mastery of your material. Ask to be kept in mind when your supervisor is appointing faculty members to committees and task forces dealing with pedagogical issues. Ask, too, to be considered when that person must nominate faculty members for awards related to teaching recognition, such as Professor of the Year and the like.

- *Become involved with a center for teaching excellence.* Nearly every college or university has a center that works to improve the level of teaching and learning on that campus. Make a conscious effort to be widely known at this center at your institution. Take as many workshops on innovative teaching techniques as possible. Offer to provide workshops on some teaching strategy that you have found particularly effective. Serve as a mentor to other faculty members who are working to improve the quality of their own instruction. Your participation with your local center for teaching excellence will give you a constant source of new energy and ideas for continuing to make progress in your instruction. At the same time, it will enhance your reputation as the go-to person when people want to talk about superb teaching.

- *Seek recognition for your teaching from disciplinary associations.* Many associations provide annual awards to stellar teachers. Get yourself nominated for these awards, year after year if necessary, until you are successful in receiving one. If your association has a committee on pedagogy within the discipline, ask to be appointed to it. Use this recognition that you are receiving from outside your institution to enhance the level of recognition that you receive for teaching excellence within your institution.

- *Apply for grants that support instruction.* Finally, work with your research and sponsored programs office to obtain external funding for the improvement of teaching at your institution. Many foundations and other agencies provide financial support for workshops, equipment, travel to training programs, and other opportunities that you can use to make a demonstrable impact on the quality of instruction at your institution. Receiving grants of this sort has a double benefit for you. First, the actual project funded by the grant will have a direct effect on the quality of your teaching itself. Second, as the person who "brought in that grant to enhance our established excellence in teaching," you will gain immediate recognition as one of your institution's key players in the area of teaching excellence. For more information on how to locate and apply for grants, see the next chapter, "Writing a Grant Proposal."

Thomas R. McDaniel, senior vice president, professor of education, and acting dean of graduate studies at Converse College in Spartanburg, South Carolina, offers the following excellent advice for faculty members interested in taking the next step toward excellence in their teaching:

> The professor's life is defined somewhere within the normal parameters of scholarship, service, and teaching—but the essential task of the professor is teaching. In research institutions, scholarship is most valued and rewarded, while community colleges often emphasize the importance of service. Nonetheless, most professors are drawn to the academy because they want to teach, enjoy teaching, and believe in their hearts that they have something to teach of value to the next generation. This is not only the central task of the professor but the one that is ultimately most challenging. That may be so in our current era in part because teaching can no longer be viewed as merely transferring the knowledge that is in the professor's head (acquired through years of rigorous study) to "blank slates" arrayed passively (yet receptively) before the revered, wise, sage on the stage.
>
> Kahlil Gibran says in his famous essay on teaching in The Prophet: "If [the teacher] is indeed wise he does not bid you enter the house of his wisdom, but rather leads you to the threshold of your own mind" (p. 56). That requires more pedagogical skill than most professors realize. Yes, the professor should be wise, knowledgeable, articulate, and (even) entertaining. But the "essential college professor" is one who has mastered the ability to lead students to the "thresholds" of their own minds, awakening in them the same passion for learning that first motivated the professor to seek an academic career. Of his "poor scholar" Chaucer declared: "And gladly would he learn, and gladly teach." The professor who would be remembered long after a student's graduation is the teacher who communicates successfully his or her passion for learning and love for teaching, remembering that (as Gibran concludes) ". . . the vision of one man lends not its wings to another man" (p. 57). Or woman. The teacher who remembers that he or she is also a learner can become that professor remembered forever by those "gladly" taught. (Personal communication, November 16, 2007)

If you take the three steps outlined in this chapter, you will discover that you have made not merely a few minor improvements in your teaching, but a major, transformative difference in your entire approach to instruction. You will have gone from being a good teacher to being a model for others to emulate. Turn to sources such as the *Teaching Professor* and the *Journal on Excellence in College Teaching* to remain current about new trends and developments in college teaching. (For more on the *Teaching Professor*, see Chapter 25, "Overcoming Research Block.") Even better, make it your goal, as you reach that next step in teaching, to contribute articles to these and other journals so that your colleagues in higher education can benefit from your experience. Finally, remember that the backwards design approach has plenty of applications outside of course revision. In its most general form, it becomes the second of Covey's Seven Habits of Highly Effective People (1989): "Begin with the end in mind" (p. 97).

REFERENCES

Covey, S. R. (1989). *The seven habits of highly effective people: Powerful lessons in personal change.* New York: Simon & Schuster.

Gibran, K. (1923). *The prophet.* New York: Knopf.

Walvoord, B. E., & Anderson, V. J. (1998). *Effective grading: A tool for learning and assessment.* San Francisco: Jossey-Bass.

Wiggins, G., & McTighe, J. (2006). *Understanding by design* (2nd ed.). New York: Prentice Hall.

RESOURCES

Bain, K. (2004). *What the best college teachers do.* Cambridge, MA: Harvard University Press.

Baiocco, S. A., & DeWaters, J. N. (1998). *Successful college teaching: Problem-solving strategies of distinguished professors.* Boston: Pearson.

Bean, J. C. (1996). Engaging ideas: *The professor's guide to integrating writing, critical thinking, and active learning in the classroom.* San Francisco: Jossey-Bass.

Boyle, E., & Rothstein, H. (2003). *Essentials of college and university teaching: A practical guide.* Stillwater, OK: New Forums Press.

McKeachie, W. J., & Svinicki, M. (2006). *McKeachie's teaching tips: Strategies, research, and theory for college and university teachers* (12th ed.). New York: Houghton Mifflin.

Moore, S., Walsh, G. A., & Risquez, A. (2007). *Teaching at college and university: Effective strategies and key principles.* New York: Open University Press.

WRITING A GRANT PROPOSAL

Writing a successful grant proposal can benefit your scholarship in many different ways. To begin with, most institutional systems for evaluating faculty members count the receipt of a major external grant as a significant achievement in scholarship. Creating a winning proposal entails an advanced level of research, planning, and effective writing. To be sure, even writing an unsuccessful grant proposal is likely to have required an extensive review of the literature that deals with the issue or problem you are interested in investigating. Second, any project that is funded by external sources usually involves an extremely important or innovative area of research. Sometimes grants are received for the enhancement of teaching or for the expansion of service projects, but the vast majority of grants support original research or creative activity. Because neither foundations nor other types of funding sources are likely to fund a project that they don't regard as important, that external endorsement means that your research has been validated as superior in quality by an impartial observer. Finally, the receipt of one grant can often be used as the basis for receiving other, perhaps even larger grants later on. As we'll see in just a moment, acting as an effective steward of research funding is of great importance to funding sources when they make their allocations. In addition, grant writing involves learning a particular set of skills to phrase your ideas in an effective manner. Once you have mastered these skills, you can use them effectively when you write additional grant proposals, and you are likely to increase the rate at which your proposals will be funded. This chapter is intended primarily for college professors who do not yet have experience in writing successful grant proposals. To get you started, we'll divide the basics of the process into eight steps:

1. Be an Effective Steward of Research Funding
2. Locate Possible Sources for External Funding
3. Use Your Institution's Resources
4. Work Closely with a Program Officer from the Funding Agency
5. Be Willing to Modify Your Proposal

6. Adhere to the Five Guidelines for Effective Grant Applications
7. Seek Maximum Buy-In from Your Institution
8. If Your Application Is Not Funded, Try Again

Step One: Be an Effective Steward of Research Funding

As we just saw, demonstrating that you can execute a funding project responsibly, adhere to deadlines, and produce a tangible product at the end of the process is extremely important to most funding agencies. The best way to do this is to obtain a series of small grants, many of which are funded internally by colleges and universities themselves, before applying for external funding. In addition to proving that you are a responsible steward of resources, these small grants can also serve as seed money to demonstrate the feasibility of a larger study, clarify the nature of a problem, or prove the reality of the need that your larger grant proposal will seek to address. Work closely with your institution's research and sponsored programs office to discover whether your school makes internally funded grants available for research purposes and, if so, which of their programs best suits your idea. In many cases, you can apply for an internally funded start-up grant through a fairly simple process. Most institutions use a brief form that requires the faculty member to describe the project in general outlines, identify in perhaps a paragraph or two what the funds will be used for, and specify the product or outcome that is likely to result from the project. By successfully completing this small project, you will be able to demonstrate to external agencies that your own institution found your project worthy of initial funding and that you produce meaningful results when you receive grants. So, even though the funding you receive from internal sources may be quite small, be sure to handle all record keeping appropriately, expend the money wisely, and conclude the project with a demonstrable result or product.

Step Two: Locate Possible Sources for External Funding

Your institution's research and sponsored programs office will probably have access to many different databases that can tell them of new opportunities for project funding. Once you've successfully handled a few small grants, make an appointment with one of your institution's research officers or grant writers, outline in general terms the project for which you'd like to seek external funding, and allow that office to determine a list of agencies that may be interested in your type of project. If you teach at a very small college or an institution that does not yet have a long history of seeking grant support, there may not be an actual research office for you to turn to. In that case, you may need to identify a few funding sources yourself. Here's how to begin:

- *Grants.gov* is a comprehensive source for finding and applying for all types of grants that are administered through the federal government. Its search engine permits keyword searching, browsing, searching by specific agency, searching by deadline date, sorting by eligibility, and a host of other options. If you are trying to locate a funding source on your own, this is probably the first source that you should check.

- *The Federal Register* provides information about all grant programs involving the U.S. federal government. Programs that are currently under consideration are also discussed, so this is a good source of information about opportunities that are pending or that could arise in the future. The online version is searchable (www.gpoaccess.gov/fr/index.html). A microfiche version, updated daily, can be purchased through the U.S. Government Bookstore (http://bookstore.gpo.gov).

- *The Foundation Center* sponsors a website (http://foundationcenter .org) that contains information about many grants offered by private, nongovernment organizations. Though many of its services are subscription based, the center does offer free searching of its foundations database by name and location. Once a foundation is identified, the website provides such information as the foundation's contact information, assets, total giving, and most recent IRS filing. In addition, the Foundation Center offers both online and classroom training in grant writing. (For more information about the Foundation Center, see Chapter 38, "The Faculty Member as Fundraiser.")

- *Guidestar.org* is another subscription-based service that offers a broad range of online grant information. Through monthly or annual subscriptions, the user can quickly search grants by keyword, location, size of grant, and a variety of other options.

- *The National Endowment for the Humanities* (NEH) funds projects, primarily to cultural institutions such as colleges and universities, that fall within its areas of primary concern, including languages, linguistics, literature, and so on. NEH grants are both browsable and searchable on its website (www.neh.gov/grants/index.html), and a bimonthly periodical listing of upcoming NEH grants is available from the U.S. Government Bookstore (http://bookstore.gpo.gov).

- *The National Endowment for the Arts* funds creative projects in such areas as dance, design, music, opera, theater, and the creation (as opposed to the study) of literary works. Upcoming funding opportunities are listed at www.nea.gov/grants/apply/index.html.

- *The National Science Foundation* annually offers a wide array of funding opportunities in the sciences as they are broadly defined. The foundation's funding opportunities are searchable at www.nsf.gov/funding and, through links at the same site, it regularly posts a valuable and frequently updated proposal guide that can assist scholars who are new to grant writing.

- *The National Institutes of Health* (NIH) and its Office of Extramural Research sponsors an extensive range of grants related to various aspects of human health, health education, and basic research in the areas of its primary focus. The Office of Extramural Research also provides a great deal of information explaining how to apply for its grants, how proposals will be evaluated, and where you may be able to locate workshops on effective grant writing (see http://grants.nih.gov/grants/oer.htm). In addition, if you are considering applying for an NIH grant, there are several excellent guides such as Gerin (2006) and Yang (2005) that can simplify the process for you.

- *The Fulbright Scholar Program*, administered in part by the Council for International Exchange of Scholars (CIES), provides teaching and research opportunities abroad for U.S. scholars, as well as programs that can bring international scholars to institutions in the United States. In addition to opportunities that support individual researchers, CIES also sponsors programs for institutions that can enhance their efforts in global education (see www.cies.org/Institutions).

- *The Chronicle of Higher Education* (http://chronicle.com), a weekly publication, includes a feature called "Deadlines" that lists upcoming opportunities for fellowships, grants, workshops, and the like. Although the deadlines for some of these opportunities may appear in print too late for you to write a complete application according to the principles outlined in this chapter, it is worth scanning the "Deadlines" feature each week to get ideas of possible funding sources that, if you are unable to take full advantage of now, may prove to be opportunities for you during their *next* cycle.

In addition, your state's official website is likely to provide links to funding opportunities for which your institution is eligible because of its location, so be sure to check these listings frequently. Although some faculty members may claim, "There just aren't grants available in my area," even a small amount of searching will indicate that projects in any academic field do have funding sources available to them. Moreover, because of the ease of Internet searching and the large number of databases available, these sources are increasingly easy to identify.

Step Three: Use Your Institution's Resources

Many colleges or universities have experienced grant writers on the staff of their centers for research and sponsored projects. These writers can help you shape an idea into a project that funding agencies are likely to find appealing. They can guide you in the language to use in phrasing a proposal, the amount of detail to use in building your budget, and the development of an effective assessment strategy that can help determine the impact of your project. At some schools, staff members in the office of research will actually do most of the writing themselves, once the principal investigator has provided the central idea and answered a series of questions. At others, the staff member will polish, edit, and improve the draft created initially by the researcher. In either case, this process takes a great deal of time, and the faculty member responsible for the grant will need to begin the process long before the deadline. Other internal resources that can be important in the preparation of a grant proposal are the school's institutional review board (IRB), which makes sure that research projects, particularly those involving human subjects, are done ethically and in accordance with the law and accepted procedure. Because IRB members tend to be experienced researchers, they can also help faculty members tailor a proposal so that it will be likely to achieve significant results and be recommended for funding. If you are a member of a scholarship network (see Chapter 27, "Seeking and Providing Peer Support for Scholarship"), your colleagues in that group can also be extremely important resources in refining your proposal and increasing the probability that it will receive funding.

Step Four: Work Closely with a Program Officer from the Funding Agency

Most funding agencies, particularly those associated with the state or federal government, prohibit the officers in charge of specific programs from speaking in favor of or against individual applications while the selection committee is reviewing them. The program officer, the argument goes, should be an impartial figure who treats all applications equally; the selection committee will then use its professional judgment in recommending the best possible applications without being swayed by the biases of the program officer. Nevertheless, even though that is how the system is intended to work, it remains true that grant writers who consult regularly with a program officer throughout the proposal process have a far greater likelihood of being funded than writers who simply submit a proposal before the deadline without prior consultation. Indeed, at some granting agencies, the funding rate for proposals that arrive over the transom, as previously unseen proposals are often described, is virtually zero. So, if program officers usually cannot defend particular proposals, why do the applications on which they are consulted stand a greater chance of being funded? For one thing, program officers can tell grant writers about particular interests of the funding agency that may not be immediately clear from the published guidelines. They can suggest terminology that may make a particular proposal more likely to be funded, refer the author to previously funded proposals that can serve as a guide, and recommend ways in which the focus of an application might be slightly modified to make it more appealing to the selection committee. During the review process itself, although the program officer is unlikely to be asked his or her opinion of a particular proposal, the committee often asks the program officer factual questions about a proposal if a matter seems unclear. If the program officer has already discussed the project with you on several occasions, he or she is in a much better position to be able to answer these questions, thus making the selection committee more likely to vote in favor of your grant. For this reason, you should never submit a grant proposal without at least talking about your proposal with the officer in charge of the particular program whose support you are seeking, hearing that person's suggestions, and then *following* those suggestions to the letter.

Step Five: Be Willing to Modify Your Proposal

Though we all imagine that our ideas for research projects are compelling enough to be immediately fundable for their own sake, we are rarely fortunate enough to encounter a funding agency that is interested in funding precisely the project that we have in mind. After all, foundations and government agencies have their own interests, missions, and charges, which you will need to keep in mind as you develop your proposal. As you read the guidelines for the program to which you are applying, look for key phrases that suggest a special interest or concern that must be addressed in order to qualify for the program. Be sure to incorporate these keywords into your application, featuring them prominently if it is possible to do so. Here is an area where a program officer can be invaluable as you flesh out your idea. "I know that the guidelines say that we'll consider research on any health-related issue," the program officer might say, "but lately the selection committee has been giving priority to prion diseases and conditions related to aging. And I know that they've been backing off from endowing faculty lines, even though that used to be a major part of what we did. The recent proposals that were successful tended to be those that targeted critical areas of basic research, included support for equipment purchases that an institution couldn't fund internally, and had a likelihood of leading to publishable results within three to five years." In this short conversation, the program officer has just given you a great deal of information about what you need to do in order to submit a proposal that has a good possibility of being funded. It may be, of course, that there is no way in which you can modify your proposal so that it addresses prion diseases and conditions related to aging. However, it may also be that although this area was only going to be a secondary or tertiary concern in the idea you had originally conceived, your proposal can be rethought to place the area of interest to the foundation in the forefront of your request. In much the same way, you may be interested in traveling to a foreign country to conduct research on site at a particular author's home and gain access to that author's personal papers. Unfortunately, the only grants that you can find available support teaching and not research in the country where you wish to travel. It is perfectly possible for you to apply for a teaching award and then, in your spare time while you are in the host country, begin gathering materials for your research project. In general, don't be surprised if you cannot find a funding source that supports exactly what you wish to do. Seek instead a source that supports projects as close as possible to what you have in mind, and then be flexible enough to modify your proposal so that it suits the needs of your granting agency. Remember, too, that if you are funded to pursue an interest you already have, you only build on areas already related to your field of research. However, if you are willing to consider alternative projects similar to your original area of interest, you may discover a whole new field of research possibilities.

Step Six: Adhere to the Five Guidelines for Effective Grant Applications

There are five guidelines every good grant writer should keep in mind at all times while developing an application for funding. These guidelines are as follows:

- *Keep your audience in mind*. Remembering who will be reading your proposal is so important to effective grant writing—and, as we shall see, to getting a book accepted by a publisher (see Chapter 24, "Writing a Book Proposal") and creating a curriculum vitae that successfully advances your career (see Chapter 31, "Creating an Effective Curriculum Vitae")—that it merits its own essential principle:

Whenever you are writing any type of document, keep in mind not only what you want to say but also to whom you are trying to say it.

As we just noted, the selection committee that will review your proposal will have its own concerns and areas of interests. They are not going to fund your project simply because you are a nice person who really needs this support to carry out your research. On the contrary, they are going to fund you if they believe you can achieve a goal that is important to *them*. Keep in mind, too, what the selection committee is likely to know. Will they be aware of the major resources in your field? Will you need to explain basic concepts mentioned in your proposal or can you take this knowledge for granted? You don't want to insult them by defining terms that they use every day; you also don't want to confuse them by using jargon with which they are unlikely to be familiar. For this reason, learn as much as you can about the sort of people who serve on the selection committee and tailor your proposal to their concerns, level of knowledge, and prior funding history. Some granting agencies keep the identities of review panels secret, but if you can determine who the reviewers are, this information will be of great value to you.

- *Ask yourself, "Why should the people associated with this funding source care about my project?"* Frequently we become so close to our own work that we assume everyone is going to care about migration patterns in sixteenth-century Holland, the mating rituals of the emperor goose, prenatal care in sub-Saharan Africa, or whatever else is the focus for our research. Particularly in the case of research projects that benefit those in need or seek to improve human health, we may become indignant at the mere question of why our research is important. We have to keep in mind that the problems people face in the world are so varied that a need that appears obvious and critical to us may not yet have become this obvious to other people, all of whom are focusing on their own ways of improving the world. Effective grant applications, therefore, are not those that assume a need, but those that make the case, clearly and compellingly, that an area of inquiry is worth pursuing.

- *Develop the application in a timely and systematic manner.* Grant applications are all too frequently completed only on the day they are due and then rushed, faxed, or emailed to the funding agency. Though these proposals may be successfully funded, they are far less likely to be as effective as they could have been—because following the guidelines outlined in this chapter takes time. Most successful grant applications are begun at least six months to one year before the due date. This allows the writer the opportunity to work with a staff member in the research and sponsored programs office, discuss the proposal (perhaps several times) with a program officer, be sure that the proposal is broadly supported throughout the institution (see below), and revise the application thoroughly so that it flows smoothly and is free of typographical errors. Rushed applications are far more likely to contain mistakes. It is not uncommon for funding agencies to reject applications simply because they appear to have been poorly edited. "If the people requesting this money are not careful enough to check their spelling and grammar," selection committees sometimes ask, "how are they going to be careful enough in spending the grant properly?" In addition, some programs, such as the Fulbright Scholars Program, receive so many applications for each available slot that they often use spelling and neatness as a preliminary screening criterion. You will only have sufficient time to create a well-crafted proposal, revise it, and then improve it once more if you start your application process early.

- *Focus on deliverables.* Too many grant applications devote a great deal of attention to establishing a need for the research project, discussing the methods that will be used to complete the plan, and summarizing the credentials of the investigators, but then overlook what is likely to *result* from the project itself. It is true that, in many cases, you simply don't know what the result of the research will be; that is why you are requesting the grant in the first place. But try to view the matter from the perspective of the selection committee: they are not interested in funding projects simply because the basic idea seems attractive; they are interested in results, in solving problems, and making the world better in some way. So, how will your research project do that? What is the product that you are likely to deliver at the end of the project? A report that ends up sitting on a shelf is never of interest to a funding agency. A product or activity that has some demonstrable benefit is far more likely to pique their interest. So, be sure to mention what you expect to do at the end of this project that you cannot do now. Whom will the project serve? How will it benefit them?

- *Include a description of how you will assess this project.* In addition to describing what you will be able to do if the project is successful, you also need to outline how you will *know* if the project is successful. Are there certain benchmarks along the way that would indicate success? Are there certain trigger points that, if you do not attain them, will tell you that you need to change your approach? What are the outcomes that you hope to attain through the project? How will you measure those outcomes and, most important, what will you do with the measurements that you obtain? Review committees want to know not merely that you are promising to do what you say you will do but that you are documenting this success in some way, that you have a plan in case setbacks occur, and that you have a strategy for improving the project while it is still under way. Several of the techniques that we discussed in connection with teaching in Chapter 10, "Assessing Student Learning," can be adapted to writing grant proposals.

Step Seven: Seek Maximum Buy-In from Your Institution

If you have planned ahead and are not submitting your application at the last minute, you will now be able to improve your chances for successful funding by obtaining as much buy-in from your institution as you can. Many institutions, particularly those with well-established research and sponsored programs offices, will have a formal sign-off procedure for every grant that is submitted. At a sign-off, representatives from all the offices that are likely to be affected by the grant meet together, consider the impact that the grant would have on their areas, and formally sign the proposal. For example, the principal investigator's department chair and a representative from the dean's office would be present to acknowledge that they understand the impact the grant might have on the courses that could be offered during the grant period, suggest alternative staffing for those courses if that is desirable, and indicate whether the amount budgeted to "buy out" a faculty member from a teaching assignment has been adequately reflected in the grant. A representative from the business office or the president's office might be present if matching funds are promised by the grant proposal. This representative can indicate the institution's willingness to provide those matching funds and may even suggest a funding source. A representative of the office of research will be present to explain how the budget for the grant was prepared, how the rate for indirect costs was determined, and to approve any last-minute changes authorized at the sign-off. Through this type of procedure, no office on campus is caught unawares by receipt of a grant that requires a commitment from them, and everyone has an opportunity to ask questions before the application leaves campus. The advantage of a sign-off is that everyone connected to the grant is physically present in the same room at the same time so that questions may be easily asked and answered.

If your institution does not conduct formal grant sign-offs, you may need to take other steps to promote widespread support for and understanding of your proposal. Make your own appointments with all the offices that could be affected by the grant. Be sure that everyone understands his or her commitments, and underscore the benefits that will be derived from the grant if it is funded. If the funding agency allows it, and it will fit within your page restrictions, you may even wish to request a letter of support from the president, provost, or dean stating why the grant would be important to the institution, what benefits would result, and how long after the granting period the institution would support this project. Letters of this type can be invaluable in making your case to the funding agency.

Step Eight: If Your Application Is Not Funded, Try Again

Only a minority of grant applications are funded. Even fewer applications are funded the first time they are submitted. So, if your proposal is funded immediately, you have been extraordinarily successful. But if it hasn't been funded, it is not the end of the world. Certainly you will be disappointed, and you may wonder what else you could have done with all those hours you spent writing the grant proposal. Let this disappointment subside quickly, however, and contact the program officer for the review committee's comments. These comments can be extremely useful as you revise your proposal and resubmit it for the next deadline. What do the comments reveal about concerns of the reviewers that you hadn't addressed in the proposal? What do those comments reveal about parts of the proposal that the committee misunderstood? (Don't be angry that the selection committee simply misunderstood an aspect of the application that you thought was completely clear. View this result as an indication of where you can revise your proposal to supply even greater clarification.) Were there items requested in your budget that are not funded by this particular program or that the reviewers regarded as excessive? Were your statement of needs and summary of potential benefits clear? Was your assessment strategy sufficiently detailed? Be sure to address all the reviewers' comments, revise the proposal, and resubmit it for the next cycle. Remember that revising a proposal is far less work than creating a proposal from scratch. The comments of the committee, though they can at times be distressing, are ultimately the best advice on how to get your project funded for the future.

Writing a successful grant proposal is a skill that comes easily to some, but others acquire it only after much effort. The important thing to keep in mind is that it is a skill that *can* be acquired. Remember to read the grant guidelines carefully and address all the questions that are asked. Adhere to the page limits you are given, even if you feel that you need far longer to explain the merits of your idea. Present your project in language that matches the funding agency's areas of greatest interest. Keep in mind who the reader of the proposal is likely to be and what that person probably knows and doesn't know. If, after taking all of these steps, you still are unsuccessful, revise the proposal and resubmit it. In the end, your efforts will pay off handsomely.

REFERENCES

Gerin, W. (2006). *Writing the NIH grant proposal: A step-by-step guide.* Thousand Oaks, CA: Sage.

Yang, O. O. (2005). *Guide to effective grant writing: How to write an effective NIH grant application.* New York: Kluwer Academic/Plenum.

RESOURCES

Carlson, M., & O'Neal-McElrath, T. (2008). *Winning grants step by step* (3rd ed.). San Francisco: Jossey-Bass.

Hall, M. S., & Howlett, S. (2003). *Getting funded: The complete guide to writing grant proposals* (4th ed.). Portland, OR: Portland State University Press.

Miller, P. W. (2009). *Grant writing: Strategies for developing winning government proposals* (3rd ed.). Munster, IN: Patrick W. Miller & Associates.

Miner, J. T., & Miner, L. E. (2005). *Models of proposal planning and writing.* Westport, CT: Praeger.

New, C. C., & Quick, J. A. (1998). *Grantseeker's toolkit: A comprehensive guide to finding funding.* New York: Wiley.

New, C. C., & Quick, J. A. (2003). *How to write a grant proposal.* Hoboken, NJ: Wiley.

Ogden, T. E., & Goldberg, I. A. (2002). *Research proposals: A guide to success* (3rd ed.). San Diego, CA: Academic Press.

Smith, N. B., & Works, E. G. (2006). *The complete book of grant writing: Learning to write grants like a professional.* Naperville, IL: Sourcebooks.

Wason, S. D. (2004). *Webster's new world grant writing handbook.* Hoboken, NJ: Wiley.

24

WRITING A BOOK PROPOSAL

Despite changing technologies, many disciplines still consider a book-length work of original scholarship published by an established academic press to be the ultimate product of research. Though this perspective may be more common in the humanities and social sciences than in many of the natural sciences, fine and performing arts, and applied fields, there are few disciplines that would not regard the publication of a well-researched and well-received book as a significant achievement. Nevertheless, not all books are alike. A monograph is technically a book-length work of scholarship that addresses a single subject. Frequently, however, the term *monograph* is used for a work of scholarship that is somewhat shorter than a book but that nevertheless appears in a volume of its own. A monograph thus bears to a book something of the same relationship that exists between a novella and a novel. A textbook is an extended publication that contains little or no original research but that is intended primarily for pedagogical purposes. Frequently, of course, books that were originally published as works of original research become assigned on the reading lists of college-level courses. These books, although we all call them "required texts," are quite different from actual textbooks, at least in terms of how they are regarded in the evaluation systems of most colleges and universities. As the primary purpose of a textbook is to report or popularize information rather than to add to the overall body of knowledge in a discipline, many schools weigh textbooks as achievements roughly equivalent to the publication of a scholarly article. Others even place the publication of a textbook in the category of teaching or service rather than scholarship. Still others give textbooks more importance than individual articles, but still value them less than entire books devoted to original research. Finally, there are books consisting of creative works, such as novels, poetry, short stories, plays, and the like. Creative works tend to count a great deal in most institutions' evaluation systems if these works are relevant to the scholarship of the discipline. In other words, a book of poetry published by a professor of creative writing may be regarded as a very important scholarly achievement, but a book of poetry published by a mechanical engineer may count very little in that professor's annual evaluation. To be sure, many colleges and universities regard it as important for members of their faculty to be well rounded, and they are delighted when professors of accountancy publish novels or professors of history publish plays. But schools are also well within their rights if they credit these works as relatively insignificant to a faculty member's overall achievement as their relevance to that person's primary responsibilities is indirect at best.

As the publication of a book remains such an important scholarly product for so many fields, how do you go about getting a book published? Certainly, you can write the book first, and then submit it to a publisher for review. This approach has worked extremely well for many people. On the other hand, many faculty members who pursue this course later discover that what they end up with is a completed manuscript that no one is willing to publish. A far more fruitful approach is to develop a book proposal relatively early in your writing process, secure the interest—and helpful suggestions—of a publisher, and then complete the book with a publication agreement already in hand. In this chapter, we'll explore the various steps involved in creating and submitting a proposal for a book-length project that a college professor can complete within a year or two.

Cultivate Personal Relationships with Publishers' Representatives

We saw in Chapter 23, "Writing a Grant Proposal," that speaking to a program officer *before* submitting an application for external funding is extremely important. In many cases, grant applications have almost no likelihood of success without these conversations. Successful book proposals often involve the same principle. By developing a relationship with a publisher's representative, you can gain invaluable insight into what the editors of that particular press are looking for and how you might be able to adapt your proposal to meet their needs more effectively. Furthermore, publishers' representatives, unlike program officers for grants, are perfectly entitled to speak in favor of proposals that they believe have merit. These are people whom you most definitely want "on your side." So, how do you get to know a publisher's representative if you aren't already acquainted with one? Well, there are three primary ways, and you would be well advised to pursue all of them to increase the chances that your book will be published.

- *Conferences in your discipline.* Most professional conferences include a hall where book or media products in the discipline are sold or displayed. Though the representatives at these meetings are primarily interested in selling current publications, they can also be an excellent source of information about the possibility of your idea being of interest to their firms. Ask these representatives if you can speak with them about a book proposal that you would like to develop. Be understanding if they prefer to meet with you at a time when they are likely to be less busy answering questions about publications already in their catalogue. Be understanding, too, if they say that they are not the right people with whom to have this conversation; simply ask for the name and contact information of the appropriate editor or representative and realize that you now have a line of access that you did not have previously. If the representative is willing to discuss your idea with you, present it in a clear and concise manner, ask how it relates to that publisher's current list and plans for the future, and request a copy of that publisher's guidelines for submissions, if they exist. A week or two after the conference, follow up with the representative, thank the person again for his or her time, and provide a realistic goal for when your full proposal will be forthcoming, if it still seems appropriate to send it.

- *Publishers' agents on your campus.* In addition to working at conferences, publishers' representatives frequently visit campuses, meet with faculty members individually in their offices, describe new additions to the publishers' catalogues, and inquire about that faculty members' needs in the areas of teaching and research. Although these representatives, who may be some of the same people attending conferences in your discipline, are likewise more interested in selling existing books than in learning about ideas for new publications, they can nevertheless be extremely useful sources of information. Follow the same procedure that you would with a representative at a conference. Ask if you can discuss your idea for a book and, if the representative demurs, request contact information for the appropriate person. Follow up on this conversation in a timely manner and submit your proposal in cases where success seems possible.

- *Publishers of books on related topics.* A third source of information about possible venues for your book is to contact the representatives of publishers who have released books on topics related in some way to your idea. Scan your bookshelf and determine who has published a significant number of the sources you will use in your own book.

Find out where these publishers are located either through the copyright page of the books themselves or by means of an Internet search. The best way to proceed when contacting a publisher "cold" (that is, without previous contact or an expression of interest) is by telephone. Call the number that you have uncovered through your research, state that you would like to discuss an idea for a possible new publication with an acquisitions editor, and ask to be connected to that person. Do not be surprised if you have to explain what you would like to several people before you reach the appropriate editor or representative. Then follow the same procedure that you would follow with a publisher's representative at a conference or in your office. Mention that you believe your idea would be appropriate for this publisher in light of their published books on similar topics. Express a willingness to follow this initial conversation with a full proposal if the publisher is interested. Understand that you may be refused at this point or after your proposal has been received. In such a situation, simply find the publisher who has released the *next* greatest number of works in your field and start over again.

Book Proposal Guidelines

Many publishers will provide guidelines for new submissions that will tell you exactly what they'd like to see in a book proposal. For example:

- *Oxford University Press* sponsors a Web page of advice, information, and resources for authors in various disciplines (www.oup.com/authors), provides clear contact information for editors in different academic disciplines (www.us.oup.com/us/corporate/contacteditor/scholarlypopular), and specifies its own guidelines for what a book proposal should contain (www.us.oup.com/us/corporate/proposal submissionpolicy/guidelines).

- *Harvard University Press* provides a detailed guide on how manuscripts should be prepared for its consideration (www.hup.harvard .edu/authors/pdf/general.pdf), which items should be included in a formal book proposal (www.hup.harvard.edu/authors/ms_guidelines .html), and how to contact its acquisitions editors (www.hup.harvard .edu/authors/editors/index.html).

- *Princeton University Press* offers different guidelines depending on whether the author is preparing a manuscript using a conventional word processor or a typesetting and layout program (press.princeton .edu/about_pup/authors/authors.html) and even has a downloadable checklist available (http://press.princeton.edu/about_pup/authors/conven_checklist.doc) to make certain that those who are submitting proposals have provided all relevant information.

- *Cornell University Press* provides an extensive guide to contributors (www.cornellpress.cornell.edu/guide/author_guide.pdf) and offers a detailed list of disciplines in which they publish (www.cornellpress.cornell.edu/cup8_authorguidelines.html).

- *The University of North Carolina Press* maintains a website for potential authors that lists the disciplines of its special interests and general guidelines for authors (http://uncpress.unc.edu/browse/page?section_name=For+Authors).

Many other academic presses provide similar information either on their websites or as a brochure that can be requested. If you are interested in submitting your idea for a book to a publisher that does not specify what should be included in a proposal, simply follow the guidelines that are provided by any of the presses just listed or base your letter on the following general outline:

- *Concept.* Write two or three sentences summarizing your central thesis or describing what your book will be about. If you feel that you are unable to convey your idea in only two or three sentences, this inability is probably a sign that you have not sufficiently refined your topic. Remember that the publisher will need to tell potential readers about your book in only a few lines in a catalogue or on a website. People who consider buying your book will be making up their minds based on a short paragraph on the book's cover. So, keep focusing your idea until you can express it clearly and succinctly.

- *Format.* Provide a brief description in terms of what your book will look like. How long will the manuscript be? Will you need to include illustrations, tables, or an index? Will the book incorporate material from other works for which rights will need to be obtained? How many chapters will the book be?

- *Audience.* Remember the essential principle that we considered in Chapter 23, "Writing a Grant Proposal": whenever you are writing any type of document, keep in mind not only what you want to say but also to whom you are trying to say it. In fact, when you are writing a book proposal, you really need to keep *two* audiences in mind: the potential audience for the book and your current audience for the book proposal. With regard to the potential audience for the book, describe whom you envision as most interested in buying the book. Is it intended only for advanced scholars in the discipline? Is it suitable as a textbook? If so, at what level? Would it appeal to general readers? One way of getting a clearer idea of the people who might be most interested in your book is to think of appropriate conferences or events at which this work might be a welcome addition to the book exhibit. The audience for that conference or event will be a good indication of the probable audience for your book. Then, as you write the book, keep this audience vividly in mind in terms of what they know and do not know, what their interests are, and what may require additional explanation. With regard to the audience for the book proposal, you may need to realize that the reader could have a different set of assumptions and background knowledge from that of your ultimate audience. Be sure to explain technical terms, abbreviations, and references that someone outside your discipline may not understand. Identify people who, although well known in your field, may be unfamiliar to most people. Give the reader of the proposal, in other words, all the information needed to make an informed decision about your idea.

- *Context.* What are some of the major works in your field to which your book will be similar? How will your book be different from those other works or make a new contribution to your discipline? Who are some qualified authorities in your discipline that could review your proposal for the publisher? (Don't just include the names of friends or close colleagues; try to think objectively about the most qualified people to evaluate the merit of your proposal.)

- *Sample.* Include one or more sample chapters from the proposed book. In most situations, you will be submitting the proposal when the book is not yet complete, in case the publisher would like you to modify the idea based on comments from reviewers. However, you should be far enough along in developing this project that it could be completed within a year or two. For this reason, include a sufficient amount of the manuscript so that the reader can form a clear idea of what the final product would be like, but don't be surprised if you are asked to modify your original idea to some extent.

- *Timetable.* Provide a reasonable projection of when the work will be completed.

If the publisher doesn't specifically ask for some of the information requested above, supply it anyway in your brief cover letter. Also state in your cover letter whether you are giving the publisher the right of first refusal (which most publishers will want and some will require before considering a proposal) or submitting your idea to several publishers simultaneously.

———————————

The process of moving from original idea to published book usually takes several years. Most academic publishers prefer to consider an initial proposal rather than a completed manuscript so that they can help guide the book's development along the way. The sample chapters that you include with your proposal do not have to be the first chapters in the book. In fact, because introductory chapters often provide a general overview of the argument to be made and the methods that will be used, it is not uncommon that these are the final chapters that authors will write. Even if your book proposal is declined a number of times before it is finally accepted, the review process can be extremely valuable in helping you clarify your vision and theme for the finished work. Moreover, when you do finally receive a publication agreement, there can be no stronger impetus to stay on task and get a work completed than a publisher's looming deadline. With all of the distractions that are possible in academic life, a fixed deadline can provide a focus for one's energy and ensure that what is now a wonderful idea soon becomes a tangible reality.

RESOURCES

Boice, R. (1990). *Professors as writers: A self-help guide to productive writing.* Stillwater, OK: New Forums Press.

Derricourt, R. (1996). *An author's guide to scholarly publishing.* Princeton, NJ: Princeton University Press.

Germano, W. (2005). *From dissertation to book.* Chicago: University of Chicago Press.

Germano, W. (2008). *Getting it published: A guide for scholars and anyone else serious about serious books* (2nd ed.). Chicago: University of Chicago Press.

Harmon, E., Montagnes, I., McMenemy, S., & Bucci, C. (Eds.). (2003). *The thesis and the book: A guide for first-time academic authors* (2nd ed.). Toronto: University of Toronto Press.

Luey, B. (2002). *Handbook for academic authors* (4th ed.). New York: Cambridge University Press.

Rabiner, S., & Fortunato, A. (2002). *Thinking like your editor: How to write great serious nonfiction—and get it published.* New York: Norton.

Rankin, E. (2001). *The work of writing: Insights and strategies for academics and professionals*. San Francisco: Jossey-Bass.

Silverman, F. H. (1998). *Authoring books and materials for students, academics, and professionals*. Westport, CT: Praeger.

Silverman, F. H. (1999). *Publishing for tenure and beyond*. Westport, CT: Praeger.

Silvia, P. (2007). *How to write a lot: A practical guide to productive academic writing*. Washington, DC: American Psychological Association.

25

OVERCOMING RESEARCH BLOCK

There are two experiences that nearly every college professor encounters at least once during his or her career.

- *Being in the zone*, that wonderfully exhilarating sensation when everything seems to be going just right with your research. Ideas come easily, the writing goes smoothly, acceptances (whether of articles, book proposals, or grant submissions) arrive in rapid succession, and everything appears to be falling into place with surprisingly little effort.

- *Being blocked*, that incredibly frustrating experience when nothing seems to be working out. New ideas simply won't come. Even if the ideas do come, it is extremely difficult or even impossible to put them into words. After struggling gamely to find the words, one article or proposal after another is turned down. You start to wonder whether an academic career was the right choice after all. You believe that this slump will last forever. You just can't seem to make any headway in your scholarship. You are blocked.

There are several important lessons to be drawn from these scenarios. First, although research block can be an extremely isolating experience because it may appear that "everyone else" is progressing well in the area of scholarship, it is far from a rare experience. Nearly all academics and creative artists encounter it from time to time. So, don't regard the frustration or temporary setback as a permanent character flaw. It comes with the territory. Second, all of us have ebbs and flows in our scholarly productivity. Although far too many systems of faculty evaluation assume that every college professor will have an unbroken line of scholarly productivity from the receipt of the terminal degree to the granting of emeritus status, real life tends to be far more complicated. The stresses of private life, the multiple pressures of developing new ideas at the same time that one is trying to be an excellent teacher and a solid institutional citizen, and the mere fact that not every bright idea pans out all mean that some periods in our careers will be far more productive than others. The worst mistake you can make, either in playing the stock market or evaluating your own productivity, is to assume that whatever trend is occurring now is likely to last forever. There will be easy times, and there will be hard times. We simply have to allow for them. Third, and most important, because research block is common and only temporary, there are specific steps you can take to shorten its duration. A few of the most beneficial strategies for ending research block will be the subject of this chapter.

Before considering those strategies, however, we need to understand that although research block can feel like a single, massive problem, it actually has two rather different manifestations that can appear either separately or together.

- *Inspiration block* is what we experience when the *ideas* won't come. We can't figure out the solution to a problem, don't know the next direction to take in our research, or simply feel bored by a field from which we used to draw a great deal of interest and excitement.

- *Writer's block* is what we experience when the *words* won't come. We may know what we want to say but can't determine how to say it. Or we work laboriously over a single sentence, drafting and redrafting the words for hours on end, achieving fairly little in the way of productivity for all the effort we expend.

As these two problems are handled in slightly different ways, let's consider them each individually.

Strategies for Overcoming Inspiration Block

Inspiration block tends to occur when people are so locked in to one way of viewing a problem or situation that they become locked out from other possibilities for creativity and insight. Many of the most productive approaches to overcoming inspiration block involve shaking things up a little so that you feel compelled to view matters in a different light. How you decide to shake things up will depend a great deal on the nature of your discipline and the research project in which you are involved. But in order to develop a fresh perspective when you are running short on ideas, consider what might occur if you were to spend even a short time looking at your project with a different:

- *Method.* If you work in a discipline that primarily uses quantitative methods to gather and analyze data, what might you be able to learn if you temporarily adopted a qualitative method for a while? If you regularly use qualitative methods, historical analysis, close reading, stylistic analysis, or the like, what might you learn if you temporarily adopted a more quantitative method? Certainly, specific methods are integral to certain disciplines but if you can't change your overall methodology, what *can* you change in your approach to the problem?

- *Medium.* How might it change your perspective on an issue if you were to summarize your data as a story or attempt to convey it poetically? Could you create a Venn diagram, flow chart, or any other visual representation of what you have thus far been viewing in non-visual terms? If you have been poring over sets of data on a computer screen, print them out and view them on paper.

- *Location.* If you usually work at your desk, try working outside, while taking a bath, or at the library. If you're accustomed to working where it is busy, find a quiet place; go to a crowded coffee shop if you've always assumed that you need complete quiet to generate new ideas. Go for a drive, or even just sit in your car for a few minutes, allowing new ideas to come to you. Find a local art gallery or museum where you can sit and think for a while. Go anywhere; just change the scenery and environment of your workplace. If physically changing location is not possible, try changing the space virtually: dress differently from how you ordinarily do, neaten a cluttered space or clutter an overly neat space, burn a fragrant candle, open the window, or alter the lighting.

- *Point of departure.* If you regularly work on a project sequentially with a clear starting point and a clear ending point, try jumping in to the problem at a different point. Start at the end and work backwards. Choose a random point in the middle and just start writing, keeping track of assumptions you are making and points you will have to introduce earlier in the work so that you can go back and address these points later. However, if your methods tend to be more free-form, force yourself to go through the ideas more systematically. Choose a particular theme, idea, or data set, and trace it through from beginning to end.

- *Point of view.* If your project has any sort of visual element, even if it is only a table, chart, or diagram, see if you notice anything different by turning it on its side, inverting it, or developing a mirror image. If you have any type of data that you have not yet given a visual form, try graphing it in various ways, and see if it makes sense to interpret it as a scatter plot with a trend line, a pie chart, a bar graph, or some other form. You can also view information differently by regarding it from another person's point of view. If you are the physician, view the matter from the perspective of a patient. If you're interpreting the protagonist's motivation in a novel, see that character through the eyes of one of the minor characters. If you are attempting to collect oral histories from a group of victims, see if you can get into the thoughts of the person or group who victimized them.

Not all of these approaches are appropriate for every single project or discipline. The key approach to keep in mind, however, arises in answering the following question: is there any way in which you can alter how you have been seeing the problem so that new ideas about it can freely emerge? Changing your perspective in some fashion frees your view from the ways in which you have been locked until now. But if none of the techniques that we have discussed so far helps you to overcome your inspiration block, there are still several other steps you can take.

- *Consider the most outrageous idea that you can develop.* One very effective way of breaking out of a cycle of unproductive thought is to pursue an idea that is wholly implausible, impractical, or even downright impossible. What, in your field, would be a hypothesis that is so completely outrageous or unprovable that it would never have occurred to you before? Sometimes while conducting these exercises, you will discover that the impossible and ludicrous contains seeds of the very answer you needed all along. Usually, however, you will find that forcing yourself to think in new ways provides you with the freedom you need to discover an answer that hadn't occurred to you before.

- *Take a break from your current project by working on something else for a while, getting away, or clearing your mind.* As we saw earlier, changing your location can help free you from being unable to generate new ideas. One of the reasons why this approach works is that, in new environments, we tend to think differently. But we also tend to think differently when our focus changes in other ways. Many cases of inspiration block can be addressed by simply working on a different project temporarily. As you direct your attention elsewhere, your mind subconsciously continues to generate new ideas and work on your problem. Many people are familiar with the experience of struggling to remember a particular name or term only to discover that it will not come to them no matter how hard they concentrate; as soon as they turn their attention to a different topic, however, the name or term suddenly pops into their minds. Coming up with new ideas, approaches, or solutions works in much the same way. You may also have discovered that many times your best ideas are developed when you are not actually working. People often say that they do their best thinking in the shower or when walking their dogs. Try something similar the next time you feel your inspiration is blocked. Go for a walk. Listen to some music. Engage in your preferred form of physical exercise. Let the problem go and, in many cases, the answer will arrive on its own. You can often prompt your creativity by applying less pressure to it rather than more. Try not to intentionally clutter your leisure time by forcing yourself to seek a solution or a new idea in any conscious manner. Rather, when you work, work; when you relax, relax. Our best ideas usually do not appear because we call them; they appear because we *let* them.

- *Brainstorm for ideas.* Another way in which to overcome inspiration block is to set yourself a specific period of time (at least a half hour to a full hour), take out a legal pad, and write down every idea or approach you can think of, no matter how ridiculous or unlikely. If you find yourself getting stuck after a while, take down a book from the shelf, open it, and find the first word you come to: develop an idea that incorporates that word. Then find another word and do the same. Don't allow yourself to stop until the full time period is used up. Also, don't allow yourself to stop writing for too long a time. Force yourself to keep writing something. When the entire time you've allocated has elapsed, go through your ideas and put them into order of priority. Are there any ideas that can be fruitfully combined in some way? What is the most improbable suggestion that you made? Why is it improbable? How does it differ from the sort of idea you were seeking?

- *If you find yourself at a loss about the next direction in which to take your research, try to brainstorm for titles.* Just as in the last brainstorming exercise, set aside at least half an hour and assign yourself the task of generating possible titles for presentations, articles, or books until the time runs out. Be as creative and idiosyncratic as you can. If you find it difficult even to get started, remember that in certain disciplines the standard formula for the title of an academic article or presentation is

AMBIGUOUS PHRASE: ATTEMPT AT A WITTY REMARK.

The ambiguous phrase that appears at the beginning of the formula usually contains at least one word that can be interpreted differently, depending on the context. After the colon, academic authors frequently place a humorous phrase that is a pun or some other type of joke.

Generate as many possible titles as you can in the time allotted. You may find that some of the most outrageous titles you come up with actually begin to direct your thoughts to the most productive new areas.

- *Explain your project to an intelligent and inquisitive person who happens to know very little about your field.* Identify a friend or colleague who is intelligent and inquisitive but who has no particular knowledge of your discipline. Describe your challenge to this person or discuss projects in your field that have interested you before. What you will discover is that sometimes an intelligent nonexpert will ask you a question that forces you to think about matters in a way that you have not considered before. At times, too, the person to whom you are speaking will approach the challenge from the perspective of his or her own specialty, and this new point of view will suggest new slants to your problem. Even more frequently, however, you'll discover that the mere act of having to describe your thoughts in different words to someone who does not understand the technical terms and assumptions of your discipline will cause you to see an issue differently, and a new idea or solution will occur to you. This solution to inspiration block is one of the primary reasons for establishing a scholarship network, as we'll discuss in Chapter 27, "Seeking and Providing Peer Support for Scholarship."

- *Remind yourself that new ideas ebb and flow in our lives.* There are times when new ideas seem to come to us in great numbers. There are times when we seem to run dry of ideas. Recognizing the inevitability of this pattern allows you to prepare for it. At those times when new ideas continually occur to you, keep track of them in a notebook or a text file on your computer. Then, when inspiration block comes (and it will), consult your list of ideas and pursue one of your earlier possibilities. You may also find that the act of reading over a list of earlier ideas stimulates new inspirations.

- *Read something about creativity or creative people.* One final method of seeking inspiration is to read the accounts of creative people and how they sought their inspiration. Authors like Wright and Wright (2002) may prompt you to think, "Well, I can't come across new ideas in exactly the same way that, say, David Cole and Larry Witte did in the Wrights' book, but what I *can* do is . . ." Reading about creative people thus helps prompt our minds to be creative almost in imitation of the case study that we are reading. For this reason, you should always keep a few books on your shelf that include accounts of creative or innovative people. Bobonich (2002) and Esser (2002) are good places to start whenever you feel that you need a fresh jolt of inspiration.

Strategies for Overcoming Writer's Block

Writer's block occurs when, although we have ideas to express, we cannot find the words to express them. Some of the techniques that we considered in the discussion of inspiration block also work with writer's block. If you find yourself temporarily at a loss for how to continue, change your location, go for a walk, work on something else for a while, or do anything that helps you break your routine. In cases of more prolonged writer's block, however, you will need to take more aggressive measures. The following strategies are useful in instances where your writer's block has lasted longer than a month or where you are trying to prevent a recurrence of this problem in the future.

- *Stop writing in midsentence.* Sometimes our hardest task is getting started. It is often difficult to come up with an effective opening sentence or first paragraph. Yet when we do, we usually find that our writing flows more easily. In a similar way, it can become difficult to get back to a writing project after we've been away from it for a day, a few weeks, or an extended period. Having to get ourselves back into the mindset we had when we last were working on that project can be the biggest challenge that we face. If it becomes difficult enough, these interruptions can lead to writer's block. For this reason, an effective writing strategy is to end each session not at the end of a paragraph or section but right in the middle of a sentence. Picking up where you left off the last time thus becomes relatively easy and, with this running head start, you can help overcome the difficulty of getting back into an interrupted project.

- *If you have an established routine for writing, break it. If you don't have an established routine for writing, create one.* In other words, anything we do that causes a change in our habits or approach can help free us from the habits and approaches that are interfering with our writing. Some writers thrive on the regularity of their routines. This was the case, for instance, with the behaviorist B. F. Skinner:

> The circadian rhythm of his writing schedule did not miss a beat. A timer rang at midnight signaling him to arise, move to his desk, and write until signaled to stop at one o'clock. He returned to bed

and arose again to the sound of the timer at five o'clock and com- posed until it buzzed two hours later. He wrote three hours a day, seven days a week, holidays included. As the years passed, these three early morning hours were, as he often said, "the most reinforcing part of my day." The other twenty-one hours were arranged to make the writing time as profitable as possible. (Bjork, 1993, p. 217)

Skinner, like the novelist Jane Smiley, developed a routing for writing that was based on working each day for a particular period of time. Other authors, like Anthony Trollope and Graham Greene, created rou- tines based on writing a certain number of words each day. The exact nature of your writing routine is likely to be highly personal and one that will work best with your own discipline, interests, and way of life. It is the mere matter of having a set routine, however, that can help you break your writer's block. If you force yourself, as painful as it may be at first, to write five hundred words each day beginning precisely at 3:00 P.M. and not allowing yourself to leave your chair until those five hundred words are written, you will soon find the words coming more easily and the quality of your writing will improve. But what if you've successfully used a routine for several years but now it is no longer helping? Then it's time to take the opposite approach and abandon your routine. Write between phone calls on a busy day. Write while you are waiting for your lunch order to be served. Write late at night or when you feel that you just can't sleep. Write after a walk in the park. Write while on a long trip by air or train. Do whatever you *haven't* been doing. Change is one of the keys to overcoming writer's block. As what you have been doing hasn't been working, try something else. You may well solve your problem with just this single action. At the very least, this remedy is highly unlikely to make your frustration any worse than it already is.

- *If you find yourself unable to write productively on your current proj- ect, write something useful and productive anyway.* Writing is a skill that gets easier the more you practice. When you write a great deal, you discover that your words flow more readily and that starting a new project or section of a project becomes less of a chore. So, to keep yourself in good shape as a writer, keep writing on some useful project even if you find that you simply cannot continue with your current book or article right now. Some excellent opportunities for keeping up with your writing include:
  - *Salem Press* (www.salempress.com), which each year publishes a number of reference works in various fields. Salem Press

regularly issues calls for requests to contribute on specific topics. Each submission is regarded as a work for hire and must fit into specific guidelines for length and focus. Because entries in the volumes issued by Salem Press are not peer reviewed, they tend to count relatively little in the faculty evaluation systems of most institutions. Nevertheless, they provide excellent opportunities for scholars to write about subjects that they know very well, teach a writer how to meet a strict deadline and adhere to a limited word count, and ensure that you keep up your academic writing. Salem Press even pays contributors for their work.

- *Book reviews*, which appear in most academic journals. Although publishing book reviews is unlikely to win you tenure or promotion, they do provide opportunities that will keep you writing, expose you to new developments in your field, and help expand your personal library since you almost always get to keep the book that you review. In the back of many journals is a section titled "Books Received." These are new works submitted to the journal by authors or publishers that are awaiting review. Contact the book review editor of the journal and ask to review one or more of the titles on the list. While you may discover that the books you request have already been assigned to other scholars for review, the editor will now be aware of your interest and may keep you in mind when similar titles appear in the future.

- *The Teaching Professor* (www.teachingprofessor.com) is published ten times a year by Magna Publications in Madison, Wisconsin. Sometimes when it is difficult for us to continue the writing of a new research project, it feels much easier to write about our teaching. In all probability you have discovered some valuable method of presenting information in your discipline, designing courses, or providing nonclassroom learning experiences for your students. This insight can be shared with your fellow college professors, and you may find that writing about something you know very well can help you overcome your block in writing about new subjects. *The Teaching Professor* is an excellent resource on various aspects of college-level instruction. Each piece is relatively short, and new contributors are always sought. For author guidelines, see www.magnapubs.com/aboutus/authorguidelines.html.

Truly severe cases of research or writing block may require consultation with an academic job coach who often can help a college professor identify and then address the underlying problem (see June, 2008). Most cases, however, are not serious enough to require outside intervention and result from following habits that, although once productive, are now hindering either the researcher's inspiration or writing. The best solution in these instances is to identify ways in which those habits can be broken by acting in a significantly different manner. Each person will discover what type of change works best in his or her individual situation. You may need to try different approaches until you find the solution that is right for you. The important thing is simply not to let this new solution become a new habit, or you may someday discover that the strategy that helps now eventually becomes just another frustrating routine in the future.

REFERENCES

Bjork, D. W. (1993). *B. F. Skinner: A life.* New York: Basic Books.

Bobonich, H. M. (2002). *Seeing around corners: How creative people think.* Pittsburgh: Dorrance.

Esser, T. A. (2002). *The venture cafe: Secrets, strategies, and stories from America's high-tech entrepreneurs.* New York: Warner Books.

June, A. W. (2008, September 26). Job coaches help professors back on track. *Chronicle of Higher Education*, pp. A1, A10–A11.

White, S. P., with Wright, G. P. (2002). *New ideas about new ideas: Insights on creativity from the world's leading innovators.* Cambridge, MA: Perseus.

RESOURCES

Creswell, J. W. (2009). *Research design: Qualitative, quantitative, and mixed methods approaches* (3rd ed.). Thousand Oaks, CA: Sage.

De Bono, E. (1993). *Serious creativity: Using the power of lateral thinking to create new ideas.* New York: HarperBusiness.

Denzin, N. K., & Lincoln, Y. S. (Eds.). (2005). *The Sage handbook of qualitative research* (3rd ed.). Thousand Oaks, CA: Sage.

Glatzer, J. (2003). *Outwitting writer's block and other problems of the pen.* Guilford, CT: Lyons Press.

Merriam, S. B. (1998). *Qualitative research and case study applications in education.* San Francisco: Jossey-Bass.

Ogle, R. (2007). *Smart world: Breakthrough creativity and the new science of ideas.* Boston: Harvard Business School Press.

Patton, M. Q. (2002). *Qualitative research and evaluation methods* (3rd ed.). Thousand Oaks, CA: Sage.

Stage, F. K. (Ed.). (2007). *New directions for institutional research: No. 133. Using quantitative data to answer critical questions.* San Francisco: Jossey-Bass.

Staw, J. A. (2003). *Unstuck: A supportive and practical guide to working through writer's block.* New York: St. Martin's Press.

Williams, F., & Monge, P. (2001). *Reasoning with statistics: How to read quantitative research* (5th ed.). Orlando, FL: Harcourt.

26

BALANCING SCHOLARSHIP
WITH OTHER DUTIES

College professors, particularly those who have not yet been granted tenure, frequently feel as though they are being pulled in many different directions at once. They are told that they need to build a successful record in research or creative activity in order to qualify for tenure and promotion. Their departments want them to receive excellent teaching evaluations year after year. They are constantly sought out for committee assignments. In their personal lives, they may be starting a family, taking care of their parents, or simply trying to have a meaningful social life despite their other commitments. The question then arises: how do you set priorities among a number of competing activities, each of which may legitimately be described as "the most important thing you have to do right now?" Moreover, even if you set those priorities, how do you make sure that an activity that is very significant, although maybe not your highest priority of all, still receives an appropriate amount of attention? These are the issues that we'll discuss in the following pages.

Seek Single Activities with Multiple Benefits

One of the traps that college professors can fall into occurs when they isolate their various activities into separate and airtight compartments. They view teaching, scholarship, and service as different activities and become anxious when scholarship "interferes" with their teaching or vice versa. Even worse, they may view the preparation of conference presentations, the writing of articles for a peer-reviewed publication, and the development of a scholarly book as distinct activities and wonder, "When will I have time to complete my book when I'm also expected to speak at professional meetings and publish papers?" One alternative to this type of mindset is to develop an approach to your work in which single activities have multiple benefits. For instance, suppose that your ultimate goal is to produce a book of research on some specific topic. A strategy that unites the numerous activities expected of you, rather than setting them at odds with one another, might look like this:

- *Step one: Create an abstract.* Take a portion of the overall project that can exist as an independent unit and write it up as a one- to two-page abstract to be submitted as a proposal for a conference presentation.

- *Step two: Move from abstract to draft.* Flesh out the abstract so that it becomes an initial draft of your presentation. Choose one of your classes and distribute this draft as part of your assigned readings. The draft thus becomes included in your course materials, and you are likely to gain some feedback as to which passages still need further clarification, where the flow of your argument is not as smooth as you would like it to be, and whether your central thesis is sufficiently clear.

- *Step three: Move from first draft to second draft.* With the information you have gained from your class's response, revise the paper and offer it as a presentation in a departmental or campuswide forum. This audience will give you further ideas about how your presentation can be improved for its final draft and, depending on your topic and how your institution weighs on-campus presentations, you will have performed a visible contribution either to scholarship or to service.

- *Step four: Make the conference presentation.* Having tested this presentation twice before, you should be confident now as you deliver this material at the conference in your discipline. The presentation will itself be regarded as a contribution to scholarship and, in the questions or discussion that occurs after your presentation, you will gain additional insight into how your ideas may be refined further. Moreover, there is almost always some downtime at conferences. If you contacted your institution's development office before you left for the conference, you might have the name of a donor or potential donor who lives in the area where the convention is located. By making a courtesy call either on the telephone or over a meal, you can perform a valuable act of service at the same time that you're pursuing your scholarship (see Chapter 38, "The Faculty Member as Fundraiser"). Alternatively, there may be a high school in the area from which your institution draws—or wishes to draw—potential students. By collaborating with your admissions office, you may be able to perform an act of service by making a presentation at the school or representing your institution at a college fair.

- *Step five: Transform the presentation into an article.* Based on what you learned at the conference, you are now ready to rewrite your presentation as a chapter that can be submitted to a refereed journal. The resulting article will be regarded as an even more significant contribution to scholarship than your presentation itself. The referees for the journal may well have further suggestions as to how your article can be revised and improved. And when the article appears, it can be included among your course materials as a contribution to instruction.

- *Step six: Transform the article into a book proposal.* With the article now complete, it need only be slightly revised to serve as a sample chapter in the proposal for the book that you were intending to create all along (see Chapter 24, "Writing a Book Proposal"). For at least one other chapter, you can follow these six steps again from the beginning, moving from the creation of a paper that enhances your teaching to a book that serves as the ultimate product of your scholarship.

Due to the many variations that occur in institutional mission, the specific emphasis of your position, and disciplinary differences, the plan just outlined may need a great deal of modification before it fits your circumstances. Nevertheless, the overall goal remains the same: finding a way to organize the many different opportunities and obligations that compete for your time into a logical progression of activities. Through careful planning, your various efforts at teaching, scholarship, and service should not compete with one another, but rather support and complement each other. With the strategy outlined above, in a year or less, a faculty member will have leveraged each activity in such a way that he or she may well be offered a publication agreement for a book without having stinted all of the other professional activities in which you are expected to engage. If that is not a suitable goal for your college or discipline, try constructing an alternative model that would work for you. In every possible aspect of your schedule, look for single activities that produce two or even three different beneficial results.

Understand the Full Trajectory of Faculty Work

Go back and reread Chapters 4 through 8. Although at times it can feel as if you are expected to be nothing less than stellar in teaching, scholarship, and service at every single stage of your career, there is a discernible rhythm or trajectory in academic life that can affect what your priorities should be at any particular time. Most institutional evaluation systems do not tell you this in precisely these terms, but untenured faculty members are usually expected to direct most of their energy toward teaching and scholarship, with service given far less attention. Midcareer faculty are usually expected to direct most of their energy toward scholarship and service, with the understanding that their teaching should by this time be developed to a sufficiently high level. Full professors are usually expected to have one area of exceptional performance—which could be either teaching, scholarship, or service, depending on their individual interests and achievements—and their contributions in the other two areas need not reach that same high degree of distinction. At a number of institutions, faculty members can choose tracks in which the weighting of these three areas of evaluation changes according to the established goal of the faculty member. Even in a college or university that does not currently offer separate faculty tracks, if you are feeling harried or oppressed by competing demands for your time and seemingly incompatible expectations, it is time to have a candid talk with your department chair (or your dean, if appropriate) about what your highest priorities should be right *now*. In most cases, you will have the following essential principle reinforced for you:

> Nearly every college professor is expected to demonstrate excellence in teaching, scholarship, and service over the course of his or her career. Nevertheless, because of the trajectory of the typical professorial career, few institutions expect stellar performance in each of these categories at every stage of professional development.

Take Full Advantage of Your Resources

Conflicting demands for one's time can make a college professor feel extremely isolated. It can appear at times as though everyone else is exceeding at this monumental challenge, whereas you alone have trouble balancing competing priorities. This impression, though false, can be so daunting that it immobilizes faculty members at the very time when they need to be making the most progress. The solution is to learn what resources are available at your institution and in your community that can help reduce the pressure of these conflicting demands and allow you to focus on your priorities. Among the resources that you should explore are:

- *Your institution's center for teaching and learning (under whatever name it may be known locally) and writing center.* These resources can introduce you to effective strategies that increase student engagement and learning at the same time that they reduce your overall workload. Moreover, the center for teaching and learning may have opportunities for you to engage in projects that deal with the scholarship of teaching (yet another way to pursue a single activity that has multiple benefits; see Chapter 28, "Alternative Forms of Scholarship"). In addition, the writing center at most institutions allows faculty members to submit drafts of works in progress for critique on the flow of thought and adequacy of argumentation. The advice you receive from the writing center can help you move more swiftly from draft to accepted article or book proposal.

- *Establish or participate in an existing scholarship network.* As we'll see in greater detail in Chapter 27, "Seeking and Providing Peer Support for Scholarship," scholarship networks are support groups of colleagues who provide encouragement throughout research projects, assist one another with meeting deadlines and keeping on task, and provide constructive criticism that results in overall stronger scholarly products.

- *Social service agencies or social workers* in your area can be invaluable sources of assistance and information if you are trying to balance your responsibilities as a college professor with those as a family member and caregiver. Increasing numbers of adults need to care for aging parents either locally or at a great distance. Social workers, who often hold positions with the county or municipality in which you live, can ease your challenge in this area. They can tell you of additional resources, options that you may not know you have, and solutions that have worked for others. They can make inquiries for you, reducing the amount of time that you need to devote to these tasks. Many college professors are not aware of the wide range of social support available to them as caregivers because these challenges are new to them. But social service agencies and social workers can help you fulfill your obligations to your family even while you complete your professional responsibilities.

Use To-Do Lists, but Do Not Become Enslaved to Them

Many faculty members try to solve the problem of balancing scholarship with their other duties by creating to-do lists that itemize the various tasks they have before them and help them to set some priorities. To-do lists are certainly valuable tools as long as they are used correctly. Over-reliance on such lists can lead to further frustration with the number of tasks that are still undone and become counterproductive because the time spent in creating, reorganizing, and updating the list could have been better spent actually performing one of the tasks on the list. The following are some guidelines for how to make to-do lists more effective (Buller, 2006):

- *Never record any item too large to be accomplished in a single session.* Any task that is too large to be finished in one day should be broken down into multiple tasks that can be accomplished in a single session. Checking off these items as they are completed provides a greater sense of accomplishment and keeps you from being overwhelmed by a long list of tasks that never seem to get checked off as completed.

- *If an item has remained on the to-do list for more than a few weeks, it should be removed from the list.* Any item that gets carried over from list to list for several weeks is unlikely to be completed anyway. Rather than being tyrannized by these items that never seem to get done, simply refocus your attention to tasks that you can and will accomplish.

- *At the end of each day spend no more than ten minutes reorganizing the list for the next day's priorities.* A small amount of time spent on setting priorities can become a useful exercise in focusing one's energy. Too much time spent on this task, however, simply becomes one more unnecessary distraction.

Track Your Use of Time

Rather than wondering where all your time goes, conduct a short exercise to find out. Keep a brief time log that records how your time is being spent each day, and then group these blocks of time into various categories. Once you see how your time is being used, you can find ways in which certain tasks can be done more efficiently or perhaps even discarded entirely in favor of more productive activities. For instance, if you discover that your appointments and meetings tend to go overtime, why does this occur?

- Does the person who is conducting the meeting focus on its primary purpose immediately, or does it take some time to get to the main topic?

- Do people tend to linger and talk long after the main purpose for the meeting has been completed?

- Can the meeting or appointment be made more efficient with a written agenda?

Identifying those time periods that tend to be less productive can help you figure out ways in which you can carve out more time for your scholarship. Remember that even relatively short periods of time can be productive for a research project. During the ten minutes you spend waiting for a telephone call to be returned, you could outline the next two or three points you will raise in an article that you are writing, use the Internet to identify some of the sources you need to obtain at the library or through interlibrary loan, or specify a few of the vexing questions that you still need to explore. As you grow more accustomed to productive use of these little "puddles" of time, you'll discover that your need for the great "seas" and "oceans" of uninterrupted time will diminish.

Balancing scholarship with other duties is frequently a matter of learning the most productive use of your available time, leveraging activities so that a single effort produces several different results, and setting appropriate priorities. If you ask almost anyone how things have been going lately, the person is likely to tell you that they are busier than ever or that things are increasingly hectic. Juggling priorities isn't a challenge you're facing alone. You can take comfort in the universality of this problem at the same time that you see how your colleagues have effectively addressed it. All of us are busy, but by following the principles outlined above you can help to transform simply being busy into an even higher level of productivity.

REFERENCES

Buller, J. L. (2006). Sharpening focus. In J. L. Buller, *The essential department chair: A practical guide to college administration* (pp. 41–45). Bolton, MA: Anker.

RESOURCES

Bland, C. J., Weber-Main, A. M., Lund, S. M., & Finstad, D. A. (2005). *The research-productive department: Strategies from departments that excel.* Bolton, MA: Anker.

Bubb, S., & Earley, P. (2004). *Managing teacher workload: Work-life balance and well-being.* Thousand Oaks, CA: Sage.

Corley, E. A. (2005). How do career strategies, gender, and work environment affect faculty productivity levels in university-based science centers? *Review of Policy Research, 22*(5), 637–655.

Crenshaw, D. (2008). *The myth of multitasking: How "doing it all" gets nothing done*. San Francisco: Jossey-Bass.

Gappa, J. M., Austin, A. E., & Trice, A. G. (2007). *Rethinking faculty work: Higher education's strategic imperative*. San Francisco: Jossey-Bass.

Levin, S. G., & Stephan, P. E. (1991). Research productivity over the life cycle: Evidence for academic scientists. *American Economic Review, 81*(1), 114–132.

Morgenstern, J. (2004). *Never check e-mail in the morning and other unexpected strategies for making your work life work*. New York: Fireside.

Stack, L. (2004). *Leave the office earlier: The productivity pro shows you how to do more in less time . . . and feel great about it*. New York: Broadway Books.

Tobis, I., & Tobis, M. (2002). *Managing multiple projects*. New York: McGraw-Hill.

SEEKING AND PROVIDING PEER SUPPORT FOR SCHOLARSHIP

Most college professors are already far more involved in peer support for scholarship than they realize. For instance, they might ask a colleague to look over a paper they wish to submit for publication and to comment on how it could be improved. If they are interested in finding out more about a particular research topic, they ask another professor if he or she could recommend works that would help with this research. Informal peer support for scholarship, in other words, is going on around us all the time. In this chapter, we're going to explore ways of developing this type of casual conversation into a more formal—and frequently far more beneficial—structure, the type of support mechanism that is known as a scholarship network. The origin of scholarship networks follows the rise of quality circles that have been found in many Japanese businesses since the 1960s. In a quality circle, a group of employees at a company volunteer to meet periodically to discuss ways in which the quality of this or that product can be improved, the safety of their physical plant enhanced, or the techniques used to create their products made more efficient. Quality circles were based on the philosophy that workers themselves are often in a far better position than managers to determine how improvements can be made to their products and their environment. Moreover, peers learn from one another, each person enhancing his or her own performance based on the experience of others.

Bernstein (1996) borrowed the idea of quality circles and adapted it to the academic environment, creating teaching circles. According to a definition proposed by Pat Hutchings (1996), teaching circles may be viewed as "a variety of arrangements through which (1) a small group of faculty members (typically four to ten . . .) (2) makes a commitment to work together over a period of at least a semester (3) to address questions and concerns about the particulars of their teaching and their students' learning" (p. 7). In much the same way that quality circles arose from voluntary efforts to improve the nature of a product, so were teaching circles voluntary efforts by professors to improve the quality of instruction at their institutions. Though many institutions had experimented with occasional brown-bag lunches to discuss various ideas related to the quality of instruction, teaching circles made this type of approach more systematic. Members of the group would set specific meeting times throughout the semester, devote an extended period either discussing a new instructional technology or a book that dealt with a new pedagogical approach, and examine their own individual challenges in instruction that semester. If one faculty member encountered a particular problem—such as disruptive behavior in the classroom or the need for creative ways to engage students with rather uninspiring material—the other members of the teaching circle were available to help, and they could offer suggestions based on similar situations that they themselves had encountered. Many college professors found this type of colleague-based support so successful that, beginning in the mid- to late-1990s, faculty members in the College of Liberal Arts and Social Sciences at Georgia Southern University expanded the approach, creating scholarship networks, an experiment that applied the same basic philosophy of quality circles and teaching circles to their research and creative activities. Both teaching circles and scholarship networks are examples of faculty learning communities that are becoming increasingly common at colleges and universities as ways for college professors to seek and provide peer support.

Scholarship networks function usually as follows:

- A department chair, dean, or provost expresses support for the idea and offers to handle the logistics of contacting people and scheduling the first meeting. It is also possible for a group of faculty members to engage in a grassroots effort to develop their own network, simply making their occasional conversations about current research projects a little more formal and systematic. Even though the networks operate independently without ongoing administrative supervision, some initial support from a supervisor can be desirable. It gives the scholarship network an official standing and, since administrative offices tend to have more clerical support than do individual faculty members, they can be extremely helpful in identifying appropriate times and places for meetings.

- Once either administrators or the faculty members themselves have expressed interest in forming a scholarship network, the participants divide into groups of five to ten members each. Some scholarship networks will prefer to consist of individuals who all work in similar fields so that they will understand each other's methodology. Others will prefer a more varied group. (The latter approach has several advantages that we'll consider later.) A planning meeting is then devoted to discussing frequency of sessions. Most successful scholarship networks meet every other week, although other groups prefer to meet less often. More frequent meetings tend to conflict with other obligations and don't give members enough time to act on the suggestions they received at the last session. Holding meetings less than once a month may not allow groups to coalesce, and thus the meetings cease altogether.

- The structure of the individual meetings depends on the preferences of the members. Some groups prefer to start their discussions by grappling with one or two chapters of a difficult book that is of interest to all of them. Other groups prefer to proceed immediately to discussing the status of their own research. Each member in turn then reports on what he or she has accomplished in the area of research since the last meeting, whether the goals set at that meeting have been kept, and whether any particular challenges or difficulties have arisen in their scholarly projects. If challenges have occurred, the other members of the network suggest possible solutions. Then, after the members have all reported on their current progress, they each state a clear goal for the next meeting. The goal should be something measurable and attainable: a goal to "do more library research into the writings of Marianne Moore" is not as helpful as a goal to "create an annotated bibliography of at least twelve books or articles on Marianne Moore that are relevant to my current project." Whenever possible, each member's goal should focus on some tangible product such as "writing an additional six pages of my first draft," "revising my entire first draft to a form that can be presented to this group," or "submitting my paper proposal to the conference." Stating the goal in these terms will make it very easy to determine whether that goal has been achieved by the next meeting. Failing to meet a goal is acceptable, of course, as unexpected situations always arise. But if a particular member fails to meet goals in meeting after meeting, the scholarship network can begin to function as a support group, helping the person be either more realistic in goal setting or more productive in his or her work.

- If any member of the network has a work of scholarship that is far enough along to share—perhaps a second draft of an article or a presentation that is nearly ready for a conference—the other members of the group then review it. Some groups find it easier to discuss suggested improvements if the papers are read aloud. Other groups prefer to read the papers silently to themselves, either at the meeting or between meetings. Each member of the group then provides comments on the work of scholarship, always with the aim of making it better. Comments are expected to provide constructive criticism. Praise that is offered simply for the sake of being nice is less valued than candid ideas about how the work can be improved. Weaknesses are not identified in a manner that will humiliate or embarrass the author. The fundamental objective of the scholarship network is for any paper, article, presentation, or book chapter produced by a member of the network to be as strong as possible.

- When a member of the scholarship network is practicing a conference presentation, other members of the group will help the faculty member prepare by asking the sort of questions that could arise at the conference itself. Though it is impossible to anticipate the precise questions that will emerge, the practice session helps faculty members learn the art of thinking on their feet and allows them to go to the conference with greater confidence and poise.

The Benefits of Scholarship Networks

Participants in scholarship networks report a number of positive experiences resulting from their participation in this type of colleague-based support. For instance, the Social Science and History Research Network at Georgia Southern University characterizes the benefit that its members have received from working together over the course of a decade in the following way:

> One of the most valuable and unexpected aspects of the Network has been the extent to which we have become actively involved in each other's work. On more than one occasion, one of us has stumbled across a document, book, or piece of information that is not relevant to her project, but is useful to another person in the group. In addition, we frequently exchange specialized knowledge. The more technologically savvy members have assisted those who are technologically challenged. Members who are adept at reading and interpreting the census and land records have helped other members work with those documents. In one case, a member who is a lawyer made a special trip to a courthouse in a nearby county to retrieve legal documents that were essential to another's research. We have helped each other with a variety of issues related to publication, ranging from dealing with journal editors who "sit" on manuscripts for long periods of time . . . through responding to readers' reports . . . to filling out author

questionnaires for publishers' marketing departments. (A. Simms, personal communication, October 24, 2007)

Each scholarship network will discover its own advantages in their mutual collaboration, but the following are several additional benefits that can be expected to result from this type of peer-based support.

- Most participants in a scholarship network report that they are more productive than they would have been working independently. The mere fact that you are working collaboratively with a group of peers whose opinion and respect you've come to value means that you will probably be very reluctant to let them down when you have publicly announced an ambitious goal. If you set yourself a personal goal, such as "By next week at this time, I will have completed ten manuscript pages on the first draft of my article," no one but you will know or care whether you actually achieve that goal. But members of scholarship networks tend to hold one another's feet to the fire. If you set a goal of writing ten pages and fail to complete it by the next meeting, the other members of the scholarship network are likely to express sympathy. But if you still haven't met that goal by the following meeting, your peers are likely to express concern. You won't want to disappoint them, and they are likely to cajole and encourage you until you meet your goals. Whereas before it may have been difficult to complete even one article within a single academic year because of conflicting commitments, you may find that the support and expectations of your peers mean that you now produce two articles, a conference presentation, and several book reviews within that same period. Each person's productivity varies, but it generally occurs at a higher level once they begin participating in a scholarship network. As but one example, Georgia Southern's Social Science and History Research Network has traced its scholarly activity in annual reports since its inception, with the following results typical for a single year. In 2002–2003, six members of the network produced (A. Simms, personal communication, October 24, 2007):

  - Two books that were released

  - One book in press

  - One book in progress

  - One book chapter in press

  - Three refereed articles published

  - Three newsletter articles published

- One article in press
- Two articles undergoing revisions prior to resubmission
- One article nominated for an award

Participants in the network all agreed that their individual productivity would almost certainly have been lower without the support of their colleagues.

- Most participants in a scholarship network find that they think of many more new and interesting research possibilities than they did when they were working independently. Just as hearing other presentations at a conference frequently inspires us with a number of ideas for possible new research projects, simply listening to other scholarship network members talk about their work can often encourage us to think of our own ideas. Scholarship networks are also fertile breeding grounds for collaborations. As participants learn about each other's research, they see possibilities for joint projects, interdisciplinary studies, or the benefits of approaching the same subject or set of data from the perspectives of different disciplines simultaneously. Indeed, a common pattern for scholarship networks is to spend their first year or two providing mutual help and support for independent projects but, from their third year on, to serve increasingly as a mechanism for producing collaborative projects. Many faculty members discover that though they may initially be attracted to networks composed almost exclusively of members of their own discipline, they soon gravitate to more diverse groups where interdisciplinary, transdisciplinary, and multidisciplinary projects more commonly develop. (On the differences among these terms, see Chapter 28, "Alternative Forms of Scholarship.") In this way, participants in scholarship networks tend to be more productive researchers than their peers elsewhere at the institution, not only because their colleagues help keep them focused on their scholarly projects, but because the "hothouse atmosphere" of a scholarship network tends to generate new types of projects over time.
- Scholarship networks are easily adaptable over time as the needs of their members evolve. When the idea of scholarship is first introduced, it is not uncommon for the most eager participants to be junior faculty members. After all, they are the people who tend to find themselves faced with high expectations for publications, conference presentations, juried exhibits, and other forms of scholarly and creative activity—but with relatively little training in how to be successful at these activities. The mutual support that junior faculty

members receive from their colleagues in a scholarship network is thus of tremendous help as they meet their disciplines' expectations for tenure and promotion. But once most participants in a scholarship network have passed these milestones, they usually continue to engage in peer-based support. They find that, as their own needs change, the focus and operation of the network can change as well. As they become senior faculty members, the scholarship network shifts away from providing peer advice on such topics as how to get an article accepted for publication or how to make certain that a paper is well prepared for a national conference. Instead, the network provides the faculty member with an important testing ground for new research ideas, a source of advice on how to move into new research areas, and colleagues who can readily support collaborative projects.

- Scholarship networks can be an invaluable aid to faculty members whose research assumes nontraditional forms or occurs in nontraditional areas. As we shall see in the next chapter, certain types of research and creative activity do not easily lend themselves to peer review before they are released, are not necessarily distributed in print, or do not meet any of the other expectations people usually have of traditional scholarship. For instance, a recital, production of a play, or dance performance cannot be peer reviewed before it occurs in the same way that an article can be refereed before it appears in print. Indeed, many of these creative activities are transitory by their very nature and cannot even appear in print in the way that articles, monographs, and books of research do. Nearly every institution is familiar with the experience of having to defend emerging forms of scholarship as acceptable for the purposes of promotion and tenure or "just as rigorous and valuable" as are traditional, peer-reviewed publications. Scholarship networks can play an important role in helping colleges and universities deal with this problem. First, they serve to educate their own members—and, through those members, other professors at the institution—about the full spectrum of scholarly activities that now take place at colleges and universities. Discussion of the disciplinary standards outlined in Diamond and Adam (1995, 2000) can serve as a good starting point for these issues. Second, they provide an early alert to faculty members who are engaged in nontraditional forms of scholarship about ways in which they present their scholarly contributions to promotion review committees that may not immediately understand the significance or importance of this new scholarship. Because participants in scholarship networks are frequently on the cutting edge of new types of research, they tend to deal with these challenges before they become apparent to the faculty as a whole. They can thus be seen as filling an institutional need that extends far beyond the needs of the members of the network itself.

Scholarship networks are one of the rare initiatives that have practically no disadvantages. They are extremely cost effective as they require little or no funding to create. They begin to improve the quality and amount of scholarly activities by their members almost immediately. And they provide an important faculty-centered initiative that can improve the job satisfaction of everyone who engages in them. There is no department chair, dean, or provost anywhere in higher education who would resist the positive contributions that this fruitful type of peer-based initiative can help create.

REFERENCES

Bernstein, D. J. (1996). A departmental system for balancing the development and evaluation of college teaching: A commentary on Cavanaugh. *Innovative Higher Education, 20*(4), 241–248.

Diamond, R. M., & Adam, B. E. (Eds.). (1995). *The disciplines speak: Rewarding the scholarly, professional, and creative work of faculty.* Washington, DC: American Association for Higher Education.

Diamond, R. M., & Adam, B. E. (Eds.). (2000). *The disciplines speak II: More statements on rewarding the scholarly, professional, and creative work of faculty.* Washington, DC: American Association for Higher Education.

Hutchings, P. (1996). *Making teaching community property: A menu for peer collaboration and peer review.* Washington, DC: American Association for Higher Education.

RESOURCES

Borgman, C. L. (2007). *Scholarship in the digital age: Information, infrastructure, and the internet.* Cambridge, MA: MIT Press.

Cox, M. D., & Richlin, L. (Eds.). (2004). *New directions for teaching and learning: No. 97. Building faculty learning communities.* San Francisco: Jossey-Bass.

Zahorski, K. J. (2002). Nurturing scholarship through holistic faculty development: A synergistic approach. In K. J. Zahorski (Ed.), *New directions for teaching and learning: No. 90. Scholarship in the postmodern era: New venues, new values, new visions* (pp. 29–37). San Francisco: Jossey-Bass.

28

ALTERNATIVE FORMS OF SCHOLARSHIP

Traditionally, the products of scholarship at most colleges and universities were expected to demonstrate three important qualities:

- They had to be published.
- They had to be peer reviewed.
- And they had to involve original research.

Making presentations at academic conferences was, many institutions concluded, a fine and worthwhile activity. As a *complement* to refereed books and articles, a history of successful conference presentations was even considered to be quite admirable. But as a *substitute* for traditional publication, presenting papers and serving as a moderator on a panel left quite a bit to be desired. No one ever gets tenured, the common wisdom went, by making conference presentations alone. Even at institutions or in disciplines where they do, they'll never be promoted to the rank of full professor. The general consensus at colleges and universities was that the highest form of scholarship was only that which grew out of research, was then vetted through a careful peer review process and ultimately appeared in a prestigious journal, was released by a major academic press, or was published in some other acceptable manner.

This traditional view of scholarship has had to be reexamined on a number of different fronts. We have already seen that certain fields, such as the fine and performing arts, simply do not fit this structure easily. The creative works that are ranked as significant products of scholarship in those disciplines often do not lend themselves to appearance in print, cannot be peer reviewed before they are displayed or performed, and are the result of creativity, research into the work, and an advanced level technique as opposed to *discovery* in the sense this term is used by many other disciplines. For other fields as well, it has become apparent that the attainment of patents, grants, and licenses may often be better indicators of scholarly contributions than published research articles. Moreover, certain conferences are so distinguished that having a paper accepted for them must be regarded as a significant achievement in scholarship. In addition, technological developments have significantly changed the meaning of the word *published*. A large number of academic journals remain peer reviewed and highly selective but have abandoned their printed forms in favor of electronic versions. The ability of personal computers to create films, Web pages, and other sophisticated forms of multimedia have greatly expanded the notion of what an "article" or a "book" may be. Finally, most colleges and universities have broadly reconsidered the very idea of what constitutes scholarship and have realized that this category includes far more than research alone. In this chapter we'll explore the implications of these ideas on the evolving notion of scholarship and examine the opportunities and challenges that arise from alternative forms of scholarship.

Boyer and the Reconsideration of Scholarship

In 1990, Ernest L. Boyer's landmark book *Scholarship Reconsidered* began questioning the traditional definition of scholarship in place at many institutions of higher education. By equating scholarship with research, Boyer noted, colleges and universities have oversimplified the intellectual contributions that professors have made and unnecessarily restricted the scholarly activity of the faculty. As we saw in Chapter 3, "What Kind of Professor Are You?" Boyer noted that there is not merely one type of scholarship that should be important in higher education, but rather four complementary types.

- *The scholarship of discovery* is "closest to what is meant when academics speak of 'research.' No tenets in the academy are held in higher regard than the commitment to knowledge for its own sake, to freedom of inquiry and to following, in a disciplined fashion, an investigation wherever it may lead" (Boyer, p. 17).

- *The scholarship of integration*, which involves "making connections across the disciplines, placing the specialties in larger context, illuminating data in a revealing way, often educating nonspecialists, too. . . . The scholarship of integration also means interpretation, fitting one's own research—or the research of others—into larger intellectual patterns" (Boyer, pp. 18–19). Though many researchers assume that the scholarship of integration only refers to interdisciplinary methods, it can also include transdisciplinary and even some multidisciplinary approaches. Interdisciplinary approaches are those that combine the methods and outlooks of two or more disciplines to create a genuine synthesis. Art history is by its very nature interdisciplinary as it fuses the aesthetic criticism of the fine arts with the identification of chronological patterns of cause and effect that is practiced by historians. Transdisciplinary approaches use the primary sources of information and certain scholarly methods commonly found in one discipline to elucidate the primary sources of information most commonly found in another discipline. For instance, building a historical theory on the basis of perspectives gained from poems or films is an example of a transdisciplinary approach, as is conducting a controlled experiment as part of a research project in the humanities. Finally, multidisciplinary approaches incorporate the techniques and material of several different disciplines simultaneously but make no attempt to synthesize them in any meaningful way. A volume that explores the art and economics of ancient China may be considered multidisciplinary if it treats both of these topics without an explicit attempt to relate them to each other.

- *The scholarship of application*, which is also commonly known as applied research. "New intellectual understandings can arise out of the very act of application—whether in medical diagnosis, serving clients in psychotherapy, shaping public policy, creating an architectural design, or working with the public schools. In activities such as these, theory and practice vitally interact, and one renews the other" (Boyer, p. 23).

- *The scholarship of teaching*, which involves not merely instruction itself but research into new pedagogical approaches and the development of strategies that lead to student success in both mastering disciplines and conducting their own research. "Teaching, at its best, means not only transmitting knowledge, but *transforming* and *extending* it as well" (Boyer, p. 24).

As higher education continued to undergo significant changes following the publication of *Scholarship Reconsidered*, it became clear that even Boyer's four-fold taxonomy could be further elaborated or refined. For example, at many institutions it is now customary to speak of:

- *Scholarship of creativity*. To many observers, the term *scholarship of discovery* is most applicable when there is some preexisting truth, principle, or entity that is "waiting" to be discovered. But a composer does not "discover" a sonata; he or she creates it. A poet does not "discover" a poem; he or she brings it into being. The same observation can be made about many types of innovation throughout the fine and performing arts. Yet originality and innovation are also found in all other disciplines. The holder of a patent, the entrepreneur who develops an important new business opportunity, and the mathematician who is responsible for an elegant theorem all have created something entirely new; they haven't merely discovered something that already existed. The scholarship of creativity is thus vitally important to the academic enterprise, even though it doesn't quite fit into Boyer's four original categories.

• *Scholarship of experience.* The importance of experiential learning has led to curricular reforms at many institutions all over the country. The value of internships, study-abroad experiences, and community-based learning opportunities is increasingly being recognized as academic programs are revised or enhanced. Yet even though it is commonly acknowledged that these experiential learning opportunities are invaluable for students, relatively few institutions of higher education have developed methods of assessing and recognizing the scholarly contributions made by the faculty members who create, supervise, and implement these programs. The scholarship of experience is an academic endeavor that can sometimes be demonstrated through traditional, peer-reviewed publications, such as books and articles that document the important pedagogical contributions of experiential education. But an essential part of this scholarship is derived from the experience itself. For example, the faculty member who is immersed in another culture while spending a year as a Fulbright fellow has performed a genuine act of scholarship merely by promoting cross-cultural awareness and by becoming intimately acquainted with another society and its values. (On the Fulbright Scholar Program, see Chapter 23, "Writing a Grant Proposal.") The faculty member is not content merely to supervise an internship, but also creates entirely new ways for students to obtain internship experience, has contributed to a discipline's knowledge base in a manner no less meaningful than if he or she had published an article. If institutions believe that there can be a pedagogy based in experience, then we should acknowledge there must also be a scholarship of experience. This type of scholarly contribution is all too frequently ignored by evaluation systems today.

• *Scholarship of service.* Falling somewhere between what Boyer termed the scholarship of application and what we have termed the scholarship of experience is a type of scholarly contribution that is rooted in service. As we shall see in Chapter 30, "Service Reconsidered," the very notion of what constitutes academic service is undergoing a wholesale reconsideration by a number of colleges and universities. Community service-learning has already become a widely accepted pedagogical form that can be of tremendous value to students. But when faculty members engage in service projects, their supervisors often assume they are applying knowledge they have already attained rather than adding to the knowledge base of their discipline as a whole. Yet we as academics tend to be very clear about the difference between service and *service-learning* when we define these concepts for students: service occurs when you simply apply a skill that you already have; service-learning occurs when there is a significant development of new concepts, perspectives, or modes of understanding as the result of a service contribution. A student who engages in service seeks to help others; a student who engages in service-learning seeks to be transformed in some significant way through the experience of helping others. That same distinction can well be applied to the notions of faculty service and the scholarship of service. When college professors apply their existing knowledge in a manner that benefits their institutions or communities, we are dealing with a contribution that falls in the realm of service; yet when a faculty member engages in service, not merely to benefit others, but also to develop new insights into the perspectives, values, needs, and priorities of those who are being served, scholarship of service comes into play. This is the realm that Kelly Ward (2003) calls "the scholarship of engagement" (see also O'Meara, 2002).

Because of this expanding notion of what constitutes scholarly activity at an institution of higher education, many colleges and universities have revised their faculty evaluation procedures to reflect this broader definition. For instance, the section of the faculty handbook that deals with scholarship at Georgia Southwestern State University (2008) contains the following very broad definition:

> Scholarship is not limited to publications or conference presentations but can include a number of professional activities where expertise in the discipline or in the area of professional education is utilized, demonstrated, or enhanced. The principal standards should always be quality, rather than quantity, and consistency with the teaching mission of the University. Examples of scholarship may include, but are not limited to:

a. Professional awards and recognition

b. Conference presentations and publications, particularly those which are peer reviewed or invited, whether in the discipline or in professional education

c. Conference participation as a panelist, discussant, or session chair

d. Generation of creative products including recitals, compositions, exhibitions, patents, and other discipline-appropriate artistic performance or creative activities

e. Peer review, either in the discipline or professional education, of publications, recitals, exhibitions, contests, performances, and other discipline-appropriate activities

f. Submission of and/or participation in grants, fellowship programs, or other externally funded support for scholarship activities

g. Attendance and/or active involvement in professional organizations

h. Participation in formal course work, special courses, and workshops to improve professional competencies, including emerging technologies

i. Achievement or maintenance of professional certification or licensing pertinent to area of teaching or professional education

j. Continuation of practical experiences outside the University pertinent to teaching duties such as professional work with schools and/or outside entities

k. Other discipline-appropriate academic or developmental activities as defined by the respective units.

Even such a detailed listing of potential scholarly products as this cannot possibly encompass all the different manifestations of scholarly work that are now possible or that may someday become possible through new developments in technology and the continued expansion of how academic work may be performed. For instance, faculty members at many colleges and universities currently disseminate their scholarship through websites, podcasts, films, and multimedia creations. The print-on-demand publishers that were mentioned in Chapter 22, "Taking the Next Step in Your Teaching," such as Xlibris, iUniverse, and Lulu, provide scholars with the option of creating a work that has not been vetted by peer review prior to publication but that may well be reviewed by professional journals only after it appears in print. As we've seen, other products of scholarship are inherently transient, such as works of live performance, service as a moderator or discussant at an academic conference, and temporary installations of three-dimensional art. Furthermore, even disciplines where collaborative work was previously uncommon have noticed increasing numbers of works that are produced not by an individual scholar, but by an entire team of scholars. For this reason, many institutions have elected not to enumerate the various types of works that are acceptable as evidence of scholarly activity, but to outline what they hope to accomplish by promoting scholarly activity and why achievements in this area are important to the institution. A good example of the latter approach may be found in the "Guidelines for Annual Faculty Evaluation, Merit Determination, Promotion and Tenure" that have been adopted by the Eberly College of Arts and Sciences at West Virginia University (1998):

> Research involves the creation, the discovery or synthesis of knowledge, the creation of new approaches to understanding and explaining phenomena, the development of new insights, the critical appraisal of the past, artistic creation, and the application of knowledge and expertise to address needs in society and in the profession. These activities result in products which may be evaluated and compared with those of peers at other institutions of higher learning. . . . Although often discipline-focused and individual, research also may be interdisciplinary and collaborative. In most disciplines, refereed publications (print or electronic) of high quality are expected as evidence of scholarly productivity. An original contribution of a creative nature relevant to one or more disciplines may be as significant as the publication of a scholarly book or article. Quality is considered more important than mere quantity. Significant evidence of scholarly merit may be either a single work of considerable importance or a series of studies constituting a program of worthwhile research. Faculty members are expected to undertake and demonstrate evidence of a continuing program of studies, investigations, or creative works.

In this definition, we notice that rather than attempting to identify every type of scholarly activity that would be regarded as acceptable at the college, the institution focuses on five key elements. It suggests that scholarship:

- *Can occur in a broad range of activities, not simply in traditional research alone.* By this definition, scholarship thus includes all four of Boyer's categories from *Scholarship Reconsidered*, as well as the three additional forms of scholarship that we explored.

- *Results in a product that may be long lasting*, such as a print publication or a painting, or may be quite fleeting, such as a live performance or the application of research to a temporary problem.

- *Should be evaluated in terms of its quality.* Although the definition anticipates that peer review of most scholarly products will occur before they are released, it is clear that other scenarios are possible. The quality of a faculty member's scholarship will be determined by comparing it to similar works by peers at other institutions to judge whether it meets or exceeds the standards of excellence expected elsewhere within the academy.

- *May be interdisciplinary or identified with a specific discipline* as well as collaborative or individually produced.

- *Is part of an ongoing commitment by the faculty member to scholarly activity.* Products of scholarship that are generated solely to be submitted for a promotion or tenure review carry far less weight than does a demonstrated history of scholarship.

Engaging in Alternative Forms of Scholarship

In much the same spirit that led to the concepts of research and creative activity seen at West Virginia University, in 1995 a task force of the faculty senate at Oregon State University undertook a revision of tenure and promotion guidelines, resulting in the following definition of scholarship: "Scholarship is creative intellectual work that is validated by peers and communicated—including creative artistry and the discovery, integration, and development of knowledge" (Weiser & Houglum, 1998). This definition, though broad enough to include both alternative and traditional forms of scholarship, reinterprets two of the three qualities of research with which this chapter began: scholarship must be validated by peers (not merely peer reviewed prior to its appearance in print) and communicated (not merely published). Even more importantly, the Oregon State University guidelines "Recognize that peer validation and communication are separate processes that can occur in a variety of ways including, but not limited to, peer-refereed publications. When peer validation and communication are accomplished in nontraditional ways it is the faculty member's responsibility to clearly describe and document how peer validation and communication were accomplished" (Weiser & Houglum, 1998). Thus, scholarship that differs from traditional forms in any of the three ways outlined earlier—publication, peer review, or consisting primarily of original research—may require additional clarification by the scholar. This type of clarification is likely to be necessary for evaluation committees to understand how the alternative form of scholarship is comparable to traditional scholarship. Even if this requirement is not in place at your institution, it contains good advice for anyone engaged in nontraditional scholarship. If you are involved in alternative forms of scholarship and are about to undergo a performance review or appraisal for the purposes of a promotion or tenure consideration, you should probably give serious consideration to providing substantial explanation to any of the following areas that are relevant to what you do:

- *Alternatives to publication.* Identify the reasons why the form or medium used to communicate each product of scholarship was appropriate to your purpose. Who was the intended audience for the work? What could be achieved through the form or medium you selected that would have been impossible or less desirable through traditional publication? If the work was inherently ephemeral, what evidence can be provided that it made a positive impact when it occurred? If the work has been recorded or is otherwise accessible to the review committee, how can it be retrieved?

- *Alternatives to peer review.* Identify how the quality of the work was evaluated and by what standards the work may be regarded as significant. Was it reviewed after it was released? Can it be critiqued by experts in your field who will be able to comment on its quality? Who, inside and outside your institution, is most qualified to consider whether the methods that you used and the standards that you achieved were representative of excellent work in your field? Refer to the criteria for evaluating alternative forms of scholarship in Glassick, Huber, and Maeroff (1997).

- *Alternatives to original research.* Identify the contribution that you made to your discipline through the work. What sort of preparation was necessary for the production of this work? How did the creation of this work require you to develop beyond the level of training and expertise that you possessed prior to the work? How was either your audience or discipline enhanced by the work that you created?

- *Significance to the discipline, institution, and academic community.* Identify the value of the work in light of the mission of your field and your institution. What benefits resulted from the creation of this work? Whom did it help? How is the work that you have done beneficial to the mission of your discipline, department, and institution? What loss or detriment would have been felt if this work had not been created?

Diamond (2004) provides several excellent examples of how to document the impact of scholarship that does not consist of traditional research and publication. Diamond's examples include directing a play, serving on a mayor's task force, developing an exhibit for a regional museum, and creating a new software system. Even if the type of scholarship that you do is not closely related to one of Diamond's examples, his process of establishing a rationale for the achievement, selecting proper documentation of excellence and impact, and tying the project to existing institutional criteria is easily adaptable to many other types of work.

―――――――――

Changes in the academy and in emerging forms of technology have made possible new types of scholarship that would not have been recognized even a few decades ago. These alternative forms of scholarship open up many exciting possibilities for faculty members who may feel that the traditional route of published and peer-reviewed research is not appropriate to their discipline or to the contribution they wish to make. Nevertheless, even though many systems of faculty evaluation are expanding to accommodate a broader definition of scholarship, those who pursue these alternative forms of scholarly activity are well advised to provide clarifications as to why their contributions are equivalent in both rigor and significance to the scholarship of their peers.

REFERENCES

Boyer, E. L. (1990). *Scholarship reconsidered: Priorities of the professoriate.* Princeton, NJ: Carnegie Foundation for the Advancement of Teaching.

Diamond, R. M. (2004). *Preparing for promotion, tenure, and annual review: A faculty guide* (2nd ed.). Bolton, MA: Anker.

Georgia Southwestern State University. (2008). *Faculty handbook, section II: Faculty affairs.* Retrieved September 30, 2007, from www.gsw.edu/̄aaf/handbook/faculty.htm

Glassick, C. E., Huber, M. T., & Maeroff, G. I. (1997). *Scholarship assessed: Evaluation of the professoriate.* San Francisco: Jossey-Bass.

O'Meara, K. (2002). Uncovering the values in faculty evaluation of service as scholarship. *Review of Higher Education, 26*(1), 57–80.

Ward, K. (2003). *Faculty service roles and the scholarship of engagement.* San Francisco: Jossey-Bass.

Weiser, C. J., & Houglum, L. (1998). Scholarship unbound for the 21st century. *Journal of Extension, 36*(4). Retrieved September 29, 2007, from www.joe.org/joe/1998august/a1.php

West Virginia University. (1998). *Guidelines for annual faculty evaluation, merit determination, promotion and tenure: Eberly College of Arts and Sciences.*

Retrieved September 29, 2007, from www.as.wvu.edu/forms/guidelines_for_ annual_ faculty_ev.htm

RESOURCES

Creswell, J. W. (2003). *Research design: Qualitative, quantitative, and mixed methods approaches* (2nd ed.). Thousand Oaks, CA: Sage.

Creswell, J. W., & Plano Clark, V. L. (2007). *Designing and conducting mixed methods research*. Thousand Oaks, CA: Sage.

Denzin, N. K., & Giardina, M. D. (Eds.). (2006). *Qualitative inquiry and the conservative challenge*. Walnut Creek, CA: Left Coast Press.

Diamond, R. M., & Adam, B. E. (Eds.). (1995). *The disciplines speak: Rewarding the scholarly, professional, and creative work of faculty*. Washington, DC: American Association for Higher Education.

Diamond, R. M., & Adam, B. E. (Eds.). (2000). *The disciplines speak II: More statements on rewarding the scholarly, professional, and creative work of faculty*. Washington, DC: American Association for Higher Education.

Hart, C. (1998). *Doing a literature review: Releasing the social science research imagination*. Thousand Oaks, CA: Sage.

McKinney, K. (2007). *Enhancing learning through the scholarship of teaching and learning: The challenges and joys of juggling*. Bolton, MA: Anker.

O'Meara, K., & Rice, R. E. (2005). *Faculty priorities reconsidered: Rewarding multiple forms of scholarship*. San Francisco: Jossey-Bass.

Reason, P., & Bradbury, H. (Eds.). (2008). *The SAGE handbook of action research: Participative inquiry and practice* (2nd ed.). Thousand Oaks, CA: Sage.

Reinharz, S. (1992). *Feminist methods in social research*. New York: Oxford University Press.

Saukko, P. (2003). *Doing research in cultural studies: An introduction to classical and new methodological approaches*. Thousand Oaks, CA: Sage.

Weimer, M. (2006). *Enhancing scholarly work on teaching and learning: Professional literature that makes a difference*. San Francisco: Jossey-Bass.

Yin, R. K. (2003). *Case study research: Design and methods* (3rd ed.). Thousand Oaks, CA: Sage.

29

TAKING THE NEXT STEP IN YOUR SCHOLARSHIP

In this chapter, we're going to build on your successes in scholarship, research, or creative activity and begin by assuming that you've already laid the essential groundwork in these areas. This chapter will take for granted that you're now a full-time faculty member at a college or university and have successfully completed at least four projects that would be regarded as significant scholarly activities in your discipline. These scholarly projects may consist of refereed articles, solo exhibitions, recitals, productions, presentations at highly selective and distinguished conferences, or any other forms of research or creative activity that are broadly recognized in your field. In almost all cases, you will have obtained the terminal degree in your discipline as this is the degree that specifically prepares graduate students to engage in extensive works of research or creative activity. It is somewhat less likely that you have already published a book or monograph in your field, although that is also possible. It is also somewhat less likely that your colleagues in your discipline already regard you as one of the leading theorists, researchers, or artists in your area of specialty.

If you do not fit this profile in any major way, then this chapter is not yet for you. You still have some foundations to prepare before returning to the activities of this chapter later. Go back to some of the earlier material in this book and follow the guidelines that appear in such sections as Chapter 9, "Taking the Next Step in Your Career," Chapter 23, "Writing a Grant Proposal," Chapter 24, "Writing a Book Proposal," and Chapter 27, "Seeking and Providing Peer Support for Scholarship." This chapter is not about getting started in scholarship; it's about taking an established record of first-rate scholarly activity and making it stellar, a model for others to emulate. We're going to explore a few ways of making you a recognized authority in your area of scholarship—and we're going to accomplish this goal in only six steps.

Step One: Identify the Objective

The first thing that we're going to do in our effort to enhance your scholarly record is to identify precisely what being an absolute star in scholarship means to you. In establishing this objective, you should keep three important principles in mind. First, choose a goal that will be clearly recognized when you've reached it. For instance, if you choose as your goal something like, "Be acknowledged by my colleagues as a leader in research," what evidence will you ever obtain that you have achieved this objective? It will be extremely difficult for you (or anyone else) to conclude that you've reached this goal. More useful is a statement specifying that you will receive some particular recognition for your research, such as a national award in your discipline or five successive years being ranked as "extraordinary" in the scholarship category of your departmental evaluation. In these cases, it will be immediately apparent when you have accomplished what you set out to do. Second, try not to select goals relating to specific scholarly projects such as, "Have a book published by a major academic press" or "Be awarded a research grant of $1 million or more." As we'll see, these are *means* by which we'll reach your goal for scholarship; they are not ultimate goals in themselves. In this way, "Releasing a professional, studio-recorded CD of German art songs" is not the sort of objective we're looking for here; "Receiving no fewer than five highly positive reviews of my CD in national publications and at least one major award for its quality" is the type of goal you should identify. We want goals that bring you *recognition* for your success in scholarship, not mere additions to your résumé. Third, be sure to set your goals high enough. It may be wonderful to be recognized as "Researcher of the Year" in your department, but is that a lofty enough goal? Does your professional association give regional or national research awards, book prizes, or similar recognitions? There may also be national awards for research that are appropriate to your discipline, such as:

- Ruth L. Kirschstein National Research Service Award in fields related to human health (see http://grants.nih.gov/training/nrsa.htm)
- Sabbatical Fellowships in the humanities and social sciences offered by the American Philosophical Society (see www.amphilsoc.org/grants/sabbatical.htm)
- E. Mead Johnson Award for achievements in pediatrics and nutrition (see www.aps-spr.org/SPR/Awards/EMJ.htm)

- Any of the numerous awards for research into various areas of chemistry offered by the American Chemical Society (see www.acs.org)
- John Simon Guggenheim Memorial Fellowship for advanced professionals in the natural sciences, social sciences, humanities, creative arts, and constitutional studies (see www.gf.org)
- Award for Research in psychiatry offered by the American Psychiatric Association (see www.psych.org/MainMenu/Research/Research TrainingandFunding/APAResearchAwards.aspx)
- Faculty Research Awards in the humanities, offered by the National Endowment for the Humanities (see www.neh.gov)
- Decade of Behavior Research Award in psychology by the American Psychological Association (see www.decadeofbehavior.org/award/index.cfm)
- C. J. Goodwin Award for Merit and the Prize for Scholarly Outreach in the classics, awarded by the American Philological Association (see www.apaclassics.org/Administration/awards.html)
- Lifetime Achievement Award for Excellence in Research Ethics, offered by Public Responsibility in Medicine and Research (see www.primr.org)

Nearly every field of academic interest has at least one national award for research. Some of these awards are recognitions for contributions that have already been made. Others fund research that will take place in the future. All of them, however, require the applicant to have achieved a high level of distinction in scholarly contributions to his or her academic discipline. Receiving one of these awards is, therefore, one of the most tangible ways for you to demonstrate that you have achieved an extraordinary level of excellence in your scholarship.

For this reason, a highly desirable goal in scholarship is to locate the most relevant national award to your field of scholarship and actively pursue it. Work with the resources provided by the national association in your discipline to identify a specific national award in research, scholarship, or professional activity that will clearly indicate to you and others at your institution that you have reached the highest level of scholarly achievement in your field. Find out what the criteria for selection are in the case of this particular award. Review the profiles of recent awardees. Contact the individuals or the committee in charge of this recognition. Then, using the information that you have gathered from all of these sources, develop your own action plan for receiving the award.

- How many articles, books, or other scholarly products do the previous winners of this award tend to have?

- What are the scholarly journals or other research outlets in which the work of previous recipients tended to appear? What were the presses that released their books and monographs?

- Are there identifiable areas or types of focus that tended to appear in the scholarly work of past recipients? Is there a way in which you can legitimately describe your previous scholarship as occurring in this area? If not, is it possible for you to refocus your current research activities so that they align more closely with this area?

- Are there specific criteria for selection that do not yet apply to you? For instance, is the award only open to individuals of a certain rank or with a particular number of years of service that you have not yet obtained?

- Have you been active in events sponsored by the organization offering the award? For example, have you attended its meetings or served on one of its committees?

With all of this information before you, you are now ready to begin developing your plan for obtaining the award or recognition that you have set as your goal.

Step Two: Develop an Action Plan

Once you have identified the recognition for scholarship that you will pursue, you may feel that even the basic requirements to achieve it are quite intimidating. For instance, you may have discovered that in order to apply for the award, you will first need to be promoted to the rank of full professor, have amassed at least fifteen years of service as a faculty member, and have published no fewer than three books and twenty peer-reviewed articles. If you are currently an assistant professor with only four years of full-time college-level experience and five published articles, achieving that bare minimum can seem a lofty enough goal for the time being. But the method outlined in this chapter requires you to add to that bare minimum at least three very different major research accomplishments *before* you will even make your initial attempt to receive the recognition. Why are we imposing this extra requirement? Because your goal is not simply to *qualify* for the achievement, but to *receive* it and to do so by a unanimous (or near unanimous) acknowledgment that you deserve it. In other words, carrying your scholarship to the next level involves ratcheting up your efforts to an entirely new level of academic achievement, reaching standards much higher than you had ever anticipated when you entered your field. The objective of this chapter is not merely to help you fulfill your dreams, but to establish even more impressive dreams than you currently have, and then to exceed those. The surprising truth is that as impossible as all of this may seem right now, you really can do it. But the first thing you need is a clear plan.

What do we mean when we talk about "three distinctly different scholarly projects"? Well, your answer will vary according to your discipline and the type of institution where you work, but they may be along the lines of the following:

- A book of original research published by a first-tier academic press
- A research grant of at least $250,000 from a nationally recognized foundation
- A sabbatical year travel fellowship that provides access to archives in another country

Or your list of three projects may be more similar to the following:

- An international solo exhibition of at least twenty paintings, none of which has yet been completed
- Purchase of three or more works by top-tier museums or galleries
- A catalogue or retrospective of works published by a major press in the arts

No matter which goals you establish, keep in mind that they should be ambitious, distinct, and clearly beyond the minimum requirements of the award or recognition that you have established in Step One. Remember that it is important for you to vary these significant scholarly accomplishments. For the purposes of this endeavor, three books are less desirable than the combination of a book, a multimedia project, and an invitation to serve as keynote speaker at an international research symposium. As you plan your strategy, think creatively and be sure to stretch your goals as far as you dare. Remember that you are not trying simply to receive the recognition that you have specified but to be the clear and obvious choice to receive it.

At this point you may be thinking, "All of this sounds fine, but it would take me twenty years or more to do all of that. How will I have time to write fifteen more articles, publish a book, receive a grant, go off for a semester-long period of research travel, and still meet all of my current obligations for teaching and service?" At this point, it may be advisable to go back and reread Chapter 26, "Balancing Scholarship with Other Duties." What you're going to do next is refine your plan so that it does not contain twenty or thirty separate and unrelated objectives, but a sequenced program of small efforts leading to a single overall objective. Look over the entire list of criteria that you have created for receiving the recognition you specified in Step One, along with the three new major scholarly goals that you have added in Step Two. How can you coordinate these so that the goals overlap and integrate? For instance:

- If you have specified that you need to have published a certain number of articles to qualify for a major research award, can those articles then become individual chapters or even parts of chapters in the book that you are planning?

- If you are going to pursue a travel grant to do international research, how can the topic of your book be modified so as to incorporate that research?

- If you need to earn promotion to a higher rank to be considered, how can you develop a timetable so that several of the scholarly projects you need to obtain the national research award will also help you receive your promotion?

- How can you tailor the topic of the research grant for which you'll apply so that it results in the creation of several articles that, in turn, can be revised as chapters for your book?

- As you look at the committees on which you may serve for the national organization that offers the scholarly recognition you are seeking, which committees are most closely related to research, creative activity, or some other area that will benefit you in the area of scholarship?

  By approaching the task in this way, you will combine what may initially appear to be a highly disparate list of scholarly achievements—and what will impress outside observers as an amazingly diverse set of accomplishments—into a single, carefully structured, and interrelated plan. Your conference presentations will lead to grants, which will lead to refereed articles, which will lead to book chapters. Or your concerts will lead to invitations for recitals in distant venues, which will lead to recordings, which will lead to national reviews of your work. Small grants will be used as the basis for larger ones. Occasional consultancies will lead to the creation of your own consulting firm. So, before going on to the next step, consolidate all the scholarly activities that you have before you into a single research agenda with all of your different objectives as steps leading you sequentially to your goal. By creating this type of scaffold, you will discover that although it may still require seven to ten years to achieve your ultimate objective, it will not take you the twenty or twenty-five years you had originally thought. But if you find that your goal is obtainable much more quickly (say, in two or three years rather than seven to ten), then it is possible that you have not been sufficiently ambitious in choosing your ultimate goal. Remember that you are trying to transform your research in a significant manner so that it reaches a new level of excellence, not merely polish it a bit. So, if it seems as though you'll complete this plan too quickly, go back and ratchet up your expectations even further.

Step Three: Achieve the First Objective on Your Plan as Quickly as Possible

Because you may still be feeling, at least on some level, that the plan you've developed is far too ambitious to be attainable, it's extremely important that you obtain proof of how you actually can achieve everything you've set out to do. Go to the very first objective that you have established in your overall plan and immediately set out to achieve it. If you have structured all of your objectives as outlined in Step Two, this initial goal is likely to be a much easier objective to attain than, say, objectives number 10 and 15. It may consist of creating an abstract of a paper that you will present at a national conference (which then will form the basis of an article, grant application, and book chapter), learning a new set of musical compositions, creating a new artwork, or some other similar task. Estimate a reasonable amount of time that you believe will be required to complete this initial task. Then take that amount of time and reduce it at least 30 to 50 percent. This first goal is going to become your new highest priority, and you will use it to get your revised, more ambitious research plan under way. So, if you think that it'll take you a month to prepare an abstract for that conference, do it this weekend. If you estimate that it may take six months to learn those new pieces of music, give yourself three months. Set an ambitious deadline, mark it on your calendar, and then stick to it. If you are going to bring your accomplishments in scholarship to an entirely new level, it is going to take not only more ambitious goals but also a much more ambitious schedule to obtain them. So, accelerate your anticipated progress to the stretching point. Use your calendar to block out as many "puddles of time" as you can between courses, meetings, and other obligations. Devote an extra half hour each evening to achieving your first objective.

And don't allow yourself any excuses, including illness and unforeseen circumstances, to keep you from attaining this first goal. Achieving your objective will be an important part of the confidence that you'll need to carry you through the entire plan. Pursue this first objective as though you were already within sight of attaining your ultimate goal. Then, once you have accomplished the first task that you have set for yourself, use that achievement to spur yourself on to the next set of objectives. Whenever the task seems impossible, keep reminding yourself, "Well, I wasn't sure I could achieve that first objective in such a short amount of time. But if I did that, then I can achieve this next objective as well!" Having a clear example of success as a reference point will help give you the motivation you'll need to sustain your effort along the way.

Step Four: Seek an Initial or Intermediary Level of Recognition

Once you have accomplished between 30 to 50 percent of the goals that you established in your plan, it is time to seek an initial level of recognition. For example, if your ultimate goal is to receive a national award for research, ask someone to nominate you for a college-level award for research, if one exists. If you have chosen some other type of goal, such as five successive years of rankings as "extraordinary" in the scholarship category of your departmental evaluation, see if you can begin by receiving this recognition in two successive years. Then, after you have attained this goal, complete roughly another third of your objectives and then begin seeking a slightly more ambitious goal, such as a research award from a state or regional association. These initial or intermediate recognitions will serve as part of your overall strategy for achieving your ultimate objective. After all, the committees that choose recipients for national awards are much more likely to honor an individual who has a history of similar recognitions at successive levels. Moreover, these periodic victories will provide you with reinforcement that although your final goal may have seemed impossibly difficult at first, you are consistently getting closer to achieving it.

Step Five: Develop a Strategy to Achieve Your Goal

When all of your preliminary objectives have been achieved, it is time to develop your final strategy for achieving your goal. If it is an award for which you must be nominated, consider whose nomination is likely to carry the most weight. Getting your president, dean, or department chair to nominate you is likely to seem more impressive to the review committee than receiving a letter from one of your colleagues. In a similar way, if you have had contact with a scholar who has a national or international reputation in your discipline, a nomination from that person will probably be more significant than a letter from an individual unknown to the selection committee. Moreover, even if an award or recognition does not require a nomination, it can benefit your candidacy to be nominated rather than to apply on your own behalf. Your intermediate recognitions and the objectives that you have achieved along the way will make it much easier for the person nominating you to make a compelling case. When you ask someone to submit a letter on your behalf, don't simply send the request; supply a full set of materials, such as *a curriculum vitae*, a few bulleted talking points, and information about the recognition you are seeking. Doing so makes the job easier for the nominator, but also results in a stronger, more detailed, and more effective letter of nomination.

Examine the criteria for the award carefully and review the list of documentation that you will need to submit. Just as you wanted to make your nominator's job easier, you will also want to make it as clear as possible to the selection committee that you qualify for the award. If you are asked to write a letter of application, you may even want to cite the criteria for the award in boldface type and then address how you meet each criterion. For example:

Recipients must hold the rank of associate professor or professor with at least fifteen years of full-time teaching experience . . . I was promoted to the rank of full professor at North-by-Northwest State University in [YEAR], after having served seven years at the rank of associate professor. Before my arrival at North-by-Northwest State, I held a full-time, tenure track position at Research State University, thus serving for a total of twenty-one years in various full-time academic positions.

. . . **and have attained a high level of distinction in scholarship.** Two of my books, *Meaningful Research in Important Fields* and *Weighty Tome of Scholarly Merit*, were cited as "Important New Contributions to the Disciplines" by the American Society of Pedantry. Before leaving Research State University, I was twice awarded my college's "Scholar of the Year Award." At North-by-Northwest

---

State University, I have received citations for scholarship at the department, college, and university levels, and I was recently awarded the Chancellor's Medallion for Scholarship in recognition of my four academic books, thirty-two peer-reviewed articles, and fifty-one essays or reviews.

Addressing the criteria in this way frees the selection committee from having to sort through all the supporting material you have provided to locate the qualifications relevant to each criterion. Because you know your record far better than a panel of strangers, you might also provide information that they would have missed anyway. Finally, addressing the criteria point by point makes it highly likely that your application will survive the committee's first screening of applications as "qualified" and "unqualified."

Step Six: If You Are Unsuccessful in Achieving Your Goal, Try Again

Even with all your careful planning, it is possible that your initial effort to reach your ultimate goal will not be successful. Remember what we said earlier: the very reason that you set out to attain this goal was not because it was an easy thing to accomplish, but because it was a difficult and impressive challenge. There are likely to be numerous other scholars who also have a strong record of research, creative activity, and other accomplishments, and some of them may also be nominated for this award. So, don't take an initial lack of success as rejection or as an indication that you have wasted your efforts. Take it as confirmation that this recognition is truly difficult to receive and that when you *do* receive it, you will have earned all the accolades that accompany it. For this reason, revise your materials, accept any critique you may receive from the selection committee, and try again. You've put far too much effort into this process to give up now, and it is not uncommon for many recipients of truly prestigious awards to have been considered five or more times before they are eventually successful.

Taking your scholarship to the next level involves clearly articulating how you would recognize genuine success in this area, outlining the various efforts that will take you there, consolidating those efforts so that each project becomes a part of a larger and more important goal, and redoubling your efforts if you meet resistance anywhere along the way. Although it is a wonderful thing to be truly surprised by an unexpected recognition from your peers, most college professors receive awards in those areas where they have pursued a plan of growth and achievement. If you have decided to make your mark in scholarship, research, or creative activity, the six steps presented here will provide you with a clear strategy for helping you achieve that ultimate goal.

30

SERVICE RECONSIDERED

Service has long been treated as the maligned stepchild of the academic triad. Though many college professors have used teaching and research as pathways to a successful career, it's the rare faculty member who reaches the rank of full professor due to a record of exemplary service. In fact, in those evaluation systems where professional contributions are weighted, it sometimes occurs that service accounts for a mere 5 to 10 percent of a faculty member's annual performance, while "teaching first" institutions may weigh instruction as much as 50 percent, and research universities may weigh scholarship up to 75 percent. Even many community colleges, where service to their region may be discussed extensively in their mission statements, place greater emphasis on teaching (and at times even on scholarship) than on individual faculty service. In sum, as college professors, we tend to be "graded" on our teaching and scholarship; service is largely treated as "pass-fail." And nearly everyone knows at least one distinguished professor who rose to the highest ranks despite never having served on a single department committee, having been minimally involved in professional organizations, and having played virtually no role in community life. It is no wonder that, for many members of the professoriate, service has become an afterthought. In Chapter 6, "Special Challenges for Junior Faculty," we encountered this essential principle: few, if any, faculty members ever earn tenure and promotion primarily through service. Given this fact, it is no wonder that many college professors engage in only enough service to "get by."

The lack of respect often given to service is particularly unfortunate because, no matter how you look at it, faculty members work in a service profession. Indeed, it's not an exaggeration to say that everything we do in academic life can be defined as a type of service:

- Teaching is the service we provide our students.
- Scholarship is the service we provide our discipline or to society at large.

- And what is generally deemed "service" in most faculty handbooks is merely the service we provide our department, school or college, institution, and larger community.

It seems particularly ironic that at the very same time that community service-learning programs are being promoted as essential to the education of many college students, the importance of service by faculty members is still largely unappreciated. Higher education desperately needs a new paradigm that reflects what faculty responsibilities really are and how service plays, not a secondary, but a leading role among those duties. We have already seen that Ernest Boyer's *Scholarship Reconsidered* (1990) brought a radically new approach to how institutions should view professional-level scholarship and defined the potential of what scholarship can become (see Chapter 28, "Alternative Forms of Scholarship"). In a similar way, the appearance of *Learning Reconsidered* (Keeling, 2004) introduced an entirely new appreciation of how learning occurs in a student's undergraduate program and where that learning occurs. What is needed now is a parallel effort in the area of service, something that we might call "Service Reconsidered," that can help both college professors individually and institutions globally develop a clearer understanding of what academic service is, what it can be, and the role it should play both in the evaluation of faculty members and in the mission of a college or university.

Let's begin our reconsideration of service with an understanding that one of the primary reasons why service tends to be so undervalued at many colleges and universities is that most institutions use an extremely narrow definition of what counts as service. If you were to ask most faculty members to offer you examples of their service, they will usually provide you with a list of committees on which they have served or the roles they have played in their professional organizations. Certainly these are important service contributions, but they only begin to cover the broad range of ways in which faculty members use their expertise to help others. As Bruce Macfarlane (2007) has noted, "'service' consists of much more than administrative and committee work. It also refers to activities like counseling students, mentoring junior or less experienced colleagues, developing links with employers or community groups, interacting with professional groups or contributing to a university committee or working party" (p. 15). Consider, for example, the following ways in which college professors serve their institutions, disciplines, and communities:

- They collaborate with representatives from such offices as student life and residence life to provide the sort of comprehensive development programs in leadership, teamwork, creative problem solving, and other areas that are outlined in Keeling (2004, 2006).

- They participate in targeted recruitment events sponsored by their departments in collaboration with the admissions office, where high school students learn about the institution while experiencing a brief but intense immersion into a single academic program, such as choral singing, chemistry, theater, Spanish, and the like.
- They provide lectures, concerts, and exhibitions that help bring the community to campus or raise funds for a particular project.
- They help students find employment long after those students have graduated.
- They cover courses for their colleagues or advise students when illness, parental leave, jury duty, and other matters prevent a fellow member of the discipline from being able to come to work.
- They referee papers submitted to conferences or journals. They provide their professional opinion on the merits of book proposals. They serve on grant review committees and select recipients of awards or fellowships.

Moreover, there are also several types of service activity that arise for faculty members in specific disciplines. For instance:

- Professors of accounting complete tax returns for the elderly and indigent.
- Professors of political science hold workshops on how to register to vote, issues that are likely to arise in upcoming elections, and post-election analysis of trends.
- Professors of foreign languages sponsor folk festivals, demonstrations of international cuisine, and presentations on events abroad. They translate documents for immigrants and assist with visa applications.
- Professors in nursing programs provide public information about resources available in the area for child and maternal health.

And we could easily add dozens of other examples. Many of these contributions are the type that may not even be reported by faculty members in their annual statement of professional activities, and yet neither the discipline nor the institution could fulfill its community mission without them. Again, in the words of Bruce Macfarlane (2007): "Service activities are essential in keeping academic communities and the universities they work in going and connected to the world around them. . . .

They directly support teaching and research activities through service work such as teaching observation, mentoring, reviewing of academic papers and the organization of conferences" (pp. 15–16). At times, these contributions go unreported because they don't fit the very narrow definition of service that appears in many faculty handbooks. For instance, institutional policies may define service as "service to the department," ignoring all the other ways in which contributions are made to the discipline, institution, and community. Or reporting forms may simply request examples of committee membership and the offices that a faculty member held, failing to ask for all the other ways in which service may be demonstrated. For example, the faculty handbook of Mary Baldwin College (2006) lists the following among its criteria for promotion: "Contribution to the whole College through committee work, involvement with student activities, and other means of maintaining and improving the ongoing life of the College" (p. 70). This definition, although it initially appears quite broad, does not, at least on the surface, provide faculty members with an opportunity to receive credit for promotion from any *other* type of service, such as service to the local community or to the discipline as a whole, because of the way in which this criterion is phrased. According to a strict interpretation of the language in the handbook, an individual who performed truly significant service to his or her academic field by serving as president of a major national association and who was widely recognized by the community through numerous, unremunerated acts of professional service, could well be regarded as unsatisfactory in the area of service simply because those contributions do not fall within the institution's definition of service.

Service to Whom?

One question that institutions frequently forget to ask when establishing policies on or criteria about service is: when we speak of service, whom should college professors serve? If we fail to ask this question, we're likely to develop a definition of service that is excessively narrow, calling service "contributions that support the department" or, as we saw in the example above, "[c]ontribution to the whole College through committee work, involvement with student activities, and other means..." If, however, we pursue our question and ask whom we expect members of the professoriate to serve, we are compelled to deal head-on with an even more comprehensive question: Why do we credit service for faculty members in the first place? What is it about service that is so essential to the academic mission that it ranks among the three traditional areas of faculty evaluation? It is easy to understand why teaching and scholarship are regarded as important when we evaluate faculty members; the instruction of students and the discovery of new insights are fundamental aspects of what colleges and universities do. But why does service deserve to stand alongside them? Among the answers to this question that we might suggest are:

- It is important for faculty members to serve their department and discipline because these units are involved in critical areas of shared governance. It is essential for faculty members to have a voice in the decisions that must be made about the future of their academic fields.

- It is important for faculty members to serve the college or school in which their departments are located, as well as the institution as a whole, as the individual perspectives of each discipline cannot be overlooked in such matters as promotion, tenure, curriculum development, and strategic planning.

- It is important for faculty members to serve their community and, indeed, the greater good because many institutions have an explicit mission to enhance their regions through economic, cultural, and intellectual development and because *all* institutions benefit from developing positive, mutually supportive relationships with their local communities.

- It is important for faculty members to serve one another because accepting one's fair share of responsibilities in their disciplines, the life of an institution, and the profession of higher education are central to our professionalism and collegiality.

Seen in this light, the answers to the questions we raised earlier become very clear. *Whom do we expect faculty members to serve?* Faculty members should serve one another, their departments, their disciplines, the school or college in which their appointments are located, the institution that employs them, the community in which they live, and the greater good of society. *Why should faculty service be regarded as important?* Faculty service is an integral part of each college professor's professionalism and collegiality. It is a visible demonstration of our commitment to academic citizenship. Moreover, service is a direct result of our commitment to shared governance. In England, Bruce Macfarlane (2007) has reexamined the role that service plays in higher education and concluded that service should be redefined as good academic citizenship. In North America, a similar approach could hold a great deal of promise. Rather than the excessively narrow definitions of service that we find in many faculty handbooks and evaluation procedures, it would be far more useful if institutions adopted a policy similar to the following:

Academic Citizenship

At [NAME OF INSTITUTION], we are dedicated to a strong culture of academic citizenship, which is important to us because it reflects our institutional values of community engagement and mutual support. Even more importantly, it is through academic citizenship that we as faculty members model our core principles to our students. In light of our institutional mission, we define good academic citizenship as any uncompensated activity that helps to promote:

1. Service to one's department and discipline, including such activities as regular participation in the work of committees, effectively holding positions of leadership, accepting and fulfilling one's fair share of departmental duties, advising and mentoring students, representing the department and discipline at public events, and the like.

2. Service to one's college and institution, such as cooperative interaction with other offices (including those with responsibilities outside the teaching and research missions of the institution), constructive participation in institutional shared governance, effective participation in the meetings and ceremonies that are essential to our institutional culture, and officially representing the institution to external constituents or agencies.

3. Service to one's community and to the greater good, such as speaking to community groups, making presentations to the public, applying one's professional expertise to assist the public at large, active membership in a service organization, building ties to employers and other academic institutions, and promoting the reputation of the institution among the general public.

4. Service to one's profession, including active membership on the committees of a professional organization, holding office in an academic or cultural organization as an officer, serving

as a reviewer, referee, or judge of professional work, activities
that develop or expand programs in one's academic discipline,
and the like.

5. An exceptionally high level of collegiality, professionalism,
and responsibility, demonstrated through service as a mentor
or role model to other members of the institution, promoting
a positive and constructive working environment, demonstrating support for the initiatives of colleagues, helping to fulfill
the responsibilities of others in emergencies, contributing to
an atmosphere of teamwork or collaboration, and the like.

Whenever possible, contributions that result from one's role as a
good academic citizen should identify the individual as affiliated
with [NAME OF INSTITUTION] and as a member of his or her
department.

This approach to academic citizenship has several advantages. First, it
directly addresses the two questions that we've identified by providing a
clear context for service activities. Second, this approach outlines clear
expectations for activities that will be credited as service. For instance, it
specifies that service activities should not be compensated. Paid consultancies, though they may be important for a faculty member's professional
growth and for the contacts they develop, are different from the type of
activity that should be characterized as service. In fact, most colleges and
universities have developed policies that restrict or at least monitor the
work for which a college professor is paid by outside entities. Not only
does the institution want to ensure that it is receiving full-time effort from
an individual who is being paid for a full-time position, but there are also
risks resulting from conflict of interest if a faculty member receives compensation from an individual or organization with other ties to the institution. For all of these reasons, it is commonly said that contributions by
faculty members should be rewarded only once. If an activity involves payment of any kind, then that salary is the faculty member's compensation;
but if the activity involves an unpaid contribution of one's time and effort,
then that activity should be compensated by being credited in one's workload as service. Moreover, in addition to stating the expectation that a college professor's service should not be compensated, the policy makes it

clear that the faculty member's institutional and departmental affiliation should be indicated whenever possible. After all, one of the reasons why institutions recognize and reward the public service done by their faculties is because of the goodwill that these contributions develop for the college or university. If one's institutional affiliation is not made clear or if the service is performed by the college professor simply as a private citizen, the college or university receives no particular benefit from the action and thus may well have relatively little interest in it. The resulting situation is parallel to what occurs when college professors make personal financial contributions to charities and causes that are important to them: the institution may well be pleased that its employees are such public-minded citizens, but it rarely rewards these contributions by counting them as service or by acknowledging them in any other manner.

The third benefit found in the academic citizenship policy above is that, while it suggests several ways for faculty members to serve, it does not restrict the definition of service to the examples provided. The policy provides guidance for faculty members who are looking for ideas about how to make an important service contribution, but it does not exclude other ideas. Moreover, deans or department chairs who do not feel that a particular faculty member is performing his or her fair share of an institution's service expectation will find in the policy specific advice about what that individual should do in the future. Fourth, the policy ties the importance of good academic citizenship to the institution's mission and to the pedagogical role that faculty members play in serving as role models for their students. Finally, and perhaps most important, the concept of academic citizenship relates the service that each faculty member performs to the critical issue of collegiality. As discussed in Buller (2006), several significant court decisions have established that colleges and universities have a right to consider collegiality when evaluating faculty members, even if institutional policies do not specify that collegiality is a criterion for employment. Collegiality can be regarded as an implied requirement of employment, much as showing up for work on time and accurately representing one's credentials are expectations that every institution has even if they are not set forth in a contract or employment manual. Despite these legal precedents, however, it is far easier for colleges and universities to address uncollegial behavior when expectations are clearly stated, as in the policy above. Moreover, by explaining the role that collegiality plays within the overall concept of academic citizenship, the policy preserves a positive focus on what faculty members *should* do (and why they should do it), rather than a negative focus on activities that are discouraged or prohibited.

An institutional policy that elevates the significance of service—and that gives due attention to the scholarship of service—can help advance important institutional goals of inclusiveness and diversity. As O'Meara (2002) has noted, "[t]he faculty most heavily engaged in service scholarship . . . [tend also to be] the most marginalized within academic culture—i.e., women, faculty of color, [and] assistant professors" (p. 75). If colleges and universities truly wish to attract and retain a broader spectrum of talented faculty members, their system of roles and rewards must be expanded to reflect the areas of contribution that frequently matter most to historically underrepresented segments of the professoriate.

> Given that service and teaching are two primary scholarly interests of women and faculty of color, should we be surprised that these faculty, more than any other, experience less satisfaction with the academic workplace, endure more subtle discrimination, and have greater concerns that they are taken seriously as scholars? . . . Faculty who commit their professional expertise to service scholarship should have the same opportunity to achieve recognition, respect, and standing in the academic hierarchy that faculty involved in other scholarly work are afforded. Institutions committed to attracting and retaining a diverse faculty might consider exploring the forms of scholarship their faculty most value and, if consistent with their mission, find ways to integrate this scholarly work, values, and commitments into their reward systems. (O'Meara, 2002, p. 76)

A reconsideration of service is essential if institutions wish to elevate service to the same level of importance that service-learning, community service, and related activities now receive in policies regarding students. A faculty member's service should be viewed not as a mere obligation that is undertaken to keep the day-to-day activities of a college or university effectively operating, but as part of each college professor's rights and responsibilities as an academic citizen. Service, collegiality, and mutual support are integral to a faculty member's role in shared or collective governance. Pedagogically, these activities are important because they demonstrate behaviors that we expect students to imitate. Although individual faculty members cannot be expected to revise institutional policies on their own, they can initiate the type of dialogue that will eventually lead to broader changes.

REFERENCES

Boyer, E. L. (1990). *Scholarship reconsidered: Priorities of the professoriate.* Princeton, NJ: Carnegie Foundation for the Advancement of Teaching.

Buller, J. L. (2006). Promoting collegiality. In J. L. Buller, *The essential department chair: A practical guide to college administration* (pp. 50–55). Bolton, MA: Anker.

Keeling, R. P. (Ed.). (2004). *Learning reconsidered 1: A campus-wide focus on the student experience.* Washington, DC: American College Personnel Association & National Association of Student Personnel Administrators.

Keeling, R. P. (Ed.). (2006). *Learning reconsidered 2: A practical guide to implementing a campus-wide focus on the student experience.* Washington, DC: American College Personnel Association & National Association of Student Personnel Administrators.

Macfarlane, B. (2007). *The academic citizen: The virtue of service in university life.* New York: Routledge.

Mary Baldwin College. (2006). *Mary Baldwin College faculty handbook, 2006–2008.* Retrieved April 17, 2009, from http://mbc.edu/docs/admin_docs/fac_hndbk.pdf

O'Meara, K. (2002). Uncovering the values in faculty evaluation of service as scholarship. *Review of Higher Education, 26*(1), 57–80.

RESOURCES

Johnson, B. T., & O'Grady, C. R. (Eds.). (2006). *The spirit of service: Exploring faith, service, and social justice in higher education.* Bolton, MA: Anker.

Kecskes, K. (Ed.). (2006). *Engaging departments: Moving faculty culture from private to public, individual to collective focus for the common good.* Bolton, MA: Anker.

Seldin, P., & Miller, J. E. (2008). *The academic portfolio: A practical guide to documenting teaching, research, and service.* San Francisco: Jossey-Bass.

Silverman, F. (2004). *Collegiality and service for tenure and beyond: Acquiring a reputation as a team player.* Westport, CT: Praeger.

Ward, K. (2003). *Faculty service roles and the scholarship of engagement.* San Francisco: Jossey-Bass.

31

CREATING AN EFFECTIVE CURRICULUM VITAE

Most college professors are familiar with how to update a curriculum vitae. At many schools, faculty members need to provide current vita information each year as part of their annual reports. In addition, colleges and universities sometimes collect vitas as part of the supporting materials they supply to accrediting agencies. When a faculty member wishes to be reviewed for promotion or tenure, an updated vita will also be required. There are dozens of other reasons why faculty members need to keep the information in their résumés current. Even so, faculty members may give relatively little thought to the design and structure of their vitas. They keep adding new items to a document that they may have first prepared in graduate school or even earlier. They don't reflect on how their lives have changed and on how a professional vita should be organized in order to be as effective as possible. They don't ask themselves which of the items that were useful earlier in their careers can now be excluded from this material, which sections should be regrouped or reordered, and which sections might be streamlined to make them as clear as possible. In this chapter we're going to examine the ways in which the structure and content of your vita should change under different circumstances, as well as many issues every college professor should consider when revising or updating a curriculum vitae.

A Résumé Versus a Curriculum Vitae

For most academic purposes the terms *curriculum vitae* and *résumé* are used interchangeably. Technically a résumé (French for *summary*) should be a shorter form than a curriculum vitae. It is customary, for instance, for a résumé to be no longer than a single double-sided page. Moreover, if you ever seek an administrative role, you may be asked to prepare an *action résumé*. This is a type of document that outlines your major achievements in broad terms. For instance, an action résumé might include a set of bulleted items such as "Increased contributions to the annual fund by over 70 percent" without specifying the actual dollar amounts that you raised. Or your action résumé might say, "Added five new degree programs" without indicating what those programs were. Administrators thus frequently submit both an action résumé from which a reader can quickly glean the highlights of their accomplishments and a curriculum vitae from which the reader can learn all the details. For most college professors, however, the distinction between a résumé and a vita will be insignificant. If you create the sort of vita resource file that will be discussed later in this chapter, you will be able to assemble either a short résumé or a more detailed curriculum vitae depending on your particular need at the moment.

The Difference Between a Vita and a Curriculum Vitae

Curriculum vitae is a Latin phrase meaning "the course of [one's] life." It is thus intended to serve as a synopsis of important actions and achievements in the life of its author. The term *curriculum* should not be associated only with an academic curriculum, such as the degrees one has earned or the courses one has completed. Rather the expression *curriculum vitae* refers to the entire course of one's career, not merely the course of study that made that career possible. The term *vitae* in this expression is a Latin genitive form meaning "of life" and should never be used in isolation. If you omit the term *curriculum*, drop the final *e* and refer to your document as a "vita" This change is thus somewhat similar to the difference between saying "This is my mother's ticket" and "My mother will arrive tomorrow"; you would never say "My mother's will arrive tomorrow." For this reason, writing a sentence such as "I have enclosed six copies of my vitae, as you requested" is both improper and likely to cause certain readers to give your application less consideration in much the same way they would if you had made a lapse in English grammar or spelling. Where this error tends to occur most frequently is in the heading of a document. A person may write something like "Parker K. Jones, *Vitae*" rather than "Parker K. Jones, *Curriculum Vitae*" or "Parker K. Jones, *Vita*." The wisest and safest choice is simply not to include the term in your heading at all. After all, if you have to *tell* someone that a document is your curriculum vitae, then you probably haven't created a very good one.

The Purpose of a Curriculum Vitae

A curriculum vitae is two things simultaneously. It is a factual document in the sense that every item recorded in your vita should be accurate, unambiguous, and verifiable should the reader ever decide to check it.

But it is also a rhetorical document in the sense that its primary function is always to persuade someone of something. For instance, you may be sending out a copy of your résumé to persuade someone that you are qualified for a job, deserve a promotion, or are worthy to receive a grant. In light of this inherent dual purpose of the curriculum vitae, college professors are well advised to ask themselves two questions as they review this important document:

- *Is every item listed on this document accurate and not misleading?* If under a section labeled "Degrees," you cite a doctorate that you have not yet earned but that you anticipate receiving soon, you may inadvertently give your reader the impression that this degree is already in hand. This misunderstanding can occur even if you label your doctorate "in progress" or place a future date beside it. In a CV, you never want to leave the impression that you are claiming an accomplishment you haven't yet earned. For this reason, separating your academic record into two sections, such as "Degrees Earned" and "Work in Progress," is preferable to combining this information under a single heading. Follow this procedure for every accomplishment that is pending, such as articles that have been submitted but not yet accepted for publication, grant proposals that are under review but have not yet been funded, and any other achievement that you are projecting into the future.

- *What can I do to make it easier for the reader to say yes to me?* After you check your vita for accuracy, reflect on the goal for which you are submitting this particular copy of your curriculum vitae. What information does the reader need in order to decide that you are qualified or the best person for this opportunity? For instance, if you are applying for a job, review the list of required qualifications and preferences that appear in the position announcement. Have you made it easy for the reader to find that information in your vita? If one of the qualifications the search committee is looking for is "demonstrated success in introductory courses," do you even have information about what you teach in your vita? Put yourself in the place of your reader. Decide what you would need to know to make your decision and then structure your vita so that this information is readily apparent.

The Audience for a Curriculum Vitae

Depending on why you are preparing any individual copy of your curriculum vitae, your audience for the document may vary considerably. For instance, during an annual evaluation that is conducted only by your department chair, you can count on the chair knowing some rather detailed information about you, your discipline, and your institution that other people will not know. Your chair will understand if you have used a technical term from your field, if you refer to courses only by prefix and number, and if you allude to significant scholars in your area of specialty. If you were sending your vita for review off campus, however, certain readers may not understand items that you take for granted. For example, they may be confused if you don't specify that CHE 2250 is an introductory organic chemistry course required of all majors in your discipline, that the Roger Kornberg with whom you collaborated on several articles was the 2006 recipient of the Nobel Prize for chemistry, and that your advanced research into "translation" has absolutely nothing to do with rendering texts into different languages. Even more importantly, if your vita is likely to be reviewed by a group that includes individuals who do not work in higher education, they may misunderstand even such commonly used academic terms as *theory, law, principal investigator, tenure,* and *associate professor.* Although to your colleagues, heading your CV "Parker K. Jones, Ph.D." or "Dr. Parker K. Jones" may seem pretentious, failing to use your title on a document that will be reviewed by nonacademics may lead them to conclude incorrectly that you do not have your terminal degree. Remember the essential principle that we discussed in Chapter 23, "Writing a Grant Proposal": whenever you are writing any type of document, keep in mind not only what you want to say but also to whom you are trying to say it. As you prepare your vita, always ask yourself what your audience already knows and what it *needs* to know.

Awareness of your audience, coupled with a clear understanding that the purpose of your curriculum vitae will change each time you submit it to a new set of readers, leads to one important implication: there is absolutely no reason for you to keep only a single version of your vita. Because of the flexibility that results from word processing and the high quality of results that can be produced by desktop printers, college professors should maintain, not a single, unchanging curriculum vitae, but an entire computer file of curriculum vitae materials that can be organized and adapted according to the needs of any particular version of the vita. Later in this chapter we'll consider when to include or omit certain items, as well as how to configure the different sections in various ways for different purposes, but for now it might be best to begin by making the following preparations. Go back to the computer file in which you keep your vita, save it under a new name (such as "Vita Resources"), identify all the different sections of the document, and create interchangeable parts that you can mix and match according to a specific need. If you have a very large vita, you may even decide to save different sections as individual computer files so that you can locate specific items more easily. For most faculty members, however, a single computer file with clearly labeled sections will suffice. If you use a word processing program like Microsoft Word, the Document Map within the Navigation Pane can quickly move you from section to section. In Pages for Macintosh computers, the use of sections or page thumbnails can help you locate a particular section of the document very quickly. Nearly every word processor has at least some feature that will allow you to jump to a particular section without scrolling through the entire file.

Sections of a Vita Resource File

The individual sections that you establish in your vita resource file will vary according to your discipline and your specific type of professional activity. For instance, if your discipline is one of the performing arts, you will need to include a section devoted to recitals, performances, or exhibitions. In certain fields, grant activity will be extremely important, while in others the scholarship of service (see Chapter 28, "Alternative Forms of Scholarship," and Chapter 30, "Service Reconsidered") will take precedence. Your own knowledge of your discipline will guide you as to the precise categories that you may need to include in your resource file. Nevertheless, a good starting point for most college professors is a document file that includes the following sections:

- Contact information, including your full name, an indication of the name you prefer to be called, your work and home mailing addresses, all relevant telephone numbers with area codes (work, home, cell, fax), other ways that you can be contacted (such as an Instant Messaging identity, username at a social networking site such as MySpace, Facebook, or LinkedIn, and any other means that are appropriate for you), where you prefer to be reached, your personal or professional website, and so on.

- Professional experience, including all relevant positions. At what date you begin your list of professional experiences will depend on how long you have been in the field. If you are just starting out in your career, it is appropriate to include the appointments as a teaching assistant you may have held in graduate school. Once you are tenured, however, these early positions are probably best omitted from your vita. However, if you served as a research assistant to a significant figure in your discipline or pursued a topic that is still relevant to what you do, you may wish to continue including these positions throughout your entire career. At no time, however, should you list any employment that you held while an undergraduate or earlier in your life, unless you were a nontraditional student and had significant, full-time work experience. As a general rule of thumb, jobs taken simply to support yourself while in school or to earn spending money are not appropriate in a professional vita.

- Degrees, including all earned and honorary degrees (clearly distinguished) beginning with your undergraduate program. List the degree acronym (such as B.S., M.A., Ph.D., and the like), field of your major(s), year of the degree, and the institution granting the degree. Minors may be listed if you wish, but they will be irrelevant for most of the uses you have for a professional curriculum vitae. Some people prefer not to list the year in which a degree was earned, believing that this information suggests their age, and they prefer not to be discriminated against as being too old or too young for a position or honor. Omitting the year of a degree is usually a poor practice, however; age discrimination is illegal, after all, and there are remedies to pursue if it occurs. Rather than protecting you, omitting the date of your degree could well call attention to the fact that you, unlike the vast majority of other applicants or candidates, have suppressed this information. In any case, you are far less likely to be passed over in a screening process for being too young or too old than you are for submitting a poorly constructed vita that appears to be lacking routine information. Nearly everyone lists the years in which they earned their degrees, and you should, too. Also, if you have graduated from an institution that readers are unlikely to recognize or that may be confusing to a reader (such as Cornell College versus Cornell University, Miami University of Ohio, or Indiana University of Pennsylvania), include the city and state of the institution. Be consistent: if you list the location of one institution, be sure to include the location of all your degree-granting institutions.

- Academic work currently in progress, including nondegree work as well as credits earned in pursuit of a future degree. Remember that ABD, the common abbreviation for "All But Dissertation," is *not* a degree and should not be treated as such anywhere on your vita. Most institutions adopt an expression like "admission to doctoral candidacy" when a student is permitted to begin writing his or her dissertation. By listing the date on which you were admitted to the doctoral candidacy or had your advanced proposal approved, you will be accurately indicating the level you have reached in your academic work without appearing to claim a degree that is either nonexistent (such as ABD) or not yet granted (such as the Ph.D.). Besides, if you've already been ABD for ten years or more, anyone who examines your vita will conclude that you are unlikely ever to finish your doctorate. It is better, therefore, to focus on attainments that you *have* rather than those that you attempted.

- The title or topic of your dissertation or thesis.
- Areas of your academic experience or specialization.
- Areas of your administrative experience or specialization.
- A statement of your professional goals for the next five years.
- Statements of your philosophy in such areas as teaching, scholarship, and service or academic citizenship (see Chapter 40, "Taking the Next Step in Your Service").
- Refereed publications, which may be further divided into such categories as books and articles, if you have several examples of each.
- Any of your publications that have been selected for reprinting in other journals after their initial appearance.
- Citations of your scholarship in the publications of others.
- Awards for research, scholarship, or creative activity.
- Nonrefereed publications such as essays, encyclopedia entries, book or music reviews, op-ed pieces, and the like.
- Nontraditional forms of scholarship, such as Web pages, videos, podcasts, and other ways in which you may have disseminated your research.
- Academic works in progress.
- Conference presentations and papers that were delivered before academic audiences.
- Workshops that you attended or conducted, with these two types clearly distinguished.
- Panels that you chaired and sessions for which you served as a respondent.
- Courses that you have taught.
- Indications of success in teaching, such as examples or number of students who have been placed in graduate programs or who are now successful in your field, aggregated data from student evaluations compared to departmental or institutional averages, appropriate

comments from student evaluations that indicate why you have been successful as an instructor, teaching awards received, and the like.

- Your duties as an advisor or mentor.

- Guest lectures you have given, particularly those that have been invited or that took place at institutions other than your own.

- Awards that you have received but that do not fit into any of the other award categories listed here (such as awards for scholarship or awards for teaching).

- Fellowships that you have been granted.

- Grants that you have received.

- Service contributions to the institution in which you played a significant role. (This category may include work that you did in a reaccreditation process, strategic planning initiative, large-scale curriculum reform, presidential search, and the like.)

- Academic service, indicating at which level it occurred, such as departmental service, college-level service, intercollege service, and so on.

- Service to professional organizations.

- Community service.

- Memberships in professional organizations.

- Leadership positions held.

- Languages that you speak and other professional skills that you have.

- Personal information, such as a few highlights of your family life, your personal interests, and other details that make you unique as an individual.

- Names and contact information of several professional references.

- Keep in mind that you will *never* submit a vita for any purpose that contains all of the sections outlined above plus any of the other sections that may be important in your discipline. The vita resource file is simply a document or set of documents from which you will extract information for particular purposes. Do not use it as an excuse for "padding" a curriculum vitae with information irrelevant to your immediate purpose.

Deciding Which Sections to Include in a Curriculum Vitae

Of the thirty-five sections that were outlined earlier for your vita resource file, you will probably always want to include your name and contact information (though perhaps not your personal Web page or IM identity for very formal or professional purposes), your work experience, degrees earned, and refereed publications. For this reason, you may wish to create a second file called something like "Vita Template" that contains these four sections and to which you can then add other sections—or even parts of sections—depending on the particular use you have for your vita at that time.

When you are submitting a vita for evaluation by your own institution (such as for an annual review or a tenure and promotion evaluation), you will include information that you would probably omit if you were preparing a vita to be part of a grant application or to obtain a job at another institution. For example, your home institution will be very interested in the courses that you have taught and evidence of your teaching success, whereas the same information in an application for a large research grant might well be viewed as "padding." In the same way, it would seem unprofessional to include personal information about your family and hobbies when you are applying for promotion to the rank of professor, but that information could be invaluable if you have been nominated for an award or special recognition. Why? Most awards or recognitions are presented at some type of public ceremony. The individual who will introduce you will have a difficult time knowing what to say if the only information available on your résumé is the number of your publications and the dates when you earned your degrees. On the other hand, knowing that you are also a collector of eighteenth-century German porcelain, an avid hang glider, or a published poet (despite your professional responsibilities as a tax accountant) will make you far easier to introduce. Perhaps more important, this information will make you "come alive" as a real person when the committee is selecting the recipient. Similarly, you may not wish to include all the local guest lectures you have given when applying for a job at another university, but this information can be very important if you are applying for a speaking engagement or consultancy. As you decide which sections to copy from your vita resource file to the version of your résumé that you are preparing, always ask yourself which information will be most important to those who are considering you for this particular opportunity. Include only those items and omit the sections that your readers would regard as irrelevant.

Reorganizing a Curriculum Vitae for Different Purposes

Base the structure of your curriculum vitae on the particular criteria by which applications will be reviewed. If you are being evaluated for promotion and tenure, what are the criteria that the committee will use in reviewing your materials? Most institutions base their decision largely on achievements in teaching, scholarship, and service. If that is the case at your institution, why not prepare a version of your vita that has three sections clearly labeled "Teaching," "Scholarship," and "Service"? Doing so makes the job of the committee much easier and will increase the likelihood that you'll be promoted. However, if you are applying for a position at another institution, what are the required and preferred qualifications that are outlined in the position announcement? How can you order and combine relevant sections from your vita resource file to address the particular concerns the search committee will have? If you are applying for a faculty position, you will want to give prominence to your refereed scholarship. (One of the ironies of higher education is that, even at those institutions that claim to place the highest priority on the quality of instruction, selection committees still tend to be more impressed by research than by strong teaching evaluations. So, give prominence to your scholarly achievements and place the section that deals with teaching *second* in your vita.) If you are applying for an administrative position, reorganize the sections so that your success as a fundraiser, committee chair, innovator in academic programs, and effective manager of resources is featured first in your vita. You will still want to document your record of scholarship and teaching but if you place those sections first in your vita, you may be dismissed as "too academic" to have the excellent managerial and leadership skills required of the position. Almost every list of criteria for any position, award, grant, fellowship, or other opportunity lists items in their order of priority. Use that ranking as a guide to how you organize this particular version of your vita and you will greatly increase your chances for success.

Organizational Principles That Should Always Be Followed in a Curriculum Vitae

Regardless of the reason why you are creating this particular version of your vita, you should always adhere to the following guidelines:

- List all items in each section in reverse chronological order: your most recent accomplishment should always be first in a list; your earliest achievement should be last. This order is such a widely recognized custom in preparing vitas that, if you adopt any other organizational principle (such as alphabetical, true chronological order, or "importance"), you end up misleading your readers. They will assume that the first item in your list is your most recent accomplishment, even if it is not.

- Always print your vita on plain white paper that does not have a prominent design or watermark. No matter what your vita is used for, it will probably be photocopied at some point. Colored paper or paper with a design results in copies that can be difficult to read. Be sure, too, to use a good, heavy paper for any vita that you submit in hard copy. Not only will your vita appear more substantial, but it will also keep the next page from showing through if it is copied.

- Unless specifically requested to do otherwise, never prepare your vita as double-sided. Reviewers too often forget to turn over the page and will miss important details.

- Number your pages. Best of all, use the formula "page X of N" (which word processors can insert automatically) to number your pages. If your vita is ever dropped on the floor—and it will be—page numbers in this format will make it much easier to reassemble the document and to verify that all the pages are present.

- Number the items in each section. Whether you like it or not, a review committee is going to count your publications and other accomplishments. So, make it easier for the committee and count items yourself.

- Never put the pages of a vita into individual plastic protective sleeves. Because your vita is likely to be photocopied at some point in the process, you are making a great deal of unnecessary work for a committee if you force a staff member to remove each page from its plastic enclosure, copy it, and replace it in the plastic.

- Try to group accomplishments so that most sections contain at least three items. For instance, if you are new to the profession and have only published one article and two book reviews, consider creating a section labeled "Publications" and group these items together. In most cases, however, it is perfectly acceptable to list even one book in a section all by itself.

- Run all information continuously. Gaps between sections that allow the next section to begin on its own page tend to make a vita look "empty" or "padded" to most reviewers.

- Do not use a font that is too small. In most cases, a 12- or 14-point font should be used. Avoid any highly unusual or artistic fonts, as these tend to alienate reviewers. If your vita has to be submitted electronically as a word processing document, stick to a standard font such as Times New Roman, Georgia, Helvetica, or Arial, which are installed on almost all computers. If it is possible, it is always better to submit a vita as a PDF file rather than as a word processing document, because you will then be certain that the formatting will look the same on the recipient's computer.

- Do not use the space bar to position items on the page. When you use too many spaces, the way in which text appears on your screen will not necessarily be the way it appears on the recipient's screen or after it is printed. As a general rule of thumb, any time you press the space bar more than twice in succession, you are doing something wrong. Using tabs or columns is a much more reliable way to align items.

- Be consistent in the way that you list dates, pages, and so on. For instance, if you write "pages 7–13" in one section of your vita, do not write "pp. 59–81" or even just "59–81" elsewhere.

- Multiple-authored scholarship should be clearly identified as such. If you are the second or third author in the way that credit has been assigned by a journal, retain that order in your vita even if that order makes no real difference in your discipline. Frequently in the humanities, for instance, the order of the authors' names tells you nothing at all about the amount of contribution that each author made to the work (the names may simply be alphabetical, for example). In other disciplines, however, a "lead author" is a very different thing from a "second author," and a "second author" is a very different thing from a "third author." Because a reader of your vita may come from a field different from your own, you do not want even to appear to be claiming more credit for a work than you are owed. Listing your name first on a piece of multiauthored scholarship when the journal places your name third may be utterly irrelevant in your field of study, but someone from another field may assume that it implies academic dishonesty.

- Indicate the date on which the current version of your vita was prepared, either in a header or footer or at the end of the document. This practice will keep a selection committee from wondering how recent the information in the document is. You should never, in any case, submit a copy of a vita that has not been updated within the past year.

- When listing your membership in professional organizations, it is helpful to include the years of your membership or the date on which you joined the organization.

- After you have prepared the version of your vita that you intend to submit, review it to make sure that your activities can be accounted for from the date of your undergraduate degree until the present day. Certain reviewers will assume that unexplained gaps of time conceal activities you'd prefer no one to know about. For this reason, if you have ever left full-time employment to raise a family or to care for a relative, it is often useful to make a simple indication of this fact in your listing of work experience. For instance, an entry of this type might be phrased "2001–2003: Workforce interruption following adoption of son, Dylan" or "2005–2007: Primary caregiver to elderly parents."

- Verify that your degree dates accurately reflect those on your official transcripts. You may think of the date you received your Ph.D. as the date you defended your dissertation, but the institution may list it as the date of conferral or graduation. If your transcript differs in any way from your curriculum vitae, some members of a review committee will find it a cause for concern or assume you are being dishonest for some reason.

- Never use first person forms anywhere in your vita. Even if the version of the document that you are preparing contains a section on your career goals or your statement of teaching philosophy, construct these sections without the use of "I," "me," or "my." First person forms give résumés an unprofessional appearance. Sentence fragments—such as "Goal: to serve as chair of a large department at a major research university"—or some other type of alternative phrasing is always preferable. Particularly in a statement about your philosophy or core principles, don't state that you believe something; merely state what you believe. For example, "The best college professors are those who strive for excellence in both teaching and scholarship" is a much stronger statement than "I feel that college professors should strive for excellence in both teaching and scholarship."

- Avoid acronyms, abbreviations, or jargon that would not readily be understood by any potential reader.

- Before submitting any version of your vita, proofread it at least twice. Even better, have someone you trust proofread it for you. Even minor typographical errors and misspellings can be held against you by certain reviewers.

- Do not project future events (publications, completion of degrees, and so on) more than six months into the future. Be very careful when listing any publication as "forthcoming." Certain reviewers will assume that a forthcoming publication is a work in progress, not a work that has already been submitted or accepted by an editor. The best practice is to include on a vita only items that have already occurred or appeared in print. For annual reviews or for promotion evaluations, however, you may wish to include a few items that are clearly marked as "Submitted for editorial review" or "In press" to specify their current status.

Making a Curriculum Vitae More Visually Appealing

Nearly every word processor includes templates that can be used for preparing a vita. In addition, many websites, including those maintained by the makers of word processing programs, have additional templates and vita samples. Résumés are such a commonly produced commodity these days that it is rarely necessary to start a vita design from scratch. Simply review the templates that came as part of your word processing software, do an Internet search for additional examples, and adopt a clean, crisp, and professional design that appeals to you.

The Proper Plural of Curriculum Vitae

As we have seen, the expression *curriculum vitae* is Latin, and its plural is formed in a manner different from that used for most English words. The proper plural of *curriculum* is *curricula*, just as the proper plural of *memorandum* is *memoranda*. A plural form *curricula vitae* is possible, therefore, and it is sometimes seen. Yet since the word *vitae* ("of life") further characterizes the type of curricula being discussed, it might be argued that its proper genitive plural *vitarum* should also be used. But you will never see the phrase *curricula vitarum* ("courses of lives") used to refer to more than one of these documents. Your best choice, therefore, is to find an alternative whenever you need to use this word in the plural. Adopt such phrasing as "Enclosed you will find three copies of my curriculum vitae" or ". . . three CVs," ". . . three vitas," or even ". . . three résumés." Because of all the alternatives available, you'll find that you never really have to use *curriculum vitae* in the plural, and thus you can avoid having to choose between being incorrect and using a form that will strike most readers as peculiar.

College professors need to prepare copies of their vitas for many different reasons. Each reason, however, may require a version that includes slightly different items or the same items but in a slightly different order. Therefore, adopting the practice of keeping a vita resource file from which various entries and sections may be drawn as needed will help faculty members document their achievements in a manner that makes them most successful for each position, promotion, grant, or recognition they are seeking. Also, because you will usually submit your CV along with a cover letter, it may be a good idea to review the guidelines presented in Chapter 1, "Applying for a Faculty Position," on the appropriate length and tone for most of the letters you might write to accompany your vita.

RESOURCES

Anthony, R., & Roe, G. (1998). *The curriculum vitae handbook: How to present and promote your academic career* (2nd ed.). San Francisco: Rudi.

Anthony, R., & Roe, G. (2003). *101 grade A résumés for teachers* (3rd ed.). Hauppauge, NY: Barron's.

Asher, D. (1997). *Asher's bible of executive résumés and how to write them.* Berkeley, CA: Ten Speed Press.

Buller, J. L. (2006). Helping faculty members create successful résumés. In J. L. Buller, *The essential department chair: A practical guide to college administration* (pp. 271–274). Bolton, MA: Anker.

Jackson, A. L., & Geckeis, C. K. (2003). *How to prepare your curriculum vitae.* New York: McGraw-Hill.

McDaniels, C. (1996). *Developing a professional vita or résumé* (3rd ed.). New York: Ferguson.

32

SEEKING LEADERSHIP
POSITIONS

Faculty members may be interested in obtaining leadership positions for several very important reasons.

- When committees review applications for promotion and tenure, they frequently hope that candidates have not merely served on committees and performed other types of institutional service, but have also made a positive difference and instituted needed changes.
- Establishing new directions for either your department or the institution as a whole can often be accomplished far more effectively if you have attained a leadership position, such as within a strategic planning group or the body charged with setting priorities for a capital campaign.
- Within organizations associated with a faculty member's discipline, it is often easier to set the agenda for policies and innovations that can affect the entire field if you have obtained a leadership role instead of merely serving as one of many members of a professional organization.
- At some point in a faculty member's career, it may become desirable to pursue an administrative position as a department chair, dean, provost, or president (see Chapter 39, "Exploring the Possibility of Administrative Work"). Having an established record of leadership within committees or while heading a task force can be tremendously important when being seriously considered for such opportunities.

You've probably already observed, perhaps in your own experience or from the careers of your colleagues, that successfully filling leadership positions tends to lead to other leadership opportunities. Frequently it is the person who has already demonstrated success while heading one committee who is asked to take on another major assignment, or the person elected president of the faculty senate who is invited to chair the next major administrative search committee. As this pattern is so common, how do you get started in academic leadership if you have not yet held one of these positions either on your own campus or in one of your professional organizations? Or if you've already been offered a few leadership positions but wish to advance even further or to be more successful when given a significant responsibility, what should you do?

View Your Role as a Consensus Builder

Search committees for deans or department chairs frequently ask candidates, "What's your management style?" It really isn't a very good interview question, because there is only one acceptable answer: "I'm a consensus builder. My management style is extremely collegial." (And if you ever serve on a search committee for an academic leader, remember that it is far better to ask, "How do you go about building consensus? How do you demonstrate collegiality?") But what this question does reveal is that in academic settings, people expect their leaders to be effective at promoting a unified vision. There's a good reason for this: in a system of shared governance as we have at American colleges and universities, the ability to succeed in a nonhierarchical setting, identify shared goals, and act in a collegial manner while still demonstrating the capacity to make difficult decisions is the most productive way—at times, the only possible way—for an institution to move forward. To be a leader at a college or university, a person has to be able to speak to a wide variety of constituencies, relate the individual interests of diverse stakeholders to a common goal, create an environment in which it is possible for every voice to be heard, and implement decisions without alienating or disenfranchising anyone. That's a difficult task. For this reason, when people are choosing chairs of committees or representatives on major projects, they tend to select those individuals who have demonstrated an ability to promote harmonious progress. If you can demonstrate this talent even while you are only one of several attendees at a departmental meeting or serving as only one among many members of a committee, you will increase your likelihood of being offered a significant leadership opportunity. Even more important, you will be demonstrating effective academic leadership.

How can you go about building consensus when you are not the head of your department or the chair of a committee? First, try to identify possible areas of agreements that may be hidden by layers of inconsistent vocabulary. In a surprising number of situations, people in a group feel that there is more disagreement present than actually exists because they are using different terms to describe the same thing. It can be difficult to hear these points of commonality if you are so accustomed to one set of expressions that other words seem to imply something quite different. As an honest broker, however, you may be in the best possible position to identify precisely where common views may be found. Try to articulate what you have identified as a possible area of agreement by rephrasing positions with different vocabulary or by somehow combining the terms that the different parties are using. It may be possible to say something like, "I think we're actually far closer to agreement than it seems. When you speak of X, aren't you merely suggesting that . . . ? And when you're talking about Y, doesn't that really mean . . . ? So, aren't we actually looking at just slightly different aspects of the same thing? You see, I think there's a way of taking both of these points of view into account by . . . "

Second, if the disagreement is not a mere matter of terminology, try approaching the matter from a different perspective. Seek higher ground from which you may be able to gain a sense of agreement. "It's clear that there are several different philosophies at work here. But isn't the most important issue the development of a program that best serves the needs of our students regardless of *how* that program is shaped? So, if we can all agree that the needs of our students are paramount, let's see if we can first identify those needs and only then determine how we can best meet them." By directing attention away from an area of contention—in this case, the precise nature of a curricular reform—and redirecting it to something that everyone can agree on, such as the importance of serving students or of preserving high academic standards, you can move an entire group away from what separates its members to what unites them. They may then come back to their task with a renewed sense of common purpose.

When it does not seem possible to find higher ground, a third possibility is to seek at least some sort of *common* ground. Perhaps suggest that the group temporarily set aside an issue about which there is too much disagreement and focus on some other issue for a while. You need not go too far afield. The new topic might simply be some other aspect of the main problem you are trying to solve. But what you are seeking is an opportunity for people to direct their attention somewhere else momentarily and to explore ideas that may receive broader approval. Frequently people who have disagreed on one issue but then discover that they can agree on several other points are able to return to the problematic issue with a greater willingness to compromise and explore other solutions. In other words, you are providing members of the group with an opportunity to rediscover the unity that they have rather than their single area of discord.

Fourth, when all else fails, consider the importance of terms such as *normally* or *in most cases*. Sometimes people oppose policies or initiatives because they are concerned with the occasional exception that could arise.

Merely by inserting a word that demonstrates a willingness to be flexible, such as *ordinarily* or *under usual conditions*, you may be able to find a basis for agreement. Finally, be aware of the many resources that are available to help you promote consensus on committees or during department meetings. Works such as Dressler (2006) or Williams (2006) can be invaluable in suggesting ideas for moving a project forward and promoting agreement. Moreover, by trying the suggestions made in these works and the other strategies just outlined, you'll begin to discover your own methods for achieving consensus, and the approaches that best work for you. Each of our personalities is different, and whereas some people ease tension through humor, others do so through compassionate counseling, level-headed objectivity, or attentive listening. What you most want to discover is a consensus-building technique that fits your character and works most effectively in your particular environment.

Move Ideas Forward

People tend to give leadership positions to those who have demonstrated that they can get things done. Every faculty member soon realizes that in most committee work, there's a huge difference between talking a matter through and talking it to death. Santayana may have been right that those who do not learn from the past are condemned to repeat it, but all too many committees seem bound and determined to repeat the past at every meeting. There sometimes seems very little reason even to print a new agenda for these meetings because the same issues will inevitably be covered, the same arguments made, and the same objections found. The person who can move this process forward demonstrates important leadership skills, and that person need not be the chair of the committee. If you sense that a working group has reached gridlock or at least has not made progress as quickly as it should, you can be the one who helps restore progress. Talk to the chair of the committee in advance, saying something like, "I was listening to the discussion we were having the other day, and I heard people making a lot of good suggestions. So, I simply incorporated those ideas into a proposal, and I wonder if we might be able to discuss it at the next meeting?" Committees often find that having a document of this type helps them make progress in a way that simply discussing ideas cannot accomplish. It gives them a "product" to respond to. Even if they disagree with everything in the document, you can use those disagreements to determine what people really do want to propose and achieve. Try not to be defensive about your proposal: when people find fault with some aspect of it, they're not finding fault with you; after all, what you tried to incorporate into the document are the very ideas that you heard discussed at previous meetings. Your satisfaction will come not from the validation of your initial draft or phrasing, but from being the person who transformed a philosophical discussion into a concrete plan for action.

Promote a Positive, Optimistic Environment

One important way in which you will attract leadership opportunities is by projecting an attitude of confidence and optimism. Particularly when challenges arise, people tend to gravitate naturally to those who appear calm, strong, relaxed, positive, and enthusiastic about the future. Many college professors seem to feel that the best way of demonstrating how hard they are working is by talking repeatedly about how much they have to do and constantly seeming immersed in a flurry of competing demands. It is interesting to observe, however, that the degree to which people get things done is often in inverse proportion to the degree to which they seem "busy" all the time. In any case, the faculty members who convey an attitude of being overwhelmed, harried by numerous demands, and barely able to keep up with the pace of work are rarely those to whom others turn when they are seeking leadership. Leaders tend to arise from those who are viewed as cheerful, always willing to take time to notice the good work that others are doing, and able to see the positive where most people can only see the negative. Then, when matters become extremely stressful, the leaders whose advice is sought are often those colleagues who don't lose their heads in a crisis and who understand that neither good times nor bad will last forever. They get things done even while they take steps to ensure that people feel good about themselves (see Buller, 2007).

In addition to projecting an aura of confidence and optimism in everything you do, it may also be possible to promote collegiality and optimism through more formal structures, such as by establishing an informal committee to enhance morale. For instance, Southwest Airlines, an industry leader in maintaining high employee morale through its unconventional approach to staff relations, maintains what it calls its Culture Committee:

> The committee works behind the scenes to foster Southwest's commitment to values such as profitability, low cost, family, love, and fun. . . . .
> [Its first members] were all great in their individual jobs and were handpicked for their creativity, expertise, energy, enthusiasm, and,

most importantly, Southwest Spirit. . . . For the two years they serve on the committee, members engage in leadership activities that protect the company's unique and highly valued culture. Committee members have been known to visit stations with equipment and paint in hand to remodel a break room. Others rally at one of Southwest's maintenance facilities to serve pizza and ice cream to maintenance employees. Still others simply show up periodically at various field locations to lend a helping hand. . . . Their labor is really a labor of love; their payoff is the relationships they build with other workers, the knowledge that they have sparked worthwhile and fun endeavors, and, most importantly, the satisfaction of having been a vital part of keeping the Southwest Spirit alive. (Freiberg & Freiberg, 1996, pp. 165–166)

If such a group is not yet in place in your department, college, or institution, you can begin demonstrating leadership by creating one and working to improve the atmosphere for everyone in your unit.

Always Keep the Big Picture in View

Another trait often sought in leaders is their ability to understand how the needs and challenges of their own areas fit within a larger framework. The congressional representative who is continually successful in winning contracts for his or her own district may be beloved at home, but these are rarely the people who come to be viewed as "presidential" or even "senatorial." However, the representative who can both advocate for his or her own district and make the good of the whole country an extremely high priority may well have a political future. The same thing happens at colleges and universities. Faculty members who can see no further than the interests of their department or program are not exhibiting the traits demonstrated by genuine campus leaders. Every college professor will, of course, have extremely strong loyalties to his or her academic field; it is this discipline that brought the faculty member into the profession in the first place. But to succeed as chair of the faculty assembly or the institution-wide curriculum committee, a broader perspective is usually required. The ability to understand that "It's not always about us; in fact, it's *frequently* not about us" is often what separates the successful academic leader from the person who is regarded as incapable of seeing the forest for the trees. As you work on various committees, therefore, be an effective advocate for your discipline but also provide evidence that the needs of the institution as a whole often come first. It is counterproductive to advocate for additional faculty lines, for instance, in times of extreme financial exigency. Moreover, the initiative that will best serve your students or research is often not located within your program itself. What most benefits your students may be staffing for a service course, improved access to courses in general education, an impressive new facility or residence hall that can attract stronger students to the entire institution, an expansion of a center for tutoring or advising, or any number of other improvements that initially appear unrelated to your area. Your research might be enhanced more by staff additions in the offices of sponsored programs or institutional advancement than by the purchase of new equipment in your own area. By recognizing how the good of the whole is best served, you are not only demonstrating the sort of leadership skills that you will need as a committee chair, department head, or dean, but you are also often achieving a goal that can benefit your own program in the long run.

Become the Recognized Authority in Some Area

You can also enhance the likelihood that you'll receive leadership opportunities if you develop a reputation as the recognized authority in some area. As we saw in Chapter 6, "Special Challenges for Junior Faculty," it can be extremely beneficial to your institutional identity to become known as *the* person to consult on matters such as assessment, budgeting, faculty development, post-tenure review, course evaluation, strategic planning, hiring practices, diversity development, legal issues, or curricular development. Choose one of these areas as your particular niche, conduct a literature review just as you would for a research topic in your discipline, attend training workshops in this area, and begin volunteering for campus committees and work groups that address this topic. All colleges and universities need faculty members who, in addition to being knowledgeable about their academic field, are also experts in some activity essential to the way in which the institution operates. Your reputation as the go-to person in a key area can be an important aspect of your overall role as an academic citizen, and can open up possibilities for higher leadership opportunities if you should ever desire them.

Of course, one possible area for your special expertise is in the field of leadership development itself. Many parts of the country have leadership programs sponsored by or spun off from local chambers of commerce. These programs usually have a title beginning with the word *Leadership*, followed by the name of the city (Leadership Cincinnati USA; www.lead ershipcincinnati.com), county (Leadership Palm Beach County; www .leadershippbc.org), or state (Leadership Maine; www.mdf.org/leadme/ home.html) in which they operate. Participation in one of these programs can bring several important benefits. First, leadership training will educate you about resources available in your city, county, or state and about how these political entities function. Second, it will expose you to a broad range of influential people whom you may not have the opportunity to meet otherwise. Third, it will give you practical training in developing your own leadership potential and leave you with some documented "products" of how you have succeeded as a leader. Fourth, it will provide you with insight into how other members of the faculty and staff could best be prepared for leadership roles. It might be possible, for instance, for you to develop a faculty leadership training program within your department or throughout your institution. By doing so, you will both be providing an extraordinarily important service to your colleagues and enhancing your own reputation as an emerging leader.

Develop a Solid Leadership Plan

In Chapter 4, "Career Planning for College Professors," we saw the importance of developing a flexible career plan. In much the same way, a leadership plan can be an integral part of your overall career plan, identifying those leadership opportunities you hope to pursue and why. For example, if you hope someday to be a university president, you may want to develop a strategy that enables you to serve first as a department chair, then as dean, and then perhaps takes you in a new direction. Maybe you'll want to consider the possibility of pursuing an ACE Fellowship (www.acenet.edu/AM/Template.cfm?Section=Fellows_Program1). Or maybe you'll move from the academic environment to a development office or university advancement for a few years, getting the sort of fundraising experience that you'll need as a president. Or perhaps it might be better to pursue a position as the executive assistant to a president in order to understand how these offices run and which issues tend to be addressed at this level. If you decide that a presidency of a university is not your calling, you could easily develop a similar plan that will carry you to head a professional organization in your field, chair your institution's faculty assembly, or serve as union president. In each case you'll want to identify the leadership skills and achievements that you will need to gain along the way and determine the best way to develop those skills and document those achievements.

All of this planning should be done, however, only if you truly believe that you have the appropriate temperament for the leadership position you are seeking and would find that position an effective role in which to make a positive difference. Don't seek a leadership position simply to build your résumé, increase your income, or advance a personal agenda. If these are your objectives, there are certainly easier opportunities to achieve them, such as by writing a textbook, serving as a consultant, or including summer compensation (where permitted) as part of a grant proposal. In short, the essential principle on this topic is:

Don't pursue any opportunity in your professional life simply because of the chance to make more money. Rather, identify those professional activities that you both love and excel at. Then explore the most likely way to improve your level of income by engaging in those activities.

Faculty members who seek leadership roles for any reason other than to promote the interests of the institution and academia as a whole ultimately end up doing more harm than good. Be very candid with yourself and with others about why you want to become an academic leader, and develop your plan accordingly.

Seeking leadership positions can be an important part of a faculty member's career plan as well as a major part of one's role as a good academic citizen. You can be an academic leader either among your colleagues on committees and in departments or in elected or administrative roles. The best academic leaders are those who can see the big picture, convey an air of confidence and optimism, and put the needs of others ahead of their own. Although each college professor will be expected to demonstrate academic leadership at least once during his or her career, for the right type of person, filling leadership roles can become a key element in the type of service performed on behalf of the institution, community, or discipline.

REFERENCES

Buller, J. L. (2007). *The essential academic dean: A practical guide to college leadership.* San Francisco: Jossey-Bass.

Dressler, L. (2006). *Consensus through conversation: How to achieve high-commitment decisions.* San Francisco: Berrett-Koehler.

Freiberg, K., & Freiberg, J. (1996). *NUTS! Southwest Airlines' crazy recipe for business and personal success.* New York: Broadway Books.

Williams, R. B. (2006). *More than fifty ways to build team consensus* (2nd ed.). Thousand Oaks, CA: Corwin Press.

RESOURCES

Bolman, L. G., & Deal, T. E. (2008). *Reframing organizations: Artistry, choice, and leadership* (4th ed.). San Francisco: Jossey-Bass.

Buller, J. L. (2006). Advice for future department chairs. *The Department Chair, 16*(4), 1–3.

Fisher, R., Ury, W., & Patton, B. (1992). *Getting to yes: Negotiating agreement without giving in* (2nd ed.). New York: Houghton Mifflin.

Green, R. L. (2009). *Practicing the art of leadership: A problem-based approach to implementing the ISLLC standards* (3rd ed.). Boston: Allyn & Bacon.

Preskill, S., & Brookfield, S. D. (2009). *Learning as a way of leading: Lessons from the struggle for social justice*. San Francisco: Jossey-Bass.

33

SERVING ON COMMITTEES

Service on committees is one of the most important ways in which college professors participate in shared governance at institutions of higher education. As faculty members, we use committees to approve changes to the curriculum, set new academic policies, grant exceptions to existing policies, identify and interview prospective faculty members, choose recipients for awards, chart strategies for the future, and conduct dozens of other types of business that are essential to our educational mission. Even though it is clear that the service performed by faculty members includes far more than committee membership (see Chapter 30, "Service Reconsidered"), many evaluation processes still place a great deal of emphasis on the amount of committee work each college professor has performed. Like student ratings of instruction, which tend to be overemphasized when teaching is evaluated, and refereed publications, which tend to be overemphasized when scholarship is evaluated, the number of committees on which a faculty member has served is frequently given prominence in evaluations of service because it is so quantifiable. Review committees are occasionally distracted by the illusion of objectivity provided by numerical results, and so they may write such unhelpful statements as "Professor Allen averages 3.795 out of a perfect 4.0 on annual student ratings of instruction, has published twenty-seven refereed articles in academic journals, and served on more than a dozen committees." Such a statement tells the reader nothing at all about the quality of Professor Allen's work, but evaluators have a predilection for reporting items that can be counted or otherwise reduced to a number, even if those statistics are all but meaningless. For this reason, it can be important for faculty members to demonstrate a willingness to serve on committees—and to serve on the *right* committees—even though their academic citizenship will inevitably consist of far more than simply committee membership.

Over the course of your academic career, it is likely that you will serve on many different kinds of committees. Although it may initially seem that meeting this expectation does not require guidance and preparation in the same way that you might need, for instance, if you were teaching a large course or preparing a grant proposal does, there are actually several important principles to keep in mind if you want your committee service to be as productive and rewarding as possible.

Choosing the Right Committees

As we've seen, colleges and universities rely on committees to perform a great deal of work. In fact, most colleges and universities tend to develop essentially the *same* committees. To be sure, one institution's Educational Policy Committee may be called the Undergraduate Programs Committee at another institution, but in reality these different titles refer to the body that approves curricular matters at the undergraduate level. Moreover, some of these very common academic committees are regarded as particularly important because they are broadly involved in work that is vital to the institution's ongoing success. In general, the groups that most institutions regard as especially significant include institution-wide curricular committees, the faculty senate, strategic planning bodies, and administrative search committees, particularly those outside of the faculty member's own department. Because there is some variability in the significance of particular committees at different institutions, however, be sure to talk with your chair, dean, or a trusted senior faculty member about your individual situation. This type of conversation has many benefits. In addition to receiving the benefit of that person's advice, you'll also be signaling your willingness to be a good academic citizen. In many cases, the person whom you consult will eventually nominate you for appropriate opportunities that come along later.

It is also a good idea to incorporate a focus on committee work into your overall career plan or at least your action plan for service. In Chapter 6, "Special Challenges for Junior Faculty," we discussed the importance of developing a realistic strategy for the service that you'll perform. Especially if you are relatively new to the profession, you will want to avoid serving on—or being *expected* to serve on—so many committees that it deprives you of the time you will need to develop your teaching skills and to advance your scholarly agenda. Women and members of minority groups should be particularly careful of becoming overly committed to relatively insignificant but time-consuming committees. In a well-meaning attempt to diversify hiring and to represent a cross-section of views when new policies are being developed, many institutions seek to balance virtually every committee by gender and race. Unfortunately, the problem with this approach is that because women and members of minority groups are often underrepresented on the staff, the same people get assigned to committee after committee. Because of these issues, every faculty member should work out a clear strategy with a supervisor. In an action plan for service, you will target particular committees because they are important to what you are doing or because they will be regarded as significant in your evaluations. Certainly every college professor will need to accept a rotation on a minor committee from time to time. Without these groups, the right books would not be ordered for the library, events would not be planned, support services would be ignored, and awards would not be made. If your service contribution consists solely of committees that have little impact outside of your department, however, it will be much more difficult for you to make an effective case that you have been as valuable as possible in your academic citizenship.

A good action plan for service should take into account all of your overall goals. For instance, if you are seeking a major recognition in scholarship as suggested in Chapter 29, "Taking the Next Step in Your Scholarship," you might ask yourself: "Which committees will best help me improve my scholarship and become more recognized for my success in research?" Approached in this way, your plan might be to initiate a scholarship network first in your department, then extend it collegewide, before finally serving on a committee that promotes scholarship networks across your institution. (On scholarship networks, see Chapter 27, "Seeking and Providing Peer Support for Scholarship.") Once this activity is well under way, you might ask to be nominated as your departmental representative to a committee that deals primarily with research, such as the institutional review board or the animal care and use committee. Eventually, you might seek to chair one of these committees. But if you have decided that excellence in teaching will be the area in which you will make your primary contribution, you might decide to take an approach similar to that outlined above, by developing teaching circles rather than scholarship networks. The committees on which you serve might be those that deal with curricular development, awards for instruction, and faculty review of teaching. You might contribute service by first attending then offering workshops sponsored by your institution's center for teaching excellence, perhaps eventually becoming a faculty representative to such a center. Finally, if your goal is to become an administrator, seek out committees that help to set policies for your department, then look for substantive collegewide service on curricular bodies and search committees, while also serving on (and eventually presiding over) the faculty senate. For more suggestions on how to use your service contribution as preparation for an administrative career, see Chapter 39, "Exploring the Possibility of Administrative Work."

Serving on a Committee

Because so many institutions give service less weight than teaching and scholarship when evaluating faculty members, it is easy for college professors to assign committee work a relatively low priority. Nevertheless, doing so is almost always a mistake. When you serve on committees, colleagues see you in ways that are different from any other environment. Many faculty members at your institution will never see you teach. At meetings of the department and full faculty, you may make comments rarely or not at all. On a committee, however, other faculty members see you *working*. They start forming impressions of you that it may be difficult to alter later in your career. Your colleagues may be judging your reliability, your insight, how well you communicate, your ability to compromise, your writing skills, and the extent to which you can remain focused on the topic at hand. Although you may think that committee work has relatively little to do with your teaching and scholarship, other people on the committee may, rightly or wrongly, even be making assumptions about the quality of your teaching and scholarship based on how well you serve on a committee. They may think something like, "That point was particularly well presented. Dr. Smith must be very good in the classroom," or "It took Dr. Jones so long just to get us this set of minutes. I bet students don't get their papers back very quickly either." These judgments tend to be especially important when you are serving alongside faculty members who may not know you very well, such as members of other departments. For this reason, keep the following guidelines in mind as you serve on committees:

- *Always be on time.* Although the committee may not be your highest priority at the moment, it does involve a large number of other people who are probably as busy as you are. Showing up late for a committee meeting, particularly if it occurs more than once, may well be regarded as disrespectful by the other members of the committee.

- *When minutes, agendas, and other materials are distributed in advance, come to the meeting having read all of the items and with a few constructive ideas or suggestions to make.* Material distributed before a meeting is your "homework." Just as you expect your students to come to class with their reading done and assignments prepared, so do our colleagues expect us to come to meetings ready for the discussions that will take place and the decisions that must be made. We know what we think about the student who, in response to a question, furtively glances through the textbook, desperately trying to find an answer in a chapter that has obviously not been reviewed. Nevertheless, many faculty members do precisely the same thing at a committee meeting, shuffling through pages of handouts, picking out phrases here and there to mention off the cuff, and hoping to absorb information during the meeting itself that has not been given the prior attention that it deserves. This is no way for important decisions to be made. Even such a routine matter as approval of minutes requires a bit of advance thought and preparation. In many cases, those minutes become part of the institution's permanent record, consulted when later questions arise or when accreditation visits are planned. For this reason, don't simply glance at these documents during the meeting itself and rush to vote for approval. Read them over before the meeting begins and, though not nitpicking or pointing out every split infinitive and lack of parallel structure, take time to provide corrections for true inaccuracies and clarify sentences that could easily be misunderstood later.

- *When you are new to a committee, do more listening than talking for the first few meetings.* Each committee develops its own set of working procedures over time. In addition, there are a number of issues that every committee feels it has already dealt with sufficiently and does not wish to revisit. When members are new to a committee, they can bring a fresh perspective to a discussion but they can also suggest inadvertently that the committee take on a task that it has already completed or address a topic that had been fully explored in the past. It is simply good common sense to spend a few meetings getting the lay of the land. Feel free to express your opinion, of course, but be sure that you are also discovering how this particular committee operates and what its past concerns have been. If possible, go through minutes from the last two or three years to educate yourself about matters of recent discussion in the group. Faculty members who come charging in immediately after having been appointed or elected to a committee are frequently resented by more senior members of the group who view themselves, correctly or not, in leadership roles or as mentors. Even if you are right about a point and these other members of the committee are wrong, you are likely to need their support later when matters come to a vote. So, take some time to learn the issues, find out who serves as opinion leaders on the committee, and develop an appropriate long-range strategy to accomplish what is in the best interest of the institution.

- *During discussions, contribute insights that advance the work of the committee, but try not to repeat points that have already been made.*

The time that a committee has available is necessarily short. Meetings must be squeezed in between members' teaching and research schedules, and often between other meetings. Few committees have the luxury of being mere debating clubs or discussion groups. For this reason, it is often helpful to ask yourself "How is the comment that I am about to make advancing our work?" before participating in a discussion, particularly one that has already become prolonged. Restating a position already made clear by another committee member, repeating a point that you have already made, and sharing anecdotes that are only marginally related to the matter at hand merely extend the discussion; they do not move it along. At best, these repetitions will make a long meeting even longer. At worst, they may derail the entire discussion and prevent *any* productive work from being done. In the vast majority of situations, therefore, remarks made during committee meetings should be concise and on topic.

- *Whenever possible, help the committee to advance its work by drafting a "product" or proposal.* In Chapter 32, "Seeking Leadership Positions," we saw how helpful it can be for someone, not necessarily the chair, to come to a committee meeting with a proposal or document that synthesizes the past group discussions and helps move toward an action. In most cases, people find it easier to respond to a written draft than to arguments that have been aired orally. If you are in doubt as to the appropriateness of taking the lead in drafting such a document, the best thing to do is to meet privately with the committee chair several days before the meeting. Run your draft by the chair, explain that you are merely trying to be helpful, and ask whether the document would be useful to the discussion that is about to take place. Almost always, the chair of the committee will eagerly express gratitude for your foresight and constructive work. In those rare situations where, possibly because of turf issues or because the matter is more complex than you realize, the chair declines your offer to help, accept this decision graciously. You don't want to appear to be undermining the chair's position in the committee, and there will be plenty of opportunities for you to make a contribution later. Alternatively, of course, you can offer your draft to the chair to be used however he or she wishes. This strategy is particular useful when you want to avoid the impression of making a power move and or seeming presumptuous. It has the added advantage in that the chair cannot possibly say no: you have not asked that person to do anything, and so there is no request to turn down.

Chairing a Committee

Chairing a committee requires even greater skills at planning, leading effective discussions, and managing diverse personalities than does serving on a committee. At some point in your career as an academic citizen, you will find yourself chairing at least one academic committee. At that time, you should keep in mind the following guidelines:

- *Be sure that you understand the committee's operating procedure.*
  Even if the committee that you are chairing already has an officially appointed parliamentarian, as the chair you will need to understand who on the committee has voting rights, how motions must be made, and how voting on motions should proceed. It is frequently the case that, in the heat of an intense debate, claims are made that parliamentary procedure requires you to do this or that; as most faculty members have only a general sense of whether the claim may be true, decisions can be made in haste that should have been more effectively challenged or debated. Materials such as Jones (1990), Robert, Evans, Honemann, and Balch (2000), and Sturgis (2001) will give you essential information about conducting meetings and evaluating the priority of various types of motions. In addition, there are several websites that can help you review most aspects of committee procedure and organization. Among the best of these websites are the Official Roberts Rules of Order (www.robertsrules.com), Roberts Rules of Order Online (www.rulesonline.com), and an excellent resource developed by the Student Activities Office of California State University, Chico (www.csuchico.edu/sac/student Organizations/parliamentaryProcedures.shtml). Finally, both the American Institute of Parliamentarians (www.parliamentary procedure.org) and the National Association of Parliamentarians (www.parliamentarians.org) offer a wide range of information and training materials, including opportunities for workshops and distance learning, that can give you even more detailed knowledge of how parliamentary procedure should be applied when you are chairing meetings (see Buller, 2007). Alternately, approaches such as those outlined in Susskind and Cruikshank (2006) establish effective operating procedures for committees that don't rely on traditional parliamentary procedure. Remember, unless your institution requires that meetings be conducted according to a specific system, it is relatively unimportant which set of operating procedures your committee uses as long as it is consistent in following some set of procedures.

- *Prepare, distribute, and adhere to an agenda.* A printed agenda distributed in advance helps keep meetings focused and on track. If you begin a meeting by distributing a new agenda, it becomes more difficult for the members of the group to prepare their thoughts on the issues that will be discussed. Conversations tend to wander far from the primary topic of the meeting, and time is wasted. By preparing a written agenda well before the meeting, you achieve several important goals simultaneously. First, you force yourself to think through the various results that you would like to produce from the meeting, place them in a priority order, and develop an effective strategy for dealing with them. Second, by distributing the agenda at least two days before a meeting, you are giving committee members time to collect any materials that they may wish to bring to the meeting, and to prepare their own thoughts and positions on the various issues. Third, your agenda sends a clear message about what is of the highest priority in your committee's discussions. Groups are less likely to devote extensive time rehashing familiar arguments about the third item on the agenda when there are a dozen other issues that need to be addressed. For this reason, good committee chairs prepare an agenda well in advance of the meeting, distribute it to all members, and make sure that it is followed during the meeting itself.

- *Keep the conversation focused and move the discussion forward.* Though most people will do their utmost to work as effectively as possible on a committee, even the best colleagues may get off track every now and then. They may forget an issue that was already decided several meetings earlier. They may feel that an important matter has been overlooked, when the truth is that no one else really cares about that issue. They may sincerely misunderstand a matter and thus get sidetracked on an irrelevant point. In addition to these goodhearted committee members who inadvertently slow the work of the committee, you may occasionally encounter a member who uses the group as a platform for his or her own personal agenda, feels compelled to grandstand on some issue, lets a personal difference with you or another member overshadow the committee's primary mission, or arrives late for meetings and expects issues that have already been decided to be reopened for his or her personal convenience. As chair, you have a responsibility not to let these distractions interfere with your committee's work. You must be polite but assertive in keeping to the established agenda, cutting off discussion by moving to a vote or the next topic when the conversation is no longer productive, and making sure that your members' time is well spent. You can refocus the discussion by saying something like, "That's an interesting point, but I think it may only be tangential to the topic we're discussing. Perhaps we can explore it some other time." In a similar way, you can politely offer to catch up a member on an issue after the meeting or refer to the group's minutes to illustrate that a decision has already been made. A light touch and a bit of well-intentioned humor can diffuse tension, return everyone's focus to the topic at hand, and maintain your committee's high level of productivity.

- *Ask yourself and your committee members periodically, "Exactly what problem are we trying to solve?"* Committees also sometimes get off track because they lose sight of their overall objective. Particularly in the case of standing committees, meetings can tend to occur simply because they're expected, not because they're needed. For example, some institutions undergo lengthy and expensive processes of curricular reform, not because their assessment processes have indicated that reform is necessary or desirable, but simply because there is a committee that has been charged with revising the curriculum. It's a good corrective, therefore, to ask either implicitly or directly "Exactly what is it that we're trying to fix here?" from time to time. Committees that cannot easily identify the problem they are trying to solve, the goal they are trying to achieve, or the improvement they are trying to make are likely to end up meeting and forcing people to change the way they do things for no reason at all. Remember that everyone is far too busy to revise a set of documents or procedures unless a clear benefit can be identified with that change.

- *Set as constructive a tone as possible.* The role that the chair of a committee plays in setting the tone for the committee as a whole is extremely important. If you approach your task as though it is difficult, meaningless, annoying, petty, or impossible, your committee will inevitably agree. If, however, your mood is upbeat and you approach your meetings with high energy and good spirits, people will not only enjoy working with you on the committee, they will actually do a better job. Stay positive, focus on the good that your committee can accomplish, cheerfully cancel meetings when the agenda is insufficient, and thank your committee members generously for their time and contributions.

Committees are ubiquitous in academic life. There is no point in resenting their "intrusion" on the time you need for teaching and research, because higher education could not exist without them. In fact, you wouldn't really want your institution to function without committees; they are a vital part of how shared governance is implemented at American colleges and universities. On many different levels, your essential principle should be the following:

Never make the mistake of thinking that going to meetings takes you away from your "real work." If you're a college professor, it's important for you to understand that going to meetings is an integral part of your "real work."

In light of this principle, come to view your "real work" as being a constructive, contributing academic citizen in the broadest sense possible and strive to make service on committees a productive investment of time for everyone involved.

REFERENCES

Buller, J. L. (2007). *The essential academic dean: A practical guide to college leadership*. San Francisco: Jossey-Bass.

Jones, O. G. (1990). *Parliamentary procedure at a glance: Group leadership manual for chairmanship and floor leadership*. New York: Penguin.

Robert, H. M., III, Evans, W. J., Honemann, D. H., & Balch, T. J. (2000). *Robert's rules of order* (10th ed.). New York: Perseus.

Sturgis, A. (2001). *The standard code of parliamentary procedure* (4th ed.). New York: McGraw-Hill.

Susskind, L. E., & Cruikshank, J. L. (2006). *Breaking Robert's rules: The new way to run your meeting, build consensus, and get results*. New York: Oxford University Press.

34

SERVING AS AN ACADEMIC ADVISOR

The mere placement of a chapter on academic advising in a unit that deals with service is bound to raise some eyebrows. "Advising is part of a college professor's *teaching* role," many faculty members will argue, "and that is precisely how this work is evaluated at my institution." To be sure, the best sort of academic advising is a natural outgrowth of our role as teachers, and much of the discussion that appears below will emphasize this very point. Nevertheless, in this chapter we are going to explore academic advising in the context of service for several important reasons.

- Although advising is evaluated at many institutions as part of a college professor's teaching responsibilities, that arrangement is far from universal. Many colleges and universities do regard academic advising as part of a faculty member's service load, particularly in environments where the number of advisees you are assigned can vary dramatically. In addition, some schools include advising and mentoring students as a wholly separate, fourth category of faculty workload, in addition to teaching, scholarship, and service. Though excellent advising always involves teaching students many things, including how to choose courses that help expand their worldview, balance their workload, and help them develop to their fullest potential, there is simply no universally accepted way of acknowledging the role that academic advising plays within a college professor's workload.

- More important, a college professor's role as an advisor needs to be viewed within the larger context of service as effective academic citizenship that was discussed in Chapter 30, "Service Reconsidered." Those who feel that it is demeaning to regard academic advising as "mere service" may well be thinking of service only as the type of menial work that is necessary for a department or program to function. Certainly, good advising can play a much more significant role in a student's development than a faculty member's work as a club sponsor, liaison to parents during family weekend, or warm body at yet another committee meeting. However, if we approach advising as an essential function of many faculty members' roles as superb academic citizens, it becomes clearer that academic advisors, though they most definitely teach the students they are assigned, also fulfill a much greater function that is integral to the very idea of effective academic citizenship.

• Finally, at some institutions and in certain disciplines, academic advising is no longer a faculty responsibility. Professional staff advisors are hired who work with students out of an advising center located at either the institutional, college, or departmental level. We'll argue below for the roles of advisor and mentor to be merged as much as possible, but in many environments the two functions are artificially separated. In these cases, an advisor is a staff member who helps students build their schedules. A mentor is a faculty role model who helps students advance in their lives and their careers. In recognition of this reality, we shall discuss advising and serving as a mentor separately—even though the best advisors do not limit their advice to course selection—within the general context of good academic citizenship.

Regardless of whether we consider academic advising to be part of our instructional responsibilities or more closely related to our roles as academic citizens, the most vital question is, "How can college professors become more effective as advisors?"

Take Advantage of Available Resources

Academic advising carries with it a great deal of responsibility. If you provide inaccurate advice, a student could end up delaying his or her graduation—and spending thousands of dollars unnecessarily—by taking courses that weren't needed, missing courses that were needed, or taking courses out of the proper sequence. Most institutions do, it is true, put the onus of proper course selection squarely on the student. Advisors merely provide advice, they reason; it is the duty of the students themselves to make sure that all academic policies are being followed and that they register for the correct courses in the correct order. Institutions, too, vary widely in how they respond to "advisor error." At some schools, poor advice from a professor or staff member acting in an official capacity is sufficient to warrant a waiver of requirements. At others, waivers are never given due to advisor error under any circumstances.

Most schools deal with these issues on a case-by-case basis and attempt to weigh the degree to which both the student and advisor were acting in good faith. No matter how much responsibility your institution assigns to you as an advisor, it is important to realize that there are several excellent resources available for advisors.

- In-house training for advisors often takes a number of forms. Depending on the size of your institution, advisor training may be provided within the department itself, or it may be offered centrally by the college or university. Frequently workshops on advising may be offered by a center for teaching excellence or a professional development office on campus. Even if participation in these workshops is not required, advisors should consider participating in them every year or two because requirements change, prerequisites for courses are added or deleted, and alternative means of completing requirements are sometimes developed. Many schools have developed extensive handbooks for academic advisors, and some even offer online workshops that professors can complete from their own offices and in their own time. This in-house training is particularly valuable as programs are so different from one school to the next, approaches to general education vary widely, and the precise focus of a major at one school may not be at all similar to the emphasis of that major at other institutions.

- The single best general resource for academic advisors is Gordon, Habley, Grites, and Associates (2008). In an extensive work that spans more than five hundred pages, the authors provide insight into best practices on all aspects of advising from the philosophical basis of the advisor's task to specific techniques for assessing the effectiveness of advising procedures. Among the other topics addressed are the legal foundations of academic advising, exemptions to the Family Educational Rights and Privacy Act of 1974, diversity issues in advising, individual versus group advising, additional resources for advisors, exemplary practices in academic advising, and a great deal more. This compendium of information is so complete and valuable that a copy of it needs to be on the shelf of every faculty member whose duties include advising students.

- The National Academic Advising Association (NACADA; www .nacada.ksu.edu) hosts regional and national conferences on issues related to advising, sponsors Webcasts, conducts training institutes for administrators and on the assessment of advising, offers seminars on the technology of advising, and even provides online courses.

NACADA's Consultants Bureau can audit existing advising procedures at institutions and provide assistance on how academic advising
can be improved. Its awards program recognizes individuals or institutions who have made significant contributions to the field of advising students. Twice a year NACADA offers grants of up to $5,000
for research into advising. The association also provides printed and
electronic resources for advisors. The *NACADA Journal* appears
biannually and covers a range of issues related to the scholarly study
of advising. Its quarterly electronic publication *Academic Advising
Today* has a more applied focus and allows advisors to discuss best
practices in dealing with the challenges and opportunities related to
advising. NACADA membership is valuable, not just for full-time
staff advisors, but also for faculty members whose duties include
service as an advisor.

Duties of Academic Advisors

- *Understand in detail the curricula and requirements of all the
  programs about which you'll be advising students.* The academic
  advisor's primary responsibility is to be knowledgeable about the
  programs for which he or she is expected to provide advice. If the
  students you'll be advising are unlikely to have completed their
  general education requirements, be sure that you understand your
  school's general education program in full detail. Do certain courses
  count toward the fulfillment of more than one requirement? Are
  there degree requirements that do not involve taking credit-bearing
  courses, such as maintaining an academic or extracurricular portfolio,
  attendance at a certain number of cultural events, or engaging in a
  specific amount of community service? If you are likely to be advising
  students in majors outside your own, be sure that you understand
  how those programs work, which courses need to be taken early in a
  student's career because they are prerequisites for later courses, and
  whether certain courses are beneficial when students are preparing for
  their senior thesis or capstone experience. For majors that students
  frequently complete in order to be admitted into graduate or professional programs, are there courses that may not be required for the
  major itself but are required or highly recommended for admission
  into the graduate program? If a student is attempting a double or
  triple major, be sure you understand how many credits, if any, may be
  applied toward more than one degree simultaneously. Most colleges
  and universities make tracking these issues as easy as possible through

degree audits and worksheets for monitoring a student's progress in the general education program, major, and minor. Many times these worksheets are automated, either in the institution's central information or enterprise resource planning system, such as Banner or Oracle, or as independent Web pages, spreadsheet templates, or electronic forms. As a result, there are numerous tools available to help you determine which requirements a student needs to complete at any stage in his or her academic program.

- *See each advisee as a complete person.* Like committee work, advising should never be viewed as a distraction from your "real work" of teaching and research. Each individual advisee will have a different set of needs based on his or her past academic history, level of ability, personality, background, career goals, life goals, and immediate challenges or circumstances. A good advising session should be about more than just choosing the right courses for the next term. It should even be more about helping a student attain his or her objectives in terms of a degree and a profession. A good advising session should also be a good mentoring session. Take the time to get to know each student as an individual. Not only will this approach help you to provide that student with better advice, but also your meeting with the student could turn out to be the only substantive one-on-one contact with a college professor that this student receives (see Chapter 15, "Teaching One-on-One"). Don't simply ask which courses the student is interested in taking or needs to complete. Ask, too, what sort of person the student would like to become, who his or her role models are, and what he or she hopes to accomplish in life. Provide true advice to each student: encourage your advisees to stretch a bit and take courses that force them to move beyond their comfort zone. Remember that they will only be able to ask you about what they already know. There may be disciplines or individual professors that could greatly enhance the educational experience of students, but the students may not think to ask about them because they are not as familiar as you are with the institution or academic life in general. Most of all, understand that each student selects and registers for classes only a few times while at your institution. It is easy to get frustrated with someone who doesn't seem able to find the information that he or she needs or who is having trouble with the process of online registration. But remember that though you deal with these matters frequently, these procedures need to be followed only a few times in a student's life, and thus an extra measure of understanding may well be required.

- *Help each student begin to take responsibility for making appropriate decisions that are in his or her long-term best interests.* An advisor's ultimate goal should be to prepare all of his or her advisees to the point where they can serve as their own advisors. Initially in a student's academic program, an advisor's guidance is often essential. Some students will look for the easiest possible way to fulfill requirements or even look for exceptions to every inconvenient policy. Others will want to take only courses that they like or that they believe will be fun. Still others will try not to venture far from their own comfort zone and will hope merely to continue learning what they already know and to have their assumptions about the world validated by others. Good advisors do not merely assist students in selecting courses; they also teach their advisees how to take advantage of opportunities, strengthen areas of weakness, and expand their horizons. They teach advisees about the importance of delaying gratification and putting their long-term interests ahead of their short-term desires. In this way, each advising session becomes a lesson in how to make decisions and balance competing goals. As we saw in Chapter 20, "Maintaining Appropriate Faculty-Student Relations," the client-profession relationship that exists between student and professor-advisor is necessarily focused on meeting a student's needs, not on satisfying his or her desires. Just as physicians try to teach their patients to take some appropriate degree of responsibility in securing their own treatment, so do good advisors try to bring their advisees to the point where they can identify for themselves how their needs are best addressed through courses and other opportunities that may not be easy and fun but that are far more beneficial in the long run.

- *Introduce students to the resources that can help them solve problems and make well-informed decisions.* One of the ways in which advisors can help students take responsibility for their own academic programs is to ensure that all of their advisees understand the resources available to them. An advisor may wish to verify that his or her advisees are fully aware of the services provided by the campus career center, understand how the testing center can inform them of application deadlines for graduate and professional school exams, know when job fairs will occur on campus and why these opportunities are important even for students who are not immediately looking for a job, and have access to all the other information that they need. An advisor might even consider making a call on behalf of the student or walking the student over to a center that can provide a needed service. A student may be reluctant to make use of a disabilities services center because he or she is embarrassed to admit that he or she could have a learning disability or because the student doesn't understand the full range of accommodations that such a center can provide. A student's academic work could be suffering due to financial concerns, emotional challenges, or illness that could be addressed by the financial aid office, counseling center, or health center, if only the advisor would provide support for this choice or offer to make an introduction. Just as we saw that students may be unaware of some of the procedures involved in registering for courses because they do so very rarely, we need to remember that colleges and universities can be confusing environments for many students. As college professors, we take the organization of our institutions for granted; we work in this environment every day, and it doesn't occur to us that someone may not understand the difference between a registrar and a provost, the business office from the business administration department, or the bursar's office from the financial aid office. But for students, particularly those who are new to the institution or who are the first in their families to attend college, this environment can be very confusing. Good advisors see their roles as guides through the often baffling complexities of institutional procedure and don't assume that students will just pick this information up on their own.

• *Monitor your advisees' academic progress even when it is not an official advising period.* Many institutions have early warning procedures in place for students who are not attending classes regularly or who are off to a poor start on their first few assignments. As an advisor, if you have access to these early warnings about your advisees, it can be important to take the initiative, summon the student to a consultation, and try to determine the cause of the problem. Sometimes, as we've seen, there will be a nonacademic challenge that is affecting the student's academic performance; you can encourage the student to seek the help he or she needs before the situation worsens and an entire course or even an entire term is wasted. At other times, the student may be best advised to withdraw from the course while there is still time, even if it means delaying graduation. No student, of course, is eager to spend an extra year and a great deal of added money for additional tuition and room and board because it is not possible to graduate on schedule. However, for certain students, college is best completed more slowly but also more successfully rather than quickly and poorly. In any case, you will not be able to consider these possibilities with the student if you do not monitor your advisees' academic progress throughout the entire semester.

- *See your role as both advisor and mentor.* As we'll see in the next chapter, faculty mentors assume a range of responsibilities that extend far beyond those of an academic advisor. Nevertheless, academic advisors are often the best people to serve as mentors to students at both the undergraduate and graduate levels. You have already established a close working relationship with your advisees, and they are used to coming to you for a broader perspective on their academic programs. They are used to meeting with you independently or in small groups as a way of planning strategies that will help them achieve their goals. It is a natural progression to enhance this relationship from providing advice about course selection and academic programs to providing advice about career opportunities, choices in life, and the entire spectrum of success or fulfillment. Often relationships that began as those between advisor and student simply develop into more complex roles as mentor and protégé. Sometimes this development requires an explicit effort on the part of the advisor or student. In any case, you're particularly well positioned to provide meaningful advice to the student on a wide range of topics. You know the student's academic record, understand a bit about his or her abilities and aspirations, and have engaged in a conversation with the student that has extended over several semesters or years. If your advisee has never taken a class with you, your relationship with the student is bound to be different from that of someone who has had to evaluate that student's work and assign grades. The student may feel more comfortable conversing with you about fears or challenges, because you're not the person who will be rendering a "judgment" in the classroom. But even if your advisee has taken several courses with you, a mentoring relationship is still possible. You will need, of course, to make it clear that information shared in confidence has no bearing on the student's grades or how you will treat that student in class. Indicate that the discussions that you have with the student as an advisor and mentor are privileged and, as long as you don't violate this trust, it is likely that the student will be able to differentiate your role as a teacher from your role as a mentor.

Create a Master Advisor Program

One of the best ways to enhance one's own skill as an advisor is to work closely with another faculty member who is widely regarded as skilled in advising. Nearly every college or university has professors who fall into this category. Students eagerly clamor for this advisor. If the institution allows the practice, even some students who are not majoring in that professor's field want this person as an advisor. Thank-you notes arrive in great numbers, often from students who have graduated years earlier and are still benefiting from the superb guidance provided by their very memorable advisor. If you're the type of college professor who fits this description, share your insights with others. If you're not this kind of person but you know someone who is, encourage that person to participate in or create a master advisor program where highly regarded faculty advisors assist others in improving their skills. Master advisor programs can occur at any level of the institution: departments, divisions, colleges, or university-wide. If your school already has an award for advisor of the year, consider encouraging past recipients to form the basis of a new master advisor program. If your school does not yet have such an award, developing one can be one of the first initiatives of a new emphasis on excellence in advising. As a way of providing peer support for scholarship, an advising community can be the perfect complement to the teaching circles, scholarship networks, and service alliances that are discussed in Chapter 27, "Seeking and Providing Peer Support for Scholarship," and Chapter 40, "Taking the Next Step in Your Service." With an advising community, teams of colleagues can discuss important changes to academic programs, successful strategies in advising, insights gained from the meetings or publications of groups like NACADA, and individual problems they are encountering. Master advisor programs and advising communities can be instrumental in encouraging institutions to recognizing the importance of superior advising and rewarding it properly. Moreover, if you are still seeking your own niche in your department or field, developing a reputation as a master advisor—perhaps even achieving recognition on a national level—can create possibilities for your own unique identity and achievements.

Although the distinction is sometimes ignored, what academic advisors provide is *advising*, not *advisement*. The word *advisement* means "careful reflection and consideration," as in the expression "I'll take that under advisement." It is the word *advising* that means "the contribution of guidance and suggestions." Although each school's students must ultimately take responsibility for their own academic schedules, it is the duty of advisors to be well informed about any academic program in which they may need to advise students, understanding that individual advisees have differing needs and personal situations, and be willing to intervene on an advisee's behalf when such action is called for. No matter whether your school considers advising to be part of your teaching duties or a critical component of your service role, good advising requires taking time to be informed and, most important, listening to the needs of your advisees.

REFERENCES

Gordon, V. N., Habley, W. R., Grites, T. J., & Associates. (2008). *Academic advising: A comprehensive handbook* (2nd ed.). San Francisco: Jossey-Bass.

RESOURCES

Brown, S. D., & Lent, R. W. (Eds.). (2005). *Career development and counseling: Putting theory and research to work.* San Francisco: Jossey-Bass.

Frost, S. H. (1991). *Academic advising for student success: A system of shared responsibility.* San Francisco: Jossey-Bass.

Gordon, V. N. (2006). *Career advising: An academic advisor's guide.* San Francisco: Jossey-Bass.

Gordon, V. N. (2007). *The undecided college student: An academic and career advising challenge.* Springfield, IL: Charles C. Thomas.

Gordon, V. N., & Sears, S. J. (2009). *Selecting a college major: Exploration and decision making* (6th ed.). Paramus, NJ: Prentice Hall.

Kramer, G. L. (Ed.). (2003). *Faculty advising examined: Enhancing the potential of college faculty as advisors.* Bolton, MA: Anker.

Luzzo, D. A. (Ed.). (2000). *Career counseling of college students: An empirical guide to strategies that work.* Washington, DC: American Psychological Association.

35

SERVING AS A MENTOR

In the *Odyssey*, Mentor was the trusted counselor of Odysseus. Too old to join the expedition to Troy, Mentor stayed behind in Ithaca where he began to serve as a role model and provide advice to Odysseus' son, Telemachus. From this bit of literary and mythological history, we can conclude two important things:

- The term *mentor* began as a proper name, unlike words such as *advisor* and *grantor* that have a verbal base. In other words, you can *advise* someone or *grant* a person something, but you can't *ment* anyone. As a result, *advisee* and even *grantee* are actual words, but the recent coinage *mentee* is etymologically meaningless. It's a little like referring to a wise but long-winded person as a Nestor, after Homer's garrulous king of Pylos, and then calling every member of the audience who suffers through the speech a *nestee*. The correct terms to describe a person supervised by a mentor are *advisee, protégé* (feminine: *protégée*), and *apprentice*.

- Just as the original Mentor counseled both Odysseus and Telemachus, good mentors today frequently serve as role models to more than one person. If someone is effective as a mentor, word tends to spread very quickly, and others will want to benefit from that person's advice and experience. In addition, one's skill as a mentor increases over time and, the more opportunities a person has to act in this capacity, the better mentor a person will become.

In the last chapter we saw that academic advisors should see their roles more as mentors than as mere repositories of information when students are selecting courses. This bit of advice immediately raises the question: is there any difference between an advisor and a mentor? If so, what precisely is the nature of that difference? In the best of all possible worlds, an advisor should always aspire to be a mentor, although a mentor need not always also act as an academic advisor. To understand why this is so, it's necessary to examine the various responsibilities involved in being a mentor in a bit more detail.

The Role of the Mentor

The relationship between mentor and protégé is different from most other relationships we encounter in life. Relationships between spouses, friends, colleagues, and teammates are based on—or at least aspire toward—equality. Relationships between teacher and student, doctor and patient, lawyer and client, and even advisor and advisee all contain an inherent element of inequality: one person in the relationship has a need, and the other person has a specialized type of knowledge that can address that need. The relationship between mentor and protégé falls somewhere between these two extremes. It contains an inherent inequality, because the mentor is seeking to address a need that the protégé has. An implicit power differential exists because, of the two parties in the relationship, the mentor is more experienced, (usually) older, and often has significantly more authority. Nevertheless, a mentor-apprentice relationship is also based on a potential for equality; in fact, that potential is the very essence of the relationship. A physician does not treat a patient in order for the patient to become a physician; he or she does so in order for the patient to become well. An attorney does not advise a client in order for the client to become an attorney; he or she does so in order to protect the client's rights. But a senior scientist may serve as a mentor for a budding young scientist precisely in order for this apprentice to become as accomplished and eminent some day as the mentor is right now. In other words, good mentors plan for their own obsolescence. Doctors do not assume that, if they treat one illness, their patients will never again require medical care, and attorneys do not assume that, if they resolve one issue, their clients will never again be in need of legal advice. But mentors strive to make themselves unnecessary; if they are effective, their apprentices will no longer require a mentor. In fact, if they are truly effective, their apprentices will serve as mentors for others.

Both advisors and mentors serve as trusted counselors. Mentors, however, carry this task even further by becoming good role models. They assist the individuals for whom they are responsible not just through their words, but also through the actions they perform. Sometimes these actions provide a passive benefit to the advisee: the mentor is observed taking responsibility, making appropriate decisions, achieving desired results, and demonstrating for the advisee how the job is supposed to be done. At other times, the mentor takes a more active role in benefiting the advisee: the mentor makes calls on the advisee's behalf, opens doors to new opportunities, overcomes obstacles, and helps in other ways not be possible for the advisee to do on his or her own. The best sort of mentors are those who do not merely do a good job but who simultaneously live a good life. Although mentors frequently provide career advice and even use their own networks to help an apprentice advance in his or her career, excellent mentors are positive examples in a broader sphere of activity. They demonstrate how professional activity fits into a well-balanced life and show how priorities should be set in order to achieve success on several different fronts. Even though mentors will undoubtedly be well respected as professors, accountants, poets, scientists, or in any other field, their most important value is to be found in the fact that they are excellent and compassionate people.

Mentoring Faculty Members

One other important reason for treating the topics of advising and mentoring separately is that although academic advising tends to take place solely between a student and a faculty or staff member, mentoring relationships can occur at any level of the institution. In fact, faculty-to-faculty mentoring has become an increasingly important component of faculty development programs. At some colleges and universities, a faculty mentor is assigned as part of a comprehensive faculty first-year experience program. Such a mentor can provide advice about implementing a research agenda, enhancing teaching skills, and building a network outside of one's immediate academic area. Particularly in cases where the mentor works in a different department or division, this relationship can provide newer faculty members with a broader institutional perspective and an objective point of view. For faculty members who arrive at a school after having worked elsewhere, the mentor can provide background into procedures, institutional history, and the reasons why certain units or policies may have developed a bit differently from those of other schools. Mentors can smooth the way for faculty members making the transition from one type of institution to another, provide introductions to people who can help with problems or concerns, and offer an understanding ear when the faculty member simply needs to give voice to occasional frustrations. Even for faculty members who have served a number of years at an institution, mentors can help people deal with the type of challenges that we discussed in Chapter 25, "Overcoming Research Block," enhance their skills as instructors, introduce them to new service opportunities, and generally help them become as engaged and motivated as possible. Formal mentoring programs arise out of the recognition that at any point in a faculty member's career, a trusted counselor and role model can be far more effective in fostering his or her success than any number of workshops, handbooks, or institutional procedures. Even in cases where no formal mentoring program exists, faculty members frequently find individuals who fill the mentor's role, even if no one ever uses that term. We all can benefit from the objective guidance and support of a more experienced role model and then, when we ourselves have amassed a great deal of experience, can benefit further by helping those who are rising in our ranks.

Mentoring Students

Regardless of whether a faculty member works as a student's advisor in such areas as course selection, thesis supervision, and general academic advice, it is possible to act as that student's mentor. Among the many important duties fulfilled by faculty mentors of students, these role models:

- Provide career advice and use their network of contacts to increase the student's chances of meeting the right people, securing interviews, and being given every opportunity for making a successful start in his or her career

- Offer insight into the special emphases of different graduate and professional programs, the specialties of the faculty members who teach in each program, and the types of students that tend to be successful there

- Serve as the student's advocate with other faculty members and the administration when it is warranted

- Act as a sounding board when the student is exploring different options, seeking an objective point of view, or simply in need of a sympathetic ear

- Present a positive example of how to balance professional concerns with one's private life, make choices among equally attractive or difficult options, and set priorities

If all of a student's faculty members provide information, professional insight, training in appropriate methods, and enhancement of critical and creative thinking, the mentor often supplies the key to how all of that is applied to the lives of successful people who work in that field. A good mentor is part colleague, part guru, and part oracle. It is only through a combination of experience and pure instinct, however, that mentors learn when it is best to adopt each of these roles.

Basic Principles for All Mentors

All mentors—those who work with undergraduate students, graduate students, adult students, faculty members, and peers from outside of the institution—are likely to follow certain principles in order for their work with their protégés to be as beneficial as possible. Among the most important of these principles are the following four:

- *Come to agreement with your apprentice on the nature and goals of your relationship from the start.* Because the relationships between mentors and advisees range so widely, it is important for the two of you to establish from the start what your apprentice is hoping to gain from the relationship and what you feel you are able to offer. If this agreement is not established early in your work together, later misunderstandings are not merely likely, they are all but inevitable. For instance, you may see your role with a graduate student as providing objective guidance during the preparation of his or her dissertation, making some contacts and opening some doors when it is time to look for work, and serving as a good role model should the student decide to follow an academic career. All of these goals are admirable, unless the student assumes that your role will largely be one of advocacy on his or her behalf with a very difficult thesis committee, support and validation for his or her work when others seem to offer only criticism, and a willingness to step in as dissertation advisor of last resort if the relationship the student has with the committee breaks down entirely. In such a case, lack of agreement about goals and the nature of the relationship is more than a problem: it creates a situation that is worse than if the student hadn't had any mentor at all. For this reason, your first several meetings with anyone you are mentoring should be devoted to exploring some goals, ground rules, and a timetable that the two of you can agree on. In certain situations, a memorandum of understanding, which both of you can sign, might even emerge from these discussions. Then, as the relationship develops, you might review these goals from time to time as a way of making sure that you're accomplishing what you set out to do and keeping your relationship focused on what is most important to you both.

- *Be patient and understand that mistakes will occur.* Your protégé has not chosen or been assigned to you because he or she was already fully developed as a professional in your field. Rather, you became that person's mentor because your apprentice needed your help and guidance, and that need will continue throughout your relationship.

You should not feel that you have failed as a mentor, therefore, if your advisee makes mistakes, does not always take your advice, or fails to profit immediately from your work together. As we saw in Chapter 17, "Reducing Grade Anxiety," mistakes can be powerful learning experiences. Rather than wasting time by upbraiding your protégé or (even worse) ending your relationship because he or she did not take your advice and consequently made a mistake, use the situation as a learning experience. Review the reasons why you recommended the course of action that you did and explore possible ways to rectify the situation. Your apprentice is much more likely to benefit from having made mistakes (as unpleasant as they may have been) and to trust you more in the future if you accept that occasional problems will arise than if you act in such a way that your apprentice feels bad after every error or difference of opinion. From your own experience, you have probably realized that you are more likely to open up to those who accept you than to those who frequently criticize you. Your protégé is likely to feel the same. Try to view each situation from that person's perspective and realize that ultimately you can only offer advice and a positive example; you cannot control that person's decisions.

• *Help your apprentice become successful on his or her own terms, not necessarily according to your standards.* The goal of the mentor is to help each apprentice succeed, not to become a clone of the mentor. Although most people regard the various choices they have made in their lives and careers as the "right" ones, those choices were right for those people, not necessarily for everyone. This is yet another reason why it is important to find out as much as you can about the apprentice's goals and aspirations early in your relationship. The advice and opportunities that you provide each apprentice will differ according to what that person wants from a career, as well as his or her general goals in life. Certainly, any academic advisor understands that an advisee may choose not to follow his or her own precise academic specialty. In much the same way, mentors—who serve as role models in a far broader way than do academic advisors—should not be surprised if many of the choices they have valued in their own lives and careers are ultimately regarded by their protégés as inappropriate for them. The person whom you are mentoring may want a completely different type of experience in graduate or professional school, prefer working in a large corporation while you would be happiest in a small, privately owned business, have little interest in marriage and a family whereas you cannot imagine a complete life without them, or differ from you in any of a dozen other ways. The goal is always to help the apprentice find his or her own best career path and to live his or her own best life, not to replicate yours. The best mentors are those who take pride in how diverse the choices are that their protégés have made and how each of them is successful on his or her own terms. The most frustrated mentors are those who feel that there can be only one path to success, either in life or in one's career, and try to restrict their advisees into following only that path. At the end of the day, whether you "allow" them to do so or not, apprentices will live their own lives, not relive yours for you.

- *Keep a schedule of contact with your advisees.* Mentors are sometimes reluctant to establish too formal a relationship with their advisees. "I think regular appointments just make these discussions artificial," a mentor might say. "Just contact me whenever you need me. I'll be around." That type of flexible arrangement may sound attractive, but productive contact between most mentors and their apprentices tends not to occur unless you make a special effort to see that it occurs. All of our lives are busy, and our schedules tend to fill up before we know it. Unless we make plans to get together with those we're mentoring on a regular basis, those meetings tend to occur sporadically, infrequently, and finally not at all. No single schedule will be appropriate for every mentoring relationship. With certain advisees, getting together several times a week will not be too often. With others, a brief conversation once or twice a year will not be too rare. Explore the possible frequency of your conversations with your advisee during your initial contact. As with the goals for your entire relationship, you should be able to tell whether you are both on the same page with regard to the frequency of your meetings. For instance, if you suggest getting together for a conversation or update every other week, and your advisee seems surprised or hesitant, it could be that the two of you have dramatically different expectations about what you will try to achieve together. Ask whether that seems too often or not often enough. Try to achieve some compromise that doesn't overburden either of you with meetings that take place excessively often but are not particularly productive. Always allow for some flexibility in meeting times and the possibility to get in touch between your regular sessions; you may come across some information about an opportunity that you'll have to share with your advisee right away or he or she may face an emergency that either requires your immediate attention or necessitates postponing your conversation. In all cases, however, a flexible schedule for consultations is far better than no plan at all.

Mentoring Mistakes

Just as there are four principles that all mentors should follow, no matter whether they are working with students or peers, there are also four mistakes that all types of mentors should try to avoid.

- *Don't allow your role to expand into that of a personal counselor or therapist.* Advisees will bring all sorts of problems and challenges to your attention, particularly as they become increasingly comfortable with you. It can be easy for someone you've helped overcome a professional challenge or take better advantage of a professional opportunity to assume that you can fulfill a similar function in his or her personal life. Certainly personal and professional matters can become easily entwined. A sick parent can cause a student to fall behind in coursework, and a stressful tenure appeal can strain a marriage. Nevertheless, no mentor should take on the role of being a professional counselor without a license. Use the personal information your protégé shares with you to understand matters in a larger context, but don't try to provide guidance in matters that clearly go beyond your professional responsibilities. If it's appropriate, recommend that the person see a trained counselor or therapist or even offer to make a referral. Especially in cases where people appear to be seriously depressed or a danger to themselves or others, handling these situations effectively requires specialized training that most mentors don't have.

- *Don't try to control too much.* As we saw earlier, your goal is to help your protégés become the best possible version of themselves, not duplicates of you. You'll need to give each apprentice a certain amount of latitude, as well as the freedom to do things differently from how you would have handled the situation. Your duty as a mentor is to serve as a trusted counselor, a positive role model, and a sympathetic supporter. At times your function in providing an opportunity for your protégé to vent may need to take precedence over your function as a guide or teacher. Though you would never want someone for whom you're responsible to make a mistake that causes severe, lasting, or irreparable damage, you should allow your apprentice enough freedom to make mistakes that can be learning opportunities. No mentor can guarantee that his or her apprentice will never become frustrated or experience setbacks. What good mentors do, however, is to turn both positive and negative experiences into opportunities for their apprentices to grow professionally and to discover their own ways of solving problems.

- *Don't keep your relationship from evolving.* We saw earlier that one of the distinctive features of the relationship mentors have with their protégés is that it holds the potential for equality. Over time, your way of interacting with your protégé will gradually change. Although an undergraduate advisee will not really become your equal while in your charge, even this development is possible once the student has completed graduate school and entered the profession. More commonly, however, we see a gradually evolving status between the mentor and the graduate student whose research becomes increasingly innovative and important, the intern who grows into a fully competent and confident colleague, and the faculty peer whose teaching, scholarship, and service fully come into their own. As this natural progression occurs, any differential in status between mentor and protégé becomes less and less significant, and the person who was once in a supervisory role assumes the status of an equal. This transition can seem uncomfortable for some mentors. They derive a sense of self-worth from the degree to which their advisees need them. But this attitude is contrary to the very spirit of the mentor relationship. We mentor others not so that they will always look up to us, but so that we can bring them to our own levels or perhaps even higher.

- *Don't discourage an appropriate amount of risk taking.* It is natural to want the people for whom we are responsible to feel comfortable and be protected from unnecessary disappointments. But certain kinds are disappointments are necessary if a person is to develop to his or her full potential. Overprotective mentors, out of a well-intentioned desire to protect their advisees from harm, sometimes stifle the very initiatives that could be most beneficial in the long term. They may try to provide a shortcut to experience and assume that what did not work for them will not work for anyone. But good mentors encourage a certain amount of risk taking. They know that without taking chances, new discoveries are often not made and exciting opportunities are sometimes passed by. Good mentors understand that part of their job is to encourage their advisees to explore beyond their comfort zones and, when disappointments arise, to help their advisees see even rejection as a chance for personal growth.

Resources for Mentors

Faculty members who have served as mentors for a number of years have probably already developed their own list of favorite resources, since material on this topic is plentiful. If, however, you are new to mentoring, you might wish to begin with the following important resources.

- Daloz (1999) and Zachary (2000) provide excellent introductions to the process of mentoring. Daloz focuses on experiences with adult students, although much of what he describes is easily transferable to other situations, and incorporates personal anecdotes, the theories of Joseph Campbell and William Perry, and an engaging, conversational style into his advice for both novice and experienced mentors. Zachary provides clear and useful advice on the concept of mentoring as a partnership and offers guidance on how mentors can inspire their protégés to reach new levels of excellence that they may not have believed possible.

- EDUCAUSE maintains a website called the "Mentoring Information Kit" (www.educause.edu/mentoring) that, although originally intended for those who work in the area of information technology, may be easily applied to other situations. The "kit" includes a useful section about the various stages of the typical mentoring relationship, advice to apprentices on how to select an appropriate mentor, and a summary of the skills that mentors should strive to develop, as well as links to many other resources.

- MentorNet (www.mentornet.net) provides an electronic community for students to receive advice and support from professionals in the field. Experienced mentors in disciplines closely related to engineering and natural science might wish to consider applying their expertise to building relationships and serving as a role model through this medium. MentorNet also provides a one-on-one e-mentoring program, resources about women and minorities in the STEM disciplines, and a résumé database.

Effective mentoring is hard work and requires a strong commitment from both mentor and protégé alike. However, good mentors receive more than the satisfaction of knowing that they have helped others succeed. They also have an opportunity to examine their own priorities objectively and critically, improve the retention of students or colleagues at their institutions, and learn at least as much as they teach. Mentors can make a difference in ways that textbooks and policy manuals cannot. They can help put strategies for success into their proper context and even help redefine what success is. Though an outgrowth of a faculty member's teaching and service roles, many college professors find that their mentoring relationships bring benefits that could never be recorded on a résumé or annual activities report. At its highest level, mentoring is nothing less than helping to shape the future, one life at a time.

REFERENCES

Daloz, L. A. (1999). *Mentor: Guiding the journey of adult learners* (2nd ed.). San Francisco: Jossey-Bass.

Zachary, L. J. (2000). *The mentor's guide: Facilitating effective learning relationships.* San Francisco: Jossey-Bass.

RESOURCES

Abbott, I. O. (2006). *Being an effective mentor: 101 practical strategies for success.* Washington, DC: National Association for Law Placement.

Benisimon, E. M., Ward, K., & Sanders, K. (2000). *The department chair's role in developing new faculty into teachers and scholars.* Bolton, MA: Anker.

Ensher, E., & Murphy, S. (2005). *Power mentoring: How successful mentors and protégés get the most out of their relationships.* San Francisco: Jossey-Bass.

Harvard Business School Press. (2004). *Being an effective mentor: And a receptive protégé.* Cambridge, MA: Author.

Johnson, W. B., & Ridley, C. R. (2004). *The elements of mentoring.* New York: Palgrave Macmillan.

Jonson, K. F. (2008). *Being an effective mentor: How to help beginning teachers succeed* (2nd ed.). Thousand Oaks, CA: Corwin Press.

Zachary, L. J. (2005). *Creating a mentoring culture: The organization's guide.* San Francisco: Jossey-Bass.

36

HANDLING CONFLICT WITH
A SUPERVISOR

The vast majority of college professors maintain perfectly congenial relationships with their chair, dean, and president. Certainly, all administrators expect some grumbling from time to time about this or that decision, and periodic venting about one's boss is so common that it is regarded as a time-honored tradition in the American workplace, but relatively few supervisors ever take this type of harmless complaining personally. In fact, it is not unheard of for upper administrators to voice their frustrations over faculty members every now and then, particularly when they believe that there has been unnecessary resistance to certain decisions. These same administrators are, however, almost universally among the faculty members' strongest supporters and, despite occasional differences in outlook, nearly all effective chairs, deans, provosts, and presidents still view themselves as faculty members at heart.

The difficulty arises when the expected level of goodwill breaks down. What do you do when, for whatever reason, you find yourself in a continuing state of conflict and tension with one of your supervisors? We're not going to be concerned in this chapter with the faculty member who is properly reprimanded for violating an important policy, consistently performing at an inadequate level, or being overtly rude to his or her supervisor. In these situations, the best advice one can give the faculty member is to apologize and make a sincere commitment to do better in the future. This chapter will be devoted to what you might do if you feel that because of a personality difference or some other matter that you can't control, your relationship with a supervisor is deteriorating. How do you improve things if you observe your colleagues being praised and rewarded for the same activities that receive little or no positive response when you engage in them? What should be your response to a supervisor who won't "ever give you a break" or "cut you any slack"? How can you continue to be effective in your job when your relationship with your chair, dean, or president is affecting your morale, job satisfaction, and performance? As we begin our examination of these questions, we'll consider several significant implications that result from the following essential principle:

It takes two people to keep a conflict going.

Reflect on Your Own Attitude and Actions

Even though we began this discussion by saying that we will not be exploring situations in which you are clearly at fault, it is still important for you to consider whether the conflict is one where you are "unclearly" at fault. In other words, can you identify any of your actions, statements, or attitudes that could have caused this problem? Even the largest universities can often seem more like small towns than big cities. They frequently harbor a tremendous amount of gossip and backbiting. Is it possible that something that you did or said "in private" was reported to the administrator? Though supervisors try to be thick-skinned and accept a certain amount of griping among employees, they are also human and have normal reactions in upsetting situations. If your chair, dean, or president thinks of you as an ally but then learns that you were unjustly critical or demeaning in a private conversation, this may feel like a betrayal. You may have inadvertently caused the conflict yourself by appearing to be a hypocrite. In a similar way, if your supervisor is a strong advocate for some idea or policy, and you have been viewed as a strong opponent of this initiative, you may be sensing hostility over what you have done as a roadblock to progress. It may be true that you have said nothing privately that you would not have said openly, that your opposition was to the idea and not to the person who developed it, and that supervisors really should be able to differentiate between personal and professional disagreements, but none of this matters at this point. It often happens that even when people know better, they invest a great deal of themselves in a proposal and take it personally when their ideas are criticized. For this reason, before you dismiss the conflict as wholly your supervisor's fault, examine very carefully what role you could have played—intentionally or not—in causing the problem. It does you relatively little good to dismiss the whole matter by thinking, "But a supervisor should be a bigger person than that!" Even if your role in initiating the conflict was extremely small, you *did* have a role to play, and your problem may only be solved if you consider ways of rectifying or making amends for your own behavior. A candid conversation (see below) or an apology may be necessary before you can proceed to reestablishing a more constructive relationship.

Change Your Response to the Conflict

As we shall see in Chapter 37, "Handling Conflict with Colleagues," keeping a conflict going can require an amazing amount of energy. In an odd way, a prolonged conflict depends on an ongoing commitment from both parties. Many people are familiar with coworkers who have managed to extend a feud or personal disagreement with someone for ten years or more. Eventually these situations develop into their own "relationships": the participants develop a sense of identity as being "the person who hates so-and-so." People can gain a feeling of moral superiority, almost of "purity" from the belief that "I don't put up with the sort of thing" the other person represents—whatever "that sort of thing" may be. To outsiders, this longstanding conflict can seem astonishing, even amusing. What sort of satisfaction do the participants derive, we start to wonder, from keeping this argument going? Yet the participants themselves would never dream of ending the conflict, largely because this dispute helps them reinforce who they are and why they matter. From our point of view, we outsiders can see how each party could end the whole unpleasant affair at any time. These types of disputes give rise to another essential principle, a corollary to the one we encountered earlier:

Although it takes two people to keep a conflict going, it only takes one to end it.

In other words, simply because you're on the receiving end of your supervisor's hostility or poor behavior, you are under absolutely no obligation to repay this treatment in kind. As we saw in the case of the two coworkers who prolonged their dispute for many years, both of them must have had an investment in the argument to keep it going. However, you can adopt a different strategy. You can simply refuse to play along. You can respond to rudeness with politeness. You can try killing the other person with kindness. You can reply calmly when you are falsely accused. You can refuse to acknowledge or escalate outrageous behavior. You can treat the whole situation not as your problem, but as a reflection of the other person's mood and personality. You can, in other words, "win" simply by not playing along.

Some faculty members will find this strategy unacceptable. "I don't want to be a doormat," they may say, or "I didn't get this far in life by being treated this way." Other people may be concerned that by seeming to tolerate a supervisor's reproaches and hostility, they would be acknowledging that this treatment was justified. Untenured faculty members in particular may be afraid that unless they "defend themselves" somehow, their future careers may be in jeopardy. Still other college professors will argue, "Someone in my supervisor's position should be held to a higher standard. I have to look out for myself because no one else will." Nevertheless, in the vast majority of cases, what the faculty member views as justified "self-defense" will merely escalate an insignificant matter into an actual and serious problem. We all have bad days, and it is perfectly conceivable that what you regarded as a harsh criticism was simply your supervisor's ill-conceived but ultimately understandable annoyance over another matter altogether. Even the best supervisors find themselves occasionally giving a highly valued colleague short shrift because there was just news of a severe budget emergency, or because of a personal life crisis, or because this is the twentieth problem that had to be addressed that day, and their energy is running low. Good supervisors do sincerely try to leave these other issues at the door when they are meeting with you about an unrelated issue, but even the best boss is only human and sometimes makes mistakes. If you nurture your grievance and allow it to grow, you may end up transforming a problem that originally had nothing to do with you into a new crisis that's all about you. Remember that it's not servility to suffer occasional ill treatment in silence; it is a sign of maturity and good judgment. In a surprising number of cases, it can even be your best strategy for alleviating a problem.

Most people discover that they can endure the relatively infrequent slight or rude remark from a supervisor by dismissing it as "just one of the prices we pay for working here." But it can be much harder to maintain this strategy over the long haul. So, what do you do if, day after day, you find yourself receiving unwarranted rudeness, poor behavior, or mistreatment? What do you do if this problem has already been going on for a long time? Later in this chapter we'll consider several effective strategies that you can adopt, but in the meantime, keep in mind that when repaying bad behavior with good, actually abating the problem may require a bit of time. If we've been in a situation where for many months we've thought another person was being rude to us or believed that person had wronged us in some way, we are unlikely to revise our opinion simply because that person received our cold shoulder with a smile or a kind word once or twice. Barriers between people that took a long time to build can take an even longer time to be worn away by a gentle touch. If your supervisor believes that you were the one who started the conflict or that you have not been collegial in some way, it can take weeks or months before that person realizes you're not "playing along" with the conflict anymore. He or she may have become conditioned to treating you in a certain way, and reconditioning a new response takes time. Except in the most extreme of situations—those where your career or livelihood is truly threatened—you will discover that it feels like a great relief to treat the other person well and conclude, "At least this conflict is no longer *my* problem. If my supervisor continues to act this way, it will be *that* person's problem from now on." Just when you think that the only satisfaction you're ever going to get from the situation is that your supervisor's mistreatment no longer disturbs you, you may be surprised to notice that the conflict has ceased. You have ended it by redefining yourself as a person who refuses to participate in conflicts that aren't productive.

Distinguish Constructive Assertiveness from Hostility and Rudeness

"That's all well and good," you may be thinking, "but it won't work in my case." After all, your supervisor may be a truly bad boss. He or she might be a bully, have difficulty controlling anger, maintain an extremely low regard for faculty members, be unable to communicate effectively, or have some other serious problem that could be manifesting itself in this conflict. As gently as you respond to the poor treatment you're receiving, you may not be able to "fix" the problem by simply refusing to play along. So, if you've tried ending the conflict in the ways that we've discussed and you discover that your boss's bad day is rapidly becoming a bad year or even a bad career, what do you do? Well, the first thing you can do is to understand that a polite and gentle response to conflict does not exclude your ability to be constructively assertive. Certainly, an occasional ill-considered remark is best ignored because it is not worth elevating a small matter into a serious problem. And some people are more comfortable than others about tolerating harsh treatment from a supervisor. But if you've tried other approaches and you feel that the most appropriate strategy is to stand up for yourself or a colleague, try to do so in a manner that will be productive, not in a way that will merely satisfy your immediate desire to do something. Be calm, be assertive, and be sure to focus on the statement or action that caused the problem, not on the supervisor's personality or merit. It may seem that there is a very small difference between the statements "You were incredibly rude to me just now" and "The way in which you spoke to me just now was extremely inappropriate," but these remarks have completely different implications. The first statement is addressed to the *person*, and it implies that the supervisor is ill-mannered or a poor manager. The second remark is directed toward the *action*, and it suggests that the supervisor could have been more effective in achieving the desired result. If you believe that a conflict has resulted from your supervisor's anger, rudeness, or lack of consideration, then you will make matters worse by demonstrating your own anger, rudeness, or lack of consideration. State your concern calmly and politely, listen to the reply, and be assertive without being insubordinate or disagreeable.

Just as there is a difference between hostility and assertiveness, so is there a difference between a supervisor who is being malicious and one who is being forceful. Sometimes it becomes necessary for a chair, dean, or president to *insist* that an action be done in a particular way. Although we college professors may feel uncomfortable with the idea of someone "giving us orders," there are situations in which a supervisor is entitled to issue instructions and to expect that they will be carried out. For this reason, ask yourself whether you genuinely have a conflict with your supervisor or whether that person is merely being appropriately assertive in his or her job. Simply because we may disagree with certain policies, we don't have a right to ignore them when they have been implemented through established procedures. We don't have a right to pick and choose the parts of our jobs that we like best, to ignore a decision about which we disagree, or to disobey an instruction we've been given. So, even as you pursue your own right to be assertive without being insubordinate, be sure that you have not overlooked your supervisor's right to be assertive without being demeaning. If the cause of your conflict is ultimately that you disagree with an action taken by your chair, dean, or president, then you should express that disagreement in the appropriate manner and venue. But keep in mind that you don't have a right to ignore the decision, undermine it, or to criticize it at inappropriate times, such as during class or in locations where students are present.

Discuss the Conflict with Your Supervisor

Part of constructive assertiveness involves handling a conflict in an appropriate manner and place. One of the best ways you can achieve this goal is to make an appointment with your supervisor, meet in private, and discuss the situation both openly and candidly. In some cases, the appropriate place to do this is over lunch at some quiet location off campus; neither one of you will be on your own turf: in an environment different from that associated with the conflict, you have the best possible chance to resolve it. Open your conversation in a calm and nonaccusatory manner. Seek information and insight, not the mere scoring of "points." You might begin the discussion by saying something like, "For some time now, I've noticed that there seems to be a level of tension between us, and it really concerns me. After all, I think you've done a really good job with [state one or two accomplishments about which you can be both positive and honest], and yet I frequently notice that our conversations still result in conflict. Have you noticed it, too, and, if so, do you have any ideas about how we may be able to put that behind us?" When the other person speaks, be an active, engaged listener and, as you respond, seek only to understand, not to be defensive about your own behavior. After all, there will be other opportunities in which you will be able to respond to false accusations and to present your actions in the proper light. Your purpose now is to try to understand the origins of the conflict so that you will later be able to develop a plan to deal with it. As you listen to the issues that your supervisor raises, try to see them from his or her perspective. For instance, you may think that your new service project is the most important contribution you can make at this point, but your chair may believe that it is taking you away from your research and, even worse, setting a bad example for new members of the department. Your dean may feel that you allowed your personal feelings about a colleague to cloud your judgment during an earlier tenure decision and may now find it difficult to know when you're acting on principle and when you're prompted by other motives. Your president may feel that one of your remarks ruined his or her opportunity to secure a new gift from a donor, even though you had no idea of the effect your words may have had. If you immediately leap to defending your actions during this discussion, you may only make the matter worse. Seek instead to understand the cause of the conflict, apologize for anything you may genuinely need to apologize for, and, most important, see if the two of you can discover a way to resolve the conflict and improve relations for the future.

Most administrators will respect you a great deal simply for taking the initiative to resolve the situation in this way. Some of them may even be surprised by the conversation because they did not know that you perceived their actions as indicative of a conflict. At times, however, a supervisor may not yet be ready or willing to talk about the situation. Each person is different and, although you have worked things out in your own mind so that you are ready for a resolution, the other person may not have reached that same point. The response you receive may simply be "Oh, everything's fine" or "I don't know what you're talking about." If that is the case, follow up with one or two illustrations, phrasing them in such a way that you do not make your supervisor become defensive about his or her actions. As before, focus on the behavior or statement that caused you concern; do not imply that the supervisor is guilty of a character flaw or not up to the job. If you find yourself prompting a defensive response or one that deflects the fault toward you—"Oh, that? That was nothing. I was just annoyed because the meeting was running on too long. You shouldn't be so sensitive"—try providing a few more examples. If you are still unsuccessful, you might prompt your supervisor for a positive concluding remark. "So, we're OK? There are no lingering issues between us? I don't have to be concerned about how I'm going to be treated in the next faculty meeting or on my evaluation?" By raising these questions, you are providing your supervisor with every opportunity to address any concerns he or she may have. In addition, you are making it clear to your boss, politely but unmistakably, that you expect a change in behavior for the future.

Learn How Others Perceive the Conflict

The reactions of other people can be an important corrective in situations where we may have lost our own objectivity. If you've tried the approaches we have discussed so far—determining whether anything you have done may have contributed to the conflict, refusing to prolong the conflict yourself, being assertive but cordial in making your position clear, and discussing the matter candidly and privately with your supervisor—your next step is to learn how other people perceive the situation. Some colleagues will show support for you simply because they are your friends, but others may be frank in telling you that you're overreacting or handling the matter inappropriately. Naturally you will want to be careful in selecting the people with whom you share information. You don't want to start rumors, make the problem worse, or promote misunderstandings.

If you do find that other people have observed the conflict, understood that you've tried to resolve it, and concluded that you are being mistreated, then one approach you might consider is to take full advantage of the regular evaluation process. Nearly every institution has adopted some type of formal administrative review. In many cases, these evaluations are conducted either online or through written responses. In other situations, the individual or group who is responsible for evaluating the administrator will offer opportunities for people to discuss positive achievements and situations that may be a cause for concern. Use this evaluation process for the purpose it was designed to achieve. In answer to open-ended questions, you don't have to provide so much information that your identity becomes obvious to your supervisor when he or she reads the review. You can say something like, "The dean seems to have an unresolved conflict with a member of our department, regularly making unprofessional and demeaning remarks that seem uncalled for." A comment like this does not provide any evidence that you are the person whom the dean has publicly humiliated. Supervisors read these comments and, even though faculty members at times don't believe it, often change their behavior when problems are pointed out in a constructive way. In addition, the person or board to whom the supervisor reports will see these comments and, in cases where multiple responses suggest that a problem exists, may exert added pressure for the behavior to change.

Pursue a Formal Grievance

In order to protect the rights of college professors, a wide variety of formal processes are usually in place. Most institutions have a procedure for conducting a formal grievance hearing. In a unionized environment, the bargaining unit will have a mechanism in place for dealing with complaints against a supervisor. But even in nonunionized environments, the faculty senate or faculty assembly will frequently act to investigate serious accusations made by a college professor against a supervisor. When no other options are available, you should remember that every boss has a boss: your chair reports to a dean, the dean to a provost or president, the president to a board. If every other solution has been tried, you can always go to the next level. But these options should be pursued only in the most extreme of situations. If a faculty member's livelihood, professional standing, and career are in jeopardy, invoking these protective measures is appropriate. In fact, situations such as these are why these procedures exist. However, if a faculty member merely feels underappreciated, uncomfortable, or inconvenienced by a supervisor's attitude or actions, it can be counterproductive to resort to such measures. A department chair who appears not to appreciate you is unlikely to feel that sense of admiration grow when forced to undergo a long defense against a formal grievance. Formal processes are created to deal with severe problems that cannot be solved through informal mediation or working matters out on your own. (On more formal types of mediation, see Chapter 37, "Handling Conflict with Colleagues.") At best, it trivializes the grievance process when people use it for other purposes. At worst, the really serious problems can go unaddressed because the system becomes clogged with handling minor matters. So, though you should certainly not hesitate to avail yourself of these protections when they are called for, you should always exhaust all other remedies before you resort to such extreme measures as a formal grievance.

Conflict with another person is always disturbing. It can be particularly disturbing, however, when a conflict occurs with someone who makes important decisions about us. Bad bosses exist in higher education just as they do in all fields. Most administrators, however, are truly trying to do what is best for the institution as well as for everyone who is connected with it. Talking with them calmly and openly about the conflict, the difficulties it is causing you, and your desire to resolve it can go a long way toward creating a more positive work environment for everyone concerned.

RESOURCES

Crawshaw, L. (2007). *Taming the abrasive manager: How to end unnecessary roughness in the workplace.* San Francisco: Jossey-Bass.

Fisher, R., Ury, W., & Patton, B. (1991). *Getting to yes: Negotiating agreement without giving in* (2nd ed.). New York: Houghton Mifflin.

Haight, M. (2005). *Who's afraid of the big, bad boss? 13 types and how to survive them.* West Conshohocken, PA: Infinity.

Scott, G. G. (2006). *A survival guide for working with bad bosses: Dealing with bullies, idiots, back-stabbers, and other managers from hell.* New York: AMACOM.

Sharpe, D., & Johnson, E. (2007). *Managing conflict with your boss.* San Francisco: Pfeiffer.

37

HANDLING CONFLICT WITH COLLEAGUES

All college professors have days when they are tempted to agree with Jean-Paul Sartre's conclusion that *l'enfer, c'est les autres* ("Hell is other people"). You know what happens. Students are late in completing their work. Chairs and deans impose demands that are impossible to fulfill in the time available. The support staff seems unavailable precisely when you need them most. And one or more of your colleagues have apparently adopted a special mission to annoy, frustrate, or impede you. These experiences are, in the grand scheme of things, relatively insignificant and, if viewed with a bit of detachment and common sense, may even lead you to start wondering, "If everyone around here seems to be getting on my nerves, maybe the problem isn't them; it's me." The solution in most of these cases is simply to take a deep breath, get matters back into perspective, and approach the situation with compassion and humor. But what do you do if your problem is not with everyone but with just one or two of your colleagues? And what if this situation is not confined to a single day or week, but is ongoing and interferes with your work? What do you do if you find yourself in a situation where you have a serious conflict with a coworker?

Reflect on the Severity of the Conflict

Not every type of conflict is the same. In fact, not every type of conflict is undesirable. At times, tension with a colleague can cause us to do our jobs better. For instance, we may proofread our documents more carefully because we know that an "annoying" coworker is going to "nitpick them to death." We may choose our words judiciously in public meetings so that we are not misunderstood and, through this very process, discover a clearer way of expressing our ideas. We may even find ourselves becoming more productive as scholars and more innovative as teachers simply because we don't want to be outdone by someone whom we find irritating, unpleasant, or boring. These are instances of positive conflict, and they remind us that we don't go to work to be comfortable; we go there to make a positive contribution. So, if a colleague irritates us but ultimately does not interfere with and possibly even enhances our ability to make a positive contribution, we may want to reconsider whether solving this "problem" is really desirable. Annoying people are found in every line of work, and higher education is certainly no exception. Although you may feel that your current irritant should be relocated to the other side of the planet, remember that his or her replacement could be even worse.

In contrast to these beneficial situations, a conflict with a colleague becomes problematic when it interferes with the quality of your work, threatens your livelihood, or causes you to miss out on opportunities that would be in the best interests of the institution, your students, or you individually as a college professor. For instance, it is a significant problem when a personality conflict between two colleagues is severe enough that it causes one of them to lose objectivity about the other's accomplishments during a tenure evaluation. In a similar way, it is a problem when a colleague refuses to assign graduate students to another professor for reasons that are ultimately unrelated to his or her professional qualifications. Other examples include departments that can no longer meet to discuss important issues because their members "just can't get along," grant proposals that miss deadlines because professors are unable to communicate effectively with one another, and a decline in student retention caused by a "bad atmosphere" that permeates an entire program. In such situations, simply ignoring the problem or hoping it will go away is no longer an option, and you will need to take action, both for your own good and for the good of your program.

Break the Cycle of the Conflict

When you find yourself involved in a conflict with another person, it may seem there is no way out of the situation: you simply don't like the faculty member, and nothing will change your point of view. Keep in mind, however, that we are under no obligation to like our colleagues; we simply have to work effectively with them. Resolving the conflict that you have with your colleague does not necessarily mean that you need to start having lunch together on a regular basis, invite each other to your homes, or expand your working relationship into a deep and abiding friendship. As academic professionals in a free country, we are all entitled to choose our own friends and to like or dislike whomever we wish. But personal preferences are not the issue here; your effectiveness as a college professor is the real issue. If conflict with a coworker is interfering with your department's ability to attract and retain students, secure its necessary resources, provide a high quality of education, or produce the level of scholarship to which your college or university aspires, then whether you like the other person is irrelevant. You need to find a strategy for working together. The situation is similar to what you may encounter in your classes. All of us have students whom we like and others who, for whatever reason, we find less interesting or who may even annoy us. Nevertheless, in our role as instructors, we set those feelings aside and work on behalf of every student's academic progress. In much the same way, we have to function effectively with colleagues even when we dislike them or are irritated by them. We are failing in our responsibilities as academic citizens if we allow conflict with a coworker to prevent the mission of the institution or program from being fulfilled (see Buller, 2006).

Longstanding conflicts can be particularly difficult to resolve. After all, it is one thing to settle a dispute that arose a week or two ago, but it's far more challenging to put an end to tension that has been building over several months, even years. As we saw in the last chapter, however, conflicts that are protracted require a great deal of "commitment" to keep them going. It can be exhausting to renew your angry or contemptuous feelings for someone day after day. For this reason, most disagreements between people dissipate after a short time. One of the participants in the conflict will approach the other and say something like, "Isn't there any way that we can put this all behind us?" and the other person will usually be relieved at the prospect of doing so. But long-term conflicts are another matter. People do not sustain a conflict beyond a few weeks unless they "gain" something from it. What they gain may be a sense of identity or self-worth; it may be a perverse sort of satisfaction. No one may think of it in precisely these terms, but it could be that a person feels obliged to extend a conflict because "I am the person who supports high academic standards at this institution and, as such, I cannot tolerate anyone who threatens those standards." It may be that one party in the dispute still holds a grudge over an incident from the distant past, and the other person involved in the conflict does not even realize that an apology is still expected or desired. Or it may be that the conflict has simply become so habitual that the participants expect it to continue even when it serves little purpose. In these cases, the solution is to break the cycle of the conflict. Thus, if you're involved in a conflict with a coworker, it is up to you to take the first step toward moving your interaction in a more positive direction. It doesn't matter if you weren't the one who "started it." It doesn't matter if it's the other person who's really at fault. What matters is that it's your responsibility to end the impasse for the sake of your students and program. Doing so doesn't mean that you're giving in; it simply means that you're moving on.

Decide on a Central Message for Your Conversation

Before speaking to the colleague with whom you have a conflict, decide specifically what you intend your message to be. Conversations of this sort are always likely to be a bit difficult—there may even be some tension as you work through your issues—and you don't want this discussion to get under way when you have only a vague idea of what you hope to accomplish. Naturally, you will not be able to script every remark that both you and the other person will make, but you need to have a general idea of what you hope to accomplish during your discussion. Even more important, you will want to decide before the conversation takes place what you are *not* going to say. If there are certain issues that you know will exacerbate the matter without ending the conflict, make up your mind that no matter how much you are provoked or tempted to do so, you will not bring them up. Past history that is no longer relevant should play absolutely no part in your conversation. Even past history that, in your opinion, remains highly relevant to the conflict should likely be excluded from the conversation. Your goal, after all, must be to figure out a way to coexist with this colleague in the future, not to rehash grievances from the past. Often the only way to achieve this goal is to set aside all these earlier grievances and focus on where you will proceed from this point. Make up your mind, therefore, that your tone in this conversation will be positive and forward looking, that you will not allow yourself to be dragged back to earlier conflicts, and that your primary goal will be to create a new, more constructive relationship. Remember: you don't have to end up with warm admiration for your colleague. All you are seeking is a constructive work environment. If it is helpful, try to find at least five positive things that you can say about the other person. (*Everyone* has at least five positive qualities.) Keeping these traits in mind is a good way to help yourself begin the meeting with a positive outlook, and it will also give you some encouraging things to say in the meeting itself. For instance, if the other person accuses you of having degraded or undermined his or her performance at work, you will be able to say, "Actually, I think that you've done a lot of positive things for our program. For example, you've . . ." Remember that the person with whom you're speaking will not have prepared for this meeting in the same way that you have. Your colleague may well adopt a more negative tone and repeat accusations that you regard as irrelevant. You cannot allow any of this to distract you from your primary purpose of moving forward to a more constructive relationship. So, do not allow anyone or any statement to alter your resolution to be positive. Keep in mind the following essential principle:

It is almost always possible to disagree without being disagreeable.

Arrange a Private Meeting

To resolve the conflict and move ahead in your relationship with your colleague, you'll need to have a conversation about how you'll proceed. You've already made up your mind about what you intend to say and what you hope to accomplish, so now you're ready to begin putting these plans into operation. But don't blindside the other person. Instead of just dropping in at his or her office and launching into your discussion, stop by to suggest that the two of you have a conversation later. Even this request may surprise the other person. After all, if there has been tension between the two of you, suggesting a friendly chat will be the last thing this person expects; you will likely be asked something along the lines of, "What is this about?" There may even be suspicion or hostility in your colleague's voice, as he or she may suspect that you only want to meet in order to continue the conflict. Remember, therefore, to keep your attitude positive and be candid about your purpose. Say something like, "We've had this tension between us for a long time now. And I'd like to end it. I'm hoping you would, too. So, I'd like us just to talk about ways of having a better working relationship." Sometimes the other person will agree immediately. Sometimes he or she will say something like, "Well, let me think about it." If that happens, keep your attitude positive and say, "That's fair. Think about it for a few days, and I'll check back with you later." If, either immediately or when you follow up with your colleague, you're told that that person simply is not interested in talking with you, doesn't think it's a good idea, or can't see the point of this type of conversation, reaffirm your willingness to have the discussion if the other person ever changes his or her mind, and leave the matter there for the moment. From that point on, treat the conflict as though it were over: no longer respond to taunts from the other person; include your colleague in conversations and decisions related to departmental business as much as you are able; act generally as though, in your mind at least, the matter has been resolved satisfactorily. In a surprising number of cases, if you begin to act as though there were no conflict, eventually there will be no conflict.

By responding to negativity with a positive attitude and not allowing yourself to be drawn back into a dispute, you can frequently solve the problem even though the other person may initially be unwilling to participate in your efforts to move forward.

Regardless of how you feel about your colleague as a person, have your conversation in such a way that he or she can save face as much as possible. People tend to become defensive when they feel that a personal judgment is being made about them. So, give your colleague a dignified way to end the conflict. If a solution must be framed as overcoming "an unfortunate misunderstanding between two well-meaning professionals," then that result is better than continuing to wait for an apology that never comes. If you decide that the two of you must agree to disagree, then simply avoiding the troublesome topic in the future may well be preferable to expecting a capitulation that would only add to the tension in your department. Since your focus is on building a new relationship for the future rather than on settling scores from the past, allowing your colleague a tactful way to set aside the dispute simply makes the best sense. Whatever you do, try to resolve the conflict yourself—don't go running to the department chair or dean expecting your supervisor to solve the problem or take your side in the dispute. Such a strategy is likely to backfire. Complaining to the boss about a colleague may come across as whining, tattling, backstabbing, or simply being incapable of handling a situation on your own. Most chairs and deans regard personal conflicts as relatively petty matters that have no place on their list of high priorities. By calling a problem to your supervisor's attention, therefore, you may be inadvertently characterizing yourself as having a poor sense of judgment. If you truly need advice on how to handle a workplace conflict, see if your institution's human resources office has someone who can assist you. Personnel in these positions are frequently trained in conflict resolution, know how to keep matters confidential, and will advise you on additional strategies you can use to improve your working environment.

Consider Formal Mediation

Another service that the human resources office may be able to provide is formal mediation. In mediation, a trained professional will meet with those involved in the dispute, help you talk through the issues, remain objective, and guide you toward establishing ground rules for working together in the future. Mediators do not decide matters of right and wrong. They are not arbitrators; rather, they serve as catalysts for the type of positive discussion that, when the system works as it should, will lead the participants to agree to a solution. In many cases, mediation can occur without either your supervisor or anyone else at the institution becoming aware of the discussions. For conflicts that are too difficult to resolve yourself, mediation may thus be your best option for a discreet solution. Nevertheless, because mediation works best among peers, you should reflect carefully before requesting mediation in a conflict involving a supervisor (see Chapter 36, "Handling Conflict with a Supervisor"). In cases where power imbalances exist among those in conflict, other options, such as the administrative evaluation process, better protect your anonymity and are usually more effective in the end.

Isolate or Manage the Problem

In *The Essential Academic Dean* (Buller, 2007) administrators are asked to place a problem they are facing into one of four categories:

• Problems that are likely to be solved
• Problems that are unlikely to be solved but that can be managed
• Problems that are unlikely to be solved but that can be isolated
• Problems that are unlikely to be solved, managed, or isolated

In your attempts at an informal discussion and formal mediation, you have tried to solve the problem. If that strategy hasn't worked, it is now time to determine how the problem can be either managed or isolated. What's the difference between these two approaches? A problem is *managed* if steps are taken to reduce its severity, even though the conflict itself does not go away completely. A problem is *isolated* if even its severity cannot be reduced, but steps can be taken to limit its effects. In the case of a dispute with a colleague, you might manage the situation by meeting with the other person only when there are other faculty members present. In doing so, you should not be trying to develop a faction of us versus them, but simply create an environment in which it is more difficult for the other person to carry on a personal dispute. Though certain people enjoy grandstanding in public situations, a larger group will tend to diffuse or deflect another individual's animosity in most cases. As an added advantage, you will have neutral parties present who can tell you objectively if you said or did anything that exacerbated the problem. The other people who were present can also serve as witnesses if you should ever need them. If this solution is not effective, you might try to isolate the problem by seeking committee appointments or a course schedule that minimizes the likelihood of interaction between you and the other person. In the most severe situations, you might even request an office relocation that will reduce your chance of having unpleasant encounters.

Workplace conflict can transform a satisfying and enjoyable career into a situation where you dread coming to campus, think about applying for other positions, and find your productivity rapidly declining. College professors need to understand, however, that conflict with colleagues is not particularly uncommon, that it sometimes can be an inducement to better work, and that it frequently can be fixed either through private conversations or formal mediation.

REFERENCES

Buller, J. L. (2006). Helping to resolve personality conflicts. In J. L. Buller, *The essential department chair: A practical guide to college administration* (pp. 65–74). Bolton, MA: Anker.

Buller, J. L. (2007). Challenging employees. In J. L. Buller, *The essential academic dean: A practical guide to college leadership* (pp. 78–85). San Francisco: Jossey-Bass.

RESOURCES

Cheldelin, S. I., & Lucas, A. F. (2003). *The Jossey-Bass academic administrator's guide to conflict resolution.* San Francisco: Jossey-Bass.

Coffman, J. R. (2005). *Work and peace in academe: Leveraging time, money, and intellectual energy through managing conflict.* Bolton, MA: Anker.

Lieberman, D. J. (2005). *How to change anybody: Proven techniques to reshape anyone's attitude, behavior, feelings, or beliefs.* New York: St. Martin's Press.

Lloyd, K. (2006). *Jerks at work: How to deal with people problems and problem people* (2nd ed.). Franklin Lakes, NJ: Career Press.

Masters, M. F., & Albright, R. R. (2002). *The complete guide to conflict resolution in the workplace.* New York: AMACOM.

Matz, D. (2007). The chair's role in resolving departmental conflict. *The Department Chair, 18*(2), 12–15.

Rhode, H. (1996). *Dealing with conflict and confrontation.* Boulder, CO: CareerTrack.

Scott, G. G. (2004). *A survival guide for working with humans: Dealing with whiners, back-stabbers, know-it-alls, and other difficult people.* New York: AMACOM.

Solomon, M. (2002). *Working with difficult people.* New York: Prentice Hall.

Topchik, G. S. (2001). *Managing workplace negativity.* New York: AMACOM.

38

THE FACULTY MEMBER AS FUNDRAISER

Fundraising and admissions are two activities that many college professors primarily regard as someone else's responsibility. "They recruit 'em; we teach 'em," a faculty member might say when speaking of the admissions office. Or you may hear, "Their job is to get the money; ours is to spend it," when the topic of institutional advancement comes up. The wise faculty member soon learns, however, that matters are rarely as simple as these statements make it seem. In order to have as many excellent majors in one's program as possible, it may be well worth your time to make a few calls to prospective students, meet with them and their parents when they visit campus, make an occasional presentation about one's discipline at a local high school, or write personal notes of encouragement to those who have been admitted but who have not yet confirmed that they will attend the institution. Some professors will complain that these activities take them away from their most important responsibilities; others will realize that their duties as academic citizens involve not just offering classes and performing research, but also recruiting the best possible students, advising them, and helping them develop plans for their later careers. Even though some college professors may find it difficult to believe, fundraising, too, can be a significant part of one's service to an institution. In fact, the more global term *development* in many ways encompasses both fundraising and recruiting. As a college professor, you develop your program by attracting a sufficient number of capable students for the discipline to flourish and also by securing the funding that will be required to support your discipline's teaching, scholarship, and service missions. Of course, you can—and all too many faculty members do—leave these functions to other people at your institution. But if faculty members want a voice in what type of students their program will have in the future and how resources are allocated at their institutions, it is really in their own interests to become involved in these areas.

Faculty Can Speak Persuasively About an Academic Program

Although development officers, deans, and presidents are well accustomed to cultivating donors and making formal requests for financial support, college professors are often in an even better position to speak eloquently about the needs and possibilities of a particular academic area. Administrators probably know a good deal of general information about your discipline and how it works; as a faculty member, however, you "live" your discipline every day. You know where there would be possibilities for your students to accomplish incredible things if only more funding were available. You're aware of the exciting research that you or your colleagues could perform if only there were sufficient resources. If you ask yourself what makes you really excited about your discipline and what could increase that excitement for the future, you are already well on the way to identifying an area where you could speak most effectively about the needs of your discipline. Perhaps additional scholarship support for students who have the intellectual capacity to succeed in your field but lack sufficient economic means for education would permit a broader range of students to continue their studies in your department. Perhaps the most important thing your discipline needs is a research fund that could be used to acquire an important piece of equipment, fund a travel opportunity to an important collection, provide seed money for new initiatives, or support additional graduate students on your project. Or it may be that your program could be completely transformed if only it could begin hosting a major conference in your discipline, offer each student a substantive study-abroad experience at no cost to them in the student's junior year, build a new state-of-the-art facility, host a different distinguished visiting professor in your field each year, support a wider range of student research, or make possible any of a number of other opportunities. Consider what it would take to carry your program to the next level of excellence or ensure its success for the future. What would be needed in your program to make you absolutely enthusiastic about coming to work every day? If you can channel those ideas into a vision that excites a potential donor as much as it does you, you already have the basis for a compelling presentation about your discipline's needs.

Don't forget, too, that as a college professor, you have one asset that is invaluable in fundraising: many of your institution's alumni already know you as a professor. For a successful graduate of a college or university to be asked to make a gift by his or her favorite professor creates an almost irresistible opportunity. It may seem strange if you've not yet encountered the phenomenon before, but when alumni meet a former professor, they frequently revert to how they felt as students. If they respected or even idolized you, those emotions are likely to come rushing back as soon as they see you again. By reliving a few cherished memories, demonstrating that you remember these students, and making it clear that you *personally* would appreciate their support to the institution, you can secure a gift in a way that no one else at your institution could. To alumni, the dean or president may have seemed a somewhat distant figure. You, on the other hand, were a part of the student's day-to-day life. As a result, you have the potential to help your institution achieve its fundraising goals in a unique way. So, if you have a clear vision for how your program can be improved through external funding and possess the people skills that allow you to interact well with others in small groups, development can be a significant part of your academic citizenship.

Never Go It Alone

Nevertheless, just because you have a unique position as a potential fundraiser, you shouldn't immediately set off to secure a contribution all on your own. No faculty member should ever seek to raise money for the institution without prior consultation with both the appropriate supervisor (your chair in most cases, your dean in others) and a staff member from your local development or institutional advancement office. There are several important reasons for operating in this manner.

- Members of the development staff will understand the often highly complex legal and long-term financial implications of a gift proposal. Moreover, they will be aware of options that can simultaneously be of greater benefit both to the donor and the department than an outright gift may be. (On gift options such as an endowment, bequest, trust, lead trust, remainder trust, and gift-in-kind, see Buller, 2006.)

- Both your supervisor and development office are likely to have a good sense of your institution's financial plans from an extremely broad perspective. They may thus be able to suggest ways in which you can use your current project to leverage even greater financial support for your program in the long run.

- You may have a donor in mind for whom there are specific development plans, perhaps even much greater plans, elsewhere at your institution. The advancement office will know which potential donors are already active prospects for other endeavors at the institution. For instance, you don't want your request for a $500,000 gift to be accepted, only to learn later that the donor was about to make a gift of $5 million, which has now been put in jeopardy. Donors don't like the sense that an institution is coming after their resources from every direction at once any more than you care to be oversolicited by an organization. And the last thing in the world you want is to develop a reputation as the person who "lost $4.5 million" for your institution.

- Your supervisor and the development office will have a clear sense of where the request you wish to make fits into their overall priorities for the institution. It can sometimes be difficult to accept the truth but the priorities of any individual college professor may not reflect the priorities of the institution as a whole. For instance, your president may not want to spend some of the "social capital" that he or she has accumulated with potential donors by seeking funding for your project at the expense of other institutional needs. Although a new stadium or residence hall may not seem as central to your students' education as improved lab facilities or an endowed chair, there may be reasons for these priorities that are only visible from another institutional level. The stadium may open the institution to an entirely new source of revenue that eventually could fund improved lab facilities, several endowed chairs, and a great deal more. The new residence hall could be intended to reverse a rising rate of attrition that, if allowed to continue, would be a far greater threat to your discipline's future than will result from leaving your priorities temporarily unfunded. In a similar way, your institution's priorities may be on gifts that are budget relieving (gifts that free up money that is already being spent on current operations for other purposes) rather than gifts that add new programs. In general, your institution's strategic plan, perhaps complemented by a separate development plan (particularly if a major campaign for endowment or capital improvements is under way), will guide your supervisors and the development office in setting global priorities for fundraising. Part of being a team player is understanding that other goals may occasionally surpass those that have the greatest immediate effect on you.

Seek Development Training

Although fundraising involves a set of knowledge and skills that is probably far less complicated than what you needed to become qualified as a professor in your academic discipline, it still requires training. If your institution has a well-developed program for administrative development, it may offer its own periodic workshops in fundraising. Ask the human resources office, the professional development center, or the center for teaching excellence whether any of the staff development sessions they provide include workshops in this area. But even if no local source of training is available, you still have other options.

- The Council for the Advancement and Support of Education sponsors conferences and workshops each year that cover a broad array of fundraising issues ranging from the basics through such topics as stewardship of donors, working with young alumni, conducting annual fund campaigns, and even managing entire development offices. If you express an interest in active fundraising, your institution's development office may be willing to subsidize at least part of the cost for attending the training. For more information on the training programs currently available, see www.case.org.

- The Foundation Center (www.foundationcenter.org) offers several full-day workshops, online courses, and tutorials in such areas as the basics of locating support from foundations for academic programs, an overview of corporate giving, developing a fundraising plan, and conducting research on prospective donors. Many of the Foundation Center's training programs are free, while others are available for a small cost. Classroom training courses occur at a number of metropolitan centers, so it is often possible to locate a venue for training that is either near where you live or in another location where you will be for an academic conference. For more information about the Foundation Center, see Chapter 23, "Writing a Grant Proposal."

- Several fundraising consultants involved in higher education also offer training programs, often providing these services on local campuses. Although such workshops can be expensive, it can actually be more cost effective for your institution to bring a consultant to your campus than to send large numbers of faculty for training elsewhere. Particularly if you know that you have many colleagues who are also interested in fundraising or if the development office has recently hired several new staff members who must be trained anyway, it may be worthwhile to inquire into the possibility of hiring a consult to provide a tailored training program at your institution.

- Though good fundraising involves practice, hands-on experience, and the type of people skills that one rarely develops simply from reading a book, it is still possible to gather a great deal of information about development from good resources. Among the best are Axelrod (2006), Buchanan (2000), Panas (2002), Roth and Ho (2005), and

Worth (2002). Start collecting a small library of useful resources on the basics of fundraising, learn the relevant terminology, and keep up with recent developments in this area by consulting the *Chronicle of Philanthropy* either online (www.philanthropy.com), through subscription, or at your institutional library.

- Another excellent way to learn about how fundraising is practiced in higher education is to ask your development office if you can officially shadow one of its representatives from time to time. Understand that, in this capacity, your purpose is simply to observe procedures and absorb information; you will want to resist the urge to make suggestions or to "help" the development officer in any way, as such efforts may well end up being counterproductive. See if you can attend a development staff meeting where upcoming priorities are set. It can also be informative to witness a "moves meeting" in which different members of the staff discuss the contacts they have made since the last meeting and how they have tried to proceed with various prospects. Then you may wish to sit down with one particular development officer as a potential donor is researched. Ask if you can accompany that officer on a donor or stewardship call. Just remember that almost anything you learn in this capacity is likely to include some highly confidential information. By shadowing a current member of the development staff, you are attempting to learn processes and techniques that will enable you to be a valuable faculty ally in fundraising; you are not engaging in this activity to learn privileged information that you will share with others in an inappropriate way.

Express Your Willingness to Participate in Fundraising Activities

Almost always when a faculty member says that he or she is willing to participate in fundraising, the development office will eagerly accept this offer to help. As we saw earlier, faculty members bring certain perspectives to the fundraising process that regular development officers do not have. You shouldn't expect, of course, that the very first project with which you'll be involved will concern the closing of a multimillion-dollar gift. Your first experiences are likely to be far more modest. You might be asked initially to help draft a letter that could go out to alumni for an annual fund appeal, assist in making a stewardship call to a past donor, or serve as the guest speaker at an event for supporters of the institution. You might be asked to visit a donor or prospective donor while you are in that person's area for a conference or to give a guest lecture. These situations are all valuable learning opportunities. You'll gain insight into the best way to phrase a request for fundraising purposes, how to provide a diplomatic answer to an awkward or extremely blunt question, and just how much cultivation of a potential donor occurs before a formal "ask" is made. You'll also learn a great deal about other units of your institution that will help you in your future development activities. Your institution may adopt a certain approach toward development, perhaps involving a specific system that it follows on the advice of a consultant, and you will need to know about this as well. There are certain strategies that institutions use for the annual fund, others for building endowment or funding capital projects, and still others for planned giving, estates, and trusts. If you offer your help to the development office, you are likely to be involved in a project where you are needed most and where your current talent and abilities will do the most good. From that experience, however, you will learn what you need to make an important contribution in other areas, and you will soon be able to expand your activities.

College professors are frequently reluctant to become involved in fundraising because "I hate asking people for money" or "I feel uncomfortable looking like a beggar all the time." Fundraising, however, involves far more than just asking people for money. It involves setting priorities, phrasing those needs in a way that will most resonate with particular groups, getting to know prospective donors (and letting them get to know you), and many other activities as well. Remember that if you truly cannot make the "ask," a development officer can always handle that step of the process for you. However, if you've ever gone to your chair or dean and set out the need for a new piece of equipment, travel funding, or additional research support, then you've already made an "ask" that is more difficult, in many respects, than any request you will ever make to a donor. Fundraising is simply one more way that you and your institution have of seeing that resources are adequate to achieve your goals. For many faculty members, development activities can be an important part of their academic citizenship.

REFERENCES

Axelrod, T. (2006). *The joy of fundraising: How to stop suffering and start enjoying asking for money for your favorite cause.* Seattle, WA: Benevon.

Buchanan, P. M. (Ed.). (2000). *Handbook of institutional advancement* (3rd ed.). Washington, DC: Council for the Advancement and Support of Education.

Buller, J. L. (2006). What every department chair needs to know about fundraising. In J. L. Buller, *The essential department chair: A practical guide to college administration* (pp. 129–137). Bolton, MA: Anker.

Panas, J. (2002). *Asking: A 59-minute guide to everything board members, volunteers, and staff must know to secure the gift*. Medfield, MA: Emerson & Church.

Roth, S., & Ho, M. (2005). *The accidental fundraiser: A step-by-step guide to raising money for your cause*. San Francisco: Jossey-Bass.

Worth, M. J. (Ed.). (2002). *New strategies for educational fund raising*. Westport, CT: Praeger.

RESOURCES

Allen, R. C. (1998, November 13). Why professors should learn to be fund raisers. *Chronicle of Higher Education*, pp. B4–B5.

Buller, J. L. (2007). "But I hate asking for money...": Development tips for academic administrators. *Academic Leader, 23*(8), 1, 6.

Kuniholm, R. (1995). *The complete book of model fund-raising letters*. Paramus, NJ: Prentice Hall.

Rhodes, F. H. T. (Ed.). (1997). *Successful fund raising for higher education: The advancement of learning*. Phoenix, AZ: American Council on Education/ Oryx Press.

Tromble, W. W. (1998). *Excellence in advancement: Applications for higher education and nonprofit organizations*. New York: Aspen.

Worth, M. J. (Ed.). (1993). *Educational fund raising: Principles and practice*. Phoenix, AZ: American Council on Education/Oryx Press.

39

EXPLORING THE POSSIBILITY OF
ADMINISTRATIVE WORK

After having demonstrated success in teaching, scholarship, and service, some faculty members begin to consider the possibility of seeking an administrative assignment. It could be that after having chaired several committees, designed a few new courses, and solved a number of problems, the faculty member thinks that administrative work might be interesting or perhaps that he or she has a talent for it. It could also be that after seeing a chair, dean, or president make several mistakes or prove to be ineffective in some capacity, the faculty member thinks, "Well, even I could do better than *that*. Perhaps there's a need for someone with my perspective and experience in administration." Or it could be that after having achieved most of the goals that the person has set as a college professor, he or she begins to wonder, "What's next? Where can I find the next level of challenge?" All of these reasons for considering administrative positions are justifiable, and they are precisely the reasons why many people who are chairs, deans, and presidents today first began thinking about entering full-time administration. There is, perhaps, only one truly disastrous reason for trying to become an administrator: simply to increase one's salary. Remember the essential principle we encountered in Chapter 32, "Seeking Leadership Positions": don't pursue any opportunity in your professional life simply because of the chance to make more money. Rather, identify those professional activities that you love to do and at which you excel. Then explore the best way of improving your income by engaging in those activities. You should consider administrative work because you think it would be interesting and because you believe you've demonstrated some aptitude for it—not because you're attracted to the salary or larger office. For one thing, that position will probably not be nearly as lucrative as you believe. For another, you are likely to make both yourself and the people who report to you absolutely miserable because you will soon find yourself spending countless hours in activities for which you have little capacity and less interest.

If you are seriously thinking of trying your hand at administrative work, it is best not to do so until you have at least received tenure, possibly not until you've reach the rank of full professor. There are several reasons for delaying a move into administration. First, administrators have relatively little time to engage in research and, although they may teach from time to time, they do so less than full-time faculty members. Therefore, if you move into administration prematurely and later find you want or need to earn tenure or be promoted to the rank of full professor, you may be at a severe disadvantage when your record is compared to that of other faculty members. Though administrators have many accomplishments that they can cite during their administrative reviews, they frequently do not have anywhere near the record of teaching and scholarship that they would have obtained if they had devoted all of their time to these activities.

Second, administrators inevitably have to say no to people on a regular basis. Someone will want additional funding for research or travel, and your budget won't permit you to provide it. Someone will wish to be promoted, and you will need to tell that person that he or she is not yet ready. Someone will wish to take time off during the semester for an extended trip, and you will have to remind the member of your faculty or staff that he or she is under contract and cannot be spared. As rational as people in higher education ought to be, they do at times hold grudges because of disappointments just like these. Eventually, therefore, even the best and most compassionate administrators collect at least a small group of people who believe that they have been mistreated by the administrators, and those people often want to "get back at" the person who they believe did them harm. For this reason, even if your record as a teacher and scholar still merits tenure and promotion after an extended administrative assignment, people who are in a position to vote on your status may no longer be able to be objective about you. In the worst-case scenario, you could find yourself without an administrative position to fall back on *and* without tenure or the prospect of promotion.

Third, it takes a great deal of experience in how higher education works and how your own institution is structured before you'll be most effective as an administrator. Before you reach this point, you'll need to have done substantive work revising and developing curricular proposals, reviewing a large number of promotion files besides your own, and dealing with a variety of challenges and problems. A high level of experience simply doesn't accumulate before you're tenured—and possibly not until you've served as a faculty member for ten or twelve years—so, even if you're extremely eager for an administrative appointment, you may be better off taking your time.

Seek Leadership Positions on Committees

In this chapter we'll look at a number of constructive things that you can do while still a faculty member to prepare for an eventual administrative assignment. And the very first thing you should do is review the information contained in Chapter 32, "Seeking Leadership Positions." Whenever you apply for any administrative position, you'll need to demonstrate that you have been in charge of some project and that the project resulted in some important or useful end product.

- If you haven't done so already, try to obtain a leadership role on committees in your own department, so that you will be able to demonstrate to others that you have been effective working with other people to accomplish a significant task. At most institutions, departmental committees deemed particularly important tend to be those that deal with tenure and promotion recommendations, curricular reform and, where it exists, post-tenure review. You will want to have established a record of accomplishment in which you have chaired at least one of these committees and have demonstrated success in achieving consensus or working through some difficult issues.

- Once you've demonstrated your success as a leader in departmental committees, begin seeking similar opportunities outside the department. For instance, you might see if you can get appointed to—and eventually lead—a college-level curriculum committee or promotion and tenure review team. Also try to branch out into new areas in which you have had little or no direct experience in your own department. After all, when you apply for a position as a chair or dean, for instance, you'll need to demonstrate familiarity with a broad range of administrative assignments. So, while you are still in your faculty position you will want to gain experience in as many of these areas as possible with the goal of becoming an exceptionally well-rounded administrator.

- Volunteer for assignments that are likely to be complex, even contentious. You can hone your leadership skills by chairing grievance hearings, reviews of academic programs outside your area, broad curriculum reforms such as general education revisions, strategic planning bodies, and the like. These processes rarely run smoothly, and several of them may even extend far beyond a single academic year. It is precisely this type of experience that demonstrates your ability to handle conflict effectively, respect the rights of everyone concerned in the decision, manage complex matters over a prolonged period of time, and achieve a workable result. And if you find that long hours of committee work and extremely tense situations prove to be unbearable, you will have discovered that an administrative position may not be your best choice for a career change.

- Review the suggestions in Chapter 38, "The Faculty Member as Fundraiser," and see if you can participate in at least one significant development activity. Though it may be useful to say during an administrative interview that you have been active in supporting the annual fund, what will really matter to others is your ability to cite a large gift that the institution may not have received without you. As an administrator you will almost certainly have some budgetary responsibilities, so it is useful to be able to mention ways in which you have increased revenue either for your program or for the institution as a whole. If you are thinking about serving as a department chair, those who are interviewing you may be primarily interested in ways that you benefited your program. If you are trying to secure a position as a dean, it is important to be able to cite ways in which you have helped areas outside of your immediate discipline. Serving as the principal investigator of a grant can be quite helpful to a future administrator, but most administrative interviews tend to focus more on outright gifts from individuals and foundations.

- Run for election to the faculty senate (or the equivalent body at your institution) to gain an even broader range of leadership experience. The importance of shared governance at American colleges and universities means that it is extremely valuable for you to know firsthand how these processes work and to demonstrate that you have successfully participated in institutional governance at a high level. Faculty senate membership provides numerous opportunities for college professors to seek consensus, refine their leadership skills while chairing senate committees or the body as a whole, work collegially as advocates for their areas, and provide evidence of their administrative priorities through the initiatives they undertake.

- Volunteer to serve as a member of committees for other colleges that require outside representation. For instance, search committees frequently require the presence of faculty members or administrators from other disciplines. If you serve in this capacity, you'll learn a great deal about how other disciplines make decisions and set priorities that can be invaluable in an administrative role. Athletic committees, student life committees, and alumni relations committees frequently seek faculty representation. Don't focus solely on those areas where you already have some interest, such as athletics if you were a student soccer star or alumni relations if you're a graduate of the institution where you now work. Rather, seek out those opportunities that truly stretch your abilities and give you exposure to areas of the institution where you currently have little knowledge or experience.

Find Support Roles

At the same time that you're seeking leadership positions where you can demonstrate your ability to get things done, explore the possibility of acting in a support role where you will have plenty of opportunities to learn about detailed administrative processes. Faculty members who wish to be named department chairs might consider spending a few years serving as assistant chairs; those who hope to become deans should explore the possibility of first becoming an assistant or associate dean. These support roles will not give you many opportunities to set policies and follow your own professional agenda, but they can be invaluable learning opportunities. You will see, for example, how budgets are proposed, defended, and implemented before you are ever responsible for an entire budget yourself. They will provide you with an abundance of occasions to ask, "Why did you do it *that* way?" and to learn whether you ultimately agree or disagree with the approach taken. Other types of support roles—such positions as director of faculty development, special assistant for strategic planning, or study-abroad coordinator—can provide exposure to how higher-level administrators do their work and what these types of assignments involve. At the same time that you are improving your mastery of the many technical details of academic administration, you may also have an opportunity to work with a mentor, a senior administrator who can provide you with invaluable on-the-job training. As issues or problems arise that the office is called on to solve, you can compare the actual decision with what you would have done or how you would have handled the situation. In cases where you would have chosen a radically different course of action, discuss with your mentor how you would have approached the situation and why. Use your support role to determine which aspects of administrative work you can already do extremely well and which may require additional training or experience. As in the case of your leadership roles, you may discover while in a support position that this type of work is simply not for you, that you receive more satisfaction from work in the classroom, laboratory, or library. If that occurs, you have not wasted your time in the support position; it has actually been a valuable opportunity for you to discover what means the most to you.

Many people go through their entire professional careers without ever discovering that important truth (see Buller, 2007).

Volunteer for Accreditation Review Committees

Both regional accrediting bodies (such as the Southern Association of Colleges and Schools, the Middle States Association of Colleges and Schools, the Western Association of Schools and Colleges, and so on) and specialized bodies that offer accreditation or certification in individual disciplines (for instance, the National Council for Accreditation of Teacher Education, the Association to Advance Collegiate Schools of Business, and the National Association of Schools of Music) are continually seeking individuals qualified to review the applications for accreditation that they receive. Some of these opportunities involve off-site review of the documentation that institutions have submitted for a new or renewed status of accreditation. Other opportunities may involve travel to the institutions being reviewed to determine the accuracy of their self-studies, compliance reports, or responses to concerns that have been raised. In either case, the experience will provide you with much information about current issues in higher education policy, the ways in which various institutions address the challenges that arise in offering high-quality academic programs, and the individuals at other institutions who can serve as good resources as you develop your administrative expertise (see Buller, 2007).

Learn How Your Institution and Others Like It Work

You may already have some sense of how your institution operates, but administrators need knowledge at their fingertips about where various decisions are made and how. Do you already know the staff members and all their individual responsibilities in such areas as student life, institutional advancement, public relations, security, the registrar's office, and physical plant? While you may be seeking an administrative role that does not become involved in such issues as disputes with roommates, concerns about residence hall safety, off-campus programming, and corporate fundraising, you will certainly need to have a very clear concept of who does handle these matters on a college campus. Read such works as Altbach, Berdahl, and Gumport (1999), Birnbaum (1988), and Brown (2000) to gain insight into how American higher education works and where it might be heading. Then see if the picture that you derive from these works seems to accord with your own experience as you learn about the functions of the various offices and departments at your institution.

Stay Apprised of Ongoing Issues in Academia

No institution functions in a vacuum. The challenges that you face at your college or university have parallels at literally dozens of other schools across the country. The best practices of these peer institutions can help inform your own decisions. The problems they are addressing may well arrive at your own school in a year or two. As a result, you need to know what trends are emerging in higher education. Are the students who will be enrolling in colleges for the next few years more likely to be focused on a career or interested in serving the greater good? Are there implications of federal law that will need to be addressed on your campus? What are some of the recent developments in the areas of academic freedom, intellectual property, students and faculty members with various types of disabilities, and similar issues? To extend your expertise in these areas, the following are among the resources that you should be consulting on a regular basis:

- *The Chronicle of Higher Education* (www.chronicle.com). See Chapter 1, "Applying for a Faculty Position."

- *Dean & Provost* (www3.interscience.wiley.com/journal/121542136/home). A monthly newsletter that provides timely updates on legal rulings of interest to higher education administrators, profiles of current deans and provosts, news of concern to academic leaders, and suggestions about how to be more effective in your job.

- *Change* magazine (www.carnegiefoundation.org/change). A key resource on issues of higher education policy, improving the quality of instruction, and recent trends in academia.

- *Peer Review* (www.aacu.org/peerreview/index.cfm). Although it focuses primarily on undergraduate liberal education, it is useful also to faculty members who are interested in graduate education and professional programs because of its clear analysis of recent trends in higher education. Each issue focuses on a central topic of critical concern to academics.

- *Academic Leader* (www.magnapubs.com/newsletters/subscribe_al.html). Each issue includes approximately five articles on matters of current concern to department chairs, deans, provosts, presidents, and other academic administrators.

- *The Department Chair* (www3.interscience.wiley.com/journal/114224212/home). Each issue includes approximately ten to twelve articles on the practical aspects of leading an academic unit.

- The websites of major publishers in the field of academic administration, such as Jossey-Bass (www.josseybass.com), Magna (www.magnapubs .com), Stylus (www.styluspub.com), and ACE/Praeger (www.greenwood.com/ praeger/ace.aspx). Simply browsing the recent books being released by such publishers can provide an overview of current administrative topics of major importance. Selecting the books that interest you for your own administrative library is a useful way to begin expanding your knowledge of the issues that will be involved in being a dean. Some recommended books with which to begin this library include Bright and Richards (2001); Buller (2006b, 2007); Chu (2006); Gmelch and Miskin (2004); Hecht, Higgerson, Gmelch, and Tucker (1999); Higgerson (1996); Lucas and Associates (2000); Tucker and Bryan (1991); Walvoord et al. (2000); and Wolverton and Gmelch (2002). With a library like this as your basis, you'll soon begin to identify which areas of administrative specialty (such as assessment, faculty roles and rewards, or strategic planning) you need to reinforce through additional research.

Find a Formal Mentor

Every potential administrator can benefit from occasional conversations with someone who has gone through the same experiences that he or she is having and who knows how the system works. If your institution has not provided you with a formal mentor, take the initiative to find your own. Choose a chair or former chair in a department that has at least some similarity to your own. It is probably best that your mentor not be a former chair of your own department. Such an individual, though wanting in most cases to be as helpful as possible, is still likely to be involved (at least tangentially) in departmental politics; your "Miranda Rights" that anything you say can and will be used against you should be very carefully considered before you pursue this option. In addition, former chairs in your own department will inevitably have their own agenda and their own way of doing things; your goal is to discover the way that works best for you, not to adopt what had worked well previously for a completely different person. For all these reasons, it is best to choose a mentor from a discipline that is not so different from yours in size, mission, or focus that the individual cannot easily understand your specific experiences but also who is not in your own backyard. Remember that your mentor will provide you with advice and counsel; it is always up to you to decide whether to follow that advice (see Buller, 2006a).

Find a Confidant

Having a person to whom you can turn when you need to voice your frustrations is not the same thing as having a mentor. A good administrative mentor is a person who either is or recently was at your institution; this is the person who can guide you through the complexities of the system and warn you against proceeding in a manner that is likely to be unproductive. A good confidant is someone you can talk to freely without worrying that it's going to get back to your faculty members and other administrators. Mentors provide advice; confidants lend an ear. For this reason, the person whom you choose as an outlet for your deepest concerns and annoyances should never be a member of your current institution; in fact, the further away from your institution this person is, the better. After all, everyone needs someone to vent to every now and then. Remember, however, to do so wisely and only when it is absolutely necessary. No one likes to feel that every time they hear from someone it is about a new complaint or reason for whining. Moreover, even the things you say in the greatest confidence could get repeated to the wrong people. A secret, as the saying goes, is merely information that we publicize to one person at a time. So, choose and use your confidant carefully, and cherish a good one who comes your way (see Buller, 2006a).

Prepare for an Administrative Interview

If you've prepared yourself in all of the ways outlined above, you'll certainly be in a good position to start applying for one or more administrative positions. As you do so, begin thinking of how you will answer the various questions you'll inevitably be asked when you interview for an administrative appointment. For instance, even though it's not a particularly good question, you'll almost certainly be asked, "What is your management style?" and you should have an answer readily available. The reason why this is a poor question is that there really is only one acceptable answer to this question at most institutions: "My management style is collegial and consensus based." For this reason, you should begin thinking of ways in which you can go beyond this widely expected and overly obvious response. The best way of handling this question is to work the anticipated answer into a story that provides some clear examples of your collegial and consensus-based management style. You could respond to the questioner by saying something like, "Let me give you a few instances of the ways in which I've demonstrated a collegial and consensus-based management style in the various leadership positions I've held. The first situation I always think of was when . . ." By pointing to specific cases in which you've acted in precisely the manner that your interviewer hopes, you prove that you're not giving mere lip service to the issue of collegiality. As an added benefit, you reinforce your readiness for the position for which you're interviewing by reminding the interviewer of the leadership positions you've already held. As a result, you answer the question in a clearer and more convincing way than your interviewer may have expected and include some additional information that strengthens your candidacy.

Prepare for your potential administrative interview by imagining how you would answer the following questions, all of which are regularly asked of potential department chairs and deans:

- Why are you interested in this job?

- What evidence can you provide of your support for academic areas outside your immediate discipline?

- What evidence can you provide of success in fundraising?

- What evidence can you provide of success in increasing the budget available for your discipline?

- What makes you unique as an individual?

- Is it possible to promote a greater degree of focus in our academic programs?

- What is the best way of structuring a general education program for today's college students?

- Why should we give you this position over someone who might be more experienced in administration?

- What do you like least about your current responsibilities?

- How do you view the role for which you are applying? What do you imagine an average day would be like in that role?

- Which of the current trends in higher education strikes you as the most important?

- Which of the current trends in higher education do you believe will be dismissed in the future as having been merely a fad?

- What annoys or irritates you?

- What do you do to relax?

- How do you attract a diversity of students to our program? How do you go about recruiting a diverse faculty?

- Where do you see yourself in five years? Ten years?

- What is the biggest challenge facing academic administration today?

- What is your most significant accomplishment in your current position?

- What's the most important lesson you've learned in your current position?

- How do you go about internationalizing a college curriculum?

- What would you do to address the problem of salary compression or salary inversion? How do you identify issues of salary inequity?

- What is the best approach for colleges to take toward faculty development?

- Describe a mistake that you made in your professional life. What did you learn from it?

- How do you handle community relations?

- What is the most important contribution you've made in the area of community service?

- What is your experience in developing cooperative programs or internships with community and business leaders?

- What is the role of liberal arts in higher education today?

- What should be the proper balance between scholarship and teaching in a faculty member's responsibilities?

- What achievement would you like to look back on after your first year as an administrator?

- What experience have you had in the areas of assessment and program review?

- What is the hardest decision you've ever made in your professional life?

- What is the hardest problem you've ever had to solve?

- How would you go about allocating a budget?

- How would you describe yourself? How would other people describe you?

- How will I know when you're angry? Serious? Joking? Disappointed?

- What are some examples of your creativity and innovation?

- What's the most unpopular decision you have made in your professional life? What was its result?

- What is your favorite word in the English language? Why?
- What three sources do you use most to gain information about recent trends in higher education?
- How do you view this administrative role: primarily as the advocate for the people who report to you or primarily as the representative of those to whom you report?

When you answer questions during an administrative interview, you don't want to appear overly scripted, but you also don't want to appear as though you have never thought about the issue. Listen carefully to the question and do your best to answer precisely what you are being asked without going off on tangents. Whenever possible, try to think of one good example that you can use in answering the question you are asked. Doing so illustrates that you are not simply speaking theoretically but that you have also had actual experience in dealing with the issue about which you're being asked. Also, try not to overanswer a question, particularly if it is about a failure or weakness; if you are asked to name a mistake that you made, cite precisely one and be certain to indicate what you learned from that mistake, even if the interviewer doesn't ask you about any resulting lesson. If you cite three of four mistakes when only one is requested, you may feel that you are demonstrating candor, but the interviewer is likely to conclude that you're simply prone to mistakes.

The question "What is your greatest weakness?" is so trite in interviews that you are likely to encounter it at least once. But you should know that the standard way of answering this question—by citing a "flaw" that's really a virtue—is also quite hackneyed and thus less effective than most people believe. For instance, saying that your greatest weakness is that "Sometimes I just work too hard" or ". . . care too much" is roughly equivalent to saying that you want to be an administrator because you're a "people person." Anyone who has conducted more than a handful of administrative interviews has heard these answers repeatedly; such a response no longer sounds sincere or original. It is actually much more effective to cite an actual weakness (and we all have them), followed by the way in which you compensate for this flaw. For instance, you can say things like, "I'm terrible with people's names. So, I've learned to keep a very elaborate file of business cards so that I can brush up on these before meetings with people I don't encounter often. And, of course, an excellent secretary can be invaluable in these situations." Another good answer is, "Like most people in academic life, I sometimes tend to overanalyze things when I should trust my instincts more. I'm actually getting better at doing this, particularly since I've seen often enough that where my analytical approach takes me is almost always exactly where my instincts were directing me all along."

You are also likely to be asked during a search process if you have any questions for the person or group that is interviewing you. Many candidates who have done excellently up to this point in the process end up leaving the committee with a poor impression because they couldn't think of a single question to ask. As in a faculty interview, you should *always* have questions in mind when these are requested during an administrative interview. If you can't think of anything else you'd like to know on the spot, here are a few stock "return questions" that you can memorize for these contingencies.

- First tell me the best and then tell me the worst thing about this department [or college or institution].
- What is the one quality you are most hoping to find in this new administrator?
- If the new administrator could solve just one problem for you, what would that be?
- If you could change any one thing about this department [or college or institution], what would it be?
- What's the one thing that I haven't yet told you that you wish I'd said?

————————

Administrative assignments are certainly not for every faculty member. They require a high degree of organization, an ability to see the big picture while still coping with large amounts of details, excellent communication and people skills, a willingness to tolerate numerous meetings day after day, a thick skin, the capacity to change what needs to be changed and to build on what is already successful, and a good sense of humor. If these are traits that you possess, then exploring the possibility of administrative work can be a significant part of your own academic citizenship. Also remember that although there is almost certainly a job description for any administrative position you are considering, these positions tend to be shaped significantly by the people who occupy them. A chair who is eager for curriculum reform will come to see that as his or her primary responsibility, whereas a chair who is committed to salary equity will spend far more time on that task. A dean who is committed to fundraising will devote far more time to securing external resources than will a dean who views the position primarily as devoted to solving day-to-day problems. The previous chair or dean will have created a set of expectations (or failed to meet the expectations that were already in place). Your own sense of priorities and initiatives will in the end set your agenda at least as much as the job description will. Each administrative appointment gives you, therefore, an opportunity to *define* the role as well as to play it.

REFERENCES

Altbach, P. G., Berdahl, R. O., & Gumport, P. J. (Eds.). (1999). *American higher education in the twenty-first century: Social, political, and economic challenges.* Baltimore, MD: Johns Hopkins University Press.

Birnbaum, R. (1988). *How colleges work: The cybernetics of academic organization and leadership.* San Francisco: Jossey-Bass.

Bright, D. F., & Richards, M. P. (2001). *The academic deanship: Individual careers and institutional roles.* San Francisco: Jossey-Bass.

Brown, M. C., II. (Ed.). (2000). *Organization and governance in higher education* (5th ed.). Boston: Pearson.

Buller, J. L. (2006a). Advice for future department chairs. *The Department Chair, 16*(4), 1–3.

Buller, J. L. (2006b). *The essential department chair: A practical guide to college administration.* Bolton, MA: Anker.

Buller, J. L. (2007). *The essential academic dean: A practical guide to college leadership.* San Francisco: Jossey-Bass.

Chu, D. (2006). *The department chair primer: Leading and managing academic departments.* Bolton, MA: Anker.

Gmelch, W. H., & Miskin, V. D. (2004). *Chairing an academic department* (2nd ed.). Madison, WI: Atwood.

Hecht, I. W. D., Higgerson, M. L., Gmelch, W. H., & Tucker, A. (1999). *The department chair as academic leader.* Phoenix, AZ: American Council on Education/Oryx Press.

Higgerson, M. L. (1996). *Communication skills for department chairs.* Bolton, MA: Anker.

Lucas, A. F., & Associates. (2000). *Leading academic change: Essential roles for department chairs.* San Francisco: Jossey-Bass.

Tucker, A., & Bryan, R. A. (1991). *Academic dean: Dove, dragon, and diplomat* (2nd ed.). Phoenix, AZ: American Council on Education/Oryx Press.

Walvoord, B. E., Carey, A. K., Smith, H. L., Soled, S. W., Way, P. K., & Zorn, D. (2000). *Academic departments: How they work, how they change.* San Francisco: Jossey-Bass.

Wolverton, M., & Gmelch, W. H. (2002). *College deans: Leading from within.* Phoenix, AZ: American Council on Education/Oryx Press.

RESOURCES

Bess, J. L., & Dee, J. R. (2007a). *Understanding college and university organization: Theories for effective policy and practice. Vol. I: The state of the system.* Sterling, VA: Stylus.

Bess, J. L., & Dee, J. R. (2007b). *Understanding college and university organization: Theories for effective policy and practice. Vol. II: Dynamics of the system.* Sterling, VA: Stylus.

Henry, R. J. (Ed.). (2006). *New directions for higher education: No. 134. Transitions between faculty and administrative careers.* San Francisco: Jossey-Bass.

40

TAKING THE NEXT STEP IN YOUR SERVICE

In order to develop a strategy to take full advantage of good academic citizenship, let's begin by considering why college professors engage in service. Faculty members do, after all, have many different reasons for serving others and, as a way of developing an effective plan for success in this area, we're going to need the clearest possible understanding of our motives for service. Look over the following list of options and determine which statement best reflects your reasons for engaging in service at your college or university. If several of these statements apply to you, then select all the answers that seem appropriate, but try to place them in order of priority with the first answer reflecting your strongest motivation. There are no right or wrong answers in this exercise. Choose the statement according to what you truly believe, not according to how you think a good college professor should respond.

I engage in service activities because:

- I find them satisfying in and of themselves. I would continue engaging in service even if it were not expected of me, rewarded in any way, or noticed by others.
- It pleases me to know that I'm making a positive difference in some important way. I enjoy solving problems and making my community better.
- Service is expected of me when my performance is evaluated (for annual review, contract renewal, tenure or promotion consideration, post-tenure review, and the like), and I wish to do well in these evaluations.

(Continued)

- If I don't perform the type of service that I do, it probably won't get done by anyone else.
- Service gives me an opportunity to meet and interact with other people.
- I'm hoping to become an administrator at some point in my career, and certain types of service fit into my long-term professional plans.
- Serving others is my way of giving back to a profession or institution that has benefited me in many ways.

As you review this list, you may think that the first two points are mere restatements of the same idea but, in fact, they have entirely different emphases. The first item looks at the satisfaction one receives from the *activity* of service, the second at the pleasure derived from the *results* of service. Therefore, you might select the first point if you truly enjoy committee work, mentoring others, helping to recruit new students, participating in fundraising, and similar activities even if you never actually see any fruits of your labor. But you might give the second item higher priority if you often find yourself wearied or annoyed in actual committee meetings but as soon as you see the results of your efforts or learn of someone's gratitude for what you've done, then everything suddenly seems worthwhile.

Moreover, understanding why you engage in service provides you with important information that you'll need when you develop the career plan for your service that we discussed in Chapter 6, "Special Challenges for Junior Faculty," and Chapter 33, "Serving on Committees." Consider the following ways in which your goals might change, depending on your personal reasons for serving others:

- If your primary interest in performing service is to do well in a faculty evaluation process, then the essential goal for your service should be *visibility*. There are numerous service opportunities that will come your way but, to be frank, relatively few of them will help you achieve your goals of tenure, promotion, and successful annual reviews. The committees that tend to count are those that are institution-wide (or at least collegewide) efforts and that involve such issues as curriculum, governance, and strategic planning. You will want to target those committees, try to chair them eventually, and develop a reputation for efficient and collegial work. Outside of service on committees, focus on mentoring other faculty members, building new programs with employers or other outside agencies, and establishing new service programs that help the community in which your institution is located.

- If your primary interest is eventually to seek an administrative appointment, then the essential goal for your service should be *variety*. When you are ready to pursue administrative appointments, you'll have to demonstrate familiarity with many different aspects of higher education. Depending on the sort of position you hope to have, you may even need to become quite familiar with nonacademic aspects of college life such as student affairs, residence life, physical plant maintenance, alumni relations, fundraising efforts, and so on. For this reason, strive to gain experience broadly in different types of service activities. Try to be elected to leadership positions in these groups and work to produce clear deliverables that you will be able to identify as accomplishments to which you contributed. Outside of service on committees, focus on service opportunities that put you in contact with nonacademic units of your institution, accreditation review teams, and ad hoc work groups or task forces as these activities are more likely to result in tangible products than to engage in extended or repetitive processes.

- If you engage in service activities simply because you believe that doing so is expected of you or that these activities would otherwise be neglected, then the essential goal for your service should be *selectivity*. What you've learned about yourself is that you're engaging in service out of a sense of duty or obligation, not out of a personal commitment to the inherent importance of what you are accomplishing. We should understand that there's nothing really wrong with this attitude. All college professors have certain activities that they engage in because they enjoy them and believe they are important, and others that they are willing to do primarily because they are an expected part of the job. ("I teach for free," the old saying goes. "They pay me to grade.") Some of your colleagues for whom service is a central focus of their work and self-identity might be shocked by your attitude and try to persuade you to see things differently. For this reason, absolute candor about why you engage in service may be impolitic in certain settings. Nonetheless, your philosophical position is perfectly valid. For you, teaching and scholarship are the activities that give you the greatest satisfaction and that you see as the most important aspects of your profession; you will want to be highly selective about the service assignments you seek. Try to find those that relate most closely to the aspects of being a faculty member that you truly do enjoy.

For instance, if you see yourself primarily as a scholar, volunteer for the committee that selects recipients of student research awards or, in years when you are not applying for one yourself, faculty travel grants. If teaching gives you the greatest satisfaction, mentor another faculty member on effective teaching techniques. If you are proactive in pursuing service opportunities that you "can live with," you will be in the best position to decline those that you do not see as the best use of your scarce time. Keep in mind, though, that every now and then all of us have to serve on a committee, task force, or planning group that we'd really rather avoid. Service is an integral part of academic citizenship, and in the end we all have to do our fair share.

- If your primary reason for engaging in service activities is social networking, then the essential goal for your service should be *interdepartmental opportunities*. Unless your department is particularly large, it will not be difficult for you to get to know most of the faculty members in your area. In addition to department meetings, you probably have informal social gatherings from time to time in which colleagues become acquainted with one another beyond the roles they play as academic professionals. (If your department does not have a history of engaging in social activities, then you might make an important contribution to your area by offering to host one.) Meeting people who work in other departments or colleges is usually more difficult. In order to make contact with a broader social network, look for service activities that compel you to work outside your own department. Search committees in other academic areas sometimes look for representation elsewhere on campus; express to your chair your willingness to serve in this capacity. In a similar way, those chairing searches for new positions in athletics, alumni affairs, student life, and other nonacademic programs are frequently eager for faculty involvement. In addition, certain departments need an official liaison to other departments or programs. For example, departments in the liberal arts and sciences frequently need an official representative to interact with the College of Education about teacher training programs in their areas. Science, engineering, and business disciplines often need liaisons as many of their programs require service courses from the other colleges, and certain majors, such as entrepreneurship or bioengineering, cross traditional academic boundaries. Initiatives such as general education reform, enhancing honors opportunities, and searching for a new university president inherently require representation from multiple disciplines. By developing an action plan for service that focuses on opportunities like these, you'll both make a significant contribution to your own department (one that relatively few of your colleagues may be eager to embrace) and reach out to the type of social network you are hoping to build.

• If you engage in service activities primarily because you enjoy either the activities or their results or because you derive pleasure from giving back to a community that has helped you, then the essential goal for your service should be *balance*. Service is, in some ways, an unusual part of a college professor's responsibilities. You can't be "too good" a teacher. You can't "excel too much" as a scholar. But almost everyone encounters someone at some point who became too caught up in service. That essential principle that we encountered in Chapter 6, "Special Challenges for Junior Faculty," cannot be over-looked: few, if any, faculty members ever earn tenure and promotion primarily through service. Therefore, if you receive special satisfaction from engaging in service for its own sake, you will need to make a special effort to keep all of your academic responsibilities in balance. You don't want to become so overcommitted to service that it interferes with your ability to produce a high level of scholarly work or to become ever more effective as a teacher. Seek a balance between your various responsibilities and discuss with your chair or a trusted faculty colleague whether you have accidentally overemphasized one area of your assignment to the detriment of the other two. Go back and reread Chapter 30, "Service Reconsidered." Is there some way in which you can broaden your passionate commitment to service into a more comprehensive role as an excellent academic citizen? After all, some college professors can devote too much time to service, but no one can be accused of being "too effective" as an academic citizen.

Develop a Statement About Your Philosophy of Service

Once you've clarified for yourself why you engage in service, you may want to develop a statement about your philosophy of service that could be included in certain versions of your curriculum vitae (see Chapter 31, "Creating an Effective Curriculum Vitae"), your annual self-evaluation, or your application for tenure, promotion, or post-tenure review. While it may not be diplomatic to say something as blunt as "I engage in service simply because it's expected of me," you can summarize the role that service plays in your career in a manner that helps guide the decisions you will make and explains those decisions for others. Try to phrase your philosophy of service without using any first-person forms; doing so makes your statement appear more universal and gives it a form more suitable for insertion into a résumé or application. A good philosophy of service statement might look something like this:

Philosophy of Service

Higher education administration is best viewed as a service profession. Much as Ernest Boyer redefined scholarship in *Scholarship Reconsidered* (1997) and the American College Personnel Association/National Association of Student Personnel Administrators redefined teaching in *Learning Reconsidered* (2004), it is time for colleges and universities to reexamine service in an approach that might be called *Service Reconsidered*. In other words, everything we do in academic life is service. Teaching is service to one's students. Scholarship is service to one's profession. What universities generally term service is merely contributions made for the greater good of one's institution, discipline, and community. Thus, by using their professional talents to serve those who teach, learn, and perform research, college professors take their contributions to a new level . . . improving themselves by working for others, improving the quality of academic life by serving the needs of their colleagues.

Your own statement will, of course, reflect the values and goals of academic citizenship that you identified for yourself in the first part of this chapter. In style and focus, you'll want your philosophy of service to complement similar statements about why you teach and why scholarship is important to you that you may have developed for your curriculum vitae, teaching portfolio, administrative portfolio, or self-evaluation. (On teaching and administrative portfolios, see Seldin, 2004; Seldin & Higgerson, 2002). Together these three statements should explain to others why you make the decisions that you do and should guide you regarding decisions that you will make in the future.

Consider Joining a Service Alliance

In Chapter 27, "Seeking and Providing Peer Support for Scholarship," we saw the value of teaching circles and scholarship networks, groups of colleagues that meet periodically to provide support for instruction or research. One creative way to take your service to the next level is to form a service alliance, equivalent to the teaching circle or scholarship network. Service alliances begin by asking the question: what particular talent or resource does each of our members possess that we can combine somehow and direct toward the greater good? Just as teaching circles and scholarship networks meet on a regular basis to discuss progress and challenges relating to their areas of focus, service alliances work toward engaging in one or more innovative service projects. In the course of its discussions, a service alliance can also function as a support group to address important aspects of the other service contributions of its members. For instance, if there is a challenge facing a particular committee on which one of the members serves or there is a problem that has arisen for an organization on which a member serves as an officer, the service alliance can provide advice, counsel, and a sympathetic ear. As with other types of colleague-based support, service alliances may owe their existence to whatever particular project they are designed to undertake, but their continued value will be found in the way in which each member assists the others in improving their contributions to an important aspect of their professional lives. (For more on service alliances, see Buller, 2006.)

Taking the next step in service involves determining what it is you hope to achieve through your service contributions, developing a plan to achieve those goals, and then collaborating with other similarly minded colleagues who wish to take their academic citizenship to the next level. No college or university can succeed without the committed service of its college professors. Moreover, college professors are often idealistic individuals committed to making a positive difference in the world within the context of their academic disciplines. Good academic citizenship involves putting that idealism into positive practice. It carries your teaching to a different audience and tests your scholarship by applying it to practical situations. A high level of service promotes excellent town-gown relations, makes it easier for the institution to engage in development activities, and eliminates the false impression that academic life has little to do with the real world.

REFERENCES

Boyer, E. L. (1990). *Scholarship reconsidered: Priorities of the professoriate*. Princeton, NJ: Carnegie Foundation for the Advancement of Teaching.
Buller, J. L. (2006). Developing colleague-based support for teaching, scholarship, and service. In J. L. Buller, *The essential department chair: A practical guide to college administration* (pp. 255–261). Bolton, MA: Anker.

Keeling, R. P. (Ed.). (2004). *Learning reconsidered 1: A campus-wide focus on the student experience.* Washington, DC: American College Personnel Association & National Association of Student Personnel Administrators.

Seldin, P. (2004). *The teaching portfolio: A practical guide to improved performance and promotion/tenure decisions* (3rd ed.). Bolton, MA: Anker.

Seldin, P., & Higgerson, M. L. (2002). *The administrative portfolio: A practical guide to improved administrative performance and personnel decisions.* Bolton, MA: Anker.

EPILOGUE: A CHECKLIST FOR THE ESSENTIAL COLLEGE PROFESSOR

Every college professor will discover his or her own path to a satisfying career. Much of the information that appears in this book will need to be adapted to fit the unique circumstances of your own discipline, institution, and individual interests. Despite this need to tailor advice to your own situation, many college professors have discovered that there are certain truths that seem to transcend all the variation we find in academic life. As a way of pulling together everything that we've considered in this book, see if you agree with the following conclusions.

- *The essential college professor recognizes the need for balance and perspective.* All of us want to excel at teaching, research, service, advising, mentoring, and leadership. But trying to reach that level of success immediately after you begin your academic career can lead to more frustration than success. Even if you do achieve all of these goals at once, what triumphs are then left for you later in your profession? Most academic careers have a discernible rhythm, a clear ebb and flow. Faculty members achieve excellence in a few areas at first, then expand that level of success into other parts of their careers. Inevitably, interests change over the course of a lifetime. In fact, interests should change, or professors risk becoming stagnant by not challenging themselves sufficiently. The essential college professor makes a genuine effort to keep all aspects of life in balance. He or she has friends, families, romantic partners, interests outside of academia, and multiple facets to his or her personality. It is perfectly possible to excel at academic life while still devoting time to political causes, religious activities, or service groups. The best professors rarely make the mistake of feeling they are serving their students or disciplines by spending every available moment in the studio, laboratory, or library. They become well rounded as faculty members because they've already discovered the secret of how to remain well rounded as people.

- *The essential college professor never loses sight of why he or she chose an academic life in the first place.* Few graduate students choose an academic career because they believe this path will lead them to great financial rewards. Most college professors entered their profession because they love ideas, hoped to make new discoveries or engage in great creativity, and wanted to share advanced learning with others. Somewhere along the way, however, we occasionally lose sight of initial goals and begin feeling sorry for ourselves because others have higher incomes or work fewer hours. That type of self-pity can become a trap, and we need to resist it whenever we sense its presence. The essential college professor looks for ways of finding excitement in the life of the mind, the support of interesting colleagues, and the opportunity to make a genuine difference in the world. If we ever find that our work offers more drudgery than intellectual pleasure or that we're becoming preoccupied with a sense that we're not receiving the level of respect or compensation we feel we deserve, then something has gone seriously wrong with our expectations. The vast majority of college professors do work extremely hard and contribute to their communities in countless ways that are never recognized, but these are inherent features of our career. The essential college professor is someone who continually finds excitement in a new idea, discovery, or student's achievement. Of course, he or she should be reasonably paid, but salary and workload issues should never become fixations. The essential college professor receives satisfaction from hard work and finds that many aspects of academic life provide their own rewards.

- *The essential college professor knows that all institutions of higher education are exactly alike, even though they are all completely different.* Every college or university has its own mission and serves students who may be very different from those attending other schools. Some institutions have a research mission, whereas others view teaching as their most important function. Some admission standards are highly selective, while other schools take pride in meeting students where they are. Disciplines, too, vary widely in their needs for specific kinds of facilities or equipment, their pedagogical methods, their preferred forms of scholarship or creative activity, and the number of student credit hours they can generate per full-time faculty member. Despite these differences, however, many issues and challenges are familiar no matter where one works or which field one pursues. There's probably no institution in the world that does not believe it is underfunded, insufficiently appreciated, and too often misunderstood. Every academic department knows that it has an excellent faculty and superb curriculum,

cares about its students, and upholds high academic standards.
If you move from one institution to another, you may discover that
the names of your colleagues will change, but their personalities and
challenges remain the same. The essential college professor values
the diversity that gives American higher education its strength, while
understanding that faculty, staff, and administration of schools
everywhere share a common purpose of discovering and disseminating
advanced knowledge. For this reason, the essential college professor
never assumes that an approach that works in one environment is
automatically transferable everywhere else. At the same time, he or
she does not believe that each institution is so unique that there is
nothing to be learned from the experience of others.

- *The essential college professor has a library of indispensable works
  that relate to different aspects of academic life.* Certain resources are
  so important to a faculty member's duties that every college
  professor should have access to them. To do our jobs effectively,
  we need to remain current with both the *Chronicle of Higher
  Education* (see Chapter 1, "Applying for a Faculty Position") and
  Change magazine (see Chapter 39, "Exploring the Possibility of
  Administrative Work"). Our bookshelves should include McKeachie
  and Svinicki (2006) on teaching, Walvoord and Anderson (1998) on
  designing assignments or tests, Bean (1996) on developing critical
  thinking through written work, Wiggins and McTighe (2006) on the
  importance of backwards course design, and Gordon, Habley, Grites,
  and Associates (2008) on advising. These resources are vital comple-
  ments to the academic sources that every college professor consults
  in his or her field of specialty. They keep us informed about important
  developments in higher education and provide excellent insights into
  ways to do our jobs more effectively.

- *The essential college professor makes plans but still allows for
  serendipity.* John Lennon's famous pronouncement that "Life is what
  happens to you while you're busy making other plans" may well be
  true, but it is hardly reason to give up planning altogether. Some of
  our most important activities as college professors require extensive
  planning. We need to make plans to earn our advanced degrees,
  develop innovative curricula, keep our disciplines and institutions
  accredited, produce scholarly or creative works, and submit successful
  grant proposals. But many of our other significant accomplishments
  can never be planned or predicted. We have no way of knowing when
  that absolutely superb graduate student will ask to take part in our

research, a new fellowship will be offered in our area of expertise, the next exciting technology will transform the way we teach, or an unsolicited nomination for a national recognition will come our way. By their very nature, certain opportunities arise at moments and in ways that we can't control. Nevertheless, even for these opportunities, our plans are useful. Planning is what puts us in the best position to take advantage of the unexpected. The essential college professor plans for serendipity, knowing that it will come but not knowing the precise form it will take. It is, in other words, not luck that helps us to fulfill our plans, but our plans that allow us to take full advantage of luck when and if it occurs.

- *The essential college professor appreciates the full value that comes from networking.* The essential college professor is not content to be an isolated scholar, working alone in the library, laboratory, or studio, deriving satisfaction only from ideas and rarely from human contact. Academic life is best lived in public. The essential college professor regards it as an integral part of faculty life to share discoveries with others at symposia and conferences. He or she delights in meeting new students and colleagues both electronically and in person. The best professors are those who keep in mind how much they have to learn from others, even as they derive satisfaction from teaching others. Networking makes us better teachers and scholars. It helps us expand our perspectives, not simply when others applaud our accomplishments, but when they disagree with our views. It keeps us current with new discoveries, challenges our preconceptions, and alerts us to new opportunities. When we are frustrated or disappointed, our network supports us and helps us see our challenges in their proper context. Faculty learning communities—including teaching circles, scholarship networks, and service alliances—cause us to increase our productivity at the same time that the quality of our work improves. Networks tell us about positions at other institutions when we are looking for a change and about exciting new opportunities that we may have overlooked. The best networks involve give-and-take, and the essential college professor takes pleasure in assisting others and in receiving the support of colleagues when it is needed.

- *The essential college professor never stops growing as a teacher and scholar.* Excellence as a faculty member is not a platform to be reached, but a goal to be pursued continually. There is always a better way to teach a course, interpret evidence, draw conclusions, reach consensus, and solve problems. The best faculty members are those who take pride in their achievements but are never content to rest on them. They are constantly evolving as instructors, scholars, and academic citizens. They are excited about revising their courses in light of new discoveries and rethinking current assumptions in light of new ideas. From the moment of their first job interview until well past their final post-tenure review, they are reinventing themselves and serving as role models for future generations of essential college professors.

REFERENCES

Bean, J. C. (1996). *Engaging ideas: The professor's guide to integrating writing, critical thinking, and active learning in the classroom.* San Francisco: Jossey-Bass.

Gordon, V. N., Habley, W. R., Grites, T. J., & Associates. (2008). *Academic advising: A comprehensive handbook* (2nd ed.). San Francisco: Jossey-Bass.

McKeachie, W. J., & Svinicki, M. (2006). *McKeachie's teaching tips: Strategies, research, and theory for college and university teachers* (12th ed.). New York: Houghton Mifflin.

Walvoord, B. A., & Anderson, V. J. (1998). *Effective grading: A tool for learning and assessment.* San Francisco: Jossey-Bass.

Wiggins, G., & McTighe, J. (2006). *Understanding by design* (2nd ed.). New York: Prentice Hall.